HOW RICH COUNTRIES
GOT RICH ... AND WHY POOR
COUNTRIES STAY POOR

Since anyone who criticizes the entire systems of others has a duty to replace them with an alternative of his own, containing principles that provide a more felicitous support for the totality of effects to be explained, we shall extend our meditation further in order to fulfil this duty.

Giambattista Vico, *La Scienza Nuova*, 1725

HOW RICH COUNTRIES GOT RICH ... AND WHY POOR COUNTRIES STAY POOR

Erik S. Reinert

PUBLICAFFAIRS

New York

PublicAffairs
Hachette Book Group
1290 Avenue of the Americas, New York, NY 10104
www.publicaffairsbooks.com
@Public_Affairs

Printed in the United States of America
Originally published in 2007 by Constable, an imprint of Constable &
Robinson Ltd, in the UK
First US Edition: August 2007
First Trade Paperback Edition: October 2008

Published by PublicAffairs, an imprint of Perseus Books, LLC, a subsidiary of
Hachette Book Group, Inc. The PublicAffairs name and logo is a trademark of
the Hachette Book Group.

The Hachette Speakers Bureau provides a wide range of authors for speaking
events. To find out more, go to www.hachettespeakersbureau.com or call
(866) 376-6591.

The publisher is not responsible for websites (or their content) that are not
owned by the publisher.

A copy of the British Library Cataloguing in Publication Data is available
from the British Library.

ISBNs: 978-1-5417-6289-3 (paperback), 978-1-5417-6288-6 (ebook)

LSC-C

10 9 8 7 6 5 4 3 2 1

Contents

Foreword

When demonstrators took to the streets of Seattle in 1999, and on numerous occasions subsequently, in protest against the World Trade Organization and related international financial institutions, their protests were implicitly directed at conventional wisdom – the economic orthodoxy which has legitimized and provided the analytical scaffolding for much of their policy conditionalities and advice. At the risk of caricature, over the last two decades this theory has claimed that self-regulating markets would produce growth for all, if only the role of government was kept to the bare minimum of the 'night watchman'.

This orthodoxy had gained popularity with the advent of 'stagflation'* in the 1970s and the intellectual assault on Keynesian and development economics. The fiscal crises of welfare states from the 1970s and the later demise of centrally planned economies provided additional succour for the new orthodoxy, despite the evident failure of monetarist experiments in the early 1980s. Today, only fundamentalists at the extremes argue for either a completely self-regulating economy on the one hand or for a totally state-run economy on the other.

---

* Stagflation: Stagnation + inflation, a term coined to describe periods of recession combined with high inflation.

This book by Erik Reinert identifies the key economic and technological forces which need to be harnessed by economic policy in order to generate economic development. His development analysis also recognizes that the 'development of underdevelopment' is a result of the failure to promote and develop economic activities involving greater returns to scale and enhanced human capabilities, as well as productive capacities. Reinert creatively applies old economic lessons in new contexts.

How Rich Countries Got Rich… argues that important economic lessons can be learned from setting the historical record straight. Reinert suggests that the history of the United States has the greatest economic relevance to today's poor countries. Seventeen seventy-six was not only the year of the first publication of Adam Smith's *Wealth of Nations*, but also saw the beginning of the first modern war of national liberation against British imperialism. The Boston Tea Party was after all a mercantilist action. The economic theorist of the American Revolution was none other than its first Secretary of the Treasury, Alexander Hamilton – now recognized as the pioneer of what is often termed 'industrial policy'.

Consider what the US economy would look like today if the Southern Confederacy had triumphed over the Northern Unionists – the last third of the nineteenth century would not have seen the US economy rapidly industrialize. As the curators of the Smithsonian Museum of American History note, the huge technological gap, recognized by American participants at the Great Exhibition at Crystal Palace in 1851, would not have been bridged, and the US might not have become the world's leading economy so early in the twentieth century.

As Reinert shows us, after the Second World War the Morgenthau Plan sought to pastoralize Germany, then seen as the source of two world wars. Instead, General George Marshall contributed to the post-war Keynesian 'Golden Age' with his plan to accelerate economic recovery and reindustrialization in Western Europe and Northeast Asia to ensure a *cordon sanitaire* of economic growth around the expanding Soviet bloc. The generous American contribution to post-war recovery stands in sharp contrast to its current aid contribution, not only quantitatively, but also in terms of 'financing government budgets' and ensuring 'policy space'.

Economic development involves profound qualitative change, not only of the economy, but also of society. Reducing economic development to little more than capital accumulation and more efficient resource allocation has become a formula for perpetuating economic backwardness in many poor countries. By deepening our understanding of uneven development by drawing from his rich knowledge of the history of economic policy, Reinert's book provides both important lessons and stimulating reading.

Jomo K. S., UN Assistant Secretary-General for Economic Development and Founder Chair, International Development Economic Associates (IDEAs)

Acknowledgements

Most ideas in this book are very old, and my biggest debt is to a large number of economic thinkers and policymakers who over the last 500 years successfully created wealth rather than reallocated it. I first came in contact with this distinguished group in 1974–6 when my wife worked as a librarian at the Kress Library at Harvard Business School. This library specialized in economic theory before 1850, thus maintaining an accessible gene-bank of their ideas. My economics professor at the Hochschule St Gallen, Switzerland, Walter Adolf Johr (1910–87) retained some old continental European ideas, and at Kress I met Fritz Redlich (1892–1978), a surviving member of the German Historical School, who introduced me to Werner Sombart.

What is original in this book was embryonically there in my Ph.D. thesis written in 1978–9. Other than from the ancients, inspiration at the time came from Tom Davis, who taught economic history and development, and inspired the idea of differentiating economic activities, from Boston Consulting Group and their approach to measuring human learning and experience, and from Jaroslav Vanek, formerly of the Heckscher-Ohlin-Vanek theorem in international trade, who had come to understand how welfare-destroying international trade could be under given circumstances. His thorough deconstruction of conventional international trade theory confirmed why I had always found it counter-intuitive. Also at Cornell, John Murra opened my world to pre-capitalist societies.

xii *Acknowledgements*

Classical development economics, with Myrdal's 'cumulative causations', always formed a theoretical backdrop.

Since I came back to research and academics in 1991, five economists and economic historians of a generation or less before mine – sometimes knowingly and sometimes unknowingly – generously advised and sustained my conviction that many old ideas, in their context, were more unfashionable than inappropriate: Moses Abramovitz, Robert Heilbroner, and David Landes in the United States; Christopher Freeman and Patrick O'Brien in the United Kingdom. To them this book is dedicated. They kept alive the long reality-based economics tradition that almost died out in the Cold War crossfire between two utopias: that of planned harmony and that of automatic market harmony.

Carlota Perez' vision of how technological change takes place has been very influential and I am also very grateful for her willingness to be my most active sparring partner in ideas. In this category my Tallinn University of Technology colleagues Wolfgang Drechsler and Rainer Kattel have also been of great help. By 1991 modern evolutionary economics had been established, and Richard Nelson's 'appreciative theorizing' helped in shaping mine. So did the post-Keynesian economics of Jan Kregel, the institutional economics of Geoffrey Hodgson, the development economics of Jomo KS, and the GLOBELICS movement initiated by Bengt-Åke Lundvall. Thanks also to the participants at Other Canon seminars in Oslo and Venice, among others Daniele Archibugi, Brian Arthur, Jürgen Backhaus, Helene Bank, Antonio Barros de Castro, Ana Celia Castro, Ha-Joon Chang, Mario Cimoli, Dieter Ernst, Peter Evans, Ronald Dore, Wolfgang Drechsler, Jan Fagerberg, Christopher Freeman, Edward Fulbrook, Geoffrey Hodgson, Ali Kadri, Tarmo Kalvet, Jan Kregel, the late Sanjaya Lall, Tony Lawson, Bengt-Åke Lundvall, Lars Magnusson, Lars Mjøset, Alfredo Novoa, Keith Nurse, Patrick O'Brien, Eyup Özveren, Gabriel Palma, Carlota Perez, Cosimo Perrotta, Annalisa Primi, Santiago Roca, Bruce Scott, Richard Swedberg, Yash Tandon (who brought me to the African reality and taught me 'the imperial factor'), Marek Tiits and Francesca Viano. Colleagues and students at many universities have been exposed to my ideas in many forms, and have provided valuable feedback and insights. I particularly mention the universities where I have returned as a visiting professor: ESAN University, the Lima business school, Universidade Federal do Rio de Janeiro, and the Asia-Europe Institute at the University of Malaya in Kuala Lumpur. Teaching six years at CAPORDE (Cambridge Advanced Programme on Rethinking Development Economics) and the related courses organized by the Other Canon in the Third World gave me a chance to be part of a group that helped shape a new view of how economic development takes place. The main initiatives were all funded by the Ford Foundation, where one person, Manuel Montes, contributed significantly to create a 'new development economics'. Over the last years, participating in meetings and processes in the UN system: CEPAL/ECLA, Department of Economic and Social Affairs (DESA), South Centre, UNCTAD, and UNDP has given valuable insights and personal alliances. Thanks also to Jon Bingen and NORISS, Norwegian Institute for Strategic Studies, for supporting this study of successful national development strategies, and to Norsk Investorforum, Norwegian Shipowners' Association, and Leif Høegh Foundation for economic support to the Other Canon Project.

Back in 1999, a group of us spent two days together developing an alternative set of assumptions for economics, built from the ground up rather than from physics down (Appendix II). Special thanks to them: Leonardo Burlamaqui, Ha-Joon Chang, Michael Chu, Peter Evans, and Jan Kregel. Many thanks also to Wolfgang Drechsler, Christopher Freeman, Rainer Kattel, Jan Kregel and Carlota Perez who volunteered to read and comment on the manuscript of this book. They are not to be blamed for my stubbornness.

A special thank you to Dan Hind, then of Constable & Robinson, whose initiative started the process leading to this book. Thanks also to my editors at Constable, Hannah Boursnell and Jan Chamier, and particularly to Jane Robertson who did a wonderful job of keeping me in line.

Probably more than most others, this book has been a family project. When they were small, our two sons, Hugo and Sophus, sometimes asked, 'Why do we always have to travel to places where people are so poor?' Now, both finishing their Ph.D. theses in Cambridge, they have become valuable advisers. Both are represented in the bibliography. They were also the ones suggesting interweaving theory with personal accounts. A short version of this book was published in Norwegian in 2004, and Sophus and my wife Fernanda translated large sections. My deepest gratitude, however, is to Fernanda, who has known me since before this project was conceived in the summer of 1967. Without her loyalty, support, courage and sticktoitiveness (a term used to describe her by her Kress Library boss) in what must have been experienced as continuous assaults of exposures to new settings, new countries, new languages and new challenges – also in projects riskier and more quixotic than this one – the conditions and experience needed for writing this book would simply not have existed.

List of Figures

Introduction to the 2019 Edition

From manufacturing you may expect the two greatest ills of humanity, superstition and slavery, to be healed.

> Ferdinando Galiani (1728–87), Italian economist

There is a phase of this matter which is both interesting and serious. The farmer has always produced the foodstuffs to exchange with the city dweller for the other necessities of life. *This division of labor is the basis of modern civilization.* At the present time it is threatened with breakdown. (italics added)

> George Marshall, announcing the future Marshall Plan,
> Harvard, June 5, 1947

The final paragraphs of this book were written during the last days of December 2006, and on the next-to-last page (298), three predictions were formulated:

First of all, a major financial crisis is increasingly likely, and Keynesianism shall have to be re-invented in a new and global context. 'Free trade' as the centerpiece of the present world economic order is likely to delay the solution to future problems in much the same way as a stubborn belief in the 'gold standard' delayed Keynesianism in the 1930s.

The *first part* of this prediction proved correct: the West had a major financial crisis starting in 2007–2008. We are still suffering from the aftermath of this crisis, and its solutions have, for many people, proved much worse than the crisis itself.

The *second* part of the prediction – emphasizing the need for Keynesianism to be reinvented on a global scale – is not taking place. Instead what we have mostly been seeing – both in the United States and in the European Union – is the exact opposite of Keynesianism: *austerity*. It was probably in Peru that austerity first became an official national policy in 1978. The Peruvian government declared it the year of austerity, and a postage stamp proudly announcing the *Año de Austeridad* was issued.[1] Over the next forty years, austerity and falling real wages spread to other Latin American countries, the Second (former communist) World, and finally now to the very core of the developed First World, to the United States. In other words, Peru and many Latin American countries were early guinea pigs for austerity – sponsored by the IMF and the World Bank – which at the moment is causing political havoc in the United States and Europe alike. At the same time the de-industrialization that accompanied the austerity in Latin America is today a main cause of international migration.

While Keynesianism solved the twentieth-century crises by creating employment, today's central banks – especially the European Central Bank – attempt to solve the crisis by flooding the global economy with cheap money. The result is a growing imbalance between a growing global indebtedness, supported by an asset price inflation,[2] and falling real wages and consequently falling demand in the real economy. For decades it seemed very improbable that wages in the West would fall. I shall argue that an important reason this is now happening is the breakdown of what John Kenneth Galbraith called the *balance of counter-vailing powers*,[3] the power of big business was limited by big labor and big government, and this kept national wages rising in step with industrial productivity.[4] David Ricardo's observation in 1817 that the market price of labor always will tend toward *the minimum required for subsistence* may finally come true because of the recent absence of institutions strong enough to prevent this development.

The *third part* of the prediction, the need to remove 'free trade' as the centerpiece of the world economic order, is clearly taking place. This should not be seen as a reactionary pushback: it is only by understanding the last centuries of the history of economic policy that we may come to understand why and how this can be accomplished. The World Bank and the International Monetary Fund are also gradually changing their positions towards the theories presented in this book. When, in 2012, World Bank chief economist Justin Yifu Lin wrote 'Except for a few oil-exporting countries, no countries have ever gotten rich without industrialization first,'[5] he repeated the conclusion for which this book provides the theory and historical background. A recent paper from the International Monetary Fund (IMF) at last also admits that policies that break with free trade – which are recommended in this book – have their merits.[6]

1848 *moments and other turning points in history*

As I note in the introduction to the 2007 edition of this book, the 1989 fall of the Berlin Wall was seen as *The End of History* in a very influential book.[7] This view was supplemented by another book titled *The End of the Nation-State*.[8]

But both *history* and *the nation-state* came back with a vengeance, in a severe global backlash against free trade ideology and the creation of nondemocratic global governance institutions that imposed austerity. In the last US elections both Trump and Sanders seemed to agree that free trade was no longer in the interest of the United States, and the many tensions inside the European Union – including Brexit – testify to the same development there.

History is more than 'one damned thing after another', to use a term from a famous historian, and in this book I point to studying the *cyclicality of economic theories* (p. 43) and the *cyclicality of history* (p. 72) – obviously in terms of broad parallels, affinities, and similarities rather than literal returns to previous conditions – as being means to better cope with an apparent age of confusion. Implicit in the understanding of cyclicality is that *turning points* exist. One typical such turning point is what I have dubbed '1848 moments': when free trade, libertarianism, and nonintervention are attacked simultaneously from the political right and the political left. We are at one such moment now.

The 1840s came down in history as 'The Hungry Forties'. Towards the end of the decade bad harvests across Europe added to general economic and social problems. Already in the late 1830s the social sting in works of Charles Dickens (1812–1870) prepared the gradually more gloomy mood, and for Christmas 1845, the Danish master of fairy tales H. C. Andersen (1805–1878) published his most heartbreaking social tale, *The Little Match Girl*. The little girl sent out to sell matches freezes to death on New Year's Eve. In 1848 it was first published in book form.

In June 1846 the British government's *Repeal of the Corn Laws* (*Grain Laws*) had produced an enormous victory for the free trade movement.[9] But a countermovement soon developed. In 1847 a massive financial crisis hit at the heart of the world economy in England. The next year, 1848, produced revolutions in all large European countries, with the exception of England and Russia. Three major economic works saw the light of day in 1848, all attacking the liberal order that had been created by David Ricardo in 1817, but from very different political angles:

1. Karl Marx & Friedrich Engels's *Communist Manifesto*. As is well known, Karl Marx (1818–1883) was so radical he had to flee Germany to seek refuge in England.[10]
2. Bruno Hildebrand's *Economics of the Present and the Future* (*Die National-Oekonomie der Gegenwart und Zukunft*). Hildebrand (1812–1878) was an early representative of the German historical school of economics, and he was very critical of David Ricardo. In 1851 the democratically minded Hildebrand had to flee Germany to Switzerland.
3. John Stuart Mill's *Principles of Political Economy*. John Stuart Mill (1806–1873) is normally seen as an ardent liberalist, but he sensationally recanted on free trade, arguing that nations needed 'infant industry protection'.

Friedrich von Hayek (1899–1992) points to a key mechanism behind theoretical and political cyclicality: 'Never will man penetrate deeper into error than when he is continuing on a road which has led him to great success'.[11] In other words: when being right and successful, mankind will 'overshoot' into error. When an unregulated market is successful, it is perceived as never needing any interventions. This is the logic behind the free trade movement that preceded 1848. This triumphalism decays both economic theory and economic policy by overshooting into overly abstract theories and into irrelevance. Here economics differs from other sciences: once it has been understood that the world is not flat, but round, the idea of a flat Earth never comes back. In economics, however, there is a movement up and down in terms of levels of abstraction, producing a form of cyclicity.

Other economists have contributed, from different angles, to describing this 'overshooting' phenomenon. The Norwegian American economist Thorstein Veblen (1857–1929), for example, suggests that knowledge exists on different levels. Highly abstract and *esoteric* knowledge, like that of high priests, carries much prestige, but is – in practice – often fairly useless. On the other hand, there is *exoteric* knowledge – useful knowledge based on facts and experience, that carries little prestige. Using Veblen's terminology, we can argue that the overshooting into excessive abstractions corresponds to Veblen's idea that irrelevant education may *contaminate healthy instincts* of useful and exoteric knowledge.

The Canadian economist Harold Innis (1894–1952) suggests that scientific fashions – or in Veblen's terms, the balance of *esoteric* and *exoteric* knowledge – follow a pattern. In his scheme, scientific fashions may be driven by political power. Innis observes that science tends to become more and more abstract, and it is communicated in *Latin*, i.e., the language understood only by scientists. These exceedingly abstract theories – like David Ricardo's theory of international trade – monopolize knowledge and enter into alliances with political elites.[12] Today's *Latin* would be mathematical economics, and today a *de facto* alliance exists between mainstream (neoclassical) economics and the financial sector. I would argue that while previous economic theories limited the power of the financial sector, today the financial sector is collecting rents from irrelevant economic theories which do not separate *money* from *what you can buy for money*.

Since mainstream economics is so abstract that it does not distinguish sufficiently between the real economy and the financial sector – tending to see the financial sector as just another sector of the economy – this theory does not perceive the destructive forces that can be created when the financial sector, rather than being in a constructive symbiosis with the real economy, becomes a parasite eating away at it, as we see for example with the deepening crisis in Greece today.[13]

Previous economic theories from left to right saw the need to keep the financial sector under control. Figure 4 (p. 54) gives an illustration distinguishing the financial sector from the real economy. In volume three of *Das Kapital*, Karl Marx explains financial crises, Lenin was of the opinion that the financial sector taking over the economy would be the last stage of capitalism, and conservative economists like John Maynard Keynes and Joseph Schumpeter both had theories of finance and crises, and some German economists distinguished between *schaffendes Kapital*, capital that created wealth, and *raffendes Kapital*, capital that only grabbed value without creating it. The best theory of the role of financial capital was probably written by Rudolf Hilferding, a social democrat and Austrian Jew who was killed by the Gestapo.[14]

Today we are in the extraordinary situation wherein these economic theories – covering the whole political spectrum – have virtually disappeared from practical use. The West has failed to make theoretical sense of perhaps the only good thing that came out of the horror chambers of the 1930s and 40s: that fascism, communism, and social democracy all strengthened the real economy by bringing the financial sector under control. Our understanding of the financial imbalances of the present economic system is so poor at the moment because the diversity of economic theories that once existed – and competed for attention – has virtually disappeared. In practice there seem to be no alternatives to mainstream neoclassical theory, one which no longer differentiates the financial economy from the real economy as was once common practice.

In Harold Innis's scheme, resistance to the alliance between the ruling economic paradigm and the elites builds up among *the*

Vernacular, i.e., those who do not read or write *Latin*. A great disconnect is slowly created by a perceived misfit between the *Latin* theory of the ruling class and their high priests and reality as perceived by common people, by the *Vernacular*. A simultaneous overthrow of power and of science (of the vested interests and their overly abstract *Latin* science) may take place after a shock to the system, e.g., a financial crisis. The French Revolution of 1789, the 1848 revolutions in Europe, and the financial crisis of the 1930s were all instances in which esoteric knowledge created crises, and these crises were solved only by resuscitating alternative – sometimes near-defunct – paradigms of knowledge.

A fascinating aspect of Innis's vision of the cyclicity of science is that he sees Western Civilization again and again being saved by knowledge that for a time survives only in the periphery, by reviving previous theories. To take a more recent example from today's financial crisis: the US economist Hyman Minsky (1919–1996) was for a long time a lonely voice when he claimed that 'it' – a severe financial crisis – could happen again. As Innis would have predicted, Minsky's economics had survived only in the academic periphery: at the University of Missouri–Kansas City and at the Levy Institute at Bard College in New York State. After the crisis of 2008, Minsky's long-marginalized theories again received the attention they deserved, though not yet sufficiently to remove the financial sector from the driver's seat in Western economies. Less abstract theories – like the ones outlined in this volume – need to be brought back.

Learning from the Cold War

Taking this cyclical view of economic history and economic theory, one event is perfectly normal and predictable: that the United States – having lost its unchallenged role as world economic leader – is tilting towards protectionism. In the early 1700s, Holland was the leading economic power in Europe, and a few years after the 1720 financial crisis, Holland became more protective of its manufacturing sector. This tendency was even clearer when England was losing its economic world hegemony during the early twentieth century.[15]

The economically most powerful country has the strongest interest in free trade. In the Davos conference of 2017, it was China that sang the praises of free trade. Free trade had just been attacked from the right and the left in the US election and had been dealt a blow with the Brexit decision, but the Chinese now embraced the trade game. They are now gradually opening up their markets where it suits them, while the Western world is encountering an '1848 moment'. The ideological overshooting that created this challenge to free trade from the right and left can be traced back to 1989.

When the Cold War ended in 1989, very few people – if any – were aware of the structural similarities of the Marshall Plan–type economic policy (as opposed to economic theory) that was carried out in the West and that of communism: of the *isomorphism* of the goals of the extreme political right and the extreme political left. The economic policies both of the West and of communism rested upon the cult of manufacturing industry and new technology, e.g., producing a space race.[16] Up until and including the gradual integration of Spain into what was then called the European Economic Community during the 1980s, European policy was extremely focused on making sure manufacturing industry survived in all member nations. The goal was *symmetrical integration* between nations that all had a solid manufacturing base. In EEC's 1988 *Cecchini Report*, laying the foundations for what in 1992 was to become the European Union, the importance of manufacturing was still very much present. Paolo Cecchini estimated that around 80 percent of the benefits of the single market would come from increasing returns to scale in manufacturing. Implicitly, then, Cecchini admitted that countries – starting with Greece and Portugal – that have since lost most of their manufacturing industry might in fact lose from the single market.

The EEC integration of Spain during the 1980s represented the last prototype integration in the nation-based economic paradigm, contrasting this with the global economic paradigm that took over after the fall of the Berlin Wall. It was after the integration of Spain that the lessons from the Marshall Plan – which had long been dead in theory – also died out in practical politics. The following table attempts to highlight the main differences between the highly successful period of nation-based capitalism from the 1947 introduction of the Marshall Plan and the much less successful period of global capitalism that followed the 1989 fall of the Berlin Wall.

Table 1.

Nation-based capitalism	Global capitalism
High-tech, high-growth industries present in all countries	High-tech, high-growth industries disappear in peripheral countries (from Greece to Mexico)
Move advanced economic activities to lagging countries. Adjust exchange rates (Europe)	Move human beings from one country to the other. Freeze exchange rates (Europe)
Create jobs in order to solve crises (Keynes)	Create money in order to solve crises (Mario Draghi)
Strong government and labor unions (balance of countervailing powers)	Gradual power shift to the financial sector (the rule of the 1 percent)
Harmonization (harmony created through economic policy)	Polarization (spontaneous chaos)[17]

Appendix VI shows a Quality Index of Economic Activities, listing the factors which most strongly promote economic growth as we measure it ('high-quality activities') and its counterpart 'low quality activities'. Appendix VII, which is new to this edition, depicts the same difference between high- and low-quality activities using the actual data for fifty-one different US industries between 1899 and 1937. The industries would be different today, but the point of Appendix VII is to visualize the huge actual differences that exist between industries at any point in time. One key difference between Appendix VI and Appendix VII, however, is that Appendix VII does not factor in the degree of imperfect competition, which is a key point in Appendix VI. With perfect (commodity) competition the advantages of fast technological change are lost because prices fall immediately. Having also factored this variable into Appendix VII, the beet sugar industry (activity number 4) would not have appeared as attractive as it now does.

A key point – see the first item in the table above – is that in the nation-based economic system most countries had all of the fifty-one activities in Appendix VII. Under the global economic system, however, the winner-takes-all countries specialize in activities with the characteristics in the left part of the graph in Appendix VII, while the losing countries tend to be left with the industrial activities with the characteristics of the right side of the graph. The loss of high-growth/growing-employment industries on the left side of the graph is – from Greece to Mexico – a main reason for migration.

Cold War Economics – the theories that stood victorious after the fall of the Berlin Wall – had its roots in David Ricardo in 1817. However, recent n-gram technology has made it possible to illustrate how David Ricardo and his theory of 'comparative advantage' were virtually neglected until Paul Samuelson brought them into the core of economics at the start of the Cold War in 1948–49. Communism advanced under the utopian slogan 'from each according to his ability, to each according to his needs'. With his new interpretation of David Ricardo, Paul Samuelson produced a counter-utopia: under the standard assumptions of neoclassical economics, free trade would produce a tendency towards 'factor-price equalization': the prices of labor and capital would tend to equalize across the planet.

This far-fetched theory brought David Ricardo out of the shadows as a marginal economist. Compared to other English economists and economic philosophers, father and son James and John Stuart Mill, David Ricardo had indeed been a 'nobody' during the first 100 years after his 1817 theory.

Table 1 shows us how economic theory changed from being nation-based to being global. Indeed on the theoretical level, the

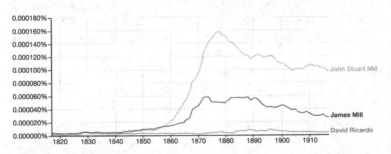

Source: Google Books Ngram Viewer, http://books.google.com/ngrams

Figure a   The frequency of 'David Ricardo' during the first 100 years after the 1817 publication of his main work, *Principles of Economics*, compared to that of two other, then much more famous, English economists.

Source: Google Books Ngram Viewer, http://books.google.com/ngrams

Figure b   Frequency of the term 'comparative advantage' from 1817 until today. As is clearly shown, the term was very little used for the first 100 years of existence, but the use of the term exploded with the start of the Cold War in the late 1940s.

Cold War (1947–1989) was fought between two *cosmo*political theories. Neither in neo-classical/neo-liberal theory nor in communism was the nation-state a unit of analysis. In both *theories* the nation-state was not seen as having a place. Neoclassical economics is built on methodological individualism – no state needed – and also in Marxism the state was supposed to wither away as obsolete after a brief 'dictatorship of the proletariat'. In practice, of course, it was not the state but the rights of individuals that withered away under communism.

Both political extremes were far too abstract to be practical guides to human societies. The implicit conclusion in 1989, however, was that because communism had proven to be wrong, neoliberalism – the other political extreme – had to be perfect. This belief has led to increasing poverty in many countries. A key economist in the historical tradition in which this book is written, Gustav Schmoller (1838–1917), clearly saw that both political extremes were unfit for practical purposes. In his 1897 inaugural speech as *Rektor* of the University of Berlin, Schmoller expressed the hope that he had seen the end of the two ideological extremes, Manchester Liberalism (today's neoliberalism) and communism. His characterization of both these ideologies was harsh: 'the naive optimism of "laissez-faire"' and the childish and frivolous appeal to revolution, the naive hope that the tyranny of the proletariat would lead to world happiness, increasingly showed their real nature, they were *twins of an ahistorical rationalism*' (Schmoller 1897, my translation, italics added).

In reality, one very positive effect of the ideological fights that dominated most of the twentieth century was that the two political extremes opened up a very wide policy space between them. Different approaches to economic policies were abundant, and it was possible for countries to learn from each other. Alternatives for different capitalisms flourished: Hyman Minsky used to say there were as many varieties of capitalism as Heinz had pickles, and that this very variety of capitalism is responsible for the success of market economies. The number Minsky had in mind is of course fifty-seven, a number well known from the Heinz ketchup bottle.

The good thing about the wide policy space that once existed was that politicians (and sometimes economists) could tailor-make solutions to the context in which they found themselves. Countries that did not have enough industry yet could protect it, countries that had a poor climate could protect their agriculture. Pragmatism – as opposed to ideology – ruled. In my own country, Norway, in the early twentieth century, a very conservative economist who was for free trade in general would admit that of course we could not have free trade with neighboring Sweden, because that would ruin our industry. Likewise conservative politicians would argue that of course the best thing would be for private enterprise to build the first railways, but since the country had so few capitalists, the government would have to do it. Very often the state would function 'as an entrepreneur of last resort', not because people were socialists, but because there were simply not enough capitalists around. A similar phenomenon could be observed with the many municipally owned businesses in nineteenth-century United States. The ideological hatred of any state intervention is a relatively new phenomenon. The end of the Cold War in a sense also became the end of pragmatism; ideology came to determine economic policy, no longer common sense.

The West has seemingly uncritically swallowed the absurd argument from the World Bank and the IMF that 'globalization has brought millions and millions of people out of poverty'. This is not true if you take China and India out of the sample, and China and India did not get richer because they opened up to free trade following the recommendations of the IMF and the World Bank. They – especially China – got an impressive economic growth because they focused on manufacturing industry and gave up economic protectionism only gradually and when it suited them. We should be aware that this was pretty much the same transition the United States had from protectionism to free trade starting in the late 1800s: we open up for free trade when it suits us, not for ideological reasons. Starting around 1820, American economists and politicians followed the policy of 'don't do what the English tell you to do; do what the English did'. The Chinese, in their turn, seem to have followed the rule of 'don't do what the Americans tell you to do; do what the Americans did'. Had US colleges and universities not stopped teaching the history of early American economic thought and the industrial policy that followed, the country would have been better prepared for the present situation.

Recognizably worrying trends recurring

Apart from free trade waning – which at this point in time seems natural – there are worrying trends, some of which are reminiscent of the 1930s. One regards ethnicity. An important factor building up to World War II was widespread poverty in Germany, partly caused by heavy reparation payments from World War I. Resentment, which always accompanies falling living standards, developed into extreme nationalism. It is also worth noting that the two countries that opted for fascism were two countries in Europe that had most recently achieved national unification: Germany and Italy.

At the moment Russia still suffers severely from the de-industrialization that followed the Shock Therapy recommended – or rather imposed – by the West in the 1990s. Real wages, industrial production, and agricultural production all fell by more than 50 percent in Russia during the 1990s, and when incomes finally recovered, they were not distributed in the same way as before.[18] The world learned from World War II that too much poverty would create war. That would be one of the inspirations of the Marshall Plan: do not repeat the *vae victis* – woe to the vanquished – that followed World War I. And while we avoided it after World War II, we seem to want to repeat the World War I mistake with a largely impoverished Russia to whom we in the West advised what amounted to a devastating equivalent to the 1919 Treaty of Versailles.

Another factor which recalls the 1930s is a term which helped Germans unite around fascism: *Zinsknechtschaft*, or *debt serfdom*.[19] At the moment, 'free trade' supported by free global financial markets brings more and more countries into large deficits on their balance of payment and into a similar nonsustainable debt slavery that helped the Nazis get power in Germany. The availability of idle capital, ostensibly created to ease the financial crisis, is clearly a part of this problem. The irony is that this time around the global capital flows generated by the huge German trade surpluses are an important source of the deficit problem. In the 1930s Germany was the big deficit country; today Germany – with the help of the Washington Institutions (World Bank and the International Monetary Fund) – imposes the same kind of deficits on other countries. In a paper written shortly before his death, Keynes argued that when a country's trade surplus is too large, this will eventually bankrupt its trading partners. This view was anticipated in Emmanuel Kant's 1795 treatise on *Perpetual Peace* in which he strongly warns against this kind of debt that entangles innocent states. 'Therefore, to forbid this credit system must be a preliminary article of perpetual peace all the more because it must eventually entangle many innocent states in the inevitable bankruptcy and openly harm them'.

One worrying aspect of this is that many nondemocratic countries seem to be doing much better than democratic ones, indicating that, perhaps, *nice guys finish last* after all. This is not merely evident from the fact that China and Singapore are doing extremely well, it is also suggested by the fact that what is probably the least democratic European country in the former communist world – Belarus – is doing much better than the two democratic countries that have most closely followed the advice of the West:

Georgia and Ukraine. In both Georgia and Ukraine virtually all segments of society are poorer in 2019 than they were under the extremely inefficient communist system in 1989. This proves one of the key theses of this book: it is better to have a relatively inefficient manufacturing sector than to have none at all. In Belarus all segments of society are wealthier than they were in 1989,[20] and wages – which used to be about the same in Belarus and Ukraine – are now about 50 percent higher in dictatorial Belarus than in democratic Ukraine.

The mechanism behind this nice-guys-finish-last phenomenon is relatively simple. Nice guys – i.e., democratically elected governments – follow the advice and conditionalities of the Washington Institutions. Dictatorships left and right, on the other hand, do not listen to the Washington Institutions, and therefore escape the worst cases of premature de-industrialization. One thing that united dictatorships and nationalist governments along the whole political axis was the conviction that manufacturing industry was important. Since Latin America in the 1970s, the IMF and the World Bank have increasingly been a threat to global democracy. Too often democracy does not deliver because democratically elected governments are forced to listen to the wrong economic advice. If the goal had been to maximize world trade, the advice of the Washington Institutions would have been appropriate. If we instead wish to maximize world welfare, their policies fail miserably.

Not only are the failed recommendations of the World Bank and the IMF a threat to democracy, they also contribute importantly to increase international migration. When I studied economics and population at Harvard in the mid-1970s, it was understood that the population carrying capacity of a nation was determined by its economic structure. Former President Herbert Hoover's 1947 report from a de-industrialized West Germany was still remembered: 'There is the illusion that the New Germany left after the annexations can be reduced to a "pastoral state". It cannot be done unless we exterminate or move 25.000.000 out of it'. Hoover had rediscovered the wisdom of the mercantilist population theorists: an industrialized nation has a much larger carrying capacity in terms of population than an agricultural state. The

Marshall Plan – reversing the de-industrialization plan Hoover here refers to – was announced about two months after this report from Hoover reached Washington. Today the mechanism described by Hoover is strongly at work in a de-industrialized Latin America and in a largely not yet industrialized Africa.[21]

The present economic strategy has already caused much harm in the European periphery. Greece caught the world's attention, but in Latvia – another country in the European periphery – the economic hardships have generally gone unnoticed. A so-called internal devaluation has cut real wages by up to 30 percent. Unemployment and low living standards force people to leave the country, and the population has decreased by around 20 percent, from 2.38 million to 1.9 million since 2000. Latvian birth statistics reveal a culture under extreme pressure, as people stop having children. In 1987 42,000 children were born in Latvia; in 2010 only 18,000. Latvia follows the classical sequence of economic decay: 1. De-industrialization (in the 1990s), 2. De-agriculturalization (death of agriculture), and 3. De-population.

During the *thirty glorious years of economic growth* between 1945 and 1975 there was no *trade-off* between democracy and increased welfare as described above. In the West people were free and wealthy, but under communism people were poorer and unfree. At the time, the logic behind the Marshall Plan – an understanding of the importance of the economic structure of a country – was still in place. The last time this type of understanding was seen was with the integration of Spain into the *European Economic Community* during the 1980s: import tariffs were lowered only gradually, and special provisions were made to strenghten the important car industry. Only now can the strong impact the 1989 Fall of the Berlin Wall had on the 1992 Maastricht Treaty be gradually understood.

Learning from the 1930s

Today's '1848 moment' – when liberalism collapses from the simultaneous attacks from left and right – calls for the same type of *zeitgeist*, the same set of theories and beliefs, that solved this dilemma in 1848 and again in the early 1930s, following the 1929 financial crisis. In 1933 John Maynard Keynes wrote a seminal article, *National Self-sufficiency*.[22] Correcting for the fact that *the minimum efficient size* of economic units is much bigger now than it was in the 1930s, this article merits rereading. The present rude awakening requires the recognition that partial deglobalization may be necessary for the international system – indeed globalization itself – to hold: that goods to a larger extent must be 'home-spun' and that finance also ought to have a more national character. This of course does not literally mean autarky or self-sufficiency, but it means returning to the extremely successful world model of development that ruled from 1947 until 1989: the vision that world prosperity requires that manufacturing industries and advanced service sectors are distributed to all nations.

As is made clear in this book, the key mechanism to wealth is not manufacturing *per se*, but activities subject to increasing returns, technological change, and consequent dynamic imperfect competition under high barriers to entry. Today such activities are increasingly found also in advanced service industries – in companies like Facebook and Google – but manufacturing appears to be a *mandatory passage point* to such advanced services.

Keynes's 1933 article didactically takes the reader through the necessary change in ideology and mind-set which was embarked upon in 1933 and upon which the West now again needs to embark. Keynes first takes us through the reasoning necessary to free the mind from a belief in free trade as a matter of 'moral law':

> I was brought up, like most Englishmen, to respect free trade not only as an economic doctrine which a rational and instructed person could not doubt, but almost as a part of the moral law. I regarded ordinary departures from it as being at the same time an imbecility and an outrage. I thought England's unshakable free trade convictions, maintained for nearly a hundred years, to be both the explanation before man and the justification before Heaven of her economic supremacy. As lately as 1923 I was writing that free trade was based on fundamental 'truths' which, stated with their due

qualifications, no one can dispute who is capable of understanding the meaning of the words.

Keynes gives us compelling arguments for deglobalization, why globalization can go too far:

> But experience is accumulating that remoteness between ownership and operation is an evil in the relations among men, likely or certain in the long run to set up strains and enmities which will bring to nought the financial calculation.

> I sympathize, therefore, with those who would minimize, rather than with those who would maximize, economic entanglement among nations. Ideas, knowledge, science, hospitality, travel – these are the things which should of their nature be international. But let goods be homespun whenever it is reasonably and conveniently possible, and, above all, let finance be primarily national. Yet, at the same time, those who seek to disembarrass a country of its entanglements should be very slow and wary. It should not be a matter of tearing up roots but of slowly training a plant to grow in a different direction.

> For these strong reasons, therefore, I am inclined to the belief that, after the transition is accomplished, a greater measure of national self-sufficiency and economic isolation among countries than existed in 1914 may tend to serve the cause of peace, rather than otherwise. At any rate, the age of economic internationalism was not particularly successful in avoiding war; and if its friends retort, that the imperfection of its success never gave it a fair chance, it is reasonable to point out that a greater success is scarcely probable in the coming years.

Global free trade did not deliver on its promise of global peace, although this was once a key argument for free trade. Obviously today's context is different than that of 1933, but my argument is that since the very same type of economic forces are at work today – although in a different context – the solution to the problem lies in similar recommendations to those Keynes offered. I am suggesting that this is the direction we need to move, but the recommendations should not be taken literally. We must keep in mind that the policies here outlined by Keynes – not a religious belief in free trade – became the foundations for the policies that produced unprecedented high economic growth in the world until the mid-1970s.

We should also keep in mind that Keynes suggested a mechanism that would have prevented today's enormous US trade deficits. He suggested a global 'International Clearing Union' which, among other things, would impose a tax on large export surpluses. This would have caused China and Germany today to revalue their currencies[23] and/or to pay an international tax on their trade surplus.

Later in the 1933 essay Keynes turns to what we today would call environmental issues:

> The same rule of self-destructive financial calculation governs every walk of life. We destroy the beauty of the countryside because the unappropriated splendors of nature have no economic value. We are capable of shutting off the sun and the stars because they do not pay a dividend. London is one of the richest cities in the history of civilization, but it cannot 'afford' the highest standards of achievement of which its own living citizens are capable, because they do not 'pay'.

> The decadent international but individualistic capitalism, in the hands of which we found ourselves after the war, is not a success. It is not intelligent, it is not beautiful, it is not just, it is not virtuous – and it doesn't deliver the goods. In short, we dislike it, and we are beginning to despise it. But when we wonder what to put in its place, we are extremely perplexed.... We are – all of us, I expect – about to make many mistakes. No one can tell which of the new systems will prove itself best.

The road ahead is now better defined than in 1933, when a planned economy was one of the possibilities open to the world. However, as a starting point we still have to get rid of what Keynes called the 'bundle of obsolete habiliments one's mind drags round'. A key obsolete notion is that all economic activities should be seen as being qualitatively alike, as is implicit in Ricardian trade theory.

Since economic activities in reality differ so widely in terms of their ability to create welfare – which this book attempts to explain – a strategy to maximize world real income and welfare requires very different policies than the present economic strategy that instead maximizes international trade.

'Free competition' – as was recognized long ago in German economic theory – may lead to a winner-takes-all situation where the declining purchasing power in the losing nations will shrink the export markets for the winning nations. Germany's huge export surplus combined with the shrinking purchasing power in the European periphery will in the long term hurt Germany's exports. China is faced with a similar dilemma. As I stated in the foreword to the Chinese translation of this book: 'It may initially sound illogical, but as wages and employment rates in many European countries and in the United States slide, it may in fact be in China's long-term interest to allow some protectionism in these countries. Protecting parts of the industrial system of the United States and Europe would safeguard the future size of overseas markets for Chinese goods.'

The devastating effects of the present crises are a direct result of the loss of a whole theoretical tradition based on quali-tative understanding of the economy – of economics as an *Erfahrungswissenschaft*, a science of experience – based on an understanding of history rather than on mathematics. In this Continental European tradition – from Karl Marx to the left to Joseph Schumpeter to the right – financial crises are a normal feature of capitalism. Because this type of theory also carries with it an understanding of the role of technology, this Continental European type of theory also explains uneven economic development. It is my hope that this kind of experience-based economic theory – in the tradition of which this book is written – again will become influential in Europe. We must recognize that

1. free trade does *not* create factor-price equalization, it does not tend to create economic harmony unless trade is *technologically symmetrical* (what used to be called *symmetrical trade*);
2. free trade is *not* part and parcel of democracy; in fact, the arrows of causality point more in the opposite direction: indus-trialism comes first. The middle classes that make democracies

stable depend heavily on a manufacturing sector[24]; and

3. the natural successor to manufacturing-based democracies may very well be a return to the system that preceded industrialism, i.e., feudalism. I have described this new version of feudalism as *post-industrial feudalism*, where the power-base is financial capital rather than land. David Ricardo's claim – quoted above – that the natural wage level is *subsistence* supports this view.

We presently face a quadruple challenge: a financial crisis, an energy crisis, an environmental crisis, and a crisis of unemployment. There is also a serious crisis of unbalance between the core and peripheral countries of the European Union. Either the uncompetitive peripheral countries become the receiving end of active economic policies – including a breakup of the Euro – or a large number of the inhabitants of these countries will physically move to the core countries. However, Greeks moving to Germany is a solution wanted neither by the Greeks nor by the Germans. There are important lessons to be drawn by Europe from how Argentina escaped from its crisis of the 1990s. *Default* and *exchange rate flexibility* are two necessary ingredients.

The Euro has proved to constitute a new version of the 'gold standard', impeding what European nations previously solved by frequent adjustment of exchange rates: economically 'irresponsible' nations have traditionally been forced to devalue. This had two beneficial effects: a) their economies were made internationally competitive again, and b) the value of the national debt, which was typically issued in the national currency, was simultaneously reduced (e.g., Italy has traditionally had a large public debt, but in lire).

Capital must be channeled from financial speculation into the employment of underutilized human resources to solve the energy and environmental crises. Polluting oil is just as unlikely to be mankind's last source of energy as horses were, but as the age of complete dependence on oil is approaching an end, we face similar uncertainties as when the age of horse-drawn carriages was coming to an end. The 1800s saw prototypes both of steam cars and electrical cars, but the best solution for the next more than 100 years came late and from an outsider, Karl Friedrich Benz, with the gasoline-powered car. Today we are facing similar technological uncertainties and therefore need to throw resources at many possible solutions. If inflation is a necessary part of quelling the dominance of the financial sector and increasing real wages, so be it. The financial crisis of the 1970s – usually called the oil crisis – was also solved partly though inflation. It has been argued that the negative interest rates of the 1970s forced capitalists into risky ventures in the real economy, like those in Silicon Valley.

Today's economic theory has lost key features of what built Western civilization, both of the Renaissance and of the Enlightenment. The core of what I call *The Other Canon of Economics*, inspired by the incredible richness of past political economy compared to what we ahistorically have come to embrace in recent decades, lies in qualitative features of societies that are not compatible – not possible to include – in the excessively formal structures of today's mainstream economics.[25]

Creating a simplified version of the Renaissance, in order to contrast this key period for the creation of Western civilization with what today is understood as 'capitalism', we find a period extremely focused on *magna facere*: creating great works and innovations in art and in the production of everything from weaponry to irrigation canals was a way of thinking big that went far beyond profit-making. What came to characterize the Western economy was that building organizations did not stop when the owner had enough money to feed his family. Renaissance *magna facere* went far beyond greed, and – as described in this book – already in the 1200s the wealth of Florence was seen as emerging from a *ben commune*, a synergic common weal that was in itself a unit of analysis.

Renaissance Florence also understood the need to prevent speculation. Transporting food out of the city was prohibited; this could feed speculation. Renaissance cities also managed to create John Kenneth Galbraith's *balance of countervailing power* referred to above. The Florentine government – the *signoria* – consisted of nine members representing different professions, and only one of them represented the financial sector. Renaissance cities also frequently rotated their elected administrators to prevent corruption, and

Florence specifically cultivated its urban culture – of manufacturing and trading – by keeping the producers of raw materials, the big land owners, away from any political power.

Two key features of the Enlightenment are also lost in today's economics: the ability to build classification systems, as Linnaeus did, and the ability to understand the limits that need to be set for private greed.[26] As I argue in this book, classification systems can also be extremely useful heuristics. A key feature of mainstream economics today is its inability to qualitatively distinguish between economic activities, and a simple taxonomy distinguishing among three types of economic activities – those subject to *diminishing returns to scale*, *constant returns to scale*, and *increasing returns to scale* – would be sufficient to demolish David Ricardo's theory of international trade and create something more realistic and sustainable.

The apparent accuracy of neoclassical economics is a direct result of its failure to make necessary – yet hard-to-model – qualitative distinctions. We all understand that if all medical doctors of Paris are put in one country and all the people who wash the floors of Parisian hospitals in another, we get one rich country of medical doctors and one poor country of cleaners. This common-sense proposition is unfathomable in Ricardian trade theory, because world trade is modeled as the bartering of labor hours, all assumed to be of the same quality. Many in the United States and Europe at the time considered this the English way of trying to convince colonies and competitors to stay with their comparative advantage in being poor and ignorant. Now, this same theory is boomeranging and making the West poorer.

Chapter 6 in this book is called 'Explaining Away Failure: Red Herrings at the End of History', and on page 216 'get the institutions right' is listed as one of the red herrings, one of the misleading paths. Not being able to correct the main flaws of neoclassical economic theory, today's economists tend to seek explanations outside their own theoretical framework. In their 2012 book *Why Nations Fail: The Origins of Power, Prosperity, and Poverty*, Daron Acemoglu and James Robinson put a heavy emphasis on institutions. The main contrast between Acemoglu and Robinson's thesis and mine is that the former tends to disregard the context in which institutions tend to develop, as solutions to existing problems. This approach risks reversing the arrows of causality.

I argue, in the continental European tradition, that the Venetians did not invent an official property register (*catasto*) around 1150 only later to create capitalism, but rather because the capitalist growth of the city created a need for a well-organised property register. The core institutions of modern society are products of the transition from feudalism to industrialism. By disregarding the history of economic policy – that prohibiting manufacturing industry was often at the core of colonial policies – Acemoglu and Robinson tend to blame the present elites of the Third World for conditions that historically have been imposed upon their countries by First World imperialism. In a sense they blame the victims.

We have still not seen the full economic, social, political, and geopolitical fallout from the 2008 crisis, a crisis born, in fundamental ways, from the hubris and mistakes of neoclassical economics.[27] I fear that things will get worse before they get better, but, in the meantime, mainstream economists should begin to be held responsible for the disastrous real-world policies they implicitly and explicitly have promoted. I argued this before the crisis, and I argue it even more forcefully now. Again and again, historical experience suggests that a system where a few wealthy actors keep the rest in thrall is unsustainable, and that backlashes can be terrible. It is a lesson that academic economics – indeed the world – tragically is being forced to relearn once more.

Introduction to the 2007 Edition

The gap between the rich and the poor on this planet is larger than ever before and still growing – at least by most methods of measuring. Even after massive economic transfers during three 'Development Decades' that began in 1970, and trillions of dollars of 'development assistance', the situation is still dismal and getting worse in many places. Half of the world's population lives on less than $2 a day, and in a number of countries real wages peaked as long ago as the 1970s. It has been estimated that in 1750 the gap between the richest and the poorest nations was at a ratio of 2 to 1; since then it has only increased.

The aim of this book is to explain the mechanisms that have produced this result, in a way that is accessible to 'the interested layperson' in any part of the world. The book must not be mistaken for an attempt to popularize ruling economic thought. On the contrary, it is an attempt to contribute to an ongoing process of refuting current policy orthodoxy and to resurrect a long-standing economic tradition, from the only laboratory available to economists – history.

The human cost of poverty is enormous. The years of human life lost due to infant and child mortality, preventable disease and general low life expectancy add up to terrifying numbers. Civil wars and conflicts over scarce resources cause pain and suffering that in wealthy countries is mostly avoidable. To these can be added the likely impact of environmental degradation on the poor. In poor societies such vicious circles are easily created, where the only way to meet demands from an increasing population is to intensify the exploitation of nature.

Since the fall of the Berlin Wall in 1989, our world economic order has – in a more fundamental way than ever before – been based on an economic theory which 'proves' the opposite of what in fact can be observed. World free trade is supposed to level out any differences in wages among rich and poor countries. If humankind does not interfere with the 'natural forces' of the market – if we apply the principle of laissez-faire – progress and economic harmony will reign. As early as 1926 John Maynard Keynes (1883–1946), the English economist who diagnosed the depression of the 1930s, wrote a book entitled *The End of Laissez-Faire.* However, by 1989 the collapse of the Berlin Wall triggered an almost messianic euphoria about a world economy that would finally conform to the expectations of theory. The World Trade Organization's first Secretary General, Renato Ruggiero, declared that we should unleash 'the borderless economy's potential to equalize relations between countries and regions'. This belief is at the core of the ideology of the International Monetary Fund (IMF) and the World Bank, and from the early 1990s, for all practical purposes, these Washington institutions took over the management of the affairs of most poor countries. For many parts of the globe, the result has been a shambles.

An abyss now separates Third World reality from the vision of Ruggiero and the Washington institutions. Where the prophets of the new world order predicted harmony, we see famine, war and progressive environmental collapse. Today we are slowly beginning to take reality into account once again. In 1992 Francis Fukuyama, American philosopher, foreign policy expert and proponent of liberal democracy, hailed the end of the Cold War as 'the end of history' in *The End of History and the Last Man,* but in 2006, in his book *After the Neocons: America at the crossroads*, he withdrew support for his own earlier views. As he now sees it, the neo-conservatives seemed to think that democracy was a default condition to which societies reverted when coercive regime change occurred, rather than a long-term process of institution-building and reform.

In this book I set out a parallel argument about the economy. Neo-liberal economists argued that economic growth and welfare would be the default condition if market interventions were removed, rather than the result of a long-term process of building a particular form of economic structure. In terms of understanding economic growth, the world *Zeitgeist* is going through a learning curve similar to that of Fukuyama between 1992 and 2006.

The world has experienced similar shocking differences between theories of economic harmony and brutal economic reality before, and there is a lot to learn from these experiences. We must move away from a theory which poses economic harmony as an automatic outcome of divinely or mathematically premeditated harmony, and move back to one in which economic harmony is a product of conscious policies. In this we are retracing the steps of one of the European Enlightenment's great champions, the French philosopher Voltaire.

On 15 and 16 January 1759, Voltaire was furtively sending out copies of his new novel *Candide, or Optimism*, to Paris, Amsterdam, London and Brussels. Once the copies arrived at these major centres of the European book-trade – in what can only be called a marketing innovation – they were published on the same, predetermined date across Western Europe. The reasons for this secrecy were twofold. On the one hand, Voltaire sought to sell as many copies as possible before they were pirated and he was cut out of the profits; on the other, he sought to bring his revolutionary message to as wide an audience as possible before the authorities realized the dangers posed by his ideas and moved to suppress them. Police around Europe seized copies of *Candide* and destroyed presses that were printing new editions. The Vatican even placed Voltaire's work on its Index of forbidden books. All to no avail: this little volume became *the* publishing phenomenon of the eighteenth century, an intellectual tsunami that not even the combined dams of political and ecclesiastical tyranny could contain.

Voltaire's story follows the young Candide as he left his home (not entirely willingly) to experience the world which he, as he had been taught by the wise Professor Pangloss, his teacher of 'meta-physico-theologico-cosmo-codology', believed to be 'the best of all possible worlds'. Voltaire was attacking the hands-off, optimistic determinism that placed on outside forces alone, whether Providence, Faith, deities or markets, the ability to bring about change and transformation. What Candide encountered, however, was a murderous world of poverty, marauding armies, religious persecution, earthquakes and shipwrecks, a world where his fiancée, the lovely Cunégonde, was cut open by soldiers 'after they'd raped her as many times as anyone can be' before being sold into slavery. All the while, Pangloss continued to preach that this was the 'best of all possible worlds', to the point where young Candide asked himself, 'if this is the best of all possible worlds, then what must the others be like?'

Through *Candide*, Voltaire sought to emancipate Europe from the mental slavery of Professor Pangloss. Many of those who preside over economic orthodoxy are in the grip of a similar, disastrous optimism and a corresponding emancipation is needed. Today's Panglossian economic theory is created from the top down, based on arbitrary assumptions and metaphors from astronomy or physics. This theory pictures a harmonious universe that happens to be tailor-made for the ruling theoretical fashion. The alternative theory that some of us are trying to revive is built up from below, based on observations of a reality that very often does not favour economic development. Rather than seeking to 'remove the obstacles' to prosperity, development must be seen for what it has always been: the outcome of conscious and deliberate policy.

One hallmark of Panglossian logic is that whatever happens is rationalized in ways that contradict reasonable modes of thought and common sense, for example, the Washington institutions sometimes argue that the dramatic mass exodus of desperately poor people from the Third World, prompted by the absence of real jobs, is 'all for the best', because their remittances to jobless relatives left behind improve the balance of payments of these poor countries. On a daily basis, innumerable immigrants risk (and many lose) their lives attempting to escape areas of superfluous population in order to reach areas of superfluous wealth. Those who survive suffer from exploitation and hostility in their new countries, so that their relatives can be saved from outright destitution.

Another feature of such thinking is that the core assumptions of the model – those who create 'the best of all possible worlds' – are hardly ever questioned. Reality tends to be filtered in such a way as to exclude observations that contradict expected outcomes. When reality gets as aggressively obtrusive as it is today, explanations are sought outside the core model. Poverty becomes a consequence of race, or culture or geography – anything but orthodox economics is to blame. Since the Panglossian economic model is assumed to be perfect, any explanation of its failure must be found in factors that lie outside economics.

Voltaire's message, and the reason why authorities at the time did their utmost to repress it, was of course that the world is not perfect, that one should actively seek to improve it rather than simply let things run their course. Maintaining civil society, let alone achieving something like 'progress', requires immense effort and constant vigilance. The reforms of the Enlightenment and the commercial societies that sprang up across Europe were heavily indebted to the spirit of *Candide*. In the twenty-first century, as we begin to realize the immensity of space and the randomness of evolution, Voltaire's insight that the world might not be perfectly designed around the whims of humankind should be all the more evident. Yet, economists and politicians today still tell us, with the certainty and authority of dead theologians, that the world would be perfect if only we would practise laissez-faire and let individual instincts (which are generally assumed to be 'rational') interact freely and without any but the most basic intervention. Some even argue that we should privatize basic institutions of society, like the legal system, and subject society in its entirety to the providential harmony of 'the market'; an assumed perfect insurance market would in this case guard us from any mischief caused by privatized justice.

But harmony is not the natural state of society. It is naive to think that the laws of the cosmos – to the extent that they may exist – should always prove positive for society, and that harmony should always result from submitting to them. Faith in 'the market' is thus often difficult to differentiate from faith in Providence or in the goodness of an ever-present deity. Why, one could ask, should the cosmos be tailored for something as idiosyncratic and historically contingent as the contemporary definition of capitalism and globalization? Once we rid ourselves of the fantasy that 'natural laws' govern the enrichment of nations, we can begin to assess how and why certain policies have worked in the past and how such successes might inform policy again in the future.

One of the main targets of Voltaire's attack in the years following *Candide* were *les économistes*, a group which in the history of economic thought is referred to as the *Physiocrats* (indicating 'rule of nature' in the same way that *democracy* means 'rule of the people'). Today's mainstream economics proudly traces its ancestry back to the Physiocrats, who believed that the wealth of nations was to be derived solely from agriculture. Historically, however, the Physiocrats did not dominate economic policy for long, and where they did – as in France – their policies created scarcity of food and poverty. Virtually all important European intellectuals of the day, from the Frenchmen Voltaire and Diderot to the Italian Abbé Galiani and Scotsman David Hume, were fierce anti-Physiocrats. Even in France, the home of Physiocracy, the most influential and bestselling economics books of the day were those of the anti-Physiocrats. And the Physiocratic movement never reached England at all. One reason for studying Voltaire's fight against the Physiocrats is that we can learn from observing similar theories: that produce the same results under similar circumstances. Today the Right to Food movement recognizes that at times there might be a conflict between human beings' right to eat and the principle of free trade; in 1774, during the build-up to the French Revolution, precisely the same argument was made by the French anti-Physiocrat Simon Linguet. Although the anti-Physiocrats won the day in practical policy terms that is not reflected in today's economics textbooks. The history of economics tends to exist in splendid isolation not only from what actually happened in real economic policy, but also from what happened in neighbouring disciplines such as philosophy, Voltaire's field.

This book begins by describing different types of economic thinking and goes on to argue why the virtual world monopoly of the current dominant theory should be broken. English economist David

Ricardo's trade theory, dating from 1817,[1] has become the linchpin of our world economic order. Even though we can see that free trade in some contexts makes people poorer, Western governments are still complacently insisting on it and are offering more aid as an incentive for accepting it. Thus, the good intentions of those who call for more aid obscure the folly of the current economic orthodoxy as it is carried out in real policies. In this way the dogma of global free trade survives, while idealism and generosity act to cover up a surreal and sometimes even criminal and corrupt reality. Understanding the problems underlying today's ruling economic theory and resurrecting alternative approaches is a necessary starting point.

Chapter 1 of this book explains the existence of different types of economic theory, and the gap that is frequently found between 'high theory' rhetoric and practical reality in terms of economic policy. Chapter 2 traces the evolution of today's canonical sequence of authors from Physiocracy via Adam Smith and David Ricardo to standard textbook economics. This tradition is contrasted with a much older and less abstract Other Canon of economics that provided the guidelines for economic policy when today's presently wealthy nations made their historical transitions from poverty to wealth; for example, England's progression from 1485 through to the post-Second World War Marshall Plan.

In Chapter 3 I argue that what Enlightenment economists called *emulation*,[2] rather than 'comparative advantage' and 'free trade', lies at the heart of successful development. In this context emulation means imitating in order to equal or excel. If the tribe across the river has taken the step from the Stone Age to the Bronze Age, your own tribe is faced with the choice of either sticking to its comparative advantage in the Stone Age or trying to emulate the neighbouring tribe into the Bronze Age. Before David Ricardo there was little doubt that emulation would be the best strategy, and historically the most important contribution of Ricardo's trade theory was that, for the first time, it made colonialism morally defensible. Today we have totally dismissed the idea that a strategy of emulation was a mandatory passage point for all nations that are presently rich: we have outlawed the key tools needed for emulation. This chapter uses the history of economic policies – the knowledge of which policies created successful development in the past – in order to create a theory of uneven economic development. In today's economics, neither of these is regarded as a legitimate academic field. Instead, in today's trade theory, economic harmony is already built into its basic assumptions.

There are plenty of good arguments for free trade, but Chapter 4 argues that David Ricardo's is not one of them. Delving deeper into the economics of production reveals that the best arguments for globalization are also the best ones for preventing poor countries from prematurely entering the world economy. Ricardo's theory appears to be right in many contexts, but is essentially right for the wrong reasons. However, aspects of Ricardian theory are deeply cherished both by the political left and the right, and criticizing it is problematic. On the political right, Ricardian trade theory provides the 'proof' that capitalism and instant unrestrained international trade are in the interests of all inhabitants of the planet. The proof of the benefits of free trade is based on what economists call the *labour theory of value*, i.e. that human labour is the sole source of all value, and the Marxist world-view is also based on this same theory. As I see it, the labour theory of value was probably better suited to make nineteenth-century industrial workers take to the streets than to explain the wealth and poverty in today's world.

Polish mathematician Stanislaw Ulam once asked American economics Nobel prizewinner Paul Samuelson – who in 1949 theorized that free trade will tend to level out world wages – whether he could point to an idea in economics that was universally true but not obvious. Samuelson's response was the 'principle of comparative advantage', according to which two countries necessarily benefit from engaging in free trade with each other, provided their relative production costs are not identical. Thus, an attack on the philosophical basis of the free trade doctrine exposes one not only to attacks from both sides of the right–left axis, but also undermines the claim of economics to be a 'hard science'. This book brings back traditions in which economics is not and never can be a 'hard science'.

Chapter 5 argues that today in many poor countries we can observe the opposite of development and progress, that is, retrogression and primitivization. The mechanisms causing this primitivization are explained, using Mongolia, Rwanda and Peru as examples. To go back to the example of the two tribes given above, logic in use only a few decades ago admitted that a higher standard of living could be achieved by entering into the Bronze Age, even though your own tribe might not be as advanced as the leading tribe. The logic that died with the Berlin Wall was that it is better to have an inefficient manufacturing sector than not to have a manufacturing sector at all, and such an approach has led to falling real wages in many countries in Eastern Europe, Asia, Africa and Latin America.

The recent responses from mainstream economics to the challenges of poverty are discussed in Chapter 6. In order to find remedies, it is necessary to distinguish core aspects of economic development from what are collateral effects or even just symptoms. It is argued that by being unwilling to critically evaluate these core metaphors, assumptions and postulates of economics, economists have recently been distracted by a string of red herrings – they have looked everywhere but at the core issues in the realm of production. The same people who were in charge in the 1990s are still the ideological leaders of what is supposed to be a reconstruction. It is rather like asking Attila the Hun for advice on urban regeneration.

In Chapter 7 I argue that knowledge of the historical process of development can prevent us from adopting policies that seem logical but are in fact very damaging. In comparison to the free trade that is forced on poor countries, rich countries restrict imports of agricultural products from the Third World and subsidize their own agriculture. Intuitively the highest priority is put on rectifying these unfair practices, but, as we shall see from eighteenth-century examples, the removal of agricultural tariffs is a long-standing weapon in the colonial armoury. However unfair the practices may seem, focusing too much on them may lead us into the Panglossian trap of assuming that if we only had *perfectly* free trade and laissez-faire, the visions of economic harmony would actually become a reality. Present World Trade Organisation (WTO) rhetoric is that the South stays poor because the North protects its agriculture. I shall attempt to show that the world is not so constructed that the starving South would get rich if they were only allowed to sell their food to the North.

We cannot make the poor rich merely through our direct and naive kindness. The world is so complex now that we have to think through the systemic and long-term effects of our actions. It is natural that people who observe backward agriculture in Africa wish to help Africa by making that agriculture more efficient. Enlightenment philosopher and economist David Hume, however, suggested that the best way to improve agriculture is through the roundabout way of first improving manufacturing industry – and we now have half a millennium of historical data to back up Hume's insight. Achieving an optimum balance between different economic sectors in a nation used to be an important part of Enlightenment economics, but has become totally lost as a theme today.

Just as we do not create more food in the Third World by eating less ourselves – at the moment famines are essentially caused by a lack of purchasing power rather than a lack of world supply – we do not create development in the Third World by closing down First World agriculture. This book argues that a deal should be struck by which the First World is allowed to protect its own agriculture (but prevented from dumping its surpluses on the world markets) while the Third World is allowed to protect its manufacturing and advanced service sectors. This is the only policy that can be consistent with successful development policy over the last 500 years.

We have collectively forgotten how to create wealthy nations – an art that was successfully employed as recently as fifty years ago – and so our responses to the challenges of poverty today, however well intentioned, amount to an attack on the symptoms of poverty rather than its deep causes. Chapter 7 focuses on the Millennium Development Goals that include worthy goals like reducing by half the number of people living on less than a dollar a day and the proportion of people who suffer from hunger, reducing diseases and child mortality, as well as educational and environmental goals. I argue that both the Millennium Goals and the campaign to 'Make Poverty History' are far too heavily biased towards palliative economics, aimed at easing the pains of poverty rather than at making the fundamental structural changes that result in true economic development. Rather than creating democracy and development, this approach – regardless of the nobility of the intentions – will produce a crippling welfare colonialism in which rich countries maintain their political power over poor countries. This is not to say we should not do what we can to relieve suffering through aid, but we must also take on the more important task of understanding how poor countries can become richer by themselves. Advocates of free trade often use similar rhetoric for their policies, but there is a crucial difference: while I argue for development over assistance as the priority for the world's poor, I want to advocate development that serves the world's poor, not passive transfers that in the end take the form of covert colonialism.

The concluding Chapter 8 charts how it is possible to create middle-income countries, where all inhabitants have a purpose and a claim on the necessities of life and at least some of its pleasures. In terms of theory and economic policy, this needs nothing more radical than going back to the practices of trade and development as they were practised in the period immediately following the Second World War, as exemplified in the 1948 Havana Charter of the defunct International Trade Organization (ITO), that is, the subjugating of the goal of free trade to other goals directly involving human welfare.

This book has three main audiences in mind. First of all, my fellow economists: the main theoretical objective of the book is to show why standard international trade theory, as it is applied today, is unsuitable – and can be outright 'primitivizing' – when imposed on nations at widely different levels of development. The book's theoretical basis is evolutionary or Schumpeterian economics,[3] to which are added elements from the historical and institutional schools, past and present. The economics of Joseph Schumpeter (1883–1950) is presently in vogue, and the book is true to Schumpeter's frequent preference for Continental economists over their British contemporaries Adam Smith (1723–90) and David

Ricardo (1772–1823). It should be kept in mind that Schumpeter's verdict on Ricardo's highly abstract construction was: 'It is an excellent theory that can never be refuted and lacks nothing but sense.'[4] As did the two most important economists of the twentieth century, John Maynard Keynes (1883–1946) and Schumpeter, this book largely defends the principles of economic theory before Adam Smith – so-called mercantilism – in its context. The material that will probably be of most interest to professional economists appears in Appendices at the end of the book.

Second, my aim is that readers without a grounding in the subject will understand what follows by the time they finish reading the book. Tightly packed into the language of economics – which the book will attempt to demystify – is the incontrovertible fact that rich countries got rich because for decades, often centuries, their states and ruling elites set up, subsidized and protected dynamic industries and services. They all emulated the most prosperous countries at the time, bringing their productive structures into those areas where technological change was being focused. In this way they created rents (a return above 'normal' income) that spread to capitalists in the form of higher profits, to labour in the form of higher wages, and to governments in the form of higher taxes. At its core, colonialism is a system that seeks to prevent these types of effects from being produced in the colonies. Poor countries specialize in activities that have one or more of the following three characteristics: (a) they are subject to diminishing rather than increasing returns, (b) they are either devoid of learning potential; and/or (c) the fruits of learning – rather than producing local wealth – are passed on to their customers in the rich countries in the form of lower prices. From this perspective, what we call 'development' is essentially a knowledge- and technology-based rent that often is reinforced, rather than reduced, by free trade between nations at very different levels of development. In this way some nations may specialize in being wealthy while others specialize according to their comparative advantage in being poor.

Both these audiences must appreciate that the main difference between rich and poor countries is that rich countries have all moved through a stage *without* free trade, which – when successful – subsequently made free trade desirable. This mandatory passage point in the history of all presently developed countries – allowing poor countries to emulate the economic structures of rich countries – is currently outlawed. Markets will not magically eradicate poverty any more than they will magically address the problems posed by global warming and environmental degradation. Only a confident and determined public in rich countries can ensure that the governments of poor countries are free to make decisions for the benefit of their own people. This means rejecting both the alleged rationality of the free trade orthodoxy and the alleged morality of a 'fairer' system of global trade. Fair trade under current conditions could easily leave extreme poverty intact. It also means keeping a close eye on our governments to ensure that they are not interfering illegitimately in the internal affairs of poor countries. This, rather than agitation for a reduction in agricultural tariffs, is likely to help the world's poorest.

And finally, a word to those who live in poor countries, my third audience. I hope that what follows will help to map the mechanisms that create wealth and poverty, creating a framework in which to discuss how extreme poverty in your countries might be addressed. Understanding the mechanisms at work makes it possible to open up a debate, and to find policies with which to fill the wider policy space that is now opening up for poor countries. Throughout I try not to prescribe what I would do to encourage development, but to suggest what the great architects of development in Europe and the United States would recommend today. If you take anything from this book, let it be this: if you want to understand the causes of American and European prosperity, study the policies of those who created it, not the advice of their forgetful successors.

1

Discovering Types of
Economic Theories

A paradigm can, for that matter, even insulate the community
from those socially important problems that are not reducible
to the puzzle form, because they cannot be stated in terms of
the conceptual and instrumental tools the paradigm supplies.

Thomas Kuhn, *The Structure of Scientific Revolutions*, 1962

Even after many years – and despite the fact I had not then read
Voltaire – the day when work on this book was started can be
determined fairly accurately. It was on one of the first days of July
1967, during my last high-school summer vacation, and I was
standing at the highest point of the largest garbage dump in Lima,
Peru. Here, with a good view of the dump itself and the nearby
slum, a man had constructed a dwelling from old steel drums. The
exterior was gaily decorated with colourful banners waving in the
wind, and the owner had invited our small group of passers-by in
for tea. I was in Peru as a guest of a Peruvian community development organization. That same autumn I was to head a campaign
among secondary school students in Norway, collecting funds for
school building in the Andes. Students in Norway, Sweden and
Finland got one day off from school, and the money we made was

donated to buy construction material for a large number of small schools to be built by the Andean villagers themselves.

Why are they so poor? My Peruvian sojourn was only into its second day and the question was gradually taking form. The background for my question was that most of the people I observed at work – the luggage handlers at the airport, the bus drivers, the hotel personnel, the barbers, the shop attendants – did not seem to be any less efficient than the people performing the same tasks back in Norway. The mature formulation of the question gradually developed into: 'What is it about this "market" that rewards people with the same level of productivity with such different real incomes in different countries?' The day after the tea party – when the stench of garbage had almost disappeared from skin and clothing – my fellow students from Sweden and Finland and I were President Fernando Belaúnde's lunch guests at the presidential palace. While it was clear to all of us that building schools was a good idea, no one seemed to have any clear ideas about the causes of poverty. I decided to look up the explanation in an encyclopaedia when I got home, but without success. My curiosity had been whetted. Why is the real wage of a bus driver in Frankfurt sixteen times higher than the real wage of an equally efficient bus driver in Nigeria, as the World Bank recently calculated? I set out to find an answer, and this book is the result.

After undergraduate studies in Switzerland and an MBA from Harvard, I started a manufacturing firm in Italy. The question from the Lima garbage dump, however, persisted. The strange thing was that so few people seemed even to be interested in the question.

In 1967, just as now, economists tended to claim that free trade would increase economic equality, levelling out wages between the rich and the poor of this world. In fact, their confidence in this theory has grown since then. Free trade is seen as a system with all winners and no losers. So why does such a collective conviction arise in certain historical periods – the 1760s, 1840s and 1990s – 'proved' by economic theory, that if high-tech engineers and people who make a living washing dishes are placed in two different countries and start trading, they will suddenly obtain the same real wages? Important social problems and even revolutions have always followed in the wake of such theories – both in the 1760s and 1840s and now – before less abstract and more practical theories take over the academic scene, repairing the social evils. American economist Paul Krugman showed great insight when he claimed that in certain historical periods previous knowledge is forgotten, and ignorance rules.

As the years passed, I came to understand that there are different types of economic theories, and that the reason my question was not asked was that the ruling economic theory worked on assumptions that not only produced the wrong answers, but also the wrong questions (see figure 1). No such thing as a theory of uneven

As in economics, inappropriate assumptions do not only produce the wrong answers, they also generate the wrong questions. Unrealistic assumptions forming its very bedrock have been the curse of abstract economic theory from David Ricardo's trade theory (1817) through to post-Second World War general equilibrium theory, affecting both liberalism and communist planned economies.

Figure 1 Inappropriate Assumptions Generate the Wrong Questions. 'Peanuts' cartoon by Charles Schulz

development existed in standard economics. This whole set of problems fascinated me to the extent that I took time off from my small firm in order to look for a possible answer through a Ph.D. in economics in the United States. I intuitively shunned theoretical abstractions that seemed to exclude features that, in practical life, could be decisive in producing wealth or poverty. Much later I found Goethe had expressed this so well: 'Grey, my friend, is all theory. Green is the golden tree of life.'

Only years later it became clear to me that Harvard Business School, over a period of two years, had intensively brainwashed me into an alternative, but now defunct, economics tradition that kept closer to the tree of real life than economics does today. The case study methodology of business schools is based on that of the German Historical School of Economics. During twelve years' study at German-speaking universities, Edwin Gay (1867–1946), Harvard Business School founder and first Dean during a period of more than ten years, had been inspired by German economist Gustav Schmoller (1838–1917) and his historical approach to economics.[1] Standard economics too often trains people to see the world through sets of methodological and mathematical lenses, and such methods create important blind spots. In contrast, the historical approach broadly gathers evidence whereby relevance is the only valid criterion for inclusion. This book analyses globalization as a Harvard Business School case study, but with the aim of maximizing real wages rather than profits. A Harvard Business School document defines the curiosity that drives good research: 'After continuously observing and studying and thinking, you stumble across something and think "I don't understand that. There's some mismatch of existing theory and my observation of reality. It doesn't fit. I think it's important – and either I've got it wrong or they've got it wrong. I want to find out."'[2] This contrasts with how research in standard textbook economics, limited by its tools and assumptions, moves along the path of least mathematical resistance[3] rather than one of maximum relevance.

Initially I studied poor countries in order to understand their poverty. Later it became clear to me that poverty is the normal state of affairs and this correlates with economists' perceptions of the world. Traditionally, wealth and poverty used to be explained by recognizing that different economic activities were qualitatively different as carriers of wealth, a perspective that has been lost in today's dominant theory, although poor country economies correspond much more closely to the conditions assumed in standard textbook economics than do the economies of rich countries. At this point it is necessary to introduce and explain two sets of key terms that describe the differences between the economic activities that typically dominate the poor countries and those that dominate the rich countries: 'perfect' and 'imperfect' competition and 'increasing' and 'diminishing' returns.

'Perfect competition' or 'commodity competition' means that the producer cannot influence the price of what he produces, he is facing a 'perfect' market and literally reads in the newspaper what the market is willing to pay. This situation is typically found in markets for agricultural or mining products. With perfect competition normally goes a situation referred to as 'diminishing returns': as production is expanded, after a certain point, more units of the same input – capital and/or labour – will produce smaller and smaller amounts of new output. In other words, if you put more and more tractors or more labour into the same potato field, after a certain point each new person or each new tractor will produce less than the last unit added. Perfect competition and diminishing returns are assumed to be the normal state of affairs in standard textbook economics.

When production is expanded in manufacturing industry, cost developments go in the opposite direction – down rather than up. Once mechanized production has been set up, the larger the volume of output, the lower the cost per unit produced. The first copy of a software product costs a lot to produce, but subsequent copies have a very low cost. Manufacturing and service industries have no immediate inputs provided by nature, no fields, mines or fishing grounds that are limited in quantity or quality. They experience falling costs – or increasing returns to scale – as volumes of production increase. It is very important for industrial companies and advanced service providers to have a large share of the market, because this larger volume also gives them lower production costs (due to the increasing returns). The increasing returns produce market power: to a large extent they are able to influence the price of what they sell. This is termed 'imperfect competition'.

It is important to understand that these four concepts are intimately connected. Generally *increasing returns* goes with *imperfect competition*; indeed, the falling unit cost is one cause of the market power under imperfect competition. *Diminishing returns* – the inability to extend production (beyond a certain point) at falling cost – combined with the difficulty of product differentiation (wheat is wheat, while car brands are very different) are key elements in creating perfect competition in the production of raw material commodities. The exports of the rich contain the 'good' effects – increasing returns and imperfect competition – whereas traditional exports of poor countries contain the opposite, the 'bad' effects.

For centuries the term 'manufacturing' was synonymous with the combination of technological change, increasing returns and imperfect competition. By cultivating manufacturing, nations captured the 'good' type of economic activities. I argue that this has been the pattern of success starting in England under Henry VII, via the industrialization of continental Europe and the United States, to the more recent successes of Korea and Taiwan. Over the last few decades, however, more and more service industries operate with rapid technological change and increasing returns, and the distinction between industry and services has become blurred. At the same time industrial products manufactured in high volumes have acquired many of the commodity attributes (but not the diminishing returns) that used to characterize agriculture.

Rich countries display generalized imperfect competition, activities subject to increasing returns, and, as I gradually began to understand, all have become rich in exactly the same way, through policies steering them away from raw materials and diminishing returns activities into manufacturing, where the opposite laws tend to operate. I also found that the key terms seem to have changed their meanings over time. Some 300 years ago English economist John Cary (1649–1720) recommended 'free trade', but at the same time was so outraged that merchants shipped raw wool abroad that he and his contemporaries discussed 'punishing the Exporter with Death'. 'Free trade' then meant the absence of monopolies, not the absence of tariffs. It was Cary's 'cult of manufacturing' that laid the foundation for Europe's wealth.

It became increasingly clear to me that the mechanisms of wealth and poverty had, during several historical periods, been much better understood than they are today. My 1980 Ph.D. thesis attempted to check the validity of Antonio Serra's seventeenth-century theory of development and underdevelopment. Serra is a very important person in this account because he was the first economist to produce a theory of uneven economic development in 1613, his *Breve trattato* or 'Brief treatise'.[4] Very little is known of Serra's life apart from the fact that he was a jurist who wrote a book when he was in jail in Naples. He sought to explain why his home town of Naples remained so poor in spite of its bountiful natural resources, while Venice, precariously built on a swamp, was at the very centre of the world's economy. The key, he argued, was that Venetians, barred from cultivating the land like the Neapolitans, had been forced to rely on their industry to make a living, harnessing the increasing returns to scale offered by manufacturing activities. In Serra's view the key to economic development was to have a large number of different economic activities, all subject to the falling costs of increasing returns. Paradoxically, being poor in natural resources could be a key to becoming wealthy.

Using the South American Andean countries as case studies, I found the development of Bolivia, Ecuador and Peru corresponded to Serra's assertions of the mechanisms at work. In the late 1970s I started collecting the genetic material of theories and practice of uneven economic growth over the last centuries, in the form of books, pamphlets and journals. In spite of the fact that many of the mechanisms of wealth and poverty were identified and described in ancient Greece, the logical starting point seemed to be the late 1400s, the time of invention of patents (Venice) and the birth of modern industrial policy with the ascension of Henry VII to the throne of England (1485).[5] Understanding and describing the mechanisms that created wealth and poverty since that time became my project.

My research restarted in 1991, just after the fall of the Berlin Wall, the event that Francis Fukuyama saw as 'the end of history'.

The centrally planned economies had failed, and it was therefore taken for granted that free trade and the market economy would make every country of the world equally rich. How this 'end-of-history' logic would develop can best be understood in light of the Cold War World View (CWWV) that developed among mainstream economists. For reasons that will be further discussed in the next chapter, the Cold War had obliterated not only theoretical issues that were seen as important in the past, but also past axes and dividing lines of agreement and disagreement. Issues that once were considered key to the understanding of uneven development had vanished without leaving traces in our contemporary discourse. It is therefore important to be able to step outside the CWWV and reconsider earlier economic theories: for example, in a CWWV, Karl Marx and Abraham Lincoln occupy positions on opposite extremes of the political axis, Marx representing the left with a big state and a planned economy, Lincoln representing the right with freedom and markets. In their own time, however, Lincoln and Marx found themselves on the same side of the economic dividing line. They both disliked English economic theory that left out the role of production, free trade that was imposed on a nation too early,[6] and slavery. There is even a polite exchange of letters between the two men. Perfectly consistent with this, Karl Marx contributed a regular weekly column to the *New York Daily Tribune*, the organ of Lincoln's Republican Party, from 1851 to 1862. This is, of course, not to say that Marx and Lincoln agreed on everything – but they agreed that what creates wealthy nations are industrialization and technological change.

In the twentieth century, the very conservative Austrian-American economist Joseph Schumpeter (1883–1950) showed that political affinity and economic understanding do not necessarily match. In the foreword to the Japanese edition of his book *The Theory of Economic Development* (German edition, 1912; English edition, 1934; Japanese edition, 1937), Schumpeter stresses the similarities between Marx's dynamic understanding of the world and his own, but observes that these similarities are 'obliterated by a very wide difference in general outlook'. In fact, the best industrial policies probably emerge when Marxists and Schumpeterians join together along the political axis, as it may be argued they did in Japan after the Second World War.

The bestselling book ever in the history of economic thought is Robert L. Heilbroner's *The Worldly Philosophers* (1969). In the last edition during his lifetime (1999), Heilbroner closes the book with the sad view that this important branch of economics – experience-based and not founded on numbers and symbols alone – was about to die out. This is the type of economics that made Europe rich, and also gave birth to the case method at Harvard Business School. Only later did I understand that I had become a necrophile economist in the tradition described by Heilbroner. Those who reasoned the way I did – and there were many – were mostly long dead. About thirty years later my book collection stands at around 50,000 volumes, documenting the history of economic thought and policy of the last 500 years. This penchant for ideas of the past, however, is combined with very wide observations of the varieties of present realities. During my careers I have been 'on the job' in forty-nine countries, on all inhabited continents, as well as having visited some just as a tourist.

During these thirty years, ideas located outside the interpretation of history and politics that accompanied the right–left axis of the Cold War World View were decidedly unfashionable. It soon became evident that economists as a group correspond to the old European definition of a nation: a group of people united in a common misconception about their own past and a common dislike of their neighbours (in this case neighbouring fields like sociology and political science). The conventional canonical sequence in the history of economic thought differs greatly from the sequence of economics books that were most studied and most influential in their time. Harvard librarian Kenneth Carpenter's carefully produced list of the thirty-nine economics texts most sold before 1850[7] contains a number of influential works that are totally neglected by historians of economic thought. In fact, the founding fathers of economics, according to the standard history of economic thought, the French Physiocrats, had only little and indirect influence on economic policies. Physiocracy never reached England, for example, where, curiously, its critics were translated long before the Physiocrats themselves. Their ideas were short-lived even in France, where they were brought down by the calamitous consequences of their implementation in the form of food scarcities and famines, and the competing ideas of the anti-Physiocrats – who are hardly ever mentioned in the history of economic thought – quickly carried the day. In fact, the spark that ignited the storm of the Bastille was when news reached Paris that the anti-Physiocrat Jacques Necker (1732–1804) had been replaced as Minister of Finance. Necker is, strikingly, also the only economist to be represented with three bestselling economics works on Carpenter's honour list.

It became increasingly clear to me that the type of economic understanding employed by the presently wealthy countries during their transition from poor to rich had been lost. The lack of general interest in my chosen subject, and the assistance of a small network of specialized book dealers, facilitated the collection of material of this now defunct, but still highly relevant economic logic. Not only were the theories that had made rich countries rich disappearing from modern textbooks and the practice of economics, the texts that had produced the successful economic policies of the past were also disappearing from libraries around the world. It was as if the genetic material of past wisdom was slowly being destroyed. The big American university libraries have a policy requiring that one of them must retain a copy of every book, but this is a strategy not without risks:[8] the Library of Congress is sometimes known to 'lose' their copy. When the only known copy of a book by one of Germany's most important eighteenth-century economists, Johann Friedrich von Pfeiffer (1718–87), was lost from the University of Heidelberg library during the Second World War, it was assumed that no copies were to be found in Germany.[9] It was therefore very satisfying to find a copy a few years ago.

In the ominous year 1984, Baker Library at Harvard University discarded all books that had not been taken out during the last fifty years, among them most of the library's collection on Friedrich List (1789–1846; an important German theorist on industrial policy and uneven growth). A Boston book dealer subsequently informed me that he had obtained books from Baker Library that 'almost have your name written on them', as he put it. Ten years later I was visiting a Harvard professor doing comparative work on Adam Smith and Friedrich List. When he complained about the lack of material on Friedrich List in Baker Library, I could explain why. In order to prove my point I faxed through the title pages of the books he needed, with the Harvard 'discarded' stamp neatly covering the bookplate.

Another case in point is the New York Public Library, which, some time in the 1970s, decided to microfilm their entire collection of pamphlets,[10] and subsequently threw the original material away as scrap paper for recycling. By a miracle the material was saved by collector Michael Zinman and resurfaced in his barn in Ardsley, New York, some twenty years later. A London book dealer informed me about this, and on two different visits my librarian wife and I spent a total of four days almost literally wading around in an esti-mated 170,000 pamphlets that had had their spines cut off to facilitate microfilming. We brought home about 2,300. Here was the whole history of US economic policy back to the early 1800s, hundreds of speeches in Senate and House (they were all issued separately) and thousands of items documenting what really happened as the United States grew from poverty to wealth. The few valuable pamphlets, the first editions of David Ricardo that had also been sent for recycling, were already gone, but these were of no interest to me because the texts are readily available. The real treasures were the obscure items that documented the debates on economic policy, not only in the USA, but in a dozen other foreign countries and languages. This debate tends to be reflected neither in the economic history of the United States – too often written in the 'manifest destiny' tradition of history[11] – nor in the history of economic thought. Small portions of the debate are found, however, in the study of political thought in the USA. To a large extent the Americans have had their own history hidden from them under a veil of rhetoric and ideology.

History reveals how rich countries got rich by methods that by now had generally been outlawed by the 'conditionalities' of the Washington Consensus.[12] Appearing on the scene in 1990, immedi-ately after the fall of the Berlin Wall, the Washington Consensus required, among other things, trade liberalization, liberalization of inflows of foreign direct investments, deregulation and privatization. The Washington Consensus reforms, as they were carried out, became virtually synonymous with neo-liberalism and 'market fundamentalism'.

By the early 1990s, the theories of Joseph Schumpeter were becoming fashionable. Fortunately, in the mid-1970s, my Harvard course in the history of economic thought was taught by Arthur Smithies – probably Schumpeter's closest friend at Harvard[13] – and essentially developed into a course on Schumpeter and his theories. Although Schumpeter himself was not interested in poverty, his theories seemed to me to describe poverty by default, and could provide a theory explaining why the Washington Consensus principles proved so damaging to so many of the world's poorest countries.

My work involved connecting several different academic disciplines: most importantly evolutionary (Schumpeterian) economics, development economics, the history of economic thought and economic history. It seemed as if an understanding of uneven economic growth would need two new academic angles: a non-Marxist theory of uneven growth[14] and the history of economic policy. Both subjects were absent, yet they were highly interconnected. The history of economic thought tells us what Adam Smith said England ought to have done, but no branch of academia seemed to worry much about what England actually did, which proved to be very different from what Smith had advised.

A passage in a letter from Niccolò Machiavelli, dated 10 December 1513,[15] describes my mood of many years:

> I return home and enter my study; on the threshold I take off my workday clothes, covered with mud and dirt, and put on the garments of court and palace. Fitted out appropriately, I step inside the venerable court of the ancients, where, solicitously received by them, I nourish myself on that food that *alone* is mine and for which I was born; *where I am unashamed to converse with them and to question them about the motives of their actions, and they, in their human kindness, answer me* [my italics]. And for four hours at a time

I feel no boredom, I forget all my troubles ... I absorb myself into them completely.

A few words now directed particularly to readers from the Third World. At first sight this may come across as an ethnocentric European book. It does not start off, for example, with Norwegian-American economist Thorstein Veblen's (1857–1929) view of capitalism as an advanced system of piracy, although history tells us that this is also a legitimate perspective. Instead I focus on how Europe created the economic power that made their dominance – their 'economies of scale in the use of force' – possible. The book does not consider the crimes and injustices committed by whites, Europeans and others, in the Third World. It tries to focus on the much more subtle – and in the long term even more harmful – effects of economic and social theories which leave out key determinants of what creates wealth and poverty. The book does not focus on slavery itself, but on slavery's legacies in productive, social and land tenure systems which block economic development to this very day. Its focus is on understanding capitalism as a system of production, and on appropriate and inappropriate economic policies.

Most civilizations that have existed have not been European, and an important part of the European story is the emulation of technologies and skills from other continents, from the Muslim world, from Asia and also from Africa.[16] In 1158, Bishop Otto of Freising repeated what had long been known, that 'all human power and learning had its origins in the East'. Recent contributions have shown how similar China and Europe were as late as in 1700.[17] It is clear that Europe and the West's view of the rest of the world has for a long time been persistently filtered through Eurocentric prejudice against other peoples and their cultures.[18] Recently, it has been argued that Eurasia had the cards stacked in their favour in terms of climate, germs and domesticable animals.[19] The role of the cow as a prototype machine producing milk, meat and manure has similarly been highlighted.

However, it is also possible to see Europe from another angle, that of a 'laggard' continent that did not consolidate its frontiers until after the siege of Vienna by Islam in 1683. During the thousand years between the time of Muhammad and the siege of Vienna, Europe was continuously defending its eastern and southern frontiers against Mongols and against Islam,[20] partly, of course, as a result of Europe's own aggression. The Mongol invasion had reached the Adriatic coast in Dalmatia and far into what is now Poland when the death of the Great Khan made the Mongols return home in 1241. Constantinople fell to Islam in 1453, marking the demise of the eastern Roman Empire and the end of perhaps the only millennial empire the world has ever seen, the Byzantine. As a consequence Islam gained control over the Balkans and the eastern Mediterranean. Venice, defender of Europe's south-eastern flank, gradually lost her possessions in the eastern Mediterranean, and a turning point in favour of the disunited Europeans came only in 1571 with the battle of Lepanto, at which the major European forces had briefly united.

What made Europe so strong subsequently? And – looking at the present huge gaps in world income – how and why was development in Europe so evenly distributed by the 1700s, from northern Sweden to the Mediterranean? Why is it seemingly impossible to repeat the same experience in Africa? Many factors clearly contributed to Europe's forging ahead: the geographic position of its sources of energy (coal); later the availability of food, wood and markets from the colonies; but also its brutality, religious zeal, organizational ability, institutional creativity (e.g. double-entry book-keeping) and intellectual curiosity.

Most important in my view were several mechanisms that emerged from Europe's large diversity and fragmentation (geographical, climatic,[21] ethnic and political). This diversity and fragmentation – which tended to be absent in the large Asian empires – created a large pool of alternative ideas and approaches in the 'market' for ideas, and was the starting point for the rivalry that created the continuous emulation among the different states. Above all, Europe's history is a history of how economic policy was able to overcome the formidable barriers to wealth that had been created by geography, climate and also culture. Travellers who journeyed to distant places like Norway 200 years ago, for example, did not envisage the country as ever being able to develop further.

The basic strategy that made Europe so evenly rich was what Enlightenment economics called emulation,[22] and the extensive toolbox that was developed for the purpose of emulating. The *Oxford English Dictionary* defines 'emulation' as 'the endeavour to equal or surpass others in any achievement or quality; also, the desire or ambition to equal or to excel'. *Emulation* was essentially a positive and active effort, to be contrasted with *envy* or *jealousy*.[23] In modern terms *emulation* finds its approximate counterparts in the terminology of American economist Moses Abramovitz (1912–2000), whose ideas of *catching-up* and *forging ahead* resonate with the same understanding of dynamic competition.

Modern economics recommends a strategy of 'comparative advantage' based on David Ricardo's trade theory, that a nation should specialize in that economic activity where it is relatively least inefficient (see Appendix I). After the 1957 Sputnik shock that made it evident that the Soviet Union was ahead of the United States in the race into space, the Soviet Union, armed with Ricardian trade theory, could have argued scientifically that the comparative advantage of the United States was in agriculture, not in space technology. The USA should therefore produce food, while the Soviet Union should engage in space technology. But in this case President Eisenhower chose emulation rather than comparative advantage. The establishment of NASA in 1958 was a policy measure in the best spirit of the Enlightenment – it was an institution created in order to *emulate* the Soviet Union – but quite contrary to the spirit of Ricardo. Ricardian economics has in fact created elements of self-referential logic, reminiscent of the worst caricatures of scholasticism. Because the dynamics that create the need for emulation have been eliminated from the theory, the Ricardian frame of mind creates counter-intuitive policy conclusions. The dynamic elements of technological change and progress that create the intuitive logic of emulation, rather than static specialization, are simply not there.

For Third World readers it is also worth noticing that the continental European economists who are the 'heroes' of this book were surprisingly mainly non-ethnocentric. Giovanni Botero (*c.*1544–1617), who successfully explored the reasons only cities were wealthy, produced a famous book on world geography, the *Relazioni Universali* ('Universal Relations'). In this work the diversity of world cultures is enthusiastically described. The Saami, the aboriginals of northern Scandinavia, are celebrated for their skills in building boats without the use of nails and for having probably the fastest means of transportation anywhere: the reindeer sleigh on snow. Two of Germany's most important eighteenth-century economists, Christian Wolff (1679–1754) – also an important philosopher – and Johann Heinrich Gottlob von Justi (1717–71), wrote books praising Chinese civilization; Justi also praised the Incas.[24] They both argued that Europe should emulate non-European institutions. In 1723 Wolff was in fact ordered to leave the University of Halle – at the time dominated by Pietists, a Protestant movement – within forty-eight hours or be hanged for his comments that Chinese philosophy and ethics were admirable and showed that moral truths could be found outside Christendom. Saved by the rivalry between the small German states, Wolff moved to a neighbouring state where the ruler had been attempting to recruit him to his own University of Marburg. In fact it may be argued that European ethnocentricity, an important ingredient in colonialism and imperialism, only became strong during the 1770s when previous 'ethnic nations' came to stand in the way of emerging nation-states and empires. (Incidentally, I have not attempted to pass the analysis of economists of the past through a filter of contemporary political correctness. When Marx and others refer to 'barbarism' and 'civilization' much in the same way one would today refer to 'poverty' and 'development', I have left the original wording intact.)

This book suggests that, based on the presence of diversity, fragmentation, emulation and rivalry mentioned above, capitalism as it developed in Europe can be usefully understood as a system of unintended consequences, subsequently systematically observed and disciplined into policy tools and institutions. This way of viewing capitalism as a somewhat 'accidental' phenomenon revives the analytical tradition of German economist Werner Sombart (1863–1941), later followed up by Schumpeter. Adam Smith (1776) remarked that we get our daily bread not from the kindness of the baker but from his desire to make money. We are fed as an unintended by-product of the baker's greed. Indeed, the discussion as to what extent private vices could be trusted to create public benefits was a key eighteenth-century debate. For centuries Europeans offered a huge diversity of approaches to technology and to institutions. The combination of diversity and emulation created a multitude of theoretical schools and technological solutions across Europe. These multitudes of ideas and their products were continuously compared, moulded and developed in marketplaces. The competition between city-states – later between nation-states – financed flows of inventions that also emerged here as unintended by-products of the emulation between nations and their rulers in war and luxury. Once it had been observed that throwing resources at problems during wartime produced inventions and innovations, this mechanism could be replicated in times of peace.

Europeans observed early on that generalized wealth was found only in areas where agriculture was absent or only played a marginal role, and came to be seen as an unintended by-product when many diverse branches of manufacturing were brought together in large cities. Once these mechanisms were understood, wise economic policy could spread wealth outside these few 'naturally wealthy' areas. Policies of emulation could, indeed, also spread wealth to formerly poor and feudal agricultural areas, but they involved massive market interventions. For laggard nations market interventions and wise economic policies could substitute for the natural and geographical advantages that produced the first wealthy states. We can further imagine that export taxes on raw materials and import taxes on finished products were originally means for raising revenues in poor nations, but that a by-product of these measures was to increase wealth through the growth of domestic manufacturing capacity. This blend of purposes was already clear in England under Edward III (1312–77).

Thus rivalry, war and emulation in Europe created a dynamic system of imperfect competition and increasing returns. New knowledge and innovations spread in the economy as increased profits and increased wages, and as larger bases for government taxation. European economic policy was based for centuries on the conviction that the introduction of a manufacturing sector would solve the fundamental economic problems of the time, creating much-needed employment, profits, higher wages, a larger tax base and a better circulation of the currency.[25] Italian economist Ferdinando Galiani (1728–87), whom Friedrich Nietzsche called the most intelligent person of the eighteenth century, stated that 'from manufacturing you may expect the two greatest ills of humanity, superstition and slavery, to be healed'.[26] Standard textbook economics which seeks to understand economic development in terms of frictionless 'perfect markets' totally misses the point. Perfect markets are for the poor. It is equally futile to try to understand this development in terms of what economists refer to as 'market failure'.[27] Compared to textbook economics, economic development is a giant failure of perfect markets.

The spread of wealth in Europe, and later in the other developed parts of the world, was a result of conscious policies of emulation: the market was a force tamed, like the wind, for the purpose of reaching a defined goal or destination. You may not necessarily be going in the direction that the wind, or the market, happens to be blowing. Cumulative factors and path dependencies cause the winds of the market to blow towards progress only when a high level of development has already been reached. The poorer the nation, the less the winds of laissez-faire blow in the right direction. For this reason, the issue of free trade and other policy decisions is one of context and timing. In the absence of a specific context, economists' arguments for or against free trade are as meaningless as doctors discussing medication without knowledge of symptoms or diagnosis. The absence of context in standard textbook economics is therefore a fatal flaw, barring any degree of qualitative under-standing. Historically successful policies have depended on 'governing the market' (Robert Wade) and 'getting the prices wrong' (John Kenneth Galbraith and Alice Amsden). Colonialism was, at its core, a system where these effects were not intended to take place, and our failure to understand the connections between colonialism and poverty is a significant barrier to understanding poverty.[28]

The doctrine of comparative advantage, originating with Ricardo, is the bedrock of today's international economic order. A prominent

American economist, Paul Krugman, claims that 'intellectuals' do
not understand Ricardo's idea of comparative advantage, which is
'utterly true, immensely sophisticated – and extremely relevant to
the modern world'.[29] I argue the reverse: that Ricardian economics,
by eliminating from economic theory a qualitative understanding of
economic change and dynamics, has created an economic theory
that makes it possible for a nation to specialize in being poor. In
Ricardian theory the economy is not going anywhere, there is no
progress and consequently nothing to emulate. With its stated confidence in comparative advantage as a solution to the problems of the
poor, the Washington Consensus has flatly prohibited the toolbox
of emulation, a toolbox we argue can demonstrate an impressive
track-record of success over 500 years, from the late 1400s to the
Marshall Plan of the 1950s and 1960s.

2

The Evolution of the Two Different Approaches

...the general reader will have to make up his mind, whether he wants *simple* answers to his questions or *useful* ones – in this as in other economic matters he cannot have both.

Joseph Alois Schumpeter,
Austrian-American economist, 1932

Aristotle was of the opinion that large centres of commerce ought to be located away from the big cities, but archaeologists can tell us that Aristotle was not listened to; in reality the trading areas were central parts of the big cities. Adam Smith's book, *The Wealth of Nations* (1776), told the English they should open up for free trade, but history tells us that in reality more customs duties were collected in England than in France during the first hundred years following Smith's book, even though France is now considered to have been the bastion of protectionism. 'Conventional wisdom' tells us England grew rich through Smithian laissez-faire policies and free trade whereas economic historians who delve into the matter consistently come up with quite different results. William Ashworth recently concluded: 'If there was a unique English/British pathway of industrialization, it was less a distinct entrepreneurial and technocentric culture than one predominantly defined within an institutional framework spearheaded by the excise (tax) and a wall of tariffs'.[1]

Today the Chicago economists – broadly representing the theoretical foundation of the present wave of globalization and of the Washington institutions – proclaim to the rest of the world that state and municipal governments should not intervene in the economy. In reality Chicago's Mayor Daley spends millions of dollars of public funds establishing incubators for high-tech industries. Even in the same city the gap between rhetoric and reality is huge.

In Washington DC, the US Small Business Administration annually uses federal money for loans and guarantees exceeding $20 billion to support private American companies. Not many blocks away, the Washington institutions – the World Bank and the IMF – continue their traditional policies of placing 'conditionalities' on poor countries that prevent them from setting up similar institutions in the Third World. A few years ago, the state of Alabama used $253 million to subsidize a Mercedes-Benz plant. State officials claim the presence of the plant created income that recovered the costs in five years, and the deal subsequently brought in four other auto plants.[2] This is the same logic that historically has been employed by poor countries when industrializing, although they generally use tariffs rather than direct subsidies. In the case of both subsidies and tariffs, although the costs are passed on to the general public, the public will find itself better off in the future. Such logic always trades off the short-term interests of consumers and the long-term interests of the same consumers in their role of producers, who will have more employment at higher wages than before. *Newsweek* hailed the entrepreneurial initiative of the state of Alabama, but normally criticizes poor countries that attempt to use the same type of mechanisms. No doubt traditional economists will criticize the existence of both the US Small Business Administration and Alabama's industrial policies. The point is that they are not listened to in the United States, where abstract 'high theory' is only permitted to determine the policies of the poor world.

In practical terms, then, lofty economic rhetoric is for export to others, while completely different pragmatic principles are adhered to for the realities at home. George W. Bush preaches free trade for the benefit of all. In reality the United States subsidizes and protects an array of products, from agriculture to high-tech industry. Paul Krugman, who has been very influential on trade and industrial policy outside the United States, complains that no one listens to standard Ricardian trade theory at home: 'the view of trade as a quasi-military competition is the conventional wisdom among policy-makers, business leaders, and influential intellectuals...It is not just that economics has lost control of the discourse; the kind of ideas that are offered in a standard economics textbook do not enter into that discourse at all...'[3]

There is an important pattern here: since its founding fathers, the United States has always been torn between two traditions, the activist policies of Alexander Hamilton (1755–1804) and Thomas Jefferson's (1743–1826) maxim that 'the government that governs least, governs best'. Alexander Hamilton was a key figure behind the establishment of the first central bank of the United States in 1791, while Thomas Jefferson fought it and contributed to its closing down in 1811. With time and usual American pragmatism, this rivalry has been resolved by putting the Jeffersonians in charge of the rhetoric and the Hamiltonians in charge of policy. Today's economic theorists have an important mission in producing Jeffersonian/Ricardian rhetoric, which, as Paul Krugman points out above, is not very influential on the domestic market.

In this the United States followed the example of England. In the 1820s a member of the House of Representatives commented that, like so many other English products, the theories of David Ricardo seemed to be produced for export purposes only. Therefore the American maxim of the 1820s, 'Don't do as the English tell you to do, do as the English did', may today be safely updated to 'Don't do as the Americans tell you to do, do as the Americans did'.

Wealthy nations have a tendency to force upon poor nations theories they themselves never have followed and probably never will. Looking behind 'high theory' in order to observe what actually happens therefore becomes an important exercise. Unlike the history of economic thought (what theorists said ought to happen), the history of economic policy (what policies were actually followed) is a non-existent academic discipline. Thorstein Veblen distinguished between *esoteric* theories, abstract theories reserved for the initiated priesthood, and *exoteric* theories, the practical theories for everyman. The problem is that the esoteric theories have had much less practical influence than the historians of economic thought have led us to believe. Since Adam Smith, however, these esoteric theories have been successfully employed as an ideological bulwark for propaganda purposes. A good example of this is today's mainstream international trade theory which 'proves' that everyone will be equally rich under a pure market economy.

A similar observation, that the richest nations generally have many more trade restrictions than their ideology professes, was made in the eighteenth century by Italian economist Antonio Genovesi (1712–69):

> There are those, who by liberty of trade mean two things: an absolute licence for manufacturers to work without regulations of measurements, of weights, of forms, of colours, etc., and one no less absolute for merchants to circulate, export, and import everything which they like, without any restrictions, without excises, without tariffs, without customs duties. But this liberty, except among adventurous people on the Moon, does not exist in any country on Earth: on the contrary you will find it nowhere less than in those nations that best understand trade.[4]

Also, historically, global free trade has been a chimera, and those who adhered to it least during the crucial moments of their development have become the world's most successful economies. The standard argument these days is to show that wealth is strongly correlated with the 'openness' of economies. This is akin to measuring the income of people still attending university with those who have graduated and are already on the labour market, and later concluding that education does not pay because university students have lower incomes. In the past, a period of protecting a manufacturing sector has been mandatory for all presently rich nations. The educational function of this period is emphasized by the term 'educational tariffs' (*Erziehungszoll*, *oppfostringstoll*) used in Germanic languages. The English term used to be 'infant industry protection', which was something virtually everyone understood was necessary. Comparing countries that have been through this stage with countries that have not is simply not meaningful.

The rhetoric–reality gap becomes even more disturbing when the same theorists use different theories for different purposes. Problems located far away are solved according to esoteric and abstract principles. When the problems to be solved are nearer to home, common sense, pragmatism and experience are allowed to enter into the picture. Adam Smith – whose *Wealth of Nations* appeared during the American Revolution – claimed that the United States would make a grave mistake if it attempted to protect its manufacturing industry. An important reason for the 1776 American fight for independence was that, as colonial masters have always done, England had prohibited manufacturing industry in the American colonies (among the exceptions were tar and masts which the English needed). Tellingly, in the same book (albeit in a different section) Adam Smith declared that only nations with a native manufacturing industry could ever win a war. Alexander Hamilton, the first US Secretary of the Treasury, had read Adam Smith, and wisely based the industrial and commercial policy of the United States on Smith's experience-based claim that only manufacturing nations win wars, rather than on his theoretical claim about free trade.

Following England's practice rather than her theory, the United States protected their manufacturing industry for close to 150 years. The theory on which today's economic order rests claims that free trade will lead to 'factor–price equalization', that is that prices of labour and capital will tend to be the same all over the world. Few economists tell their children that they might as well start a career washing dishes, where they might have a 'comparative advantage', rather than seek a career as a lawyer or medical doctor, because factor–price equalization is just around the corner. As private citizens, economists realize that the choice of economic activity will largely determine the living standard of their children. On an international level, the same economists are unable to sustain that same opinion because their toolbox is pitched at such a high level of abstraction that virtually no tools are available to distinguish qualitatively between economic activities. At this level, standard economic theory 'proves' that an imaginary nation of shoeshine boys and people washing dishes will achieve the same wealth as a nation consisting of lawyers and stockbrokers. Economists, then, advise Africa's children based on a completely different type of understanding from what they use when they advise their own children. As Thorstein Veblen has said about this type of problem: economists' instincts have been contaminated by their education.

That a nation specializes according to its 'comparative advantage' means that it specializes where it is relatively most efficient compared to another nation. Appendix I shows how this trade theory creates the possibility for a nation to achieve a 'comparative advantage' in being poor and ignorant. This happens because the trade theory that forms the basis of today's world economic order is based on nations exchanging identical labour hours – devoid of any qualitative features – against other such labour hours, in a system where production is absent. Ricardian trade theory sees a Stone Age labour hour on a par with a Silicon Valley labour hour, and therefore predicts that economic integration between these two types of economies will produce economic harmony and equalization of wages.

In very broad terms, one can distinguish between two main types of economic theory. One is based on metaphors from nature, generally from physics. Examples of these metaphors are 'the invisible hand' that keeps the earth in orbit around the sun (late 1700s) or the equilibrium metaphor, based on the science of physics as it stood in the 1880s. What this book refers to as 'standard textbook' is based on the equilibrium metaphor, which physicists themselves abandoned in the 1930s. This theory is built from the abstract metaphor downwards, and 'being an economist' essentially means someone analysing the world through the glasses and tools provided by the metaphor. This is the theory the profession uses on Africa's children.

The other type of economic theory is based on experience, built from the ground upwards, and often appears as practical policies before being distilled into theory. The city-state of Venice practised a certain kind of economic policy for centuries, long before economist Antonio Serra codified this practice into a theory and explained why it worked. Much in the same way Stone Age tribes chewed on willow bark in order to cure headaches thousands of years before Bayer codified the active substance as salicylic acid (salix = willow) and produced aspirin. Equally, early medieval sailors in the Mediterranean prevented scurvy by bringing with them oranges and lemons centuries before vitamin C was isolated in 1929. It is perfectly possible to cure illnesses, economic or other, simply by lesson-drawing without having a complete understanding of the mechanisms at work.

This less abstract type of economics is normally based on biological metaphors rather than on metaphors from physics. Ever since the codification of Roman law around AD 400, the human body has been a metaphor for the social sciences. Its most celebrated manifestation can perhaps be found in Thomas Hobbes's *Leviathan,* both in terms of its political analysis and in its impressive frontispiece showing the incarnation of the state literally formed from its citizens.[5] This type of theory is based on a qualitative and holistic understanding of the 'body' to be studied, and delivers a type of understanding where important elements, such as synergies between disparate, yet interdependent parts, are not reducible to numbers and symbols. Charles Darwin (1809–82) introduced a new kind of biological metaphor, in which changes in society, such as innovations, become like nature's mutations. While his theoretical nemesis, the French naturalist Jean Baptiste Lamarck (1744–1829), was of the opinion that acquired traits could be inherited, their two approaches actually complement each other well when transferred from the biological to the economic realm. For Lamarck's is a metaphor well suited to economics, where knowledge and experience may accumulate over generations. This experience-based theory, open to synergies as well as changes, is the one used by economists when, as private individuals, they are able qualitatively to distinguish between economic activities, and consequently advise their own children against specializing in the world economy according to a comparative advantage in washing dishes.

These metaphors all have their advantages and disadvantages. The highly abstract metaphors from physics are powerful in the accuracy of their recommendations, so that free trade will lead to the levelling out of wages across rich and poor countries (factor–price equalization). One key problem is that physics-based economics is unable to capture qualitative differences between economic activities that end up as quantifiable differences in income. The abstract physics-based models lose both the creative elements contributed by the Renaissance and the taxonomies creating order in diversity that was a key contribution of the Enlightenment. Regardless of the level of education of a person washing dishes in a restaurant, his or her wage level will never rise to the level of a high-tech engineer's. Without changing profession, the person washing dishes has specialized in being relatively poor in any labour market. That nations can also specialize in being poor is inconceivable to economists working with physics-based metaphors, because their theory lacks the tools with which to distinguish qualitatively between economic activities. These economists therefore do not accept that poor nations should attempt to manoeuvre themselves into economic activities that might increase the general wage level, as presently rich countries have all done. Physics-based models are also unable to handle novelty and innovations: that something qualitatively new can happen in the world. They also miss the synergies, linkages and systemic effects that constitute the glue that bonds economies and societies together. Margaret Thatcher's claim that 'there is no such thing as society' is a direct and logical conclusion of today's textbook economics.

Francis Bacon (1561–1626) is an important figure in the history of experience-based economic understanding. Bacon was driven by what Veblen calls 'idle curiosity', a not-for-profit inquisitive spirit. Fittingly Bacon died from pneumonia contracted while testing the effect of freezing on the preservation of meat by going out in a blizzard and stuffing chickens with snow. The chickens were preserved, but Bacon died. The reactions to David Ricardo's abstract theories were in essence – both in England by the Reverend Richard Jones (1831)[6] and in the United States by John Rae (1834)[7] – attempts to re-Baconize economics. However, such experience-based economics is generally based on biological metaphors, which are much less accurate and do not produce the same clear-cut answers. Experience-based theories bring to the surface trade-offs that rarely exist in physics-based theories, which tend to encourage the same kind of economic policies regardless of context ('one size fits all'). Free trade, for example, is absolutely necessary in order to create wealth in many contexts, but in others the same principle of free trade will reduce a nation's wealth. As a result of this, as in Schumpeter's quote heading this chapter, economics gives us a choice between simple explanations that are not very relevant and more complex explanations that are more relevant.

Using the human body as a metaphor for society has the advantage of highlighting synergies, interdependencies and complementarities in an economic system. As opposed to physics-based metaphors, the body metaphor also captures the idea of humans as spiritual beings with a creative brain as an economic factor. In the end, the basic moving force of human economic society is what Friedrich Nietzsche calls 'the capital of spirit and will': new knowledge, entrepreneurship and organizational capabilities, private and public. Recently, modern evolutionary economics has attempted to recapture these elements and apply them favourably to industrial policies in the Third World. With time this may develop into a substitute for Heilbroner's worldly philosophers.

There is, however, no need to be overly polemical, for these two types of economic thinking are in many ways complementary. We need them both, just as we need right and left feet in order to walk, as British economist Alfred Marshall (1842–1924) expressed it more than a century ago.[8] Physics-based economics gives us an illusion of order in the chaos that surrounds us, but it is important to be aware that this refuge is created at the expense of abdicating from understanding a whole range of qualitative aspects of the economic world. Forgetting that the physics-based models are not reality itself, but merely extremely simplified models of this reality, may lead to grave mistakes. One example of such a mistake is the way globalization has been introduced in the form of shock therapy. Instead of the predicted factor–price equalization, many countries now experience a factor–price polarization compared to the rest of the world. Rich nations get richer while many poor nations grow poorer. Since this cannot happen in the physics-based models, it takes the world community a very long time before any action is taken to correct this undesired development. The problem is that the physics-based models that have virtually monopolized the discourse tend to exclude precisely those factors that create wealth, factors that are present in wealthy countries but not in poor ones: imperfect competition, innovations, synergies between economic sectors, economies of scale and scope and the presence of economic activities which make these factors possible. We shall return to these factors later.

Alternative experience-based economics, the methodology still used at Harvard Business School, will be referred to collectively as the Other Canon.[9] The Other Canon is intended as a concept that unites economic approaches and theories that employ observable facts, experience and lesson-drawing as the starting point for theorizing about economics. Since the late 1400s, only the Other Canon type of economics – with its insistence that economic activities are qualitatively different as carriers of economic growth – has been able to bring nation after nation out of poverty. Once economic growth has been achieved, hegemonic nations have in sequence switched from biology-based to physics-based economics, as England did in the late eighteenth century and the United States did in the mid-twentieth century. To understand how their policies worked and why these successful nations might have shifted, the Other Canon will have to be explored in some detail.

For centuries, the experience-based type of economic theory ruled alone. Today's standard abstract theory is less than 250 years old and has its roots in the Physiocratic school that for a brief period dominated the economic policy of pre-revolutionary France. Writing after the Industrial Revolution was in full swing, Adam Smith, although categorized as an anti-Physiocrat by his own contemporaries, carried over some of the Physiocratic teachings. The abstract model really gelled only with David

Ricardo and his *Principles of Political Economy and Taxation* (1817). As we shall see, on three historical occasions these abstract principles have brought deprivation, hunger and huge social problems when applied in inappropriate contexts.

The Cold War World View brought with it the virtual extinction of the experience-based Other Canon tradition. Ricardo's theory became the only game in town – both on the political left and the political right. Figure 2 shows the family tree of economics as it was reproduced on the inside back cover of Paul Samuelson's *Economics* – the textbook that dominated the teaching of economics for more than a generation. Both communism and liberalism – both Joseph Stalin and Milton Friedman – trace their historical roots back to Ricardo. The Cold War was thus essentially a civil war between two factions of Ricardian economics, although they shared several common features: in their mature forms they tend not to recognize the importance of technology, of entrepreneurship, or any role of the state. In communism the state was supposed to 'wither away'. To achieve the mythical equilibrium, communism[10] simply replaced the market with a huge calculator. Just as social democrats tended to be the first casualties in civil wars between communists and liberalists, in the crossfire between the Ricardian right and left, the less abstract Other Canon tradition virtually died out.[11]

Traditions, though, seldom vanish entirely and many economists, dissatisfied with both extremes, have continued to work up alternatives: my work is indebted to them. Figure 3 shows the family tree of 500 years of the alternative economics. The Other Canon tradition has been the one determining economic policy in all nations which have taken the path from being poor to being wealthy. England started down this path in 1485 and continued for centuries and continental Europe rapidly followed suit. The Scandinavian countries – today so dependent on free trade due to their small home markets – followed the same policy for centuries, until (at different points in time) they were ready to compete globally. The United States did the same thing, starting just after independence in 1776, and then in the 1820s in a most aggressive way.

32   *The Evolution of the Two Different Approaches*

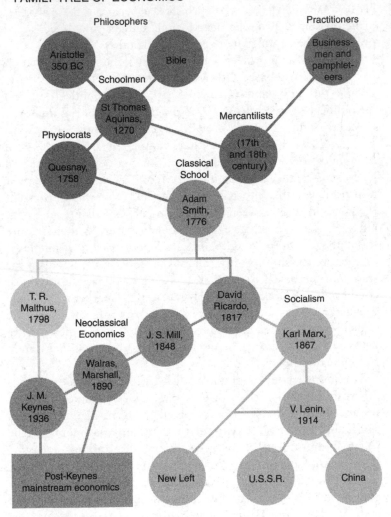

Figure 2   Samuelson's family tree of economics, 1976

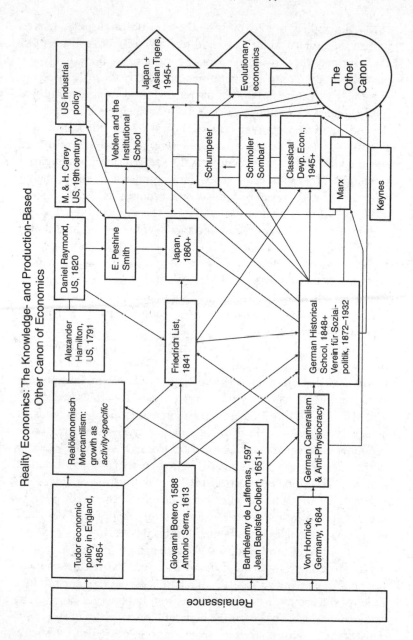

Figure 3   The Other Canon family tree of economics

My purpose is not to present the mosaic of theories I have named the Other Canon as a rigid example of eternal truths. On the contrary, the 'truth' in terms of economic policy is always an exceedingly complex phenomenon. The real world presents extremely difficult trade-offs, across time and even generations, under conditions of uncertainty. Any policy recommendation will depend totally on context and structural issues (the convenient German word is *Strukturzusammenhänge*), and therefore on specific knowledge. In Appendix II the Other Canon is compared to standard textbook economics. This comparison will probably have the greatest appeal to professional economists.

Victor Norman, an international trade theorist, describes today's standard textbook economics succinctly: 'One of the nice things about economics as a science is that it is just a way of thinking, factual knowledge does not exist.'[12] In this theoretical world, reality and factual knowledge occasionally enter as disturbing elements. When reproached by a friend that his theory did not tally with the facts, Ricardo is supposed to have replied that 'that's so much worse for the facts'.[13]

As hinted at earlier, both poles of Ricardian economics developed into something resembling a religion.[14] During the Cold War, reality-based economics – the historical schools in Europe and the institutional school in the United States – were crowded out and virtually disappeared. In Ricardian economics form tends to achieve priority over observations of reality. Standard textbook economics is created as an abstraction from an economic scenario in the same way that the game of chess is created as an abstraction of a war scenario. But just as the war in Iraq is not solved by referring to the rules of chess, the problems of world poverty are not solved by referring to an economic theory that does not contain key variables from factual knowledge.[15]

In the Other Canon tradition, knowledge on the macro level is achieved exclusively through detailed factual knowledge of what happens at the micro level. In fact, this type of understanding requires the economist to move consistently between these levels, taking the elevator between the high and low levels of abstraction. This is the opposite strategy from the one described by Victor

Norman above: here relevance is at the core, and form is only considered as it reflects relevant facts. Other Canon economics has a large toolbox and all tools that may reflect relevant reality are allowed. In today's standard economics the focus is on mathematics and precision more than on the object of analysis itself, the economy. As has been observed by others, the toolbox and the incentive system of the profession combine to make most economists prefer to be accurately wrong than approximately correct. As regards qualitative understanding, mathematical rigour has developed into a rigor mortis.

The abstract standard theory as it is used today towards the poor countries of the world assumes a world without variation and diversity, without friction, conflicts or trade-offs, where new knowledge is free and hits every person on earth simultaneously as manna from heaven ('perfect information'). Had this been a book written exclusively for economists, this would have been the place to discuss the assumptions of standard economics, assumptions which are there essentially because its proponents chose to model society based on the physics of the 1880s. However, we shall enter only briefly into the discussion of the specific assumptions, simply to flag up the mother of all assumptions: the *equality assumption*. Assuming away all differences – between human beings, between economic activities,[16] among nations – the economics profession has made its choice. Simplicity has been chosen at the cost of relevance. Economics has lost the art of organizing the world by creating categories and taxonomies which characterized the birth of modern sciences during the Enlightenment. In doing that, all factors qualitatively differentiating a twelve-year-old and his shoe-shine 'firm' based in a Lima slum from Microsoft as a firm have been eliminated. With it, any explanation as to why Bill Gates and his country are wealthier than the shoeshine boy and his country has also been eliminated. The two of them have been averaged out as 'the representative firm'. Adding bells and whistles to the basic model may satisfy the modellers – and many such models exist – but this approach is unlikely to produce the kind of understanding among the general public that is required in order to induce a much-needed policy change.

The core assumption of 'perfect information' in reality implies that humankind must consist of individuals that are all alike, cloned versions of Robert Musil's man without any qualities. [17] As nineteenth-century German economists suggested, quantification in this type of theory implied adding together quantities devoid of any qualities (*qualitätslose Größen*), labour and capital devoid of any skills. The conclusion so proudly reached by standard international trade theory, that a world trade will provide 'factor–price equalization' is in fact already built into the basic assumptions of the theory itself; a theory in which all the elements are equal and identical cannot produce anything but equality of outcome.

One result of the twentieth-century development of economics is the loss of two important dimensions: time (history) and space (geography). The world of economics became a fairy-tale world, lacking time, space and friction, a world of automatic and timeless harmony, where an oak grows to enormous proportions in the same time that is taken to cut it down (i.e. zero time). One result of this high level of abstraction is that things repeatedly happen that are not supposed to happen. One example of this is the Asian financial crisis; another is that some nations become poorer under globalization.

Today's standard economics – as applied to poor countries – fails to recognize the importance of *increasing returns* (the fact that in some economic activities costs fall as the volume of production increases), *technological change* – the possibility of which varies widely between economic activities – and *synergies,* factors that acting together produce the cumulative causations or reactions that create the structural change we call economic development. Above all, the theoretical approaches do not allow for diversity and heterogeneity. My claim is that as a result of the above factors, economic growth is activity-specific; it can take place in some economic activities, but not in others. These factors are sometimes present in the 'toy models' of the economists, even in models developed by the Washington institutions. However, perhaps as a misunderstanding of 'the scientific method', with very few exceptions standard economics admits only one factor of reality at a time.[18] Other aspects of the real world must wait outside for their turn, and are also considered in isolation. Thus the major part of the economists' toolbox always consists of physics-based tools, and as a consequence standard theory and standard policies always carry the day. In order to understand the dynamics of wealth and poverty, the Other Canon requires that all physics-based assumptions are dropped simultaneously.

Increasing returns is a principle that can be used without being fully understood, just as we saw in the cases of chewing willow bark to cure headaches, and eating citrus to prevent scurvy. Way back in history Europeans recognized the wealth-producing effects of manufacturing without necessarily relating this to increasing returns. Common sense precedes science. As Edward Misselden, an early English economist, put it in the 1620s: 'before we knew it by sense, now we know it by science'. The origin of increasing returns is normally considered to be Adam Smith's famous pin factory. As usual, what happened before Adam Smith is ignored. Xenophon (c. 427–355 BC), whose *Oeconomicus* gave economics its name, described systemic increasing returns in his book *Poroi*. In 1613 Antonio Serra – whom Joseph Schumpeter notes as 'the first to compose a scientific treatise ... on economic principles and policy'[19] – described increasing returns and the virtuous circles of wealth they produce with considerably more clarity than Smith did in 1776. German economist Ernst Ludwig Carl (1682–1743) described the phenomenon of increasing returns in his three-volume work,[20] using the very same pin factory later used and made famous by Smith.

Since Antonio Serra put them at the core of the mechanisms causing wealth, increasing returns have led a tumultuous life in the history of economic thought. Being allowed to present his ideas to the Viceroy in 1613, Serra was ridiculed and sent back to jail where he probably died a few years later. However, in the 1750s Serra's ideas were again resurrected by the first professor of economics south of Germany, Antonio Genovesi. Later, building their economic theories around the opposite phenomenon, the diminishing returns found in agriculture, increasing returns was completely abandoned by Robert Malthus (1766–1834) and his friend David Ricardo. Referring to a new edition of Serra

published in 1803, in the 1840s and 1850s two German economists Friedrich List (1789–1846) and Wilhelm Roscher (1817–94)
put increasing returns back on the map both in terms of policy and
theory. The founder of neo-classical economics Alfred Marshall
(1842–1924) keeps the reference to increasing returns,[21] but it
later disappears from neo-classical theory. Increasing returns had a
revival in the United States in the 1920s, with important articles in
1923 by Frank Graham (1890–1949) and in 1928 by Allyn Young
(1876–1929), but was promptly thrown out again in the 1930s
by another American economist, Jacob Viner (1892–1970), on
the basis that it was incompatible with equilibrium. In the 1980s,
increasing returns was reintroduced in international trade theory
by Paul Krugman, but its relevance was soon dismissed with great
authority by Jagdish Bhagwati as Krugman's 'youthful surrender
to irrational exuberance'.[22]

Politically, increasing returns is a hot potato. If you assume all
economic activities are equally subject to increasing returns – as
Adam Smith and (sometimes) Paul Krugman does, you have an even
better argument for free trade. In Chapter 4 I shall explain why.
On the other hand, if you assume that some activities (agriculture)
are subject to diminishing returns while others (manufacturing and
advanced services) are subject to increasing returns, as did Antonio
Serra, Frank Graham and (sometimes) Paul Krugman, you get a
theory clearly explaining why poor countries should industrialize
(see Appendix III). After the 1850s increasing returns was used as
the main argument for industrializing continental Europe.

During the last twenty years increasing returns has featured
prominently in research, however the increasing returns argument
is rarely freed from the 'equality assumption' referred to above;
the hugely different 'windows of opportunity' for achieving scale
in different industries are also referred to infrequently. Nor are
the different skill levels and income possibilities found in Adam
Smith's pin factory much mentioned. Economics may have
rediscovered increasing returns – there are quite public rivalries
between three American economists, Brian Arthur, Paul Krugman
and Paul Romer,[23] on the question of 'fatherhood' – yet the reluc-
tance to combine this insight with the diversity and heterogeneity

of the real world blocks the potential to use increasing returns in order to explain uneven development.

Charles Babbage (1791–1871), otherwise known for his contributions to the basic design of computers, actually went into an English pin factory with a Baconian mind and provides us with wage data.[24] The person tinning (whitening) the pin earned 6 shillings a day, while the people straightening the wire only had a wage of 1 shilling per day. Increasing returns and specialization here begin to reveal why economic growth is so uneven. The risk with globalization is that the value chains of production are broken up in such a way that the rich countries take all the high-skill jobs, in this case tinning the pin, while activities similar to the straightening of the wire are farmed out to poor countries. Poor countries tend to specialize in the economic activities which rich countries can no longer mechanize or innovate further, and are then typically criticized for not innovating enough.

The fact of the matter is that the Washington institutions force the conclusions of standard textbook economics upon the nations that are under their wings (which are most poor countries). The damage caused by excluding factors of crucial relevance varies with each nation's situation. The price of the monopoly power of an extremely abstract economic theory is in reality carried by the poor. A nation exporting goods where there is rapid technological progress, large increasing returns and important national synergies suffers little from these factors not being part of ruling economic theory: they have them in reality. Poor countries which often export articles where the same crucial elements are absent – no technical change, no increasing returns and no synergies – are the ones bearing the damage. Furthermore, a task requiring much physical strength will not hurt someone who possesses this strength, only those who don't. As we shall see later, there are plenty of good arguments for introducing free trade, but Ricardo's thesis is not one of them. In the context of a rich country, Ricardo and his trade theory are simply right for the wrong reason – a situation that causes no harm – while for a poor country he is simply wrong.

Joseph Schumpeter claimed that economics suffered from what he called the 'Ricardian Vice'; that is, building economic theory on a priori assumptions without any empirical foundations. To this we may today add a 'Krugmanian Vice', which consists in having developed theories that describe the real world better than standard theory, but refusing to use them in practical politics. We can add to this what Swedish Nobel Laureate (1974) Gunnar Myrdal (1898–1987) calls 'opportunistic ignorance', whereby we are open to a world where the assumptions of economic 'science' are juggled in order to achieve political goals. The European Common Market was promoted to electorates on a premise of increasing returns that would increase wealth (the Cecchini Report, 1988). When the same politicians needed a theory for trade with Africa, they chose Ricardo's trade theory, where increasing returns are assumed not to exist. The politicians could just as well have turned the assumptions around, and used a theory where Africa would have to build its own industry (where there are increasing returns) and where the single market would have made much less sense because of the absence of increasing returns. The choice of which assumptions are to be used under which circumstances is in the end a result of vested interests and political power. Together with the rhetoric–reality gap, economic assumption-juggling is an important tool in the power game that keeps poor nations poor: economics, power and ideology intertwine.

Technology and increasing returns, which are the main sources of economic power, create economic barriers to entry. By keeping technology and the increasing/diminishing returns dichotomy out of international trade theory, economists become useful fools/tools for the vested interests of the nations that are in power. Once this dichotomy is included, some countries will grow richer and others poorer under globalization (see Appendix III). In this real world, rich countries, specializing in the right economic activities, will develop 'economies of scale in the use of force'[25] and a 'capacity for coercion'.[26]

During the late 1700s, English economic theory diverged from continental European theory. During the first Industrial Revolution, Adam Smith – among other things also a customs official – described the world economy as a 'commercial society' focused on buying and selling, rather than on production. At the same time continental European economists, e.g. Johann Beckmann (1739–1811) in Göttingen, were writing about production, technology and knowledge as the basis for wealth creation. Inventions are also mentioned by Adam Smith, but in his theory they are produced outside the system, they are exogenous. Production, knowledge and inventions disappear from Adam Smith's economic theory because he reduces both production and trade to 'labour hours'. In 1817 Ricardo followed in Smith's footsteps, creating an even more abstract theory based on 'labour' – a concept devoid of any qualities – as the measuring rod for value. Later in the century Karl Marx wrote in the production-focused tradition of German social science on the dynamics and the social problems created by capitalism. Unfortunately, when Marx arrived at the point of providing a solution to the problems of capitalism, he reached for Ricardo's labour theory of value. This was a totally foreign element in the German tradition where knowledge, new ideas and technology were seen as the driving forces of the economy. His choice had very serious long-term consequences, allowing Ricardo's abstract thinking to rule along the whole political axis from left to right during the Cold War period and beyond. Recognizing this in the middle of the Cold War, in 1955, Nicholas Kaldor (1908–86) wrote that 'the Marxian theory is really only a simplified version of Ricardo, clothed in a different garb'.[27]

Communism and liberalism thus became, if not siblings at least cousins, abstract theoretical systems towering above the trivial details of the real world. Both theories lack what we have referred to as the capital of human spirit and will (*Geist- und Willens-Kapital*): new knowledge, innovations, entrepreneurship, leadership and organizational capabilities. The production process having been reduced to the application of identical labour hours, the world economy could thus also be reduced to the buying and selling of goods that had already been produced. Human action was similarly reduced to supplying identical labour hours, devoid of any qualities, and to being a consumer. Communism could replace the market where supply and demand met with a gigantic calculator, and claim to create the same result. With Friedrich von Hayek (1899–1992), liberalism acquired an entrepreneur who

created equilibrium in the economy. The really important entrepreneur – Schumpeter's entrepreneur who disrupts equilibrium
with his innovations and thus creates economic growth – could not
easily be formalized, and was left outside the system.

Ricardian economics' first wave of popularity peaked in
mid-1840. Social problems, finding their revolutionary outlet in all
large European nations except England and Russia between 1848
and 1871, demonstrated that the market did not create economic
harmony in the absence of wise policies. By the 1890s it was clear
that Ricardo's abstract system – where all assumptions with the
exception of diminishing returns did not reflect reality – was at
the root of all evil *both* on the political right and the political
left.[28] Two distinguished historians of economic thought who were
educated in the 1890s – Wesley Clair Mitchell (1874–1948) of the
United States and Othmar Spann (1878–1950) of Germany – both
wrote books with the English title, *Types of Economic Theory*,
and established that many types of economic theory now existed,
with the abstract Ricardian version being just one option.

In spite of this, and in spite of the total dominance of non-
Ricardian economics in the United States and on the Continent
during the first forty years of the twentieth century, the post-
Second World War push for mathematization,[29] combined with
the Cold War, brought about a resurgence in Ricardian dominance.
Again, as in the 1840s, the market was seen as a producer of
automatic harmony and the revolutions that brewed in the 1840s
were as a result of social inequities *within* nation-states. However,
similar social problems have appeared today, this time arising
more *between* nations than *within* nations.

The close kinship between communist planning and neo-
liberalism makes it easy for economists to move from one political
extreme to the other, from being Ricardians on the left to being
Ricardians on the right. Ricardian doctrine along the whole
political axis created a common front against experience-based
economics. This is one of the explanations for the problems faced
by the European Union's Lisbon Strategy, which combined the
need for innovation with the need for social cohesion. The two
pillars of the Lisbon Strategy are totally alien to standard textbook

economics, and as such met so much resistance that they were gradually watered down to something more compatible. The situation in the USA is different; here the larger rhetoric–reality gap makes it possible to apply an active industrial policy relatively undisturbed by textbook economics.

If we were to analyse the economics profession as a branch of production, a number of anomalies would soon become apparent. One is what we could call the 'primary incentive system': as Paul Samuelson pointed out in a *New York Times* interview many years ago, 'economists work for the applause of their own peers'.[30] Other sciences, such as medicine, are able to balance peer praise with feedback from the reality of recovering or failing patients. A second anomaly is that any development – from the point of view of the poor of this world it might be either progress or retrogression – is strongly path-dependent: over recent generations economics itself has followed a path of least mathematical resistance that has been unable to include such path-dependencies. Third, as Thomas Kuhn, Karl Popper and others have pointed out, 'normal science' tends to proceed within a given framework until the path has been exhausted, and a radical paradigm shift takes place. What is special about economics is that the two parallel approaches seem to exist simultaneously. To borrow a metaphor from American economist Kenneth Arrow, the Other Canon tradition 'acts like an underground river, springing to the surface only every few decades'. The existence of two parallel traditions paves the way for the opportunism and assumption-juggling we have commented on: one highbrow theory for export and a much more pragmatic theory at home. In the greater picture, the two types of economic analysis go cyclically in and out of fashion. During some periods – the 1760s in France, the 1840s in Europe as a whole and the 1990s in virtually the whole world – one extremely abstract way of thinking achieved a completely dominating position. In all cases the social costs were very high.

The choice of a tool carries with it an inherent logic. As Mark Twain said: 'when all you have is a hammer, all problems start to look like nails'. The way economics was 'mathematized' reinforced the weaknesses already inherent in the Ricardian system – its inability to include facets of reality that are important determinants for wealth and poverty. German philosophy employs the term '*verstehen*' for a type of qualitative understanding which is irreducible to numbers and symbols.[31] Philosopher Hans-Georg Gadamer (1900–2002) describes this type of understanding as something close to the essence of what it means to be a human being. If we try to understand other human beings solely through what is quantifiable – height, weight, percentage of water and trace minerals – many other key aspects are overlooked. In fact, it may be argued that through this purely quantitative under-standing, the difference between a human being and a big jellyfish consists in a few percentage points of dry matter in favour of the human being. Something similar happens to economics when economists attempt to handle society in a way that is totally dominated by quantities and symbols: the use of mathematics too often crowds out qualitative understanding. The Enlightenment created classification systems – taxonomies – to achieve a better understanding of the world around us. Creating the categories 'invertebrates' and 'vertebrates' was an initial attempt at differ-entiating jellyfish and humans. However, economics is virtually devoid of such taxonomies: it builds its accuracy precisely on the *lack* of any taxonomies, on an absence of any systematic attempt at observing and classifying observable differences. Once more than one category is introduced simultaneously, for example, increasing and diminishing returns, economic theory produces inequality and disharmony rather than equality and harmony.

As Ludwig Wittgenstein argued, mathematics tends to become self-referential. Albert Einstein expressed the same scepticism regarding the use of mathematics: 'As far as the statements of math-ematics refer to reality, they are not certain, and as far as they are certain, they do not refer to reality.' As it is generally used in economics, mathematics renders an inward-looking 'autistic' re-lationship to reality, where, for example, in international trade theory it may be argued that the conclusions follow directly from the assumptions. A system where all agents and all inputs are qualita-tively identical, applied in a world devoid of context, will necessarily produce sameness as a result. Herein lies, as I see it, the explanation as to why economics produces economic harmony as its natural outcome. The conclusions are already built into the assumptions. In their rebellion against present-day economics, French economics students seized upon this point in an amusing way when they created the movement for 'post-autistic economics'.[32]

Dissatisfaction with the state of economics is thus clearly growing. The following analysis by a well-known historian of the profession, Mark Blaug, is becoming almost mainstream:

> Modern economics is 'sick'. Economics has increasingly become an intellectual game played for its own sake and not for its practical consequences. Economists have gradually converted the subject into a sort of social mathematics in which analytical rigor as understood in math departments is everything and empirical relevance (as understood in physics departments) is nothing. If a topic cannot be tackled by formal modelling, it is simply consigned to the intellectual underworld.[33]

The same self-referential and inward-looking attitude – locking out reality – was the hallmark of the scholastics or 'schoolmen'. Any child in Denmark and Norway knows the way their countries' first great author (and economist) Ludvig Holberg (1684–1754) made fun of the scholastic traits of science in his day. Holberg lets a learned young man from the capital 'prove' to a poor and horrified country woman that she is, in fact, a stone: 'A stone cannot fly. Mother Nille cannot fly. Therefore Mother Nille must be a stone.' In *Gulliver's Travels* Jonathan Swift (1667–1745) makes fun of science in a similar way. Even early in the twentieth century, in 1926, Danish economist L. V. Birck recognized that the same type of problem was creeping back, and wrote an article called 'Modern Scholasticism'.[34]

The first to use abstract mathematics in economics were the Italian economists in the mid-1700s. After an initial enthusiasm they abandoned the attempt because they found that matters were made more complicated without adding to the analysis. In 1752 mathematician Ignazio Radicati warned his economist friends: 'You will do with political economy what the scholastics did with philosophy. In making things more and more subtle, you do not know where to stop.'[35] Today's economists somewhat naively tend to look at mathematics as a 'neutral' tool, not recognizing Mark Twain's point that the choice of tools heavily influences one's perspective.

However, I am not arguing against quantification and mathematics, I am arguing against this being the only recognized form of doing economics and am asking for room to bring qualitative analysis back to academic economics. Quantitative and qualitative understandings of the world are complementary. The problem is that most factors creating a world polarized in wealth and poverty are of a nature requiring an understanding of qualitative differences. Economists have created the same type of handicap for themselves as someone writing a thesis on various types of snow would have if she or he chose to write in Swahili. In this particular case, Saami or an Inuit language would provide much better media for communication. Like the scholastics against whom Enlightenment philosophers were fighting, economics has chosen a language which may degenerate into 'conventional wisdom' contrary to all common sense, such as 'Mother Nille is a stone'

Like standard textbook economics, in its extreme form scholasticism also 'proves' things that contradict common sense and intuition. Samuelson's factor–price equalization, which will happen under free trade, is an example of counterintuitive scholasticism in economics. Deirdre McCloskey, American economist, makes the point about standard economics proving counterintuitive propositions very clearly. The example she uses is Nobel Laureate Robert Fogel's 'proof' that the railway was not important in the development of the United States, because railways, compared to canals, only improved GDP by 2.5 per cent. This kind of reasoning would prove that the heart is an unimportant organ because it only represents 2.5 per cent of the weight of the human body. In 1971 Robert Heilbroner asked the question 'Is Economics Relevant?' The answer to that question has been increasingly 'no'.

To return to the quote from Thomas Kuhn that introduced Chapter 1: the ruling economic paradigm does not supply the tools which simultaneously grasp the most important factors that make economic development – by its very nature – such an uneven process.

Two types of economic theory
and two theories of globalization

The two broad types of theory discussed here produce different views of globalization. In fact two Nobel Laureates in economics have provided two largely conflicting theories of what will happen to world income under globalization.

In the first type of theory, based on the standard assumptions of neo-classical economic theory, Paul Samuelson 'proved' mathematically that unhindered international trade will produce 'factor–price equalization', which in essence means that the prices paid to the factors of production – capital and labour – will tend to be the same all over the world.[36]

In the second type of theory, based on the alternative tradition we have broadly labelled the 'Other Canon', Swedish economist Gunnar Myrdal was of the opinion that world trade would tend to increase already existing differences in incomes between rich and poor nations.

The economic policies of the Washington Consensus – the basis for the economic policies imposed by the World Bank and the International Monetary Fund – are exclusively built on the type of theory which is represented by Paul Samuelson. The developments of the 1990s are in sharp conflict with Samuelson's ideas, but confirm Myrdal's assertion: rich nations as a group seem to converge into a cluster of wealthy countries, while the poor seem to converge towards poverty, with the gap between them rising. Paul Samuelson's theory seems to be able to explain what goes on inside the group of rich nations, while Gunnar Myrdal's theory seems to be able to explain the development of relative wealth between the group of rich nations and the group of poor nations. Samuelson's theory is not harmful to nations which have already established a comparative advantage in increasing returns. It is, however, extremely harmful to those nations that have not passed the mandatory passage point of a conscious industrialization policy.

The kind of theory that Myrdal proposed is today almost extinct: it either exists only in fragments or in a perverted form tied to neo-classical economics as 'New Institutional Economics'. In its original form, it is rarely taught in the economics departments in today's leading universities. Economists as a group are therefore very reluctant to see that, when it comes to understanding the relationship between rich and poor countries, Myrdal might provide better tools than Samuelson.

Covering only the broad outlines of world development, Samuelson's type of theory can claim a certain degree of success in predicting the developments *within* each group of nations. The rich nations tend towards being more equally rich, while the poor seem to converge towards being equally poor. A result of this is that the 'medium-rich' or middle-income nations are disappearing, and the two convergence groups, rich and poor, stand out as isolated clusters in a scatter diagram – as in Myrdal's prediction.

In the theory based on barter and exchange – today represented by the neo-classical standard theory – the economy is a machine that creates economic harmony as long as it is left to itself. Thus today's focus is on financial and monetary variables. In this theory, the factors causing economic growth – new knowledge, new technology, synergies and infrastructure – are either kept outside of the theory, or they disappear, in an abstract search for averages, such as 'the representative firm'. The opposite happens in the production-based theory, where the financial and monetary variables become the scaffolding necessary to build the central concern, namely the productive capacity of a nation. It is precisely because the above- mentioned factors are ignored that standard theory arrives at the conclusion that globalization will benefit everybody equally, even if a country is still in the Stone Age knowledge-wise. Development, then, tends to be seen as *accumulation of capital* rather than *emulation and assimilation of knowledge*.

The differences between the two theories of economics are profound, and result from two opposing ideas of the most fundamental human characteristics, and the most basic human activity. Adam Smith and Abraham Lincoln neatly define these two different views of human nature and their resulting economic theories.

The *barter-based theory* was set out in Adam Smith's *Wealth of Nations*:

> The division of labour arises from a propensity in human nature to ... truck, barter and exchange one thing for

another ... It is common to all men, and to be found in no other race of animals, which seem to know neither this nor any other species of contracts ... Nobody ever saw a dog make a fair and deliberate exchange of one bone for another with another dog.

Lincoln described his *production and innovation-based theory* in a speech in the 1860 election campaign:

Beavers build houses; but they build them in nowise differently, or better, now than they did five thousand years ago ... Man is not the only animal who labours; but he is the only one who improves his workmanship. These improvements he effects by Discoveries and Inventions.

These two different visions of the fundamental economic characteristics of human beings lead to widely diverging economic theories and proposals for economic policy. Adam Smith does in fact discuss inventions, but they come from somewhere outside of the economic system (they are *exogenous*), they tend to be seen as free (*perfect information*) and they tend to hit all societies and all individuals simultaneously. In the same way, innovations and new technologies are created automatically and free of charge by an invisible hand that, in today's economic ideology, is called 'the market'. In their resistance to Adam Smith's view of humankind, it is notable that Abraham Lincoln and Karl Marx, generally considered opposite poles in the right–left axis of modern politics, are entirely in agreement.

The two types of theory set out two very different origins for humankind: either, for the Lincoln type, 'in the beginning there were social relations' or, for Smith, 'in the beginning there were markets'. In *The Great Transformation* (1944), Karl Polanyi (1886–1964) discusses the consequences of Adam Smith's establishing 'the bartering savage' as the axiom of economics:

A host of writers on political economy, social history, political philosophy, and general sociology had followed in Smith's wake and established his paradigm of the bartering savage as an axiom of their respective sciences. In point of fact, Adam

Smith's suggestions about the economic psychology of early man were as false as Rousseau's were on the political psychology of the savage. Division of labor, a phenomenon as old as society, springs from differences inherent in the facts of sex, geography, and individual endowment; and the alleged propensity of man to barter, truck, and exchange is almost entirely apocryphal. While history and ethnography know of various kinds of economies, most of them comprising the institution of markets, they know of no economy prior to our own, even approximately controlled and regulated by markets. This will become abundantly clear from a bird's-eye view of the history of economic systems and of markets, presented separately. The role played by markets in the internal economy of the various countries, it will appear, was insignificant up to recent times, and the change-over to an economy dominated by the market pattern will stand out all the more clearly.[37]

The two quotes from Lincoln and Smith encapsulate the two types of European economic theory as they have developed in Europe over the last 250 years, with two very different underlying views of humankind. In the English tradition, Type A, a human brain is a passive *tabula rasa* inhabiting a pleasure-calculating machine, avoiding pain and maximizing pleasure. This view leads to a hedonistic and barter-based economics with a corresponding value system and incentive system. Economic growth tends to be seen as a mechanical addition of capital to labour. In the continental tradition, Type B, the essence of a human is a potentially noble spirit with an active brain, constantly registering and classifying the world around him according to set schemata. Economics then becomes centred on production rather than barter, and on the production, assimilation and diffusion of knowledge and innovations. The driving force of the continental type of economics is not capital per se, but Nietzsche's *Geist- und Willens-Kapital*, the human spirit and will. If one believes in Type A, then Type B becomes irrelevant, and vice versa. The first view of humankind makes it possible to produce a simple, calculable and quantifiable static economic theory. The second view, of a much more complex being, also needs a much more complex and dynamic theory, the core of which is irreducible to numbers and symbols. It is important to note that 'conventional wisdom' in one type of theory may be viewed in an entirely different light in the other type. To Jeremy Bentham 'curiosity' was a nasty habit, to Thorstein Veblen 'idle curiosity' became the mechanism by which human society accumulates knowledge.

A hundred years ago, Thorstein Veblen vehemently attacked the basis of Ricardian economics. Like Polanyi later, Veblen, in his characteristic derisive style, argued that primitive economic behaviour could not be understood in Smithian and Ricardian terms: 'A gang of Aleutian Islanders slashing about in the wrack and surf with rakes and magical incantations for the capture of shell-fish are held, in point of taxonomic reality, to be engaged in a feat of hedonistic equilibration in rent, wages, and interest.' This is what economics was supposed to be about, regardless of time, space and context.

In his 1898 article 'Why is economics not an evolutionary science', Veblen attempted to form the basis for an alternative to the Type A view of man, a passive hedonistic creature thrown about by outside events, and instead bring in a Type B economic view. Like Jonathan Swift and Ludvig Holberg 150 years earlier, one of Veblen's weapons was irony:

> The hedonistic conception of man is that of a lightning calculator of pleasures and pains who oscillates like a homogeneous globule of desire of happiness under the impulse of stimuli that shift him about the area, but leave him intact. He has neither antecedent nor consequent. He is an isolated definitive human datum, in stable equilibrium except for the buffets of the impinging forces that displace him in one direction or another. Self-imposed in elemental space, he spins symmetrically about his own spiritual axis until the parallelogram of forces bears down upon him, whereupon he follows the line of the resultant. When the force of the impact is spent, he comes to rest, a self-contained globule of desire as before. Spiritually, the hedonistic man is not a prime mover. He is not the seat of a process of living, except in the sense that he is subject to a series of permutations enforced upon him by circumstances external and alien to him.[38]

In spite of this, Thorstein Veblen was later offered the honour of being president of the American Economics Association, a decision that is difficult to understand today.

From the point of view of our understanding of wealth and poverty, it may be somewhat unkindly argued that Adam Smith's most important contribution was in fact what he caused to be exogenized or removed – from later mainstream economics. Following Adam Smith, four important concepts for understanding economic development were ostracized from the mainstream model:

1. The concept of *innovation*, which had been important in English social science for more than 150 years, from Francis Bacon's *An Essay on Innovations* in the early seventeenth century to James Steuart's (1767) *An Inquiry into the Principles of Political Oeconomy*.
2. The insight that economic development results from synergistic effects and that people sharing a job market with innovative industries will have higher wages than others, both recurring themes in European economic thinking since the fifteenth century.
3. The realization that different economic activities can be qualitatively different carriers of economic development.
4. The reduction by Adam Smith of both production and trade into *labour hours* paved the way for today's still dominant Ricardian trade theory where the world economy is conceived and understood as Adam Smith's bartering dogs exchanging labour hours – void of any qualities – with each other.

Adam Smith's first work was on astronomy, and the metaphor adopted by Smith and his followers remains influential in contemporary economics: just as the planets are kept in orbit around the sun by an invisible hand, so will the invisible hand of the market economy automatically find its equilibrium as long as people do not interfere. There is, then, a very fine line dividing the invisible hand of the market and simple faith in fate and providence. In fact, we find that Adam Smith even attributed the distribution of land to providence rather than to social forces. But even so, the invisible hand would come to the aid of the poor:

> The produce of the soil maintains at all times nearly that number of inhabitants which it is capable of maintaining. The rich only select from the heap what is most precious and agreeable. They consume little more than the poor, and in spite of their natural selfishness and rapacity, though they mean only their own conveniency, though the sole end which they propose from the labours of all the thousands whom they employ, be the gratification of their own vain and insatiable desires, they divide with the poor the produce of all their improvements. They are led by an invisible hand to make nearly the same distribution of the necessaries of life, which would have been made, had the earth been divided into equal portions among all its inhabitants, and thus without intending it, without knowing it, advance the interest of the society, and afford means to the multiplication of the species. When Providence divided the earth among a few lordly masters, it neither forgot nor abandoned those who seemed to have been left out in the partition. These last too enjoy their share of all that it produces. In what constitutes the real happiness of human life, they are in no respect inferior to those who would seem so much above them. In ease of body and peace of mind, all the different ranks of life are nearly upon a level, and the beggar, who suns himself by the side of the highway, possesses that security which kings are fighting for. *(The Theory of Moral Sentiments)*[39]

Smith uses the invisible hand to produce a truly Panglossian vision of society, an attitude that carries over in today's standard economics. With the invisible hand, in unison with the four previous economic insights his system abandoned, Adam Smith created the foundations of an ideology that considers the economy a *Harmonielehre* (theory of harmony) where the market is assumed to bring automatic harmony and equalize welfare. Needless to say, the consequences of this for modern economic policy are staggering.

It is useful to think of the economy as being made up of two different spheres (see figure 4). On the one hand one has the complex, heterogeneous and chaotic world of the real economy, encompassing the production of numerous goods and services, from shoelaces to hotels and barbers. On the other hand there exists a far more homogeneous financial side, where we find all the activities of the real economy translated into dollars and cents. Today's theory of globalization tends to assume that all the different economic activities embraced by the real economy are qualitatively equal as bearers of economic development, and therefore that globalization and free trade will automatically result in economic harmony. In real life, economic inequality results from the diversity and the complexities inside the 'black box' of the real economy.

Apart from ridiculing the naive belief that free trade could produce harmony, the philosopher Friedrich Nietzsche also identified a further element, in addition to bartering and innovating, that divides human beings from the rest of the animal kingdom: humans are the only animals able to keep promises. This view raises the need for *institutions*, norms and routines, laws and rules, incentives and disincentives, whether these are expectations a society agrees to share or formal rules upheld by punishments

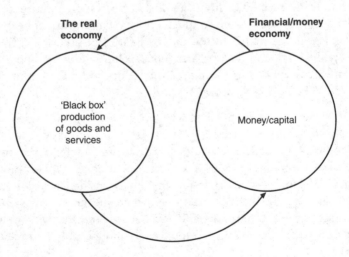

Figure 4   The circular flow of economics

for those who fail to adhere to them. The market itself is in fact such an institution, enabled to function and yet restrained by a number of formal and informal rules. Such institutions, however, have a tendency to be taken for granted in modern economics. After Francis Bacon in the early seventeenth century, economic writers long believed that institutions reflected the mode of production of any society. Today the World Bank tends to turn this insight on its head, and wants to explain that poverty arises in countries as a result of the institutions they lack, disregarding the important connections between mode of production, technology and institutions.

The first time a *barter and exchange* type of theory predominated was with the Physiocrats in France in the 1760s. The second time was in the world of the 1840s. Mainly to provide its industrial workers with cheap bread, England stopped protecting its own agriculture with tariffs and simultaneously sought to make other countries stop protecting their industry. The belief was that the growing social inequalities – what for a century would be called the 'social question' – would disappear as soon as one removed all restrictions on the economy. In the end, however, it led to even greater unrest. The modern welfare state was built from this chaos brick by brick. Germany was the first mover. A politically diverse group of economists united in the Association for Social Policy (*Verein für Sozialpolitik*) and Chancellor Bismarck agreed to their analysis of the problem and to the solutions they proposed. To a large extent this group's analysis was similar to that supplied by Karl Marx, but Marx's solution – to turn the social pyramid on its head – was not accepted. As Anthony Giddens puts it in *The Third Way*: 'The ruling groups who put up the social insurance system in imperial Germany in the late nineteenth century despised laissez-faire economics as much as they did socialism.'[40] This is the brand of economics that has virtually died out.

No historical period resembles the 1990s as much as the 1840s in terms of economic policy. Both periods were characterized by irrational, infinite optimism based on a technological revolution. Stephenson tested the first steam locomotive, *The Rocket*, in 1829, and by 1840 the age of steam was in full bloom. In 1971, Intel developed its first microprocessor, and in the 1990s a new techno-economic paradigm was again unfolding. Such paradigms, based on explosions in the productivity of specific sectors, carry with them possible quantum leaps of development. But they also bring with them speculative frenzies and numerous projects and practices which try to make normal industries perform like the core industries of the paradigm.[41] The dubious accounting practices of Enron were virtually the same as those Thorstein Veblen had heavily criticized a hundred years earlier. In the late nineteenth century, the US Leather Corporation sought to build up its stock value in the same way as the US Steel Corporation, the Microsoft of its day. At the end of the twentieth century, many companies sought to gain a similar stock value to Microsoft, but failed. In both historical periods, they were helped by a euphoric stock market which all too readily wanted to believe it could be true, and for a long time it *was* true simply because enough people believed it. But producing leather was not producing steel, and few companies had the market power of Microsoft, and as a consequence many cases had an unhappy ending.

Extraordinary Popular Delusions and the Madness of Crowds was the title of a book on stock market crashes published by Charles Mackay in 1841. In the same year Friedrich List published his book arguing that free trade had to be brought about slowly and systematically in order not to make poor countries poorer. Just as popular consciousness in such periods expects stock values to go through the roof, no matter the industry in question, at the same time a parallel illusion was created that everybody would be richer as long as the market was given a free reign. John Kenneth Galbraith called this 'market totemism'. These two periods, the 1840s and the 1990s, experienced the strongest faiths ever in the market as the only way to ensure harmony and development. In the 1840s this phenomenon was called 'free trade', today the same phenomenon is called 'globalization'. For a long period of time, the stock market failed to see the differences well enough between the enormous growth in productivity and the dominating market position of the companies carrying the techno-economic paradigm, companies like US Steel and Microsoft on the one hand, and mature industries like those producing leather and other low-tech products on the other. Even now, politicians the world over seem convinced that it has been the openness of the economy and its free trade, rather than its technological breakthroughs, that have made Silicon Valley wealthy. This illusion was catastrophic for the small investors who had put their life savings into projects that turned out to be bubbles. The parallel illusion of 'free trade' is equally damaging for the inhabitants of countries like Peru and Mongolia, who, in the name of globalization, *lost* their industry. Friedrich List committed suicide in 1846, a few months after England had seemingly succeeded in convincing the rest of Europe to abandon its tariffs on industrial products by removing her own tariffs on agricultural products. After his death, however, List's theory that free trade had to wait until all countries were industrialized, was quickly adopted in practical policy across Europe and the USA. It may be argued that List's was still the reigning theory when the European Union slowly and successfully integrated Spain in the 1980s.

The historical paradox here is that it is specifically during the periods when new technologies are fundamentally changing the economy and society – as with steam in the 1840s and information technology in the 1990s – that economists turn to trade- and barter-based theories in which technology and new knowledge have no place. One can say, in the spirit of Friedrich List, that they confuse the carrier of progress, trade, with its cause, technology. The same, ironically, can be said of Adam Smith's theory of economic development. Smith did not seem to take notice of the Industrial Revolution occurring around him as he formulated it.

During the first period of globalization – from the 1840s to the outbreak of the First World War – the rich countries became ever more industrialized, while the Third World remained technologically underdeveloped. It was this first wave of globalization that seriously dug the ditch dividing rich and poor countries in a process in which the colonies, as the practice had been for centuries, were not allowed to industrialize. As long as the latest wave of globalization builds on the same principles as the first – in other words, as long as poor countries continue to specialize in the production of raw materials – it cannot achieve more than the first one did: an increase in the difference between rich and poor, even though some new countries may join the rich.

As the great German economist Gustav Schmoller said at the founding meeting of the Association for Social Policy in 1872: 'Society today is like a ladder where the middle steps are rotten.' Society becomes polarized between rich and poor, and middle-income nations tend to disappear. The attempts from the 1950s until the 1970s to create middle-income countries by industrializing, even if their industries were not yet internationally competitive, were later destroyed by shock therapies of too sudden free trade. These countries (we will later examine the example of Mongolia) were deindustrialized and fell back into increasing poverty. If there was anything the theorists of the past, like James Steuart and Friedrich List, warned against, it was sudden changes in the trade regime. Production systems need time to learn to adjust. Continental Europe was not fooled by English attempts to remain the only industrialized nation in the world in the nineteenth century – by their vision of a global economic harmony where the rest of the world produced raw materials to exchange for English industrial goods. The rest of Europe, and overseas countries with large populations of European emigrants – the USA, Canada, Australia, New Zealand, South Africa – followed the same policy England itself had followed since the end of the fifteenth century: a relatively high tariff protection to encourage industrialization. In spite of its natural protection through high transportation costs, the USA chose to build its enormous steel industry behind tariff walls of up to 100 per cent. Although the majority of immigrants may have been farmers, the farmers were the chief beneficiaries of the existence of an industrial sector, as Abraham Lincoln noted: '[I cannot] tell the reason ... [but high tariffs will] make everything the farmers [buy] cheaper.'

Today, just as in the 1840s, we have a dominant economic theory which says these distributional problems will not happen. Although now repackaged, the myth of the bartering dogs is still at the heart of how mainstream economics understands the world economy. The financial crisis that shook Asia and the world in the 1990s was an example of a crisis economists were convinced could not happen, because the market itself would solve all problems. In the 1840s, the social crisis was largely national, as the gulf separating rich and poor grew within the borders of the individual nations, and the welfare state helped resolve this problem in Europe. Today, however, 'the social question' has acquired an international dimension, as the gulf separating rich and poor nations grows ever wider.[42]

Even in my own country, Norway, the idea that industrialization would help to build the country was extremely important. In 1814, as a result of the Napoleonic War, Norway had been ceded from Denmark to Sweden. In June 1846, the British Parliament enacted the famous repeal of the Corn Laws, allowing free trade in corn, an event today celebrated as the great breakthrough of free trade. Little is said about what happened in reality. In March 1847, less than a year after the 'great breakthrough', the Swedish-Norwegian Tariff Commission presented a report. In this report the Norwegian members argued for an increase in the taxes put on Swedish goods, while the Swedes, the 'colonial power', wanted a full customs union. One argument was that the Norwegian treasury needed the customs duties, but, as the Norwegian historian John Sanness says, 'the chief argument was that the frail Norwegian industry would have been suffocated if it was not given tariff protection against the stronger and more mature Swedish industry'. Norway was in the end awarded this, and there was no disagreement there that it was not necessary and beneficial. The great debate over economic policy at the time was not whether one should protect industry – almost everybody could agree to that – but how this should be done. Today the frail industry of the Third World is being suffocated by the same free trade Norway was able to defend itself against for a century. The fact that Norway is in need of free trade *today* neither means that it needed it 150 years ago, nor that poor countries need it now.

Norway and Sweden were competitors at the time because their exports were so similar. Norway's call for protection therefore caused outrage in Sweden. The Norwegian negotiators claimed Norway's new industry could not afford to lose its tariff protection, which even the most powerful countries at the time had not dared to do. A tariff union meant that Swedish industry would be bound to annihilate Norwegian industry, and everybody at the time knew that a country without industry was doomed to be a poor country. 'The thought process corresponded to the normal industrial protectionism of the times, as with Friedrich List,' says John Sanness. 'New industries needed tariff protection, but the tariffs should gradually become superfluous.' This is the dynamic that we have forgotten today.

Simultaneously with industrial development, from the 1840s Europe started a new race to obtain colonies, a race culminating in the Berlin conference of 1884, at which Africa was carved up among the European states. At the same time the expansion of the United States began. As a result of the war with Mexico between 1845 and 1848 the USA took possession of large areas of what had until then been Mexican territory: Texas, California, Arizona, New Mexico and Colorado. Somewhat later, while the US and Europe were still protecting their industries, China and Japan were forced, with the help of military threats and power, to sign treaties where they agreed *not* to protect theirs. For a while China and Japan became, economically, virtual colonies. In Japanese and Chinese history books these 'unfair treaties' retain an importance and are still regarded with indignation. Africans also still remember their parallel case when in 1888 Chief Lobengula was cheated into granting away excessive rights to Cecil Rhodes. Chief Lobengula's later protests to Queen Victoria were to no avail.

Since 1990 the World Trade Organization trade negotiations with the Third World have once again brought back the days of 'unfair treaties'. Empire is again not such a bad word, and the first-hand reports I receive from African delegates on the way the 'green room' negotiations take place certainly brings back visions of Chief Lobengula and his fate.

In 1994 I met one person who understood he had signed away rights he should not have. I arrived with a group at the Carondelet Palace in Ecuador's capital Quito for a meeting with President Sixto Durán Ballén. The president, an architect by profession, was a charming and grandfatherly figure, and the last president of Ecuador to serve his full constitutional four-year term. But on the day we arrived he was furious. In exchange for promises of large grants and loans, the Washington institutions had previously convinced him to abruptly remove industrial tariffs in order for Ecuador to specialize in supplying bananas to the world. The deindustrialization process had lowered employment and real wages, and in fact I was there with a group organizing micro-finance loans in order to help create new employment. The promised grants and loans had not appeared, the president said, and just before we arrived he had been informed that the European Union had slapped heavy import duties on Ecuadorian bananas. Ecuador is a much more efficient producer of bananas than the former French and English colonies in the Caribbean, not to mention the banana producers in the Canary Islands and Greece. By taxing Ecuadorian bananas, but not those of Europe and its former colonies, the European Union passed the cost for what were de facto subsidies for inefficient banana producers on to the most efficient, Ecuador.[43] Durán Ballén realized he had been cheated, but the manufacturing industry he and his predecessors had sacrificed was irretrievably gone. I awaited the publication of his memoirs[44] with interest to see if this moment of truth was referred to, but the book was dominated by the war between Ecuador and Peru during his presidency. He wanted his political memory to be associated with the war with Peru rather than his responsibility for further deindustrialization and falling real wages.

The foundation for colonialism – that it is morally defensible to keep countries as producers of raw materials only – is found in the economic theory of Ricardo. Before Ricardo, economists largely agreed that colonies were consciously made poorer. English economists sometimes made the excuse that 'if everybody else does it, then so must we'. The most important German economist of the eighteenth century, Johann Heinrich Gottlob von Justi, was of the opinion that the colonies would soon realize that they were being cheated, and rebel to obtain their own industries. In the case of the USA, who rebelled and liberated herself from England in 1776, he was right.

Today we are again in the middle of a new globalization period with the same elements present: the same vision, based on the same economists – Smith and Ricardo – of a well-balanced world with a 'natural' division of labour, with some countries exporting raw materials and importing industrial goods, and this time also advanced services. The industrial structures of poor countries become more and more like those of colonialism and the same economic theories that gave us colonialism now give us a neo-colonialism. Africa is being divided into a complex network of areas with different trade agreements – the so-called spaghetti bowl – in which the EU and the USA try to increase their fields of interest. The map of these trade agreements is not very different from the one resulting from the Berlin conference of 1884. The outcome is that the African countries are being prevented from practising the kind of trade they really need: trade among themselves that later grows towards global free trade in the Listian manner. The EU works hard to make Egypt buy strongly subsidized EU apples, thereby ousting the apple producers of Lebanon, who have traditionally delivered their produce to Egypt. The centre–periphery conditions of colonialism are strengthened again, now not only by profitable industrial goods, but also by subsidized agricultural products. Small African industrial markets are not integrated into a larger market that might have industrialized Africa. Instead, industrial Africa is increasingly fragmented, and while some countries are better off than others, each market is relatively open to the killing competition from the North. To believe that these conditions can be improved by letting poor countries export their agricultural products to the industrialized countries is an illusion. No country without an industrial sector (today we have to change the term to a combined industry-and-service sector) has ever managed to raise the wage level of its farmers.

In the first 'globalization period' direct slavery was abolished, and at the 1884 Berlin conference the European states were able to carve up Africa under a veil of rhetoric about human rights. At that time missionaries were able to remedy the worst of people's physical destitution, but their most important contribution was to calm people by promising them a better afterlife. Today many Africans see parallels with this. While Africa has been heavily deindustrialized – even the strongest advocates for globalization have to admit that most of sub-Saharan Africa has become poorer during the last twenty-five years – many organizations work, as did the missionaries, to try to alleviate the worst symptoms of poverty. And the industrialized countries contribute heavily to relieve the suffering, just as people used to contribute to the missions. After three not very successful 'development decades' under the direction of the United Nations, the world community has largely given up developing the poorest countries. In the Millennium Goals, which took over from the 'development decades', the ambition to develop the Third World has been toned down considerably in favour of an attempt to relieve the worst symptoms of poverty, by providing medicines, mosquito nets and pure drinking water. Just as cancer patients are given palliative treatment – treatment that relieves the pain without attempting to cure the disease – we are witnessing an increasing focus on *palliative economics* as a substitute for development economics.

It is interesting that even a country like Norway, so long a kind of colony itself and with several current initiatives aimed at making the world a better place, has 'forgotten' the strategy we fought for: to obtain industry and economic growth. We have forgotten that central to our own nation-building there was an industrial policy which was the opposite of the principles we today force on the Third World. After the Second World War the Labour government, aided by the Marshall Plan, reindustrialized Norway extremely successfully. Today's government, led by the same Labour party, makes a point of prohibiting the same policies for others that made us rich. Yet we have ambitions to be champions in palliative economics, in relieving the symptoms of poverty.

Stage theories

History – it has been said – was created to prevent everything from happening simultaneously. Therefore, one way economists and historians have attempted to organize history is to establish sequences of periods or stages of development.[45] For historians, the material from which humankind's tools were made (e.g. stone or bronze) has become universally accepted as the basis for establishing early historical periods: the Stone Age (Mesolithic, Neolithic), the Bronze Age. Other criteria could have been used, for instance, based on social organization, but the technology variable was chosen.

In anthropology, too, the idea that technology is an important determinant for society is an old one, the discussion of the relationship between irrigation and centralized government being a classical example. With political science and Jean Bodin's (1530–96) study of the republic, the idea of stages in human development was born. If we define sociology as starting with Auguste Comte (1798–1857), the idea of stages was there from the very beginning of that social science as well. In economics, theories of stages were central both to the important French economist and statesman Robert-Jacques Turgot (1727–81) and in the teachings of Adam Smith. In his book on the early stage theories from 1750 to 1800, economist Ronald Meek (1917–78) goes so far as to suggest that 'there was a certain sense ... in which the great eighteenth-century systems of "classical" political economy in fact *arose out* of the four stage theories'.[46] In spite of this, any concept of economic stages today is peripheral, almost alien, to economists. Each stage represented a *mode of production,* and it was obvious that each successive stage represented human progress.

Incipient ideas of stage theories are found in antiquity, both in Greece and in Rome. One may read Tacitus's (c.AD 55–120) *Germania* in such a way that 'the relative degree of civilization of the different Germanic tribes depended upon the extent to which agriculture and pasturage, rather than hunting, preponderated in their mode of subsistence'.[47] The idea of stages grew out of the idea of cycles, an old idea in political history. Cycle theories are given importance both by Arab economist and historian Ibn Khaldun (1332–1406) and by Machiavelli (1469–1527). With Jean Bodin, one of the path-breakers of the Renaissance, comes the idea that historical cycles may have a cumulative and upward trend: the idea of progress. At the same time Bodin discusses the embryonic nation-state (the republic), its institutions, laws and taxation.

Whereas Bodin puts much emphasis on geographical and climatic conditions, Francis Bacon, in his *Novum Organum* (1620), gives another explanation when discussing the startling differences between the conditions of life in the various parts of the world. Bacon postulates that 'this difference comes not from soil, not from climate, not from race, but from the arts'.[48] As already mentioned, Bacon was an important scientist in experience-based, but also in production-based, economic theory. Bacon's idea that the material condition of a people is determined by its 'arts' – by whether they are hunters and gatherers, herders, farmers or industrial workers – was central to the nineteenth-century German and North American conflict with England over economic theory and industrial policy. During the Enlightenment, historian William Robertson continued the Baconian tradition: 'In every inquiry concerning the operations of men when united together in society, the first object of attention should be their mode of subsistence. Accordingly as that varies, their laws and policies must be different.' Human institutions were determined by their mode of production rather than the other way around. Today's 'new institutional economics', based on standard textbook economics, tends to reverse the arrows of causality, blaming poverty on the lack of institutions rather than on a backward mode of production.

During the Enlightenment, particularly between 1750 and 1800, stage theories were centre-stage, particularly in England and France. From 1848 onwards, during the expansion and geographical extension of industrial society and the retreat of Ricardian economics, stage theories again became part of the economists' toolbox – this time especially in the USA and Germany. At the time, the fundamental changes which could be observed made it obvious that the world was entering a historical period that was qualitatively different from all previous ones.

The stage theories born during the first Industrial Revolution – those of Turgot and of the early Adam Smith – follow humans first as hunters and gatherers, then as shepherds of domesticated animals, then as farmers, finally reaching the stage of commerce. Most significantly, English classical economists tended from the late eighteenth century on to concentrate their analysis on the last stage of evolution, on *commerce* – on supply and demand and on prices – rather than on *production*. During the nineteenth century, German and American economists insisted on a very different interpretation of the development stages. To them, the previous stages were all built on ways of producing goods, and they saw it as a grave mistake to classify the next stage of development another way. This difference of opinion essentially laid the foundation for the ways that nineteenth-century German and American economic policy came to differ from that prescribed by English theory. To English economists the last stage was 'The Age of Commerce'. To German and American economists the last stage was 'The Age of Industry'.

This is the key point where today's standard textbook economics, the descendant of Adam Smith's 'Age of Commerce', deviates from the production-based economics I refer to as the Other Canon, a descendant of continental European (particularly German) and American economics. Having ignored the importance of technology and production, as was stated previously, modern international trade theory insists that free trade between a Neolithic tribe and Silicon Valley will tend to make both trading partners equally rich. Other Canon trade theory, on the other hand, insists that free trade is beneficial to both parties only when they have both reached the same stage of development.

Stage theories are also useful for understanding the important issues of population and sustainable development. The pre-Columbian population of North America, consisting essentially of hunters and gatherers, has been estimated as low as 2–3 million people, whereas the pre-Columbian population of the Andes, having reached the agricultural stage, has been calculated at 12 million. This gives a population density thirty to fifty times higher in the apparently inhospitable Andes than on the fertile prairies. Thus the concept of sustainability only becomes meaningful when combined with a technology variable, with a mode of production.

Because the focus of analysis was to be trade and commerce, and not production, English and, later, neo-classical economic theory slowly came to see all economic activities as being qualitatively alike. Theories of production which were later added to this Anglo-Saxon tradition of economics – today's standard theory – essentially came to regard production as a process of adding capital to labour in a rather mechanical way, similar to that of adding water to genetically identical plants growing under identical conditions. Economics developed, to use Schumpeter's phrase, 'the pedestrian view that it is capital per se that propels the capitalist engine'. Because we perceive capital as the source of growth, rather than technology and new knowledge, we send money to a pre-manufacturing Africa, capital that cannot be profitably invested. German and American economists a hundred years ago would have understood that the mode of production in Africa – the lack of a manufacturing sector – is the cause of poverty rather than the lack of capital per se. As both the conservative Schumpeter and the radical Marx agreed: capital is sterile without investment opportunities that are essentially products of new technology and innovations. American and German economists a hundred years ago also understood synergies: that only the presence of manufacturing made modernization of agriculture possible.

Standard textbook economics fails to consider how differing technological windows of opportunity create huge variations in economic activities, and consequently also widely different opportunities for adding capital to labour in a potentially profitable way. The first Industrial Revolution was essentially one in cotton textile production. The countries without that industrial sector – the colonies – had no industrial revolution. Everyone understands the importance of the Industrial Revolution, but Ricardo's trade theory convinces us that Stone Age tribes would become as rich as industrial countries if they would only embrace free trade. It is important to note that I am not constructing a straw man to attack here. As shown by the quote from WTO Secretary General Renato Ruggiero in the introduction, this was indeed the vision that shaped the world economic order after the end of the Cold War.

In one of its more far-fetched defences of free trade, the journal *Foreign Policy*,[49] in an essay entitled 'Trade or Die', argues that the lack of free trade was the reason the Neanderthals died out. The fact is that the coexistence of Neanderthals and humans took place before humans started trading, when trade was at best an insignificant ritual gift-giving between tribes.[50] Nevertheless economists are stuck with Adam Smith's fanciful invention of the bartering savage as our ancestor. However, on a different page in the same issue, when discussing the relative costs of movie tickets, *Foreign Policy* falls down on the common sense understanding of the importance of manufacturing for national wealth: 'A night at the movies is relatively cheap in countries with large domestic industries' (p. 31).

The standard economics tradition also came to disregard completely the 'soil' in which the process of adding water to the plant (capital to labour) took place, in other words the historical, political and institutional context of the process of development. Standard economic theory considers neither the obvious focusing of technical change at any point in time, nor the extreme variation in 'windows of opportunity'[51] between different economic activities which is the result of this focusing effect, nor the context in which this process takes place.

As the German historical tradition and the American institutional school died out, economists' understanding of production – of what used to be called 'industrialism' – as the true source of wealth further declined. Swedish institutional economist Johan Åkerman brilliantly explains how production was lost – right, left and centre:

> Capitalism, property rights, income distribution came to be considered the essential features, whereas the core contents of industrialism – technological change, mechanization, mass production and its economic and social consequences – partly were pushed aside. The reasons for this development are probably found in the following three elements: *Firstly*, Ricardian economic theory ... became a theory of 'natural' relations, established once and for all, between economic concepts (price, interest, capital, etc). *Secondly*, the periodic economic crises are important in this respect because the immediate causes of the crises could be found in the monetary sphere. Technological change, the primary source creating growth and transforming society, disappeared behind the theoretical connections which were made between monetary policy and economic fluctuation. *Thirdly*, and most importantly, Marx and his doctrine could capitalize on the discontent of the industrial proletariat. His teachings gave hope of a natural law

which led towards the 'final struggle', when the pyramid of income distribution would be turned on its head, the lower classes should be the powerful and mighty. In this ongoing process the technological change came to be considered only as one of the preconditions for class struggle.[52]

In short, all across the political spectrum *production* as the core of human economic activity was lost. UNCTAD's 2006 report on the least developed countries, 'Developing Productive Capacities',[53] is one attempt to bring production back to the core of development economics. The report cites several of the ideas I have presented in this book.

3

Emulation:
How Rich Countries Got Rich

Around the thirteenth century the Florentines, Pisans,
Amalfitans, Venetians and Genoese began adopting a different
policy for enhancing their wealth and power because they
noticed that the sciences, the cultivation of land, the application of the arts and of industry, and the introduction of
extensive trade could produce a large population, provide for
their countless needs, sustain great luxury and gain immense
riches without having to add more territories.

Sebastiano Franci, Milanese Enlightenment reformer, 1764

A new view of the world: from zero-sum game to innovation and growth

Since time immemorial the majority of the Earth's inhabitants have
lived simple lives, in relative poverty, in an often fragile balance
between population size and the resources available to them. As
Alfred Marshall, one of the founders of neo-classical economics,
expressed it, all migrations in history have been created by diminishing returns: an increasing density of population set off against
an unchanged availability of natural resources and unchanged

technology. We find this mechanism described in the Bible (Genesis 13: 6) when the tribes of Israel had to part because 'the land was not able to bear them, that they might dwell together: for their substance was great, so that they could not dwell together'. Although luxury goods gradually came into being, these were for the selected few, and riches were mainly gained by the conquest of new territories.

In such a world, wealth and poverty were a zero-sum game; wealth was basically acquired by already existing riches changing owners. This view of the world, which must also have existed from time immemorial, was codified by Aristotle and shaped the world-view of scholasticism, the philosophy of late medieval Europe. 'One man's benefit is another man's loss,' confirms St Jerome (c.341–420). As late as 1643 the Englishman Sir Thomas Browne (1605–82) argued that 'all cannot be happy at once because the glory of one state depends upon the ruins of another'. History tended to be cyclical, as described by fourteenth-century Arab historian and economist Ibn Khaldun. For him societies were formed through social cohesion, and there were desert societies and town societies. A desert tribe conquered a town, but decayed as it became more refined and weaker, and after a certain number of generations the town would again be conquered by a new desert tribe.

The changes Sebastiano Franci describes above as taking place in certain Italian cities have their origins in a fundamental change to the traditional world-view. This mentality switch, which asserted itself in many ways, was a product of the late Renaissance. Many factors combined to cause the zero-sum game gradually to disappear as the dominant world-view, and at the same time to introduce an element of progress over and above the cyclical nature of history. Several of these new elements can be traced far back in time, but only during the Renaissance did they gather sufficient critical mass to enable a change of traditional world-view and forge a new cosmology. These new core elements of the Renaissance – which for the first time in history created generalized wealth in certain geographical areas – have disappeared from current economic thinking. One important underlying reason for the inability to remedy world poverty today is that these discoveries of the Renaissance – and later those of the Enlightenment – are not easily formalized in the language in which modern economists have chosen to express themselves.

It was very clear to people early on that most wealth was to be found in the cities, and particularly in certain cities.[1] The cities were the home of free citizens; in the countryside, people were generally serfs, belonging to the soil and the local lord. Arising from these observations were investigations into an understanding of the factors that made the cities so much wealthier than the countryside. Gradually, the wealth of the cities was perceived to be a result of *synergies*: people of many different trades and professions sharing a community. Florentine scholar and statesman Brunetto Latini (*c.*1220–94) described this synergy as '*il ben commune*', or 'the common weal'. Most early economists, the mercantilists and their German counterparts – the cameralists – used such synergies as a fundamental element in their understanding of wealth and poverty. 'It's the common weal that makes the cities great,' repeats Niccolò Machiavelli (1469–1527) almost three hundred years after Brunetto Latini.

With this social understanding of wealth as a phenomenon that could only be understood as a collective phenomenon, the Renaissance rediscovered and flagged the importance and creativity of the individual. Without keeping both these perspectives in mind – the common weal and the role of the individual – neither the Renaissance view of society nor the phenomenon of economic growth can be understood. This theoretical ambivalence, keeping the interests of both society and the individual in mind as units of analysis, characterized continental European economic theory, particularly German, up to the Second World War, but has subsequently almost disappeared. In the twentieth century, analyses of this point led to important debates about the relationships between different forms of freedom (for instance, the trade-off between the right of the individual to carry weapons versus the right of the rest of society not to be shot). The loss of this dual theoretical perspective – exemplified by Margaret Thatcher's 'There is no such thing as society' – seriously inhibits our understanding of poverty and failing states. The methodology of standard economics too often makes it blind to genuine synergies.

Aristotle's view of the world as a zero-sum game slowly gave way to an increasing understanding that new wealth could be *created* – not only conquered – through innovation and creativity. The gradual change in the meaning of the word 'innovation' elucidates this development. In 1277 Roger Bacon (*c.*1214–94) was arrested in Oxford for 'suspect innovations', a heresy consisting of searching for knowledge outside the Bible and the works of Aristotle. When, about 300 years later, Francis Bacon (1561–1626) wrote an essay, *Of Innovations*, innovations were accepted as carriers of increased human wealth and happiness. In his utopian vision, *The New Atlantis*, Francis Bacon describes a state where innovation holds the seat of honour and people have invented self-propelling vehicles, submarines, microphones and medicines

scribes the world's first 'national
use. The growth of manufacturing
es of diminishing returns, creating
the exclusive privilege of cities:
ly mentioned, increasing returns
ds – even without technical change
unit falls. Antonio Serra (1613)
hy state as consisting of increasing
division of labour, in other words
fferent professions and activities in

England's story

how a country goes from

poor to rich

England's story is the prototype of how a country goes from poor to rich. It was policy before it became written theory, but even in 1581 author John Hales understood the importance of the manufacturing multiplier for national wealth: 'What groseness of wits be we of ... that will suffer or owne commodities to go and set straungers at worke, and then buy them againe at theyr handes.'[2] This is the basic insight found in all countries that, one after the other, industrialized. The same principles were applied in Japan and Korea in the second half of the twentieth century.

Under conditions of falling costs with increasing output – what we have called increasing returns or economies of scale – a large population was no longer seen as a problem for seventeenth-century economists. On the contrary, economies of scale in production and division of labour among all the new crafts made a large population a condition for economic growth.[3] Not only was it a necessary precondition for wealth to have a large and growing population, the concentration of this population was also exceedingly important. English economist William Petty (1623–87) therefore suggested moving the population of Scotland and other then peripheral areas to London, where the people would contribute much more to economic growth than they were able to do in the empty fringes of the island. Not until after 1798, when Thomas Malthus (1766–1834) reconstructed an economic theory built on diminishing returns in agriculture (not on innovation and economies of scale in manufacturing) did a growing population once more, as in the biblical Genesis, come to be regarded as a problem. Malthus and his friend Ricardo's reintroduction of diminishing returns as a core feature of economics, and the simultaneous dismissal of both increasing returns and innovations had dramatic consequences because with it the previous understanding of wealth as a joint product of synergies, increasing returns and innovations, was lost. The emphasis on diminishing returns gained Ricardo's economics the name a 'dismal science' and its trade theory constitutes, to this very day, both the main excuse for colonialism and neo-colonialism and the core of the mechanisms that keep poor countries poor. Also lost was an important feature of Enlightenment science: understanding differences through the creation of classification systems or taxonomies.

Early modern Europe also saw a marked connection between discoveries – geographical and scientific – and innovations, between development of theory and development of practice. A growing understanding of an infinite universe in constant expansion was a condition for the mercantilist world-view: as the whole cosmos could expand endlessly, so could the economy. Giordano Bruno (1548–1600), the scientist and hermetic magus who was burned at the stake in Rome on 1 July 1600 for, among other things, holding the universe to be infinite, thus also contributed importantly to the opening up of Europe's economic cosmology.

At the very core of the process of economic progress is the dynamic combination of synergies and innovations under conditions of a substantial specialization and division of labour. This was clearly understood by economists as early as the seventeenth century. Later we shall see how such an economic growth system was to function in the Dutch town of Delft.

Religion was slowly loosening its universal grip on society and at the same time opening itself up to innovation, resulting in a radical shift in the meaning of the term and the attitude towards it, as exemplified by the treatment of Roger Bacon in the thirteenth century and Francis Bacon in the early sixteenth century.[4] When Constantinople, the capital of the western Roman Empire of Byzantium, fell to the Turks in 1453, many philosophers moved to Italy; as a result Western philosophy and the Western Church became heavily influenced by the Eastern Church. In the process a more dynamic version of Genesis – the story of Creation – gained a foothold. The reasoning went roughly like this: if man is created in the image of God, it is our duty to try to emulate God. What, then, is God's most typical attribute? It has to be His creativity and His innovations; He had created both Heaven and Earth. Gradually it became obvious that our role on this Earth ought to be more than that of gardeners and maintenance workers in God's Creation. God had spent six days creating, and had then left the rest of the creation to humankind. Consequently, to create and to innovate became our pleasurable duty. It is our duty to populate the Earth, and as with human propagation God had also introduced incentives for us to innovate in the joy of discovering new things. Alexandre Koyré (1892–1964) puts it this way: humankind had graduated 'from being a spectator into being an owner and master of nature.'[5] Humankind had set out on an expedition to collect new knowledge, and no matter how much wisdom was absorbed, we would keep on pushing the never-ending frontiers of knowledge.

That, briefly, is the story of the evolution of the understanding of economic growth as a joint product of synergies, a large division of labour, increasing returns and new knowledge. As we shall see, it was also understood that the potential for achieving growth was, at any time, limited to certain economic activities. In other words, economic growth was activity-specific. This holistic understanding, also taking qualitative differences into account, is at best found in a piecemeal fashion in today's ruling economic theory. Elements of the story – such as increasing returns – are occasionally, and individually brought back, but no longer are all the elements in their self-reinforcing totality brought together convincingly enough to influence the economic policy that we allow poor countries to follow. Poor countries today are those where these elements are not yet found to a sufficient degree. Colonies were regions where this kind of synergetic interaction was *not* intended to take place, and Ricardian trade theory was the first theory that made colonialism morally defensible. Although the prohibition of manufacturing industries – whether explicit or de facto – is the key element in any colonial and neo-colonial policy, standard Ricardian trade theory says this does not matter. But our world economic order is based on this theory, a theory that predicts that economic integration between an indigenous tribe in the Amazon and Silicon Valley will tend to make both communities equally rich.

Emulation: strategic economic policy comes into being with Henry VII of England (1485)

That Europe's 'islands of wealth' were often also islands in a geographic sense was not lost on early economists. The wealth of a city or nation appeared, somewhat paradoxically, to be inversely related to its natural wealth. The most important areas, like Holland and Venice, had little arable land. They had therefore been forced into specializing in manufacturing industry and overseas trade. In Florence, the most important European city-state not situated on a coast, the big landowners had been for centuries kept from having any political power. Consequently, as in the coastal states, the interests of craftsmen, manufacturers and traders dominated the life of the city. Florence understood very early the basic mechanisms that created wealth and poverty. For centuries the landowners formed a perennial threat to the Florentines as potential allies of the enemies of the state. Keeping the landowners away from power had a dual purpose for the citizens of Florence: it secured both economic power and wealth through the establishment of manufacturing and political power. To avoid speculation and prevent shortages of food, Florence vehemently prohibited the transport of food outwards from the city storage places. Economic power and patronage joined in creating a flourishing of the arts as a characteristic of non-feudal societies. This historically crucial link between political structure and economic structure – between democracy and an economy diversified away from dependence on agriculture and raw materials – is another crucial historical lesson lost today when we, with great violence and at great expense, attempt to establish democracies in nations where the economic structures are essentially feudal and pre-capitalist.

For Europe's poor nations it became clear that there was an important connection between the *production structure* of the few wealthy city-states and their riches. The wealthiest city-states – Venice and those in Holland – had dominant market power in three different areas. In economic terms they enjoyed the type of rents we have referred to earlier, allowing increasing profits, real wages and taxable income. Both had very large and diversified manufacturing and craft sectors. In the early 1500s manufacturing represented about 30 per cent of all employment in Holland. Venice had 40,000 men employed in the shipyards (the *arsenale*) alone. Each controlled an important market for a raw material, salt in Venice and fish in Holland. Even in its early stages of development, and still relatively poor, Venice always fought hard to keep its dominant position in the salt markets. In Holland the invention of salted and pickled herring (an early fourteenth-century invention) had created a huge market that was controlled by the Dutch. Third, both had built up a very profitable overseas trade. This first prosperity in Europe was based on triple rents – a triple market power in types of economic activities that were all conspicuously absent in the poorer European states: manufacturing, a virtual monopoly in an important raw material and profitable overseas trade. Wealth had been created and maintained behind huge barriers to entry created by superior knowledge, by possessing a large variety of manufacturing activities that created systemic synergies, by market power, by low costs created through innovations and increasing returns – both in individual industries and as systemic effects – by the sheer scale of their operations, and by the economies of scale in the use of military might. After 1485, England emulated the triple rent structure that had been created in the resourceless city-states of Europe. Through very heavy-handed economic intervention, England created its own triple rent system: manufacturing, long-distance trade and a raw-material rent based on wool. The success of England would eventually lead to the demise of the city-states and the growth of the nation-states: synergies found in the city-states were extended to a larger geographical area. This was to be the essence of the mercantilist project in Europe.[6]

To go back briefly to economic theory: before Adam Smith it was often understood that economic development was based on collective rent-seeking, originating in synergies of increasing returns, innovations and division of labour that were found clustered only in the cities. This is the opposite of the perfect competition postulated by today's standard textbook economics. Ever since Ricardo's writings, from the pinnacle of an industrialized England in 1817, the pattern is the same: wealthy nations keep poor countries poor based on theories postulating the non-existence of the very factors that created their own wealth. As we shall see, countries that have got rich after 1485 have all done so in defiance of Ricardo's economic theories.

History's first deliberate large-scale industrial policy was based on an observation of what made the rich areas of Europe rich: that technological development in one field in one geographic area could extend wealth to an entire nation. King Henry VII of England, who came to power in 1485, had spent his childhood and youth with an aunt in Burgundy. There he observed great affluence in an area with woollen textile production. Both the wool and the material used to clean it (Fuller's Earth or aluminium silicate) were imported from England. When Henry later took over his destitute realm with several years' future wool production mortgaged to Italian bankers, he remembered his adolescence on the Continent. In Burgundy not only the textile producers, but also the bakers and the other craftsmen were well off. England was in the wrong business, the king recognized and decided on a policy to make England into a textile-producing nation, not an exporter of raw materials.[7]

Henry VII created quite an extensive economic policy toolbox. His first and most important tool was export duties, which ensured that foreign textile producers had to process more expensive raw materials than their English counterparts. Newly established wool manufacturers were also guaranteed tax exemption for a period, and were given monopolies in certain geographical areas for certain periods. There was also a policy to attract craftsmen and entrepreneurs from abroad, especially from Holland and Italy. As English wool-manufacturing capacity grew, so did the export duties, until England had sufficient production capacity to process all the wool they produced. Then, about a hundred years later, Elizabeth I could place an embargo on all raw wool exports from England. In the eighteenth century Daniel Defoe and other historians saw the wisdom in this strategy, which they labelled the 'Tudor Plan', after the kings and queens from that family. Like Venice and Holland, and by the same methods, England had acquired the same triple rent situation: a strong industrial sector, a raw material monopoly (wool), and overseas trade.

Several English historians point out that the industrial policy plan of the Tudors was the real foundation of England's later greatness. On the Continent this plan was to have significant consequences. Florence was one of the states hardest hit by the English competition. The Florentines tried to make do with Spanish wool, and they tried to diversify from wool production to silk, but the English policy was so successful that the golden age of Florence was definitely over.

Spanish wool producers were England's main competitors as producers of raw materials and in 1695 the English economist John Cary suggested that England ought to buy all Spanish wool on the market in order to burn it. England did not have sufficient capacity to process this wool, but to remove the raw material from the market would strengthen their market power:

> We could promote a Contract with the Spaniard for all (wool) he hath; and if it should be objected that we should then have too much, 'tis better to burn the Overplus at the Charge of the Public (as the Dutch do their Spices) than to have it wrought up abroad, which we can't otherwise prevent, seeing all the Wool of Europe is Manufactured somewhere.[8]

The trade war was really a fight to be able to carry out the activities yielding the highest profits, paying the highest wages and/or that could be taxed the most. It was clear to all participants that strategic trade policy was, in effect, 'war by other means'.

For several hundred years Europe's trade policy was based on the principle of maximizing the industrial sectors of each country, while often at the same time damaging the industry of other countries. As the German economist Friedrich List put it in 1841: for several hundred years England's economic policy was based on a simple rule: import of raw materials and export of industrial products. To be wealthy, countries like England and France would have to emulate and copy the economic structures of Venice and Holland, but not necessarily their economic policies. Countries already wealthy could afford a very different policy from those of countries still poor. In fact, once a country had been solidly industrialized, the very same factors that required initial protection – achieving increasing returns and acquiring new technologies – now required bigger and more international markets in order to develop and prosper. Successful industrial protection thus carries the seeds of its own destruction: when successful, the protection that was initially required becomes counterproductive. As an anonymous Italian traveller in Holland said in 1786: 'Tariffs are as useful for introducing the arts [manufacturing] in a country, as they are damaging once these are established.'[9] Here lies the key to understanding the timing of free trade. Again, this is an insight which is lost in today's economic theory as applied to large parts of the world.

The fundamental principles of Henry VII's economic policy toolbox have, since then, been mandatory ingredients in the economic policies of all countries that have worked their way up from poverty to wealth. The exceptions to this rule are few. A small city-state devoid of resources but with a huge hinterland, like Hong Kong, may get rich in the same 'natural' way as Venice and Holland did. Studying the inner mechanisms of such states, however, makes it clear that the principle of wealth creation – from the cost of a taxi licence in Hong Kong to the city's huge corporations – is not perfect competition, but rent seeking, that is, profiting from imperfect rather than from perfect competition.

The first US Secretary of the Treasury, Alexander Hamilton, with his 1791 *Report on the Manufactures of the United States*, recreated a toolbox very similar to that of Henry VII. Hamilton's stated goals were the same: a larger division of labour and a larger manufacturing sector. The same toolbox was employed by virtually all continental European countries in the nineteenth century, including my own country Norway in the European periphery. The theories of German economist Friedrich List – who had lived long enough in the United States to become an American citizen – were the main inspiration for the European nations that followed England's policies and path to industrialization. List's writings were translated into many languages and the same 'Listian' toolbox was used in Japan from the Meiji restoration in the 1860s and in Korea – a country poorer than Tanzania in 1950 – from the 1960s onwards. Poor countries are those who have not employed this toolbox, or have employed it for too short a period and/or in a static way that has prevented the competitive dynamics from taking root. The comparison between 'good' and 'bad' protectionism in Appendix IV highlights the qualitative differences between protectionist practices.

The toolbox of economic emulation and development

> ...the fundamental things apply, as time goes by.
>
> Sam, the pianist, in *Casablanca*

1. Observation of wealth synergies clustered around increasing returns' activities and continuous mechanization in general. Recognition that 'We are in the wrong business'. Conscious *targeting, support and protection* of these increasing returns' activities.
2. Temporary monopolies/patents/protection given to targeted activities in a certain geographical area.
3. Recognition of development as a synergic phenomenon, and consequently the need for a diversified manufacturing sector ('maximizing the division of labour', Serra, 1613).
4. A manufacturing sector solves three policy problems endemic to the Third World simultaneously: increasing

national value added (GDP), increasing employment and solving balance of payments problems.

5. Attracting foreigners to work in targeted activities (historically, religious persecutions have contributed to this in an important way).

6. Relative suppression of landed nobility and other groups with vested interests based in the production of raw ma-terials (from Henry VII in the 1480s to Korea in the 1960s). Physiocracy, the originator of today's neo-classical economics, represented the rebellion of the landowning class against the policies on this list in pre-Revolutionary France. The American Civil War is a prototype conflict between free traders and raw materials exporters (the South) on the one hand and the industrializing class (the North) on the other. Today's poor countries are the nations where 'the South' has won the political conflicts and civil wars. Opening up too early for free trade makes 'the South' the political winners. Standard economics and the conditionalities of the Washington institutions de facto represent unconditional support for 'the South' in all poor countries.

7. Tax breaks for targeted activities.

8. Cheap credit for targeted activities.

9. Export bounties for targeted activities.

10. Strong support for the agricultural sector, in spite of this sector being clearly seen as incapable of independently bringing the nation out of poverty.

11. Emphasis on learning/education (UK apprentice system under Elizabeth I, Francis Bacon's *New Atlantis*, scientific academies, both in England and on the Continent).

12. Patent protection for valuable knowledge (Venice from 1490s).

13. Frequent export tax/export ban on raw materials in order to make raw materials more expensive to competing nations. (This started with Henry VII in the late 1400s, whose policy was very efficient in severely damaging the woollen industry in Medici Florence.)

Spain as a frightening example of what not to do

From the mid-1500s the theatre of Europe provided further elucidation in economic theory and policy, setting an example of what a country should *not* do. Spain had long been an important industrial state. 'In Europe, to describe the best silk one once said "the quality of Granada". To describe the best textiles one once said "the quality of Segovia",' wrote a Portuguese economist in the 1700s. By then Spanish manufacturing industry was history and the mechanisms that had diminished its manufacturing capacity and its wealth in tandem were eagerly studied across Europe. Their conclusions on what had happened were virtually unanimous.

The discovery of the Americas led to immense quantities of gold and silver flowing into Spain. These huge fortunes were not invested in productive systems but actually led to the de-industrialization of the country. The landowners primarily profited from the 'funnel of gold' from the Americas, as they had a monopoly on the export of oil and wine to the growing markets of the New World. The supply of such goods is highly inelastic, and subject to diminishing rather than increasing returns.[10] To increase production, particularly to make new olive trees yield as old ones, takes a long time. This expansion would produce the opposite of increasing returns, that is, diminishing returns which cause the cost of production per unit to rise rather than fall. The result of the increased demand was consequently a sharp increase in the price of agricultural products. At the same time, nobility owning land were exempt from paying most taxes, so the tax burden fell increasingly on the artisans and manufacturers. Their competitiveness was, on the other hand, already being squeezed by the rapid rise of prices of agricultural goods in Spain. This undid the synergies and division of labour in Spanish cities, causing a de-industrialization from which Spain only finally recovered in the nineteenth century. Successful states protected manufacturing industry, unsuccessful Spain protected agriculture to the extent that it killed manufacturing.

Politically, the 'civil war' between modern urban and traditional rural activities had already been partly lost in Spain during and after the so-called Guerra de los Comuneros of 1520–21. This prototype of a modern European revolution had the long-term effect of seriously damaging Spanish manufacturing cities like Segovia. The strong political power of the sheep-owners' organization, La Mesta – to which the Spanish throne owed money – added to Spain's pro-raw material and anti-modernizing economic policies at the time. The Mesta in fact managed to wield its power in such a way that their sheep were even allowed to invade agricultural land, and some agricultural land in Spain was converted back to grazing. A comparison of Spain and England in the 1500s provides us with a useful and early example of the importance of where political power lies: in the hands of those who have a vested interest in producing raw materials (as in Spain) or with those who have vested interests in manufacturing (as in England). This is not to imply that those who have their vested interest in manufacturing are better or less greedy individuals than those whose vested interests lie in the production of raw materials. As always, capitalism must essentially be understood as a system of unintended consequences, and the unintended consequences of making profits from manufacturing are different from those found in nations where everybody makes their profits from raw materials. Once these mechanisms are understood it is possible – as it was for Henry VII – to produce the desired effects through wise economic policies. Such policies are now outlawed by the Washington Consensus.

Just as Venice and Holland were regarded as examples to be copied, in the sixteenth century Spain gradually came to be seen as an example of the type of economic policy and economic effects a nation should avoid at all costs. It became clear that the riches from the colonies had in fact impoverished rather than enriched Spain's own capacity to produce goods and services. In contrast to England – which ever since Henry VII came to power in 1485 had actively protected and encouraged her industry – Spain protected her agricultural production, like oil and wine, against foreign competition. By the end of the sixteenth century, Spain, who had had a considerable industrial production, was severely de-industrialized.

It was clear to the observers at the time that the enormous wealth, all the gold and silver flowing into Spain, just flowed out again and ended up in a couple of places – Venice and Holland. Like a slow-moving tsunami, it is possible to study the giant wave of inflation that spread through Europe with its epicentre in southern Spain. But why did this flow of gold and silver finally end up in very limited geographical areas? What distinguished Venice and Holland, where so much of the flow of Spanish gold and silver came to a halt, from the rest of Europe? The answer was that they had extensive and diversified industry, and at the same time hardly any agriculture. The realization spread through Europe that the real gold mines of the world were not the physical gold mines, but *manufacturing industry*. We find the following observation in Giovanni Botero's work on what causes the wealth of cities: 'Such is the power of industry that no mine of silver or gold in New Spain or Peru can compare with it, and the duties from the merchandise of Milan are worth more to the Catholic King than the mines of Potosi and Jalisco.[11] Italy is a country in which ... there is no important gold or silver mine, and so is France: yet both countries are rich in money and treasure thanks to industry.'[12]

In various forms, the statement that manufacturing was the *real* gold mine is found all over Europe from the late 1500s through the 1700s. After Botero we find this expressed by Tommaso Campanella (1602) and Antonio Genovesi (in the 1750s) in Italy, by Geronimo de Uztáriz in Spain (1724/1751) and by Anders Berch (1747), the first economics professor outside Germany, in Sweden: 'The real gold mines are the manufacturing industries'.[13]

In pre-Smithian economics the establishment of manufacturing came to be seen as part of a wider mission of civilizing society. Capitalism was advanced as an argument for repressing and harnessing the passions of humankind, for channelling the energies of human beings into something creative.[14] Italian economist Ferdinando Galiani (1728–87) stated that 'from manufacturing you may expect the two greatest ills of humanity, superstition and slavery, to be healed'.[15] This became the principle on which European economic policy was founded, and which industrialized European nations one by one over a long period. Building 'civilization', building a manufacturing sector, and later building democracy, were seen as inseparable parts of the same process. This conventional wisdom was also quoted by French statesman and political writer Alexis de Tocqueville (1805–59) in 1855: 'I do not know if one can cite a single manufacturing and commercial nation from the Tyrians to the Florentines and the English, that has not also been free. Therefore a close tie and a necessary relation exists between those two things: freedom and industry.'[16]

Around 1550, many Spanish economists began to realize what was happening in their country, and produced both good analysis and sound advice. As American historian Earl Hamilton, an expert on Spanish economy and economics of this period, points out: 'History records few instances of either such able diagnosis of fatal social ills by any group of moral philosophers or of such utter disregard by statesmen of sound advice.'[17] In 1558, Spain's Minister of Finance, Luis Ortiz, describes the situation in a memorandum to King Philip II:

> From the raw materials from Spain and the West Indies – particularly silk, iron and cochinilla (a red dye) – which cost them only 1 florin, the foreigners produce finished goods which they sell back to Spain for between 10 and 100 florins. Spain is in this way subject to greater humiliations from the rest of Europe than those they themselves impose on the Indians. In exchange for gold and silver the Spaniards offer trinkets of greater or lesser value; but by buying back their own raw materials at an exorbitant price, the Spaniards are made the laughing stock of all Europe.[18]

The fundamental idea here – that a finished product might cost from ten to a hundred times the price of the raw material needed for the product – would recur for centuries in European literature on economic policy. Between raw materials and the finished product lies a multiplier: an industrial process demanding and creating knowledge, mechanization, technology, division of labour, increasing returns and – above all – employment for the masses of underemployed and unemployed that always characterizes poor countries. Today, the economic models of the World Bank assume full employment in developing countries, even though in some places no more than 20–30 per cent of the workforce has what we would call a 'job'. Those who were involved in economic policy in earlier times recognized the extent of the unemployment, the underemployment and the vagrancy, and understood that the labour involved in transforming raw materials into finished products in and of itself would increase the wealth of cities and of nations. The main point, however, was that the economic activities coming into existence when the raw materials were refined into finished products followed different economic laws than did raw material production. The 'manufacturing multiplier' was the key both to progress and political freedom.

From the end of the fifteenth century until after the Second World War the main theme in economic policy – if not in economic theory – was therefore what we can call 'the cult of manufacturing industry'. This involved talking about 'planting' industry in the same way one would 'plant' useful species from foreign lands. Two different institutions serving similar purposes were both established in the late 1400s: the protection of new knowledge through *patents* and the transfer of the same knowledge into new geographical areas through *tariff protection*. Both were based on the very same type of economic understanding: the creation and geographic spread of new knowledge through the instigation of imperfect competition. An indispensable part of this process of development were the institutions that 'got the prices wrong' compared to what the market would have done if left alone: the patents that created a temporary monopoly for new inventions and the tariffs that distorted the prices for manufactured goods and enabled new technologies and new industries to be established away from the place they were first invented.

These inventions and innovations were created in a way that markets, left to themselves, would never be able to reproduce. Today's economic policy and the Washington institutions vigorously defend only one of these institutions – the patents that create ever-increasing income flows to very few and very rich countries – while the very same Washington institutions vehemently prohibit the tools that allow the geographical spread of imperfect competition in the form of new industries to other countries. Protecting imperfect competition in the rich countries is accepted, but not in the poor. This is what I have referred to as the 'assumption-juggling' of economic theory: other theories are used at home than those that are allowed in the Third World, following the old colonial pattern. The economic power game always results in the same Golden Rule principle: the one who has the gold makes the rules.

In the early 1700s a rule of thumb developed for economic policy in bilateral trade, a rule that rapidly spread throughout Europe. When a country exported raw materials and imported industrial goods, this was considered *bad trade*. When the same country imported raw materials and exported industrial goods, this was considered *good trade*.[19] It is particularly interesting to observe that when a country exported industrial goods in exchange for other industrial goods, this was considered good trade for both parties. To use a term once employed by UNCTAD: *symmetrical trade* is good for all parties, *asymmetrical trade* does not benefit the poor countries.

This was why the most eager advocates of industrialization – for tariff protection – like Friedrich List, were also the most eager advocates of free trade and globalization after all countries had industrialized. As early as the 1840s Friedrich List had a recipe for 'good globalization':[20] if free trade developed after all countries of the world had industrialized, free trade would be the best for everyone. The only thing we disagree about is the timing for adopting free trade, and the geographical and structural sequence in which the development towards free trade takes place.

As late as during the reconstruction of Europe after the Second World War, we find that this type of economic understanding was still present. After the war, US industry was vastly superior to the industry of Europe. Yet nobody suggested that Europe should follow its own comparative advantage in agriculture – on the contrary, everything was done to re-industrialize Europe through the Marshall Plan. This was essentially a plan to re-industrialize Europe using the traditional policy toolbox, including heavy protection of manufacturing industries. One difference from previous centuries was that in post-Second World War Europe farming also had to be protected. It is, however, of crucial importance to understand that twentieth-century protection of agriculture was for entirely different reasons from the protection of manufacturing. Developing a manufacturing base was aggressive protection aimed towards industrialization and higher real wages, whereas the protection of agriculture was defensive protectionism aimed at preventing the income of the agricultural sector from falling too far behind, as successful aggressive protectionism forced up the wages in the non-agricultural sectors of the economy. In other words, protecting manufacturing industry that allows the creation of new jobs and makes national wages rise is based on a very different logic from the protection of employment in agriculture from its competitors in poorer countries. The first type of protectionism is to increase the wage level in the whole country by means of the synergies that are created, the second type helps farmers and the regions where farming dominates. The need for these two different kinds of protectionism will only be fully understood when the qualitative differences between manufacturing and agriculture are explained in the next chapter.

Germany follows in England's footsteps (1648)

France and other countries were soon imitating the English strategies that had been so successful under the Tudors. These strategies became nation-building projects at a time when the small city-states had irretrievably lost their power to nations that had managed to consolidate and enlarge 'the common weal' to larger geographical areas with larger markets. In France, the famous statesman Jean Baptiste Colbert (1619–83) developed the industry and the infrastructure which united the country. The goal was to unite the country with 'perfect competition' inside and protect its increasing returns and labour intensive industries from foreign competition. Throughout the eighteenth century, in Europe, Colbert was generally referred to as 'the great Colbert'.

Now we shall take a closer look at Europe's 'delayed nation', Germany. Veit Ludwig von Seckendorff (1626–92) was the founder of German economics. His times were characterized by war and misery. The Thirty Years War (1618–48) had wiped out as much as 70 per cent of the civilian population in some parts of Germany. The war had started as an internal religious war, but gradually involved many of the great powers of Europe at the time, including Spain, France, Denmark and Sweden. The war had no winners, but it became clear to many Germans that the real loser was civilization itself. When Seckendorff was sixteen, his father – a German serving in the Swedish army – was beheaded as a presumed spy in a North German town. When Seckendorff died at the age of sixty-six, the army of Louis XIV of France had just laid waste the German state of the Rhineland-Palatinate. In the meantime Germany had had a war with the Turks, who besieged and almost managed to conquer Vienna, and two more wars with France. This had led to Strasbourg, where Seckendorff had studied, being lost to France. The Peace of Westphalia (1648) – at the end of the Thirty Years War – left a Germany fragmented into more than 300 small states. I mention this because in my view Germany's way out of this war-torn barbarism also contains important lessons for today's failed and failing states. Germany's way out was based on a *production strategy*, a building up of trade and industry consciously diversified from agriculture and raw material production. The key to success was to emulate the economic structure of a country where peace and prosperity reigned – and the example to follow was the Dutch one.[21]

With help from his father's colleagues Seckendorff found employment with another ex-officer of the Swedish army, Duke Ernest of Saxe-Gotha, called Ernest the Pious. Among other duties, Seckendorff's responsibility was the enormous library that Duke Ernest had acquired, originally from the spoils of war.[22] This library can still be visited in the impressive castle and administrative building established by Duke Ernest in Gotha. Thus the young Seckendorff had access to all the most important writings in economics and political science of his times, and one of his tasks was to present summaries of many of them to his Duke. In 1656, at thirty years old, Seckendorff published his most important work, *Der Teutsche Fürstenstaat* (The German principality), whose thesis was based around two old traditions: a detailed description of a country, its history, people, administration, institutions and resources that had been customary ever since thirteenth-century Italy, and secondly the old German *Fürstenspiegel* (literally the 'king's mirror') textbooks or 'owner's manuals' for kings and princes on how to rule their countries. Seckendorff's book remained in print for the next ninety-eight years – a very long life for a textbook.

Some years later Seckendorff travelled to the Dutch Republic with Duke Ernest. As was the case with so many other observers of the time, the affluence, peace, freedom and tolerance he experienced in Holland made a deep and lasting impression on Seckendorff. When he returned home, he felt the need to elaborate on his advice for German princes with a supplement, *Additiones*, which was published in 1664, and subsequently always printed with the main book. In this supplement we get Seckendorff's most important economic insights. His experiences in Holland confirmed the theory he had formulated in the Gotha library, about the importance of cities and industry in the creation of wealth. The works of Italian economist Giovanni Botero, whose most famous work, *On the Greatness of Cities*, was originally published in 1588, are today found in the Gotha library in thirty different editions all published before 1655. We can assume that most of them were already there in Seckendorff's time.

Seckendorff understood the importance of having many different trades and crafts represented in the cities, and that craftsmen move from the countryside to the cities, where they can earn more. At the same time he is modern in his worry over the lack of competition among the craftsmen. Duke Ernest invested in infrastructure, and a relatively unsuccessful attempt was made to make the rivers of the principality as navigable as Dutch canals. The policies of Seckendorff enabled people to move more freely, by removing duties and taxes, and in them we find the beginnings of a welfare state, with the state taking on responsibility for helping the old and the sick.

What did Seckendorff and other economists of the time see in the Netherlands that made such a deep impression? We know quite a lot about industry and trade in the Dutch city of Delft at the time Seckendorff visited the country, and without knowing whether he ever visited Delft, we can use this city as an example. German economist Werner Sombart's theories about war[23] and luxury[24] can in

Delft be seen represented by the Navy and by the art of painting as strong incentives in the development of capitalism. But with its microscope-makers-turned-scientists the city also confirmed the Norwegian-American economist Thorstein Veblen's view that idle curiosity – also independent of profit motives – is another strong moving force of capitalism. Delft in the seventeenth century exemplified how maritime warfare, art as a luxury product, and scientific curiosity can create innovations and affluence in the same, very widely diversified clusters of production. The importance of diversity per se – another factor lost in today's standard economics – is stressed by virtually all foreign observers of the Netherlands at the time. Centrally in the Delft cluster we find the manufacturers of glass lenses – magnifying lenses – that were used for quality control in the textile industry.

By the fifteenth century Flemish and Dutch painters were pioneers in the use of oil-based paint on canvas, where Italian painters painted al fresco with water-based paint on freshly plastered walls. The Dutch painters obtained their linseed oil and their linen and hemp canvas from the Navy and merchant marine, where these materials were used in the treatment of wood and in the production of sails. In the 1600s Delft took over from Florence as Europe's foremost manufacturer of glass for scientific uses. As mentioned, handheld lenses were used in the textile industry, but the lens manufacturers also found other fields of use. The Navy needed binoculars and telescopes, and some of the glass lens manufacturers started producing microscopes. Sometimes these microscope producers themselves became scientists, describing the new world revealed by the microscopes. Delft's great microscope manufacturer and scientist, Antoni van Leeuwenhoek (1632–1723), created a synergy between textile industry, microscope production and natural science, focused around the glass lenses. To register his findings, he employed artists as illustrators. The painter Jan Vermeer (1632–75), who lived right around the corner from van Leeuwenhoek, started using a sort of primitive camera with glass lenses, a camera obscura, in his painting. A recent movie about Vermeer shows this.[25] The links between art and science are strengthened when Vermeer, before his death, named van Leeuwenhoek as executor of his will.

Another result of the Navy's operations was the need for maps. These maps have a conspicuous place in many of Vermeer's paintings; indeed, one of his biographers comments on his 'map mania'. In Italy, maps had generally been produced as woodcuts. Now the Dutch started producing copperplate engravings. Copper and brass were materials used both to produce the Navy binoculars and the scientific microscopes, thus creating one more link between science, art and naval warfare. Another Dutchman, also born in 1632, who also started his career as a glass lens producer was Baruch Spinoza, the philosopher. Figure 5 illustrates the 'national innovation system' that people could observe when visiting Holland in the period immediately following the Thirty Years War. Knowledge developed in one sector would 'jump' to apparently unconnected sectors, proving the point that new knowledge is created by linking previously unconnected facts or events. Diversity per se came to be understood as a key ingredient in economic growth, and this diversity was not to be found in agricultural communities where people tended to produce the same things.[26] This has been recognized as one of the problems of areas producing raw materials: they have little to trade between them.

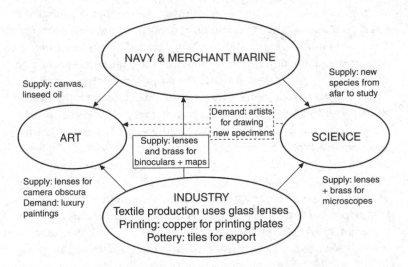

Figure 5   Delft, Holland, 1650s: an innovation system based on diversity

The Netherlands at this time was a laboratory where it was possible to observe the mechanics of economic development. To the contemporary observers it seemed clear that innovations and affluence were the results of the many windows of opportunities for invention outside agriculture, the falling unit costs of production and the increasing returns found in urban city activities, the extent of division of labour and the many different professions creating affluence as a product of synergies. Based on observation of the same phenomena in Venice, Serra describes these three principles clearly in his work of 1613, adding that 'one factor gives strength to the other'; in other words he describes a self-catalysing system of economic growth. Serra also includes a chapter on the kind of economic policy a state needs to create wealth based on this type of system. It is as if these theorists said: if you wish to estimate the wealth of a city, count the number of professions found within its walls. The larger the number of professions, the wealthier the city. The diversity of economic activities was a goal in itself that made it possible for new knowledge to 'jump' from one sector to the other as we have observed in Figure 5. These theoretical developments continued the tradition of Brunetto Latini's thirteenth-century *ben commune*, or common weal.

The goal for economic policy thus became the emulation of the economic structure found in Venice and in Holland, the bringing together of as many diverse professions as possible, all subject to increasing returns and technological change. Copying the economic policies of Venice and the Dutch Republic was never an issue. Economists at the time understood that their economic structures had come into being as a result of a strategic geographic position for maritime purposes, and the scarcity of arable land. In other words, the development strategy of Europe became one of benchmarking and emulation. Appendix V sets out the nine-point strategy of another German economist of the same century as Seckendorff, Philipp Wilhelm von Hörnigk (1638–1712), the principles that had to be followed by the laggard German-speaking states in order to emulate the economic structures of rich European countries. It is worth noticing that this strategy was directed primarily at Austria and first published in 1684, only one year after the last siege of

Vienna by the Turks. Hörnigk's book went through sixteen editions and remained in print for more than a hundred years. The edition published on the hundredth anniversary of the book, in 1784, reiterated its importance in creating the economic success of Austria. Typically, this is not a book mentioned in standard histories of economic thought.

Very early on we find the observation that a proximity to cities also improves agricultural practices. According to Botero: 'The Dutch sheep produce three or four lambs at a time, and the cows often two calves; the cows produce so much milk that one who has not seen it would not believe it.'[27] However, the key importance of the synergies between cities and countryside – the argument that only farmers sharing a labour market with a manufacturing city could ever achieve wealth – only rose to real prominence during the Enlightenment.

Josiah Child (1630–99), a governor of the British East India Company, encapsulates the attitude to worlds emulating economic policy by arguing, 'If we intend to have the Trade of the World, we must imitate the Dutch, who make the worst as well as the best of all manufactures, that we may be in a capacity of serving all Markets, and all Humours'. Similarly, Child opens his 1668 book, *Brief Observations Concerning Trade and Interest of Money*, with a comment on 'the prodigious increase of the Netherlanders' which is 'the envy of the present and may be the wonder of all future generations'. 'And yet,' he adds, 'the means whereby they have thus advanced themselves, are sufficiently obvious, and in a great measure imitable by most other nations ..., which I shall endeavour to demonstrate in the following discourse'. What was obvious to Josiah Child, however, has been lost to standard textbook economics.

The Germans were also aware that, at least in the short term, they could not emulate the more democratic political system of the Netherlands or Venice. There was a clear connection between the economic structure of a state and its political structure.[29] In the short term Germany had to live with the rulers it had. The way to develop the country was to convince the rulers to change their economic policy, which in turn – in the long term – would change the form of government in a more democratic direction. The despotism of the rulers was to develop into what Wilhelm Roscher later called an enlightened despotism (1868) and philosophers and economists, from around 1648, slowly worked to change the perception of the rulers as to what constituted a successful kingdom.

Seckendorff was an early proponent of this school of economists and political writers who were to dominate Europe in the next century, writers who convinced the kings and rulers that their right to rule a country also entailed a duty to develop the state. These were the first developmental states, predecessors of Korea and Taiwan in the late twentieth century. The enlightened ruler – the 'philosopher-king' in Christian Wolff's terms – was in charge of this 'developmental dictatorship', and the role of the economists following Seckendorff was to advise, assist, guide, correct, flatter and cajole the rulers into doing their jobs properly. Many economists also acted as one-man research councils and entrepreneurs of last resort for the kings, activities that frequently got them into financial trouble. The logic that emerged was 'the better the ruler, the wealthier the people'. Instead of judging his success by his own wealth, the ruler's success was to be based on the wealth and happiness of his people.

The first professor of economics in the world was Simon Peter Gasser, who received his chair of 'Economics, Policy and Cameral Sciences' at the University of Halle, Germany, in 1727. Almost one hundred years would pass before England got her first professorship in economics (Adam Smith was a professor of moral philosophy). The first economics textbook written by the world's first professor of economics, *Introduction to the Economic, Political and Cameral Sciences*, starts out with a poem written by Seckendorff, which describes the old ideals of a king to be an able hunter, horseman and fencer, and then goes on to describe the modern king whose success is measured by the welfare and justice found in his realm.[30]

Ireland learning from the past

In July 1980 Wilhelm Roscher's 'enlightened despotism' came to my mind. After finishing my Ph.D. I had landed my first job in an American consulting firm, Telesis. At the start of my first assignment I found myself, in the company of Telesis's managing director, in Irish Prime Minister Charles Haughey's office. Just the three of us. The assignment was to evaluate Irish industrial policy after the Second World War and to make recommendations for the future, and we were to report directly to the Prime Minister's office.

Haughey, who was an accountant by profession, had made the following statement to the Irish nation on 9 January of the same year:

> I wish to talk to you this evening about the state of the nation's affairs and the picture I have to paint is not, unfortunately, a very cheerful one. The figures which are just now becoming available to us show one thing very clearly. As a community we are living way beyond our means ... we have been living at a rate which is simply not justifiable by the amount of goods and services we are producing. To make up the difference we have been borrowing enormous amounts of money, borrowing at a rate which just cannot continue. A few simple figures will make this very clear ... we will just have to reorganize government spending so that we can only undertake those things we can afford.

Ireland had joined the European Community in 1973, and massive EC funds had floated into its agricultural sector. However, this had created over-capacity and highly indebted farmers in a very difficult market. My recollection of the meeting is that Haughey had a vision: 'Out there is a new technology coming, and I want you to help Ireland be number one in that technology'. Haughey was referring to information technology and his vision was one of emulating the rich countries, of catching up with them and forging ahead with the new technology. I was the only economist on the team in Ireland, and our advice was later made along the lines of business analysis.[31]

Today, Haughey is credited with the extremely successful transformation of the Irish economy from the 1980s onwards, based on an early move into information technology. After a while real wages in Ireland surpassed the real wages in England, the old colonial master. With his vision and leadership, Haughey had played the same role as the enlightened despots of eighteenth-century Europe.

Much of the year following my initial meeting with Haughey was spent in Dublin. From my Irish colleagues and from Trinity College Library I learned of Ireland's industrial past. In the late 1600s, Ireland – a British colony – was about to take the lead in the most important industry of the time, the production of woollen cloth. A flow of skilled Catholic immigrants from the Continent had contributed to this development. English producers of woollen cloth – who in their turn were fighting a winning battle with the wool industry of Florence – could not afford to lose her competitive edge to the Irish. They successfully petitioned the English king to prohibit all exports of woollen cloth from Ireland from 1699.

This was before Ricardo's trade theory, so everyone knew that killing the manufacturing sector and forcing the Irish to send their raw wool to England was tantamount to reducing the country to poverty. Such practices were normally defended by reference to the fact that all European powers did the same to their colonies. We have already referred to the English economist John Cary who discussed the wisdom of 'free trade and the death penalty for the export of raw materials'. The same John Cary was engaged in stopping the Irish export of woollen products. His argument was based on the economic metaphor in use at the time, that of the human body. Cary argued that England was the head of the body of the Commonwealth, while Ireland was a peripheral limb. When conflicts arose within the body of the common weal, the interests of the head had to prevail. This of course caused bitter resentment in Ireland, where the Dean of Trinity College, John Hely-Hutchinson (1724–94), wrote a book on how the commercial restraints of Ireland from 1699 had reduced her to poverty (*The Commercial Restraints of Ireland Considered in a Series of Letters to a Noble Lord*). The book, published anonymously, was condemned to be burned by the common hangman for its seditious doctrines. It was the last book in England to suffer this fate.

In nineteenth-century America, Irish immigrant workers were keenly supporting the 'American System of Manufactures', the protective system that allowed the country to industrialize. They remembered that Ireland had had her industry stolen from her, and did not want their new country to be subject to the same treatment by England (who vehemently protested against American industrialization for more than a hundred years). The situation was a bit like prohibiting Silicon Valley from exporting electronics during the 1990s. In 1699 Ireland had been prevented from emulating; in 1980 the country had its revenge when it embarked on a strategy to conquer what would become the dominating world technology for future decades – information technology. This would produce a productivity explosion that was to catapult national wage levels above that of the former colonial power. Maybe I am attributing too much importance to this, but there is almost an epic quality in the contrast between colonial Ireland in 1699 being prohibited from using the most important technology of that time – for the production of woollen cloth – for export, and its vindictive success 300 years later in the technology of our own time – information technology.

4

Globalization:
the Arguments in Favour are also
the Arguments Against

It is known that primitive nations do not improve their customs and habits, later to find useful industries, but the other way around.

> Johann Jacob Meyen, German economist, 1769

The bourgeoisie, by the rapid improvement of all instruments of production, by the immensely facilitated means of communication, draws all, even the most barbarian, nations into civilization.

> Karl Marx and Friedrich Engels,
> *The Communist Manifesto*, 1848

Globalization – as it is interpreted by the Washington institutions, the World Bank and the IMF – is in practice a very rapid economic integration of rich and poor countries both as regards trade and investments. There are many arguments for such free trade and integration; some of them are cultural, such as the observation that free trade creates contacts and understanding among different nations and cultures, but most of them are of an economic nature. If increased economic integration is done in the right way and at the right pace, it has the potential to make everyone – rich and poor countries alike – economically and socially better off. The problem lies in the timing.

The best arguments both for and against globalization are to be found in the sphere of production. One important argument is that the production of goods and services often takes place under considerable *increasing returns to scale* (*economies of scale*): the bigger the market and the more units produced, the cheaper it is to produce the goods and services we consume. There is enormous potential here for increasing the welfare of all. To build a plant that produces a life-saving medicine costs hundreds of millions of dollars. The larger the volume of sales over which this fixed cost can be distributed, the less expensive it becomes to treat each patient with the drug.

Another powerful reason for free trade is *technological change and innovation,* a product of the continuous development of new knowledge. In a larger market the costs of innovation and technical change may be distributed among a greater number of consumers, and the innovations and improvements will potentially reach each individual world citizen more quickly and cheaply. More innovations are possible in bigger markets. Had Thomas Edison and Bill Gates only operated in a small market – say Iceland, with less than 300,000 inhabitants – this book would probably have been produced with light from a kerosene lamp and with a much simpler writing technology.

A third argument is *synergies and cluster effects.* Not only does knowledge-creation thrive better where more companies – both complementary and competing – work together in networks; as we saw in the case of the Netherlands, important synergies also exist between firms and activities in the most diverse fields. Historically the most important synergy effect has been the one between manufacturing and agriculture. In a global economy each country will be able to develop its own specific clusters (other terms are 'development blocks' and 'growth poles'), where companies with complementary skills may thrive and grow in ways they could not manage alone. Also here, the larger markets created through economic integration will enable a larger division of labour, more specialization and increased knowledge.

All these arguments carry with them potentially great gains for every one of us, both in our roles as producers and as consumers. Creating opportunities for increased wages and new and/or cheaper goods and services, this set of three factors is responsible for the spectacular wealth of some countries.

These same factors – scale, technical change and synergies – work together, reinforcing each other in mutual interdependence. Although they are different theoretical phenomena, increasing returns to scale and technological progress are often very difficult to separate in practice.[1] It is impossible to recreate the technology used in today's car production in the small-scale car production of a hundred years ago. The enormous productivity increase Henry Ford achieved in car production was totally dependent on the huge volume of vehicles built. Ford understood that in order to make money he had to produce so many cars that normal people – like his own workers – could afford to buy them. He solved this in a simple way. One day in January 1914 he doubled the wages of his factory workers to $5 a day. This not only provided him with workers with purchasing power; given the monotonous nature of the assembly line work, it also established a more stable workforce. The key point here, however, is that the barriers to entry created by the combination of technical change (innovation) and economies of scale (increasing returns) made possible a huge jump in nominal wages in this particular industry, while, at the same time, the price of cars continued to fall.

Very often technological change requires increasing returns created by standardization – from that of the weights and measures of medieval city-states to that of railway gauges and technical standards for mobile telephones today. Such standardization is also a condition for network effects that create a type of increasing returns (the larger the number of users, the larger the potential benefits for the individual user). Using the telephone as an example of a network, a single owner of a phone connection will have no use for this invention until there is at least one other subscriber to talk to.

The usefulness of the network increases with its size. Economies of scale (including economies of scope and network effects) all depend on synergies created in such systems of networks. Universities are also an important part of such innovatory systems. The learning processes found at the point at which innovation, increasing returns, and synergy/cluster effects intersect and work together form the very essence of the economic development that has created wealth and welfare in large parts of the world. Today this idea is expressed in the notion of a triple helix, found in the nexus between industry, government and the university sector.

From a historical standpoint, these three factors have long been at work, and their importance has also long been recognized. The history of humankind is marked by increasing productivity, and increasing standards of living have required ever-increasing markets. We can identify the idea of systemic increasing returns in the works of the philosopher Xenophon, living around 400 BC. In 1613, Italian economist Antonio Serra, whom we have previously mentioned, grouped together increasing returns, synergies and enlightened government policy as the characteristics distinguishing the few rich city-states of Europe from the surrounding poverty. This type of theory – where the choice of economic activity determined wealth – dominated economic policy for a very long time. The choice of profession would determine the wealth of a society in much the same way that it would determine the wealth of an individual.

Towards the end of the nineteenth century, American and German economists described the history of humankind as a process that also involved a development towards ever larger economic units. This was the geographical corollary of the stage theories discussed earlier. A short version of the story goes like this: In the beginning human beings lived in family-like *clans*, organized around reciprocal work rather than markets. Income distribution took place largely as it does in the refrigerator of a normal nuclear family today, according to need. When someone married and a new house was needed, the whole group worked for free. Next time it was perhaps your own turn to need these services, and the others would turn up for work. For a group of people spending their whole lives together, such reciprocity enabled a satisfactory income distribution without markets. In this setting, market trans-actions would seem as alien as the idea of a mother selling her milk to her own baby would today.

Long-distance trade and larger villages slowly created the emer-gence of the *city-state* and qualitative changes in human society. Longer distances, increasing professional specializations (division of labour) and greater geographical mobility all led to a gradual breakdown of the old systems of reciprocity: markets appeared, first probably as sites of gift exchange between tribes, then as mech-anisms of barter with established ratios of value ('a sheep for a sack of potatoes'), then as a monetarized economy. Economic anthropol-ogists emphasize that trade first appeared between clans and tribes, not between individuals. As already noted, in thirteenth-century Europe it was clear that the wealth of the cities as opposed to the poverty of the countryside was the result of synergies. 'The common weal' – *il ben commune* – was responsible for the wealth.

The next step was the emergence of the *nation-state*. The builders of the nation-state sought to extend the same synergies that were found in the cities to a larger geographical area. Infrastructure – massive resources for roads, canals, ports and later railways and telephone lines – were key investments in the project of nation-building. The joint economic and political project that built the nation-states was called *mercantilism*.[2]

As nation-states developed, the most successful city-states – like Venice and the Dutch cities – were apparently left behind in decline and growing poverty, both relatively and absolutely. Economists at the time clearly saw how political units which did not follow in the race towards larger internal markets would inevitably be left behind economically. Much later – about a hundred years ago – it was already clear to economists who looked at the historical re-lationship between technology and geography that the next techno-economic stage would be the global economy. As in previous transitions, they noted, the financial sector would be the first to operate in the larger geographical unit.

If this is the essence of the history of humankind as it relates to geography and technology, if there are so many economic mech-anisms that will enable greater welfare in larger geographical units, if there even seems to be an iron law of increasing size of human societies that points to its inevitability, how can anyone in their right mind be against increased free trade and globalization?

A key point here is that the champions of globalization do not base their arguments on the type of reasoning above. Their analysis and their recommendations are based on static theoretical arguments which are totally devoid of any historical analysis, where technological change, increasing returns, and synergies are all absent. Their analysis is based on Ricardo's trade theory (see Appendix I), which recommends that a nation should specialize where it is most effective compared to other nations, and shows that this type of specialization leads to a gain in total welfare. Adam Smith constructed the first step that made Ricardo's trade theory possible, by reducing all human economic activity – be it production or trade – into labour hours devoid of any qualitative aspects. Ricardo's theory builds on this barter-based view of society – of Smith's metaphor of bartering dogs exchanging labour hours – that we have already discussed. The key economic factors discussed above are endogenous, they are not part of the mainstream trade theory which is the basis of our present world economic order, the ideas on which the IMF and the World Bank base their theories. More sophisticated models exist, but they do not influence policy.

There is nothing in Ricardo's theoretical construct to distinguish a Stone Age labour hour from a Silicon Valley labour hour. Since full employment is also secured, international trade theory (as it is practised today) can proudly announce that free trade between a Silicon Valley and a newly discovered Neolithic tribe in the Amazon will produce the economic harmony of wage equalization (factor–price equalization). International trade is extremely important for wealth creation, but not for the reason given by Ricardo. His static gains (see Appendix I) are completely dwarfed by the dynamic gains that are possible. However, international trade also makes possible important dynamic losses of wealth. In wealthy developed countries Ricardo is simply right for the wrong reason. In poor countries, where the factors for creating wealth are absent, Ricardo is wrong in a way which keeps them poor.

It should be noted that today's capitalist society – that essentially sees economic growth as originating in adding capital to labour – employs a trade theory based on the labour theory of value that otherwise only survived in the communist ideology. Capitalist trade theory describes production that takes place in the absence of capital. We are therefore returning to the confusion created by the common origins of Cold War capitalism and communism in Ricardian economics, an issue discussed earlier. In total contradiction to how capitalist society explains growth, the trade theory with which capitalism controls the world has no role for capital. This is an example of the assumption-juggling towards ends that ultimately become political which is a core feature of mainstream economics. Simply assuming that different economic activities can at any time profitably absorb very different amounts of capital is sufficient to invalidate and demolish the whole structure on which the world economy rests. This highlights the crucial importance of what Nobel Laureate James Buchanan refers to as the 'equality assumption' in economics.[3] This is the most important, although probably least discussed, assumption in the profession. If economic activities are all qualitatively different, standard textbook economics collapses. In standard theory, 'perfect information' and 'perfect competition' solve this problem by instantly and at no cost converting Stone Age society to Silicon Valley society. But, to quote Richard Nelson, the much respected evolutionary economist, 'that ain't the way it works'.

If we include increasing returns, effects of technology and learning and synergy effects, we can develop much stronger arguments in favour of globalization, but also strong arguments against it as it now affects the poor periphery. The factors we have analysed here allow for a theory of economic development, but also an explanation as to why this economic growth is so unevenly distributed among nations. The zealots of globalization use arguments that are static and largely divorced from the dynamics of how economic growth actually takes place. By bringing in new and dynamic factors, we have the building blocks for a theory in which globalization – if it is implemented in the wrong sequence – will lead to a situation where some countries specialize in being rich, while other countries specialize in staying poor.

Increasing returns and their absence

Not all products and services are produced under increasing returns as production expands. The first copy of a Microsoft product may cost $100 million to produce, copies number two to 200 million – if distributed electronically – may cost only a few cents or less to produce and distribute. High fixed costs create important economies of scale or increasing returns. This, in turn, creates very high barriers to entry for competitors, and leads to an oligopolistic market structure far removed from the standard assumptions of economic theory. Companies with such cost structures are very difficult to compete against.

A person making a living as a house painter faces a very different reality. Once he has learned his profession, he will not be able to paint house number two any faster than he painted house number one. His fixed costs – a ladder and brushes – will not add up to much. His low fixed costs make him an easy target for competition. The house painter will face competition from cheap labour, sometimes illegal. This is a problem Microsoft and Bill Gates do not have to face. Independently of technology, increasing returns on the one hand and the lack of increasing returns on the other are an important reason why no house painter can approach the income level of Bill Gates.

Countries specializing in supplying raw materials to the rest of the world will sooner or later reach the point where diminishing returns set in. The law of diminishing returns essentially says that when one factor of production has been produced by nature – as in farming, fisheries or mining – at a certain point adding more capital and/or more labour will yield a smaller return for every unit of capital or labour added. Diminishing returns fall into two categories: *extensive* (when production is extended into inferior resource bases) and *intensive* (when more labour is added to the same plot of land or other fixed resource). In both cases productivity will diminish rather than increase as the country increases its production. Natural resources are available in differing qualities: fertile and less fertile land, good or bad climates, rich or poor pastures, mines with high or low grades of ore, rich or less rich fisheries. To the extent that these factors are known, a nation will use the best land, the best pastures and the richest mines first. As production increases with international specialization, poorer and poorer land and mines will be brought into production. Natural resources are also potentially non-renewable: mines can be emptied, fish population may be exterminated and pastures ruined by overgrazing.

In the absence of alternative employment outside the sector depending on natural resources, a population will be forced to live solely on their natural resources. At some point it will require more work to produce the same output and this will create a downward pressure on the national wage level. Let us assume that one country, say Norway, was the country best suited in the world for producing carrots. After the best agricultural land had been converted to carrot production, the country would have to utilize increasingly marginal land in order to grow carrots. Every additional ton of carrots would be increasingly expensive to produce, but the world market price for carrots would not compensate for this. The more this country specialized in the world economy, the poorer it would grow. For resource-rich Australia, this was the key argument which prompted the country to set up an industrial sector, even if this sector would be less efficient than those of the leading industrial nations, the United Kingdom and the United States. The existence of a manufacturing sector establishes a national wage level which prevents countries from moving too far into diminishing returns, over-producing themselves into poverty and/or emptying the fish from the ocean and the mines of ore. The environmental problems resulting from letting poor countries specialize in diminishing returns activities are discussed in my article, 'Diminishing Returns and Economic Sustainability: The Dilemma of Resource-based Economies under a Free Trade Regime'.

A nation specializing in supplying raw materials within the international division of labour will – in the absence of an alternative labour market – experience the opposite effect of what Microsoft experiences: the more production is increased, the higher the production costs of each new unit of production. In this respect the house painter's profession is relatively neutral, he works under constant returns to scale. The form and speed of globalization over the last twenty years have resulted in the de-industrialization of many countries, forcing them into a situation where diminishing returns is the key feature of their production.

Economists who assume a world where increasing returns is a key feature will reach opposite conclusions as regards population compared to economists who assume a world where diminishing returns is the key feature. Around 1750 virtually all economists saw growth as emanating from the increasing returns and synergies found in manufacturing. Therefore they all saw the need for a large population to boost the national markets. As we have seen, when Malthus and his friend Ricardo later reconstructed economics with diminishing returns as the core feature, their science deservedly received the nickname 'the dismal science'. In the recent past, when overpopulation was the favourite 'red herring' explaining poverty, the confusion around this issue produced conclusions which poor countries with some justification regarded as racist. This is because typically rich industrialized countries with a high population density – say Holland with 477 persons per square kilometre – will easily conclude that the poverty of, for example, Bolivia, is due to overpopulation, although Bolivia only has 7 persons per square kilometre. The connection between mode of production and population density is as frequently overlooked as that between mode of production and political structure. In both cases the failure to connect these sets of phenomena reinforces our ignorance of what causes poverty. This leads contemporary world society along a slippery slope of theoretical red herrings (see Chapter 6), and into a situation where the symptoms rather than the causes of poverty are addressed (see Chapter 7).

Recent particularly dramatic examples of diminishing returns in action are in Mongolia and Rwanda. In Mongolia virtually all industry disappeared after a free trade shock in the early 1990s. Under such asymmetric globalization – where some countries specialize in increasing returns activities and others in diminishing returns activities – the country specializing in diminishing returns activities will easily 'specialize' in being poor. Appendix III shows this development in a numerical example provided by Frank Graham, a former President of the American Economic Association.

Rich countries specialize in man-made comparative advantages, while poor countries specialize in nature-made comparative advantages. Comparative advantages in nature-made exports will sooner or later work their way into diminishing returns because Mother Nature provided one of the factors of production in different qualities, and the best quality will normally be used first.[4] Such poor countries generally lack any social policy or old age pension provision. Having many children is therefore a rational way of obtaining the only available form of insurance. However, the increasing population resulting from this soon meets the 'flexible wall' of increasing returns as in Mongolia and Rwanda. Global sustainable development therefore depends on poor countries creating employment outside the diminishing returns sector, outside the raw material-based sector where, in the absence of an increasing returns sector, the Malthusian vicious circles of poverty and rape of nature are raging.

Technological change and its absence

The windows of opportunity for innovation and technical change are, at any time, very unevenly distributed among economic activities. At one point there was little technological change in kerosene lamps and a lot of technical change in electric lights. As we shall see, it will always be possible for a nation to specialize in economic activities where all the capital in the world will not be able to create innovation and productivity growth. This mechanism also makes it possible for a nation to specialize in being poor.

An important element in the huge 'social problem' (as it was called) that dominated nineteenth-century European discourse was the existence of so-called home-workers (*Heimarbeiter*). They produced the articles that industry had not yet managed to mechanize, as part of a production process bereft of any increasing returns and any potential for innovation. These were homemade products distributed as industrial products. Today, the outsourcing of unmechanizable products from the United States to Mexico and other neighbouring countries recreates the conditions of the nineteenth-century home-workers of Europe. In Mexico this type of industry – the *maquila* industry near the American border – grows at the expense of traditional industry, but as the *maquila* pays lower wages than traditional industry, this development is bringing down average Mexican wages. A similar *maquila* effect is found in agriculture: the mechanizable production (harvesting wheat and maize) is taken over by the United States, while Mexico specializes in unmechanizable production (harvesting strawberries, citrus fruit, cucumbers and tomatoes), which reduces Mexico's opportunities for innovation, locking the country into technological dead-ends and/or activities that retain labour-intensive processes.

The world's most efficient producers of baseballs for America's national sport are found in Haiti, Honduras and Costa Rica. Baseballs are still hand-sewn as they were when they were invented. All the engineers and all the capital of the United States have not managed to mechanize baseball production. The wages of the world's most efficient baseball producers are miserable. In Haiti they are around 30 cents an hour, some reports say down to 14 cents per hour in the mid-1990s. Every baseball is stitched by hand with 108 stitches, and each worker is able to sew four baseballs per hour. This is done by hand but with the precision requirements of a machine-made product. The balls retail in the USA for about $15 each. Following the political problems in Haiti – where the attempt of President Jean-Bertiand Aristide to raise the minimum wage from 33 to 50 cents an hour was one of the reasons for his fall from power – much of the production was moved to Honduras and Costa Rica. Here the wage level is higher, in Costa Rica slightly more than $1 per hour.

Golf balls, on the other hand, are a high-tech product, and one of the important producers – alone representing 40 per cent of American production – is found in the old whaling town of New Bedford, Massachusetts. Research and development play important roles in production, and in spite of the high wages in the area, direct labour costs represent only 15 per cent of production costs. As in an oil refinery, direct labour costs are low and the fact that they have little impact on total production, coupled with the need for qualified labour, engineers and specialized suppliers, contributes to preventing golf ball production from moving to low-wage countries like Haiti. Production wages in the New Bedford area amount to between $14 and $16 per hour. The differing wage levels in these two industrial sectors – baseball and golf ball manufacture – are a direct result of uneven technological development. The poverty of Haiti and the wealth of the United States are, for both countries, simultaneously a cause of and a result of the choice of what to produce.

The institution we call 'the market' rewards the world's most efficient producer of golf balls with an income between 12 and 36 times – from $0.30–$1 versus $14–16 per hour – more than the world's most effective producer of baseballs. Differences in purchasing power will reduce this gap, but the difference in real wages is still immense. In addition, the poor baseball producers are plagued with occupational illnesses such as the carpal tunnel syndrome. In Costa Rica, where conditions are clearly better than in Haiti, one company doctor estimates that 90 per cent of the workers at the baseball factory suffer from some kind of occupational illnesses. I have an affinity for production plants, and have always wished to observe a baseball factory from the inside. Once when I was working with microfinance in San Pedro Sula, Honduras, the sister of our host managed a baseball factory and I was told I would be welcome to look around. However, at the last minute the visit was called off, apparently on instructions from the foreign owners.

Appendix VI shows the dynamics of how technological change provides widely unequal opportunities for increasing real wages, and points to the many factors that combine to produce this effect. It shows a classification system, a taxonomy, of the quality of economic activities in terms of their ability to produce high standards of living. New technology and innovations demand and create new knowledge, producing economic activities characterized by high levels of knowledge and high levels of income. These industries are dominated by Schumpeterian and dynamic imperfect competition, high barriers to entry, high risks and high rewards. This contrasts with the perfect competition or commodity competition under which markets for raw materials operate. As innovations, products and processes mature and age, products fall like natural gravity in the index shown in Appendix VI. It is possible to show the characteristics that make baseballs a low-quality activity in terms of its potential to produce wealth, and the characteristics that make golf ball production into a high-quality activity by the same criteria.

Once a considerable gap in real wages has been created, the world market will automatically assign economic activities that are technological dead-ends – and therefore only require unqualified labour, for example, to produce baseballs – to low wage countries. Even if there should at some point be a technological breakthrough in baseball production, this will not help the poor producers. The following example will show why. In the 1980s the following product information could be found on a typical pair of pyjamas sold in the United States: 'Fabric made in the US, cut and assembled in Guatemala'. Textile production is highly mechanized, so the fabric is produced in the USA. At the time, the cutting of fabric was done mechanically, but had to be done in low piles to ensure uniform size and quality. The cutting was done by the same cheap labour that assembles the pyjamas at a sewing machine. Some time during the 1990s a new text was found on pyjama labels: 'Fabric produced and cut in the United States, assembled in Guatemala'. New laser technologies now allowed high piles to be cut automatically and with high precision, thus eliminating the need for cheap labour. Cutting the fabric could consequently be repatriated to the United States.

This section has described an important but neglected element in the mechanisms by which the market, if left to itself, will tend to enlarge rather than to diminish existing wage differences between countries. The magic of the market will tend to enlarge already existing asymmetries between rich and poor countries.

Synergies, cluster effects and their absence

Cluster effects and synergies are important, but economic activities exist where such effects do not exist, or exist to a very small degree. Baseball production in the poor neighbouring countries of the United States has no local cluster effects; all inputs to the final assembly come from the USA. The rubber core of the baseballs is produced in a factory in Missouri, the thread they are sewn with comes from Vermont and the leather comes from Tennessee.

The third factor explaining wealth, the synergy effects, is frequently non-existent in the kind of production which we farm out to the poor countries. Quite often it is even stipulated that such synergy effects shall not exist, because a usual condition for obtaining tax-exempt imports to the USA is that the inputs are imported from the USA. Such is the case in the industrializing process that the United States sponsors in Africa, by means of the African Growth and Opportunity Act (AGOA) .The Africans may export the products of their unqualified labour force to the US only if all the inputs are brought in from the USA. The Africans have to compete with the Haitians, be even poorer, to attract production. The competitiveness of a country is, according to OECD definition, to *raise* real wages while still remaining competitive on the world markets. In most of the Third World today this situation is turned upside down: wages are *lowered* in order to be internationally competitive.

Education is increasingly regarded as the key to expanding wealth in the Third World. In countries like Haiti, which specialize in non-mechanized production – in technological dead-ends – raising the level of education of the population will not help to increase the level of wealth in the population. In such countries the demand for educated personnel is minimal. Education is more likely to increase the propensity to emigrate. A strategy based on education succeeds only when combined with an industrial policy that also provides work for educated people, as happened in East Asia. A key point in the globalizing process of the last fifteen years is that this type of economic policy – which today's rich countries have had, often for hundreds of years – was outlawed by the World Bank and the IMF. To receive support from the rich countries, poor countries had to refrain from using the policies the rich countries had used and often still use. These are the 'conditionalities' of the Washington institutions.

In the earliest and most triumphalist period after the fall of the Berlin Wall, my Estonian colleagues tell me that the first World Bank consultants who came recommended that their country should close its universities because in the future Estonia would have its comparative advantage in economic activities that did not require university education. Although no World Bank economist would say the same thing today, and although the Estonians were not amused – their University of Tartu dates back to 1632 – there was a realism and honesty about this recommendation that has since been lost. Because economic activities vary so enormously in their ability to employ knowledge, it is indeed possible for a country to specialize in economic activities that do not require knowledge and education. By emphasizing the importance of education without simultaneously allowing for an industrial policy that creates demand for educated people – as Europe has over the last 500 years – the Washington institutions are just adding to the financial burdens of poor countries by letting them finance the education of people who will eventually find employment only in the wealthy countries. An education policy must be matched by an industrial policy that creates demand for the graduates.

In my experience, well-educated Haitians are very easy to find as taxi drivers in the French-speaking part of Canada. An estimated 82 per cent of Jamaican medical doctors practise abroad. Seventy per cent of all inhabitants of Guyana with a university education work outside the country. North American hospitals vacuum up poor English-speaking countries like Trinidad for nurses, while in many places in the Caribbean Cuban nurses are the ones that keep the health sector functioning. Indirectly, the USA's absorption of Caribbean nurses helps solve Fidel Castro's balance of payment problems.

The fact that well-educated people from poor countries are both wanted and can build up a far better standard of living in rich countries is a threat to the whole social fabric of many of their countries: the most competent, the best educated, flee. Even though the money these emigrants send home to relatives amounts to quite a capital sum – in countries like El Salvador this flow of emigrant funds constitutes the largest source of foreign exchange – it is generally spent for consumption, not for investments. My fellow economists in Haiti also maintain that the money transfers from emigrants in the USA and Canada ruin the incentives to work for a measly 30 cents an hour.

Thus the arguments *for* globalization – under certain conditions – also become the arguments *against* globalization the way it presently proceeds. A better understanding of the mechanisms that create economic growth also leads to clarification of the reasons this growth is so unevenly distributed among countries and individually. Logically, this means that economic policy must be tailored to the specific situation of a country, which is how it has been for centuries. In medicine, cure-alls – what the Americans often call snake oil – are considered mere charlatanism, completely unscientific. In the nineteenth century an American economist accused English economists of this kind of quackery, of offering economic snake oil, the same medicine whatever the situation of a country. Globalization as it has been promoted by the Washington institutions may easily be accused of the same approach. It is important to understand that this 'one size fits all' approach is the natural and unavoidable result of today's ruling economic theory, which is devoid of any context and devoid of any tools with which to observe qualitative differences, of any taxonomies or classification systems.

The internal logic is impeccable, but as Thomas Kuhn, whose words head Chapter I, says: the paradigm lacks the conceptual tools that would explain key socially important problems.

Instead of globalization bringing with it a levelling of prices and standards of living (factor–price equalization) in some countries, it will result in income polarization (factor–price polarization). The globalizing arguments of the Washington institutions are based on different premises from those we have mentioned, namely a trade theory which involves no capital (based on the labour-theory of value) and a theory of growth where capital per se – not knowledge and innovations – is the engine for the growth of capitalism. It is as if capital – money – will automatically embody human knowledge. This theory assumes that everybody has the same knowledge ('perfect information'), that there are no economies of scale (essentially no fixed costs), and that new knowledge is free and hits everybody in the world at the same time. The paradoxical element here – one that emphasizes the scholastic nature of modern economics – is that the assumptions needed to produce a harmonious result from international trade, i.e. factor–price equalization, are the same assumptions that also produce a situation where there would be no trade at all, except in raw materials. If we, as human beings, all had the same knowledge and there were no fixed costs, there would be no need to specialize and therefore no need to trade (except in raw materials). As Nobel Laureate James Buchanan explains: in a model 'which embodies constant returns to scale of production over all ranges of output, all of which are private, this economy would be without trade. In such a setting, each person becomes a complete microcosm of the whole society'.[5]

Paradoxes of the globalization debate

Impressive economic growth in China, India and South Korea is being held up as an example of the success of globalization. The question that is not asked, however, is: do or did China, India and South Korea take the recommended medicine – immediate economic integration? The answer is clearly *no*. Countries that have *not* taken the recommended medicine are constantly being used as proof of the excellence of globalization. China, India and South Korea have all, for about fifty years, followed variants of a policy the World Bank and IMF now prevent poor countries from following. Russia, on the other hand, is a country that followed the recommended shock therapy, with disastrous consequences. In many cases in Eastern Europe, industrial companies died even before they had a chance to figure out their own costs as is done in a market economy.

The globalization debate at its most primitive is a continuation of the binary argument of the Cold War. Market is good, state and planning are bad. The planned economies collapsed, consequently we may safely assume that markets will solve all our problems. From an Other Canon perspective the wealth of a nation is dependent on what that nation produces. The laboratory of history shows that symmetric free trade, between nations at approximately the same level of development, benefits both parties. Asymmetric free trade will lead to the poor nation specializing in being poor, while the rich nation will specialize in being rich. To benefit from free trade, the poor nation must first rid itself of its international specialization in being poor. For 500 years this has not happened anywhere without heavy market intervention.

The difference of opinion lies in the *context* and *timing* of free trade – in what contexts the different policies are followed. Free trade today may be essential for Norway, while the same free trade may be very destructive for another nation in a completely different situation. We shall see that in practice the greatest opponents of free trade in the short term have at the same time been the keenest advocates for free trade and globalization in the long run. They take the view that different situations need different solutions. Today's economic theory is so abstract that it is unable to take the situations of the different countries into consideration.

It has been mentioned earlier that today's market – and globalization euphoria – is the third of its kind in a row, the first being in France in the 1760s (Physiocracy) and the second peaking in the 1840s. François Quesnay (1694–1744) is considered the most important Physiocratic author, the earliest of the founding fathers of today's economic theory. Quesnay was originally a physician at the court of Louis XV, and at the time a common metaphor for the economy was still the human body. The shift from studying the body to studying the body politic was therefore not as unnatural as it may seem today. Quesnay's first important book, a voluminous work of 736 pages, published in 1730, was on the practice and techniques of bloodletting or bleeding,[6] which at the time was regarded as a cure for most illnesses. Quesnay's and his contemporaries' theory of bloodletting and his economic theory have at least two common elements: both supposedly cure a large number of illnesses that are produced by a whole range of different elements and factors ignored by Quesnay; both instant free trade (globalization) and bloodletting are basically harmless for the healthy, but potentially extremely dangerous for the weak. A robust and well-developed nation with a solid industry will not be hurt by Quesnay's theory about letting 'natural' market forces rule. Weakened individuals might die from the bleeding, as poor nations today experience deindustrialization and increased poverty as results of 'natural' market forces.

'The "gap" between rich and poor countries reflects the success of those countries that embraced capitalism and the failure of those that did not'

This title is a quote from an article by Martin Wolf, chief economics commentator of the *Financial Times* for the influential American journal *Foreign Policy* in 2003. In a clear and concise way it encapsulates the standard view of the reasons for wealth and poverty in today's polarized world. Some countries chose capitalism and grew rich, others chose a different system and remained poor. In our view Wolf is in fact right, but with another definition of capitalism than his own. With this alternative definition of capitalism as a *system of production,* capitalism in fact never reached the colonies or agriculture.

As the Cold War proceeded, two different definitions of capitalism crystallized. First, in 'the free world', capitalism gradually came to be defined as a system of private ownership of the means of production, where all coordination outside firms is left to the market. This developed into a definition that excludes any reference to production; as long as they bartered without central planning a Stone Age tribe would be considered 'capitalist'. Second, in Marxism, capitalism was a system defined by a relationship between two classes in society, the owners of the means of production and the workers. However, a third definition of capitalism exists, a definition that predominated until the Cold War, and was crowded out because it could not be neatly placed along the right–left axis. If we follow German economist Werner Sombart's definition of capitalism, instead of that of the Cold War, we understand why capitalism, as it is defined today, is a system within which it is possible to specialize in being rich, or in being poor.

Werner Sombart considers capitalism as a kind of historic coincidence, in which factors are brought together by a whole range of circumstances. Still, he is quite clear that economic wealth is a result of its being willed, a result of a conscious policy. The driving forces of capitalism, which create both the foundation and the conditions for the system, are, according to Sombart:[7]

1. The *entrepreneur*, who represents what Nietzsche calls the 'capital of human wit and will', the human agent who takes the initiative to have something produced or traded.

2. The *modern state*, which creates the institutions enabling improvements in production and distribution, and creates the incentives that make the vested interest of the entrepreneur coincide with the vested interests of society at large. Institutions encompass everything from legislation to infrastructure, patents to protect new ideas, schools, universities, and standardization of units of measurements, for example.

3. The *machine process*, i.e. what was long called *industrialism*: mechanization of production creating higher productivity and technological change with innovations under economies of scale and synergies. This concept is very close to what we today call the 'national innovation system'.

In Sombart's definition of capitalism, the rich countries were those who emulated the leading industrial nations into 'the Age of Industry'. With capitalism defined in this way, Martin Wolf is actually right when he claims that the rich countries are the ones that joined the mode of production that is called capitalism. However, it is more likely that Wolf had the Cold War definition in mind.

When these elements are in place, in order to function capitalism demands – still according to Sombart – the following ancillary elements to be able to develop fully: capital, labour and markets. These three elements – the very core of standard economic theory – are, according to Sombart, not at all the driving forces of capitalism, they are just auxiliary factors to the main driving forces. Without the driving forces, the ancillary elements – capital, labour and markets – are sterile. Both the conservative Schumpeter and the radical Marx agree that capital in itself, without innovations and without entrepreneurship, is sterile. Adam Smith's bartering dogs could not have created capitalism even if they had capital, labour hours and markets. Without human will and initiative, capital, labour and markets are meaningless concepts.

A chain of events, unfortunately for poor countries, led economics to lose Sombart's definition of capitalism. Adam Smith had removed production from economics by combining both trade and production into labour hours. Thus when the world economy was conceived as a system where everybody exchanged undefined 'labour hours' without technology, without economies of scale and without synergy effects – work that everybody mastered in the same way – the path was cleared for the view that free trade could be considered beneficial to all. Even adding capital per se does not create capitalism. However, for a long time American and continental European economists like Sombart had succeeded in keeping alive an alternative economic tradition, where production was at the core.

The way economics was formalized following the Second World War further strengthened the weak points of Adam Smith's theory. While economists in the inter-war period switched between open-minded common sense and self-referential models, economics became ever more introverted. Not being able to formalize Sombart's main driving forces of capitalism – not being able to reduce them to numbers and symbols with the toolbox – they were simply left out. This is another example of economics proceeding along the path of least mathematical resistance and away from relevance. As with bloodletting, the ones suffering from the regime of simplistic models were the poor and the weak. Instead of communicating in English and other mother tongues, communication increasingly became purely mathematical, and in that way lost key qualitative elements: the 'harder' the science, the more 'scientific' it became. Economics withdrew from the 'soft' social sciences like sociology, and added to its prestige by drawing nearer to 'harder' sciences like physics. However, the economists used an equilibrium model that physics had already left behind in the 1930s. The economists gradually lost their earlier ability to move between theoretical models and the real world and correct the models when they obviously went against ordinary common sense.[8] Faraway countries and races who had no political power were the victims of this development; in countries like the USA politicians saw to it that the theory was not used if it went against the interests of their own country. Pragmatism ruled at home, and high theory ruled abroad.

Combined with a general lack of knowledge of history, this led to what Thorstein Veblen had diagnosed as *contamination of the instincts*: an irrelevant education leads to an inability to communicate with what practical people see as 'common sense'. Astonishingly enough, a committee from the American Economic Association in 1991[9] pointed out the problem of universities producing 'well-educated idiot' economists: 'graduate programmes (in economics) may be turning out a generation of too many *idiots savants*, skilled in technique but innocent in real economic issues'.[10] According to the report, at one unnamed 'leading' university, graduate students could not 'figure out why barbers' wages have risen over time', but they could easily 'solve a two-sector general equilibrium model with disembodied technical progress in one sector'. This was the generation of economists the Washington institutions unleashed on the developing countries.

Amongst the tools of economics, elements like entrepreneurship and initiative, governmental policy, and the whole industrial system, consisting of technological change and innovations, economies of scale and synergies, turned out to be impossible to quantify and reduce to numbers and symbols. The only things quantifiable were what Sombart considered just auxiliary factors: capital, markets and manpower. The formal neoclassical economic theorists stopped studying the driving forces of capitalism, and went on to study only the auxiliary factors. As usual, practical policy needed some time to catch up with theory development. This only happened after the fall of the Berlin Wall. In his book in defence of globalization, Martin Wolf actually mentions Werner Sombart, but dismisses him, in one sentence, as being both a Marxist and a fascist.[11]

Theory development led to what Schumpeter calls 'the pedestrian view that capital per se propels the capitalist engine'. The

West started thinking that by sending capital to a poor country with no entrepreneurship, no governmental policy and no industrial system, they could produce capitalism. The consequence is that today we virtually stuff money down the throat of countries with no productive structure – where this money could be profitably invested – because they are not allowed to follow the industrial strategy all the presently rich countries followed. Developing countries are given loans they cannot profitably utilize, and the whole process of development financing becomes akin to that of chain letters and pyramid games.[12] Sooner or later the system breaks down, and the ones who designed it, standing close enough to the door when everybody rushes out, are able to make good financial profits, while the poor countries themselves are the losers. This is part of the mechanism that often creates larger flows of funds from the poor to the rich countries than the other way around, one of Gunnar Myrdal's 'perverse backwashes' of poverty.

It is worth noting that, according to Sombart's definition, agriculture was not part of capitalism. The colonies were also kept out (a main criterion for a colony was to keep manufacturing out) and for that very reason they were doomed to stay poor. By Sombart's definition of capitalism, then, the poverty problem is very different from the one Martin Wolf sees: Africa and other poor countries were never allowed or given the opportunity to develop capitalism as a production system.

Sombart's definition of the driving forces of capitalism is totally absent in the two definitions of capitalism that we have inherited from the Cold War. The liberalist definition includes neither the entrepreneur, nor the state, nor its dynamic institutions, nor the technological and machine processes. This definition does not really capture capitalism as a system of production rather than as a system of trade, a weakness inherited from Adam Smith; instead it focuses on the role of the market as coordinator of products already produced, on exchange rather than production. The Marxist definition is, as already noted, focused on the ownership of the means of production. What the liberalist view and today's superficial Marxist view of capitalism have in common is that these opposite poles on the right–left axis exclude both the entrepreneur, the role of the state, and the production process itself. The long economic Other Canon tradition from which Sombart came – far older than the liberalism of Adam Smith and David Ricardo – died out after the Second World War.

Technological dynamics, innovations and uneven growth

No one disagrees that new knowledge is the main factor in increases in our standard of living. Disagreement starts when this process has to be modelled. Here we take up the explanation built on Joseph Schumpeter. To Schumpeter the real driving forces of economic growth are *inventions* and the *innovations* that are created when these inventions are brought to the market as new products or processes. Innovations create a demand for investment capital, and inject life and value into otherwise sterile capital. To go back to Adam Smith's metaphor of the bartering dogs: for the dogs, capital would be bones buried for future use. Capital would not, for them, be able to produce more bones, or – as products of innovations – canned dog food or can-openers. These innovations, and the knowledge that is needed to use them, whether it is canned dog food or can-openers, were exogenized – they are produced outside of what the theory has ambitions to explain. The challenge is to endogenize them while, at the same time, letting go of the equality assumption, allowing for the heterogeneity and key variables we are discussing here.

Innovations come in different packages, and in different sizes. An example of a small innovation is the movie *Shark IV*, compared to the movie *Shark III*. There are larger innovations – like the transistor which ruined the market for radio tubes and changed the value chain in a whole industry, creating a large number of products that had never existed before. Very rarely do the really great waves of innovation roll over society and create important discontinuities, or breaks, in technological development. In the early 1980s, these great waves of innovation were named *techno-economic paradigm shifts* by Carlota Perez and Christopher Freeman.

A techno-economic paradigm shift is so fundamental because it changes the general purpose technology that underlies the whole productive system, e.g. the steam engine or the computer. In that sense paradigm shifts resemble the technological shifts we discussed earlier, when copper and bronze took over from stone as being the material from which humans made their tools, ending the Stone Age. Such a change in basic technology tends to change value chains in virtually all branches of industry, as the steam engine and the computer did. These innovations create what Schumpeter called 'creative destruction': new fields of industry with hordes of new products appear, while old established industries disappear because of a completely changed pattern of demand, and they create radical changes in the production processes of almost all industries. The economic development changes from more and more of one kind of product, like horse-drawn carriages, to more and more of something new, like cars. The manner of production changes, like the transition from cottage industry to factories. However, until the twentieth century, agriculture tended not to be part of the paradigm shifts. Productivity growth in agriculture was generally slow; only industry seemed to experience productivity explosions. As Carlota Perez points out, such radical technological change brings with it changes in 'common sense'. Soon after men and women could no longer work at home but had to come to work in huge factories, our attitude towards health care also changed radically. We were no longer born, treated for health problems, and died at home – big factory-like hospitals took over those tasks too.

Also the environmental problems changed: in the late nineteenth century huge quantities of horse manure were a threat to the health of city dwellers; now car fumes play a similar role. These inno-vations initially appear as foreign elements in the old system, creating mismatches between the old institutions and the exigencies of the new technologies. Inertia slows down the processes of change; we are not unlearning the old fast enough to create room for the new. Mismatches in learning between old and young generations also contribute to the slow speed of radical technological change. Friedrich Nietzsche describes, in a quite poetic way, an institutional inertia where ideas and opinions change first, and our institutions are only able to follow suit at a much slower pace. 'The overthrow of institutions does not follow immediately upon the overthrow of opinions, instead, the new opinions live for a long time in the desolate and strangely unfamiliar house of their predecessors and even preserve it themselves, since they need some sort of shelter.'[13]

Just like the Stone Age and the Bronze Age, techno-economic paradigms may be regarded as new and radically different ways to raise the standard of living. Towards the end of each epoch it becomes clear that the old technological trajectory is 'burnt out', it has yielded what it can possibly yield. When the perfect stone axe has been produced, the end of the Stone Age might be mistaken for 'the end of history'. There is no more room for improvements, nowhere to go without very radical change.

In modern history we can distinguish five such ways to raise the standard of living, each dominating a long period. Christopher Freeman and Carlota Perez's schematic outline is shown on the next page.[14]

A fundamental feature in any paradigm is a new cheap resource which is available in apparently unlimited quantities at a rapidly falling price. This is what we experience today with microelectronics. What is special with techno-economic paradigm shifts – what separates them from other big innovations – is that these large innovation waves change society far beyond the sphere we think of as 'economics'. These periodic shifts even change our view of, for example, geography and human settlements. Industrialism also changed our political structures, and the decline of mass manufacturing is doing the same thing again. Paradigm shifts are also a time for changing the power relations of the world; the economic leaders under one paradigm will not necessarily be the leaders under the next one. Britain reached the crest of her power under the steam- and railway paradigm, Germany and the United States took the lead during the age of electricity and heavy industry, while the United States became the undisputed leader during the age of Fordism.

The most important underlying phenomenon in a paradigm shift is the 'productivity explosion' found in the core industry. Figure 6 shows the 'productivity explosion' in cotton-spinning under the

The Historical Techno-Economic Paradigms

Period	Name of period	Important industries	Inexpensive resource	Infrastructure
1770–1840	Early mechanization	Textiles Wool	Water power Cotton	Canals Roads
1830–90	Steam and railway	Iron Transportation	Steam Coal	Railroad Steam ships
1880–1940	Electricity and heavy industry	Electric machinery Chemical industry	Electricity Steel	Ships Roads
1930–90	Mass production (Fordism)	Cars Synthetic materials	Oil	Roads, Planes, Cables
1990–?	Information and communication	Data/Software Biotechnology	Microelectronics	Digital telecom Satellites

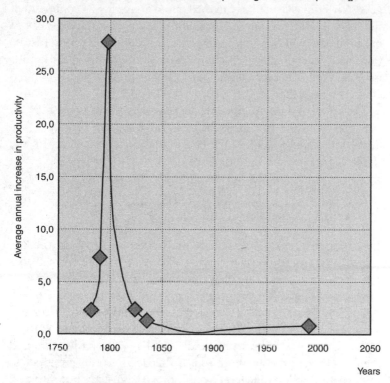

The mechanization of cotton spinning in the first paradigm

Source: Carlota Perez; *Technological Revolutions and Financial Capital. The Dynamics of Bubbles and Golden Ages*, Cheltenham, 2002; calculations from David Jenkins, *The Textile Industries*, vol. 8 of *The Industrial Revolution*, Oxford, 1994

Figure 6   An early productivity explosion

first techno-economic paradigm. At the core of colonial policy is the fact that industries with such productivity explosions are not allowed in colonies. Historically the arguments for getting such a productivity explosion industry into each country – arguments for tariff protection for the paradigm carrier – were many: this industry created employment for an increasing population, it created higher wages, it solved problems of the balance of payments, it increased the circulation of money, and – what was important for all rulers – good craftsmen and artisans and owners of factories could be taxed much harder than farmers, who were generally poor. Particularly in the United States it was commented, from Benjamin Franklin to Abraham Lincoln, that the presence of manufacturing industry in general made the supplies cheap for the farmers. Clearly such productivity explosions spread in the labour market both as higher wages and as lower prices – the combined effect is staggering.

The effect of a paradigm shift on wages can be illustrated by an example from the transition from sail to steam in Norway. The *Statistical Yearbook of Norway* for the year 1900 gives us the following monthly wages for 1895:

First mate on a sailing ship	69 kroner
First mate on a steamship	91 kroner
Engineer on a steamship	142 kroner

Even though it must have required much more skill to steer a sailing ship than a steamship, a first mate's wage was more than 30 per cent higher on a steamer than on a sailing ship, while the wage of the engineer of the steamship was more than twice that of the sailing ship mate. Thus, a shipowner who gambled on steam, and succeeded, did much to raise the wage level in his home town. These higher wages would be spent locally by the sailors of his ship and their families, and contribute to a higher level of consumption. In this way the higher wage level would spread from activities with new technology – in this case shipping – to bakers, carpenters and other artisans in the town, even to the barbers, and so they would also be able to afford to invest in new productivity-increasing technology. Society's benefits from entrepreneurship are really an unintentional side effect of the way the entrepreneur makes his money. Those who make a profit introducing new technology are far more important to a country than the shipowner who possibly made more money keeping the sailing ship industry alive. These are the same principles Henry VII of England understood when he came to power in 1485, and that could be observed in countries like Ireland and Finland over the last twenty years.

Productivity explosions, the extremely fast changes in productivity in one industry, act as catapults, rapidly raising the standard of living. However, our standard of living may be raised in two different ways: we either become wealthier because we receive higher wages, or we become wealthier because the things we buy cost less. When we become wealthier because prices fall, I call it the 'classical' model, because that is the only thing the neo-classical economists assume will happen. In reality the picture is more complicated.[15] We can call the alternative model the 'collusive' model because here the fruits of the technological development are divided among a) entrepreneurs and investors, b) workers, c) the rest of the local labour market, and d) the state, in the form of a larger tax base. This needs closer examination.

- Point a)

  The real incentive for the investments that lead to productivity development will generally be to make money, so we will have to assume that a successful investment will lead to some of the productivity increase being taken out as profit. That the first successful entrepreneurs get a high profit, which later is reduced because emulators come into the field is a standard understanding.

- Point b)

  In the same way as in the example above – the transition from sail to steam – some of the productivity increase will result in higher wages to those employed in the industry. This may be due to the fact that the new skills needed are scarce, or it may be because of the power of labour unions. Sometimes, as when Henry Ford doubled the wages of his workers in 1914, there may be an enlightened entrepreneur who realizes that he needs his own workers as customers, so it is in his own interest to see that his workers earn more. Of course, it is only under extreme circumstances, like productivity explosions, that a manufacturing firm can double wages and still survive.

- Point c)

  As the English King Henry VII observed, new technology will spread through the whole local (and gradually national) labour market, as a result of the increased purchasing power created in industries with technological change, and also of the fact that there are limits to how much wages can differ within a labour market. A wage rise in the productivity explosion sector will automatically raise all wages. Barbers have had little productivity development since the time of Aristotle, yet the wages of hairdressers in industrialized countries have – through sequences of productivity explosions – kept more or less in step with the wages of the industrial workers. Barbers in countries with no productivity explosions have stayed poor with their fellow countrymen. The Philharmonic Orchestra does not play the 'Minute Waltz' more efficiently now than it was played in Chopin's time. Still the musicians' wages have increased enormously during that period. The terms of trade between haircutting and music on one side and industrial goods on the other – between those who produce where there is no productivity increase and those of the productivity explosion sector – have improved tremendously in favour of the hairdressers and musicians. For the same haircut or the same 'Minute Waltz', hairdressers and musicians in rich countries can acquire far more industrial goods than they could 200 years ago. At the same time, hairdressers and musicians in poor countries – even if they are just as efficient as those in rich countries – are still very poor. This is the case for most occupations, particularly within the service sector: workers in poor countries are just as efficient as those in rich countries, but the difference in real wages is enormous. What we call 'economic development' is, in other words, a kind of monopoly rent from production of advanced goods and services, where the rich countries emulate each other jumping from one productivity explosion to the next.

- Point d)
  In a cartoon version of the adventures of Robin Hood, the Sheriff of Nottingham's strategy to increase tax income out of poor farmers is to hold them upside down and literally shake the last pennies out of their pockets. It did not take the European Ministers of Finance long to find out that a far easier way of boosting revenue was to increase the basis for taxation by attracting manufacturing industry. People working with machinery increased their productivity enormously and were able to pay more taxes than

those working in the fields. Also, for the Ministers of Finance, it paid to emulate the productive structures of rich countries, to enter into industrialism. With their ever-increasing tax base, rich countries were able to extend their social security network, their infrastructure and their education and health sectors.

The factors a) to d) above produce the 'collusive mode', explaining why wages in industrial countries – with frequent productivity explosions – steadily increased compared to wages in the poor countries (the colonies). Even if the colonies are now in theory independent countries, in practice they are prevented from using the emulation strategies that rich countries employed by the 'conditionalities' of the Washington institutions now just as when they were colonies. After the 'naturally wealthy' states – Venice, Holland, small city-states without agriculture – it is impossible to find examples of countries which have acquired an industrial sector without a long period of targeting, supporting and/or protecting their manufacturing sector. The only time Adam Smith mentions 'the invisible hand' in his main work, *The Wealth of Nations,* is after he has praised England's policy of high tariffs in the Navigation Acts, and then points out that after this successful protection policy it is as if an invisible hand had guided English consumers to buy English industrial goods. The invisible hand in fact replaced high tariffs when manufacturing industry, after a long period, became internationally competitive. Reading Adam Smith in this way, it is actually possible to argue that he is a misunderstood mercantilist. Also to him the key point is the *timing* of free trade. It is worth pointing out that there were 300 years of intensive tariff protection between Henry VII and Adam Smith.

Colonialism is above all an economic system, a type of close economic integration between countries. It is less important under which political heading this occurs – under nominal independence and 'free trade', or not. What is important is what kind of goods flow in which direction. To stick to the classification system above: colonies are nations specializing in *bad trade*, in exporting raw materials and importing high technology goods, whether these are industrial goods or from a knowledge-intensive service sector. Later – in the section that explains why countries which only produce raw materials cannot get rich – we shall see that within agriculture also it is possible to distinguish between typical products from rich countries (mechanizable) and products from colonies (non-mechanizable).

The same difference in wage level between industry and agriculture is also found in rich countries. Even though most of Europe's inhabitants were still farmers, in the works of Marx and the early socialists there was little trace of them for a long time. The most acute poverty was found among the industrial workers. Urban poverty is often an uglier sight than rural poverty. As the workers, with increasing political support, could further their demands for higher wages, and as they then got the benefit from the increased productivity in industry, the farmers were the ones who were economically left behind. Industry, and gradually also the workers, were protected by huge market power, could keep the prices up, and avoid 'perfect competition'. Industrialism had gelled as John Kenneth Galbraith's 'balance of countervailing powers', that is, as a system where wealth was based on extremely imperfect competition both in the labour market and in the market for products. Industrialism was a system based on triple rent-seeking by capitalists, workers and the state. The perfect competition of textbook economics was only found in the Third World.

Around the year 1900 Europe's welfare system and the triple countervailing power of industry had improved the lot of the industrial workers considerably. Slowly the understanding developed that not only could industrial workers be exploited, the farmers could also be exploited by the cities. This led to an understanding that farmers' income also ought to be protected from competition from farmers in poorer countries, or from farmers who worked in better climates. Protection of agricultural goods, then, grew out of a totally different logic than that of industrial tariffs. Industrial tariffs on industrial goods were part of an offensive strategy, to create good trade, to emulate the industrial structure of the leading nations and to bring every nation's productive sector into the areas where the productivity explosions took place, be it cotton textiles, railroads or cars. The tariffs on agricultural goods were a defensive strategy with the goal of protecting poor farmers in industrialized countries against even poorer farmers in poorer countries.

Figure 7 shows the difference in real wages between the agricultural sector and the industrial sector during a period before heavy subsidies to the agricultural sector. We can observe that in Japan farmers' wages were only 15 per cent of those of the industrial worker, in Norway 24 per cent. It is obvious that without the industrial sector, the average national wages in countries like Japan and Norway would have fallen catastrophically. Even in the world's most efficient agricultural country, the United States, we see that wages in agriculture are far below those in industry. Only in Australia and New Zealand – having an opposite climatic cycle to that of Europe and very favourable agreements with England and the rest of the Commonwealth – do wages in agriculture approach and, in the case of New Zealand, surpass those of the manufacturing sector. However, ever since these colonies were founded, Australia and New Zealand had had a very protectionist industrial policy, including against England, the mother country. By industrializing, these countries made possible the 'collusive' mode of economic growth.

Figure 7 gives a snapshot of how the presence of a manufacturing sector raises the income levels of whole nations – of the great synergy effects created by 'historical increasing returns', the

	Primary	Secondary
England, 1930	72	100
USA, 1935	40	100
France, 1930	36	100
Norway, 1934	24	100
Japan, 1934	15	100
Italy, 1928	70	100
Sweden, 1930	25	100
Australia, 1935–6	96	100
Germany, 1928	54	100
New Zealand, 1936	113	100

Source: Calculated from Clark, Colin, *The Conditions of Economic Progress*, London, 1940

Figure 7   Industrial wages set the wages for the rest of the economy: purchasing power of a median salary in the farming sector compared to the industrial sector in ten countries, 1928–36
Secondary (= Industrial) Sector = 100

combined effect of increasing returns and technical change. This was what 'good trade' and emulation managed to create not only in England, but also in all the previously poor countries whose economic policies emulated the industrial structure of England. This great synergy effect was, and still is being refused to poor countries, first through colonization, later through the Washington institutions. What we do not observe directly in Figure 7 are the second- and third-round synergy effects that originate in what we observe in that figure. A very important effect is that the know-ledge level and the high cost level in industry gradually spill over, increasing the efficiency in agriculture. Knowledge from industry influences agriculture, at the same time as the increasing national wage level makes it profitable to invest in labour-saving agricultural machinery. The geographical proximity to the industrial sector gives the farmers a market with great purchasing power. Only this will bring farming out of self-sufficiency and increase the division of labour in the countryside. Being part of the same labour market as the cities, excess labour on the farm – the younger children – will find lucrative employment in the manufacturing sector in the cities.

Even in the 1700s the connection between closeness to industry and an efficient and lucrative agriculture was obvious to anyone who cared enough to enquire. Madrid and Naples had very ineffi-cient agriculture because they had no industry. The areas around Milan, with a lot of industry, had efficient agriculture, the econo-mists of the Enlightenment observed. Proximity to industry creates cumulative virtuous circles[16] with agriculture, an effect that agriculture in poor countries without industry does not receive. Agriculture that does not share the same labour market with a manufacturing sector will not experience these synergies. This line of argument, typical of eighteenth-century Europe, was indeed the argument used, particularly after 1820, to convince the farmers of the United States that it was in their interest to industrialize under protection – in the short term to pay more for their locally produced manufactured goods than what they had previously paid for English goods – in order to create these virtuous circles of wealth in the future. Apart from the early work of Alexander Hamilton, the economists who were mainly responsible for getting this message successfully across to the American farmers were Mathew Carey (1820), Daniel Raymond (1820) and the politician Henry Clay (1887).[17] The two economists are virtually forgotten now.

Another way to measure growth and development is through learning curves. Learning curves measure labour productivity over time. Because we are interested in people's wages – and because we maintain that there are important connections between a person's productivity and his wages – we look at labour productivity and not at other kinds of productivity. When we look at learning curves, we look at the same kind of productivity explosions as in Figure 6, only from a different angle. Like the productivity explosions, the learning curves, because they measure the same thing, are characterized by a rapid descent over a relatively short time. Any epoch of time is characterized by the fact that certain products, often quite new ones, experience a tremendous productivity development, generally linked with a rapid increase in demand. According to Verdoorn's Law (after a Dutch economist), faster growth in output increases productivity due to increasing returns and technical change induced by adding new production capacity.

Figure 8 shows productivity development for a standard pair of men's shoes in the United States between 1850 and 1936. In 1850 15.5 work hours were required to produce a pair of standard men's shoes. Then a productivity explosion took place in shoe production, and rapid mechanization made it possible to employ only 1.7 labour hours to produce an identical pair of shoes fifty years later, in 1900. St Louis, Missouri, in this period became one of the wealthiest cities in the USA, based on production of shoes and beer: 'First in shoes and beer, last in baseball' was the saying about the city that showed the world its wealth when hosting both the Olympic Games and a world fair in 1904. After 1900 the learning curve for shoes flattened out. In 1923 1.1 working hours were needed to produce the same pair of men's shoes. In 1936 0.9 hours were needed. As the learning curves flattened out, pressure on wages increased, and gradually shoe production was moved to poorer regions. The USA was an exporter of shoes for a long time, now the country imports practically all its shoes. This phenomenon – that rich countries export where there is great technological development, and import where

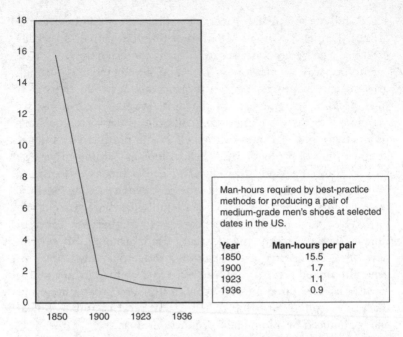

Source: Erik Reinert, *International Trade and the Economic Mechanisms of Underdevelopment*, Ph. D. thesis, Cornell University, 1980

Figure 8 Learning curve of best-practice productivity in medium-grade men's shoes, United States of America, 1850–1936

there is little technological development – is related to what in the 1970s was dubbed the product life cycle in international trade by two Harvard business school professors who described the phenomenon, Raymond Vernon (1913–99) and Louis T. Wells.[18]

What we see in Figure 8 is a typical pattern for technological development over time: rapid technological development that gradually flattens out. A new technology is born, and its potential – its trajectory – is gradually reduced and learning flattens out. This pattern is reflected in the pattern of world trade. The rich countries, where the technological innovations are found, produce and export as long as the learning curve is steep. In this period all those mechanisms are functioning, which we have described above as the 'collusive mode' of wealth creation.

As long as this cycle is not linked to the 'collusive mode' above, it may appear harmless. Standard economics focuses on trade instead of production, assumes perfect competition (meaning that everybody in the world would be able to produce shoes as they did in St Louis in 1900), and assumes that the fruits of technological change only spread in the classic way, taking the form of cheaper shoes. The toolbox of standard textbook economics does not contain tools to record the fact that at any time there are only a few industries behaving as shoe production did at the end of the 1800s, as the car production did seventy-five years later, and as the production of mobile phones does now. This form of economic theory does not take note of the activity-specific element of growth (that this happens only in a few industries at any point in time), it does not note the synergy effects spreading between industries, that high wages in shoe production helped the production of beer and the city's health sector, and that this flowering urban market created high demand and high purchase power for American farmers. In short, the virtuous circles of cumulative causation which form the essence are not recognized.

In reality the learning curve – when it has flattened out – will have exhausted most of its possibilities for increasing wealth, until, of course, a new technological paradigm hits the same product later. When a poor country gradually takes over shoe production, it will be close to impossible to increase the standard of living. This production is left to the poor countries, essentially because there is no more learning to be squeezed from the production process.

No one disagrees that innovations and learning create economic growth, but since Adam Smith this aspect of economics has been externalized. It tends to be assumed that technological change and new innovations descend like manna from heaven, available free of charge to all ('perfect information'). It is not taken into consideration that knowledge – especially when it is new – has high costs and is not generally available. The knowledge is protected by huge barriers to entry, where economies of scale and accumulated experience are important elements in creating the barrier. The larger the production volume a company has accumulated, the lower the costs. In industry the learning curves have a much-used relative, the *experience curve*, which is used for measuring just this. While the learning curves measure the development in the productivity of the workforce, the experience curves measure the development of total production costs. When several factories have the same type of technology, the factory which has accumulated the largest production volume will generally have the lowest costs per produced unit. In the race down the experience curves in the quest for lower costs, strategic pricing may actually make it profitable to price below present cost (i.e. dumping) in order to gain a production volume that, later on, will again bring the costs lower than the strategic dumping price.

In this dynamic race down the experience curves – towards lower costs – factories in poor countries with small markets and far removed from new technology have little chance. At this early technological stage it does not matter if labour costs are high, production depends upon a highly qualified workforce, and closeness to research and development. As soon as the production volume is up, costs will go down and make it possible to make money. For more than thirty years the Boston Consulting Group, an American consulting firm, has built its growth on the message of such experience curves (which have the same shape as the learning curves in Figure 8 – at first steep, then they flatten out). Only when the learning curves and the experience curves flatten out and knowledge gets into the public domain can poor countries compete, and then competition is based on their low wages and relative poverty.

Since the Industrial Revolution – with the theory of good and bad trade – the rich countries have solved this problem by seeing to it that all the countries had a part of the productivity explosions within their borders. All rich European countries built up their own textile industry – emulating the leading country – in the same way that all large countries in the twentieth century built up their own automotive industry. The countries that were not to have such industries were the colonies. For hundreds of years it was generally understood that it was better for a country to be less efficient than the leading country in the paradigm shift than to remain without modern industry at all. It was obvious that the new industries would create a higher standard of living than the old ones, in the same way that it was obvious in the 1990s that it was better to be a mediocre data consultant than to be the world's most efficient dishwasher. This was the kind of common sense that was left out of Ricardo's trade theory, which eliminated the earlier obvious logic that – in a world with a variety of industries requiring both scarce or common skills, and a variety of technologies at different points in their lifecycles – it was indeed possible to specialize according to a comparable advantage in being poor.

Situations exist, however, where the dynamics described in the learning curves can be used for making poor countries rich, by upgrading them technologically in sequence. This model was named *flying geese* by the Japanese economist Kaname Akamatsu in the 1930s (see Figure 9).[19] Another Japanese economist and

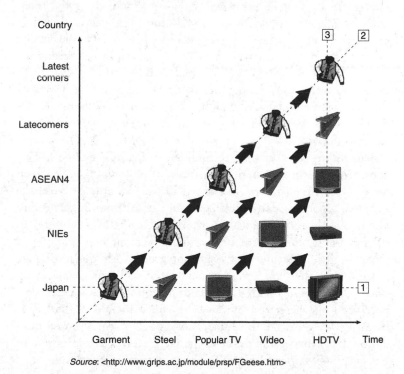

Source: <http://www.grips.ac.jp/module/prsp/FGeese.htm>

Figure 9 The 'Flying Geese' Model: Sequential Structural Transformation in East Asia

later Minister of Foreign Affairs in the 1980s, Saburo Okita, followed the 'flying geese' model and theorized that a poor country is able to upgrade its technology by jumping from one product to another with increasing knowledge content. The first flying goose, in this case Japan, breaks the air resistance for the next ones, so gradually all of them can sequentially benefit from the same technological change. For example, many years ago Japan produced inexpensive garments, achieving productivity increases which boosted the standard of living ('collusive mode') so much that a relatively unsoph-isticated product like a garment could no longer be produced prof-itably there. Production was taken over by South Korea, while Japan gradually upgraded its manufacturing to something more sophis-ticated, like TV production. When South Korea upgraded, garments were then for a while produced in Taiwan, until the same thing happened there; production costs grew too high. Production then moved to Thailand and Malaysia, and history repeated itself. Finally, production of garments was moved to Vietnam. In the meantime, however, a whole row of countries had used garment production to raise their standard of living; they had all surfed sequentially down the same learning curve, and all had become richer. Of course, this game requires that the head goose continuously gets involved in new technologies.

This model of sequential technological upgrading must not be confused with the alternative, the old static colonial model, which we can call the *dead-end model*. As in the example of baseballs in Haiti, a country can specialize statically in technological blind alleys. Should technological change happen, the poor country in the dead-end model loses the production, as in our example of pyjama-cutting. While East Asian integration for the most part has followed the *flying geese* principle, the economic relationship of the United States with its southern neighbours has for the most part been characterized by the *dead-end* principle. Canada has historically followed the European model of early emulation, although the ownership of the Canadian factories to a large extent has been in American hands. The issue of foreign ownership must be considered simultaneously with the question of the kind of production the foreigners bring into the country.

Now we can turn back to the main question of this book. The difference in the standard of living between rich countries and poor countries 250 years ago was in a proportion of 1:2. Today statistics from the World Bank show that a bus driver in Germany has real wages that are sixteen times higher than those of his just as efficient colleague in Nigeria. The phenomenon is there, and the effects can be measured, but presently no theory exists that describes these mechanisms satisfactorily. I am of the opinion that the main explanation for this is that the rich world today has confused the reasons for economic growth – innovation, new knowledge and new technology – with free trade, which just means transport of goods across borders. As did Adam Smith, the rich countries confuse the age of manufacturing with the age of commerce.

Over time, economic growth manifests itself as new products and increased productivity that meet our needs. This increase in productivity, however, is very unevenly distributed among different economic activities. As we have seen, there has been practically no technological progress in the assembly of baseballs over the past 150 years, while the manufacturing of golf balls has experienced rapid technological change during the same period. Figure 10 shows how the rich countries increase their real wages by successively skimming the steep part of the learning curve as new technologies become available. Some French economists refer to this principle as 'Fordism': the productivity increase in manufacturing spreads in the form of increasing wages in the industrial sector, and then gradually through the rest of the economy. An annual productivity increase of, say, 4 per cent has traditionally led to wage increases of 4 per cent. This system depended on a balance of countervailing power between employer and employee, and until recently, such a balance existed only in Europe and North America.

The system obviously also depended on increases in productivity. If the demands for wage increases exceed the increases in productivity, the result will be inflation. The continuous demands for wage increases provided industry with an important incentive. Compared to the cost of labour, capital – and thus mechanization – became increasingly cheaper, leading to further virtuous

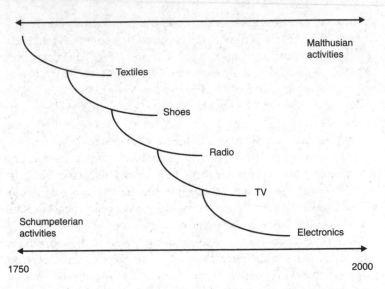

Source: Erik Reinert, *International Trade and the Economic Mechanisms of Underdevelopment*, Ph. D. thesis, Cornell University, 1980 (text slightly modified)

Figure 10   How the Wage Differentials between Rich and Poor Nations were Created Through Sequences of 'Productivity Explosions' Translated into Wage Rents

circles. As a manager of an industrial firm in Italy in the 1970s and 1980s, I experienced automatic indexing of wages[20] during an inflationary period. At first sight, the system was an irresponsible mechanism perpetuating inflation. With hindsight I find that during this period Italian manufacturing industry mechanized and achieved very high growth in labour productivity. Rising wages and inflation made it very profitable to substitute capital for labour. Higher real wages came back as increased demand and consequently created more jobs, while the very same increasing wages also gave incentives for new mechanization, which created new productivity increases, which again increased wages, all in an ever increasing spiral of increasing welfare. People employed in sectors with little productivity increase, such as barbers, got richer by increasing their prices in step with increasing industrial wages. Even if the barbers have experienced relatively little productivity increase, barbers in rich countries could improve their welfare dramatically compared to their equally productive counterparts in poorer countries. In other words, wage increases in the service sector rode on the wave of the productivity increase of the industrial sector. The real wages of a barber became dependent on who he shared a labour market with, not on his own efficiency. Based on these mechanisms, wages in the richest and poorest countries thus went from a ratio of 1 to 2 to one of 1 to 16 over time. Barbers who had no manufacturing in their labour markets stayed poor.

Fordism – understood as a system where wages increase in step with the productivity increases of the leading industrial sector – had the interesting consequence of keeping the division of gross domestic product relatively stable between labour and capital through most of the twentieth century. In my view, this kind of welfare-spiralling has, at least temporarily, largely been broken. At the moment our real wages are increasingly more dependent on falling prices than on increasing wages. This is to some extent a recurring cyclical phenomenon of deflation (falling prices) following productivity explosions, but today it is also becoming a more permanent structural feature. This results from the appearance of China and India as large players in the global economy – countries that do not run Fordist wage regimes – and also from labour unions having lost much of their power. As a consequence real wages in many countries have started falling as a percentage of the gross domestic product. This last factor in particular is a novelty, and clearly observable in countries like the USA, where recent tax cuts largely have benefited the richest strata of society, who spend the smallest part of their income, and who are more prone to buy a chateau in France with their higher disposable income than a hamburger at the corner deli. Such potential underconsumption – another phenomenon that eludes the toolkit of neoclassical economics – is a cyclical occurrence in capitalism and is not helped by US tax and wage policy. Also, for the first time since the 1930s, Europe is facing increasing pressures to reduce real wages. The periods of fastest growth in real wages have been periods of Galbraithian 'balance of countervailing powers', when – as in the 1950s and 1960s – industrialist power and labour power created Fordist wage regimes.

By studying the lifecycle of a given technology, we can see that several factors are connected. I have already discussed the learning curve in Figure 8. In Figure 11, we can see how the learning curve relates to other variables. As a new industry develops, the number of firms will tend to grow – the barriers are relatively low, and no single company has large cost advantages through accumulated volume along the learning and experience curves. Many companies will be established, but few will survive the industry shake-outs that generally accompany maturing industries. Around 1920, there were about 250 car manufacturers in the US, and only four were left forty years later. The number of match factories increased rapidly in Norway for a while, but they were in the end consolidated into one, before all match production was moved to Sweden.

Simultaneously, demand for the new product grows like a classical epidemic curve: first slowly, then exponentially until the market is saturated. Once this happens – when virtually everybody has a car, dishwasher and telephone – the growth curve levels out because only the replacement market remains. As we can observe in the market for mobile phones, it is possible to maintain this curve at a high level through minor innovations and changing fashions, by adding 'bells and whistles'. These three elements follow each other through the lifecycle of a product. On the graph, the area between the dotted lines is the area where technological change has the largest potential to increase a nation's standard of living. The wage levels in Europe's two last internal colonies – Ireland and Finland – have been catapulted by technological change over the past twenty years as the nations raced ahead, leading the pack, down the extremely steep learning curves of information and communication technology. What we must understand is that it is impossible to attain such a wage increase based on businesses with flat learning curves. Statements about countries being 'the Ireland of this-or-that-region' are empty demagoguery unless a steep and important learning curve can be tamed and internalized as it was in Ireland and Finland. Economic growth is activity-specific in the sense that, at any point in time, few economic activities exhibit very sharp learning curves.

Innovations, rather than savings and capital per se, drive welfare forwards. From both sides of the political spectrum, Karl Marx

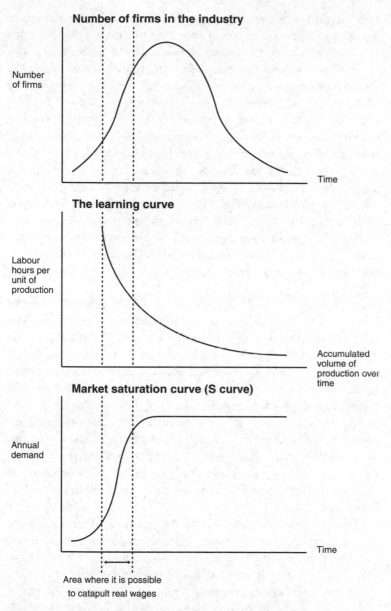

Figure 11   Industrial Dynamics: three variables

and Joseph Schumpeter agree on the sterility of capital alone as a source of wealth. The world economy functions a bit like *Alice in Wonderland*, where one of the strange characters tells Alice: 'This is how fast you have to run here in order to stand still.' In the global economy only constant innovations sustain welfare. Resting on their laurels as the world's leading constructors of sailing ships could only last until the steamship took over, when wages and employment would inevitably collapse. Schumpeter's metaphor is that capitalism is like a hotel where there is always someone living on the luxury floors, but these occupants are always changing. The world's best producer of kerosene lamps soon became poor with the advent of electricity. The status quo leads inevitably to poverty. This is precisely what makes the capitalist system so dynamic, but this mechanism also contributes to creating huge differences between rich and poor countries. The more one understands these dynamics, however, the more one can do to help developing nations out of their poverty.

The global economy can in many ways be seen as a pyramid scheme of sorts – a hierarchy of knowledge – where those who continually invest in innovation remain at the apex of welfare. The question is not really one of efficiency, as it is abundantly clear that an extremely efficient janitor in the developing world makes far, far less than an average Swedish lawyer, or even an incompetent Swedish janitor for that matter. The very bottom of this hierarchy is, for example, occupied by the world's most effective producers of baseballs for America's favourite sport, in Haiti and Honduras. Appendix VI shows the world economy as a hierarchy of skills, listing the factors that characterize the high-quality activities at the top (like golf balls) and the low-quality activities at the bottom (like baseballs).

High-quality economic activities generally emerge out of new knowledge from research. Many countries therefore invest in basic research, because it serves as a main source of innovation, even though it is often not possible to predict the results when research begins. Inventions contain important elements of serendipity, accident or results found while looking for something else. Alexander Fleming's discovery of penicillin is one such example. Often the road from invention to innovation – to the practical use of a product – is very long. The possibility of pure, nearly monochromatic concentrated light was established by Albert Einstein in 1917. But the invention of the laser (Light Amplification by Stimulated Emission of Radiation) was not translated into practical applications or innovations until the 1950s. So while basic research is a slow process, its eventual applications are many and varied. The laser went from an academic hypothesis to an important instrument in eye surgery, to guide projectiles, to uses in navigation, satellite tracking, welding, for CD-players, as substitutes for scalpels during operations, and as laser pointers. Modern information and communication technologies are now entirely unthinkable without the invention of the laser.

It is also important to keep in mind that product innovations tend to spread differently in an economy than process innovations. Product innovations tend to produce high barriers to entry and high profits, as with Henry Ford at the beginning of the twentieth century and Bill Gates today. However, when these same inventions hit other industries as process innovations – when Henry Ford's car came to agriculture as a tractor or when Bill Gates' technology is used in hotel bookings – the main effect is to bring prices down rather than wages up. The use of information technology has brought down profits in the hotel business, both in Venice and at Spain's Costa del Sol, so the hotel industry complains.

Why do countries that only produce raw materials not become wealthy?

Agriculture presents some unexpected paradoxes

1. First of all, it is obvious that shortage of food, and famines, mostly occur in countries that specialize in producing foodstuffs. The smaller the percentage of agriculture as a percentage of gross domestic product, the smaller the odds are of famine. In fact, the risk in countries with practically no agriculture is dying of eating too much. How can this strange reverse proportionality be explained?

2. Explosions of productivity were for centuries limited to industry, but, particularly in the past fifty years or so, agriculture has experienced a larger productivity growth than most industries. The productivity per acre of wheat in American agriculture has almost increased by a factor of six since 1940. Large parts of the agricultural sector have become high-tech businesses, its farmers have come to plough with automated tractors guided by GPS satellites, and a single farmer can today produce what ten used to produce only seventy-five years ago. The paradox is that the most effective agriculture in the world, in the USA and Europe, is unable to survive without subsidies and protection. Every Swiss cow is in fact subsidized with four times the pro-capita income in sub-Saharan Africa. What causes this?

3. In 1970 Norman Borlaug received the Nobel Peace Prize for the 'green revolution' in agriculture, for having produced new species that increased harvests and productivity immensely. This enormous explosion of agricultural productivity has not drastically changed the number of poor and hungry in the world. Why not?

My contention is that these three seeming paradoxes are deeply intertwined. Once this relationship is understood, it is also possible to understand why no country has been able to get rich without an industrial and an advanced service sector. It will also become clear why developing countries never will become rich by exporting food to the First World. The different economic sectors – crudely classified as the agricultural, industrial and service sectors – play different roles in the national economy, and to a certain extent follow different economic laws when they are built up or down. Failing to appreciate these qualitative differences between economic activities leads to a failure to understand why the global economy develops in such an uneven manner.

Figure 12 creates two ideal types of economic activities. I call the first category Schumpeterian activities. By means of continual innovations that lead to increasing wages, these activities create welfare and development. The second type of activity I have labelled Malthusian activities. They keep wage-levels close to the

Characteristics of **Schumpeterian activities** (= 'good' export activities)	Characteristics of **Malthusian activities** (= 'bad' export activities if no Schumpeterian sector present)
Increasing returns	Diminishing returns
Dynamic imperfect competition	'Perfect competition' (commodity competition)
Stable prices	Extreme price fluctuations
Generally skilled labour	Generally unskilled labour
Creates a middle class	Creates 'feudalist' class structure
Irreversible wages ('stickiness' of wages)	Reversible wages
Technical change leads to higher wages for the producer ('Fordist wage regime')	Technical change tends to lower price to consumer
Creates large synergies (linkages, clusters)	Creates few synergies

Figure 12   Schumpeterian vs. Malthusian Economic Activities

subsistence level, just as Malthus predicted for humanity as a whole. One, as we will see, operates principally in manufacturing, the other is found typically if agriculture and raw materials extraction are left to the forces of the market. The depression of the 1930s illustrated the difference between these two types of activities very well. In the manufacturing sector it manifested itself as unemployment, while the workers who kept their employment kept their wages. As a result of this, wages as a percentage of GDP actually increased in the US during the crisis. John Kenneth Galbraith reports that the farming sector experienced the depression as falling prices for their produce, and falling income. The ratio between farm prices and farm costs, called 'parity price', reflected the earnings of the farmers compared to the costs of the inputs they needed. In 1918 this ratio stood at 200. The fall of this ratio measures the increasing poverty of American farmers compared to the rest of the US economy. In 1929 it fell to 138, and in 1932 it reached what Galbraith calls 'a dismal, even murderous 57'.[21] The price of farm produce had fallen by more than two thirds compared to the cost of the input farmers needed from the rest of the economy. John Steinbeck's *Grapes of Wrath* depicts the situation in American farming at the time.

To further illustrate the difference between the two ideal types of economic activities, I shall peg them to two very different forms of foreign aid: the aid that rebuilt Europe and Japan after the Second World War, on the one hand, and the one generally practised today on the other. Contrary to popular opinion, the Marshall Plan was not a simple programme for transferring massive sums of money to struggling countries, but an explicit – and eventually successful – attempt to reindustrialize Europe. The basic mechanisms for creating virtuous circles harnessed by the Marshall Plan had, however, been identified by Antonio Serra more than three hundred years earlier.

The productive structures of today's developing countries have, via the Washington institutions, been subject to programmes with exactly the opposite effect. They have, I would argue, suffered from Marshall's dark twin – a Morgenthau Plan like the one implemented in Germany in 1945. When it was clear that the Allies would win the Second World War, the question of what to do with Germany, which in three decades had precipitated two world wars, reared its head. Henry Morgenthau Jr, Secretary of the Treasury from 1934 to 1945, formulated a plan to keep Germany from ever again threatening world peace. Germany, he argued, had to be entirely deindustrialized and turned into an agricultural nation.[22] All industrial equipment was to be removed or destroyed; the mines were to be flooded with water or concrete. This programme was approved by the Allies during a meeting in Canada in late 1943, and was immediately implemented when Germany capitulated in May 1945.

During 1946 and 1947, however, it became clear that the Morgenthau Plan was causing serious economic problems in Germany: deindustrialization caused agricultural productivity to plummet.[23] This was indeed an interesting experiment. The mechanisms of synergy between industry and agriculture, so key to Enlightenment economists, also worked in reverse: killing industry reduced the productivity of the agricultural sector. Many of those who had lost their jobs in industry returned to the farm, and the biblical mechanisms of diminishing returns, referred to in Chapter 2, became the dominating mechanisms in the economy. Former president Herbert Hoover, who at the time played the role of the old and wise statesman, was sent to Germany with orders to report to Washington what the problem was. His investigation took place in early 1947, and he wrote three reports. In the last, dated 18 March 1947, Hoover concluded: 'There is the illusion that the New Germany left after the annexations can be reduced to a "pastoral state". It cannot be done unless we exterminate or move 25,000,000 out of it.'

Observing the dark consequences of deindustrialization, Hoover had reinvented the old mercantilist theory of population: an industrial state could feed and maintain a far larger population than an agricultural state occupying the same territory. In other words, industry greatly increases a country's ability to sustain a large population. The fact that famines only occur in countries specializing in agriculture underlines the power of industry, of the division of labour and of the importance of the intersectorial synergies that create and maintain welfare.

Less than three months after Hoover submitted his report, the Morgenthau Plan was silently buried. The Marshall Plan was devised to produce exactly the opposite effect, namely to reindustrialize Germany and the rest of Europe. In the case of Germany, industry was to be returned to its 1936 level, which was considered the last 'normal' year before the war. Today's problem is that the dominating barter-focused economic theory fails to appreciate the difference between a Marshall Plan and a Morgenthau Plan. To return to the quote from Thomas Kuhn which opens Chapter 1, the conceptual tools needed to differentiate the two plans are not part of the toolbox of standard growth theory. A country specializing in Malthusian activities will remain poor, while countries specializing in Schumpeterian activities slowly but surely will be able to build their wage levels and their systems of production to achieve ever higher standards of living. I will quickly discuss how the two ideal types of activity differ.

As Antonio Serra pointed out, the production of raw materials and manufactured goods obey different economic laws. This argument had been used to justify the view that countries producing raw materials also needed an industrial sector. Today's economic science as it is applied to the Third World fails to recognize this, and globalization thus has destructive consequences, particularly in small, poor countries. However, not all economists have failed to recognize this insight. American economist Paul Krugman resurrected these centuries' old ideas around 1980, but his innovations had no practical consequences. In economics, ideology and methodology now interweave around the unfortunate coincidence that the 'mathematization' of the neo-classical paradigm requires assumptions that portray the market economy as a utopia of harmony and equality. Seeing the economy through mathematical filters thus had strong ideological implications, which may explain why economics has been allowed to drift into irrelevance – an irrelevance that supported certain political agendas. Krugman invented tools that made it possible to demonstrate the old dichotomy of increasing returns creating wealth, and diminishing returns creating poverty, but his theories did not meet any political demand.

Whatever their initial productivity level, agriculture, and the production of raw materials in general, will sooner or later run into *diminishing returns*. As we have mentioned, diminishing returns come in two categories: *intensive* and *extensive*. If you put more and more men to work the same field, you will eventually get to the point where a worker produces less than the one who went before him. This is the intensive variety that I previously have discussed through the example of cultivating carrots. Small, poor countries often have their entire economies directed towards the export of a single product, be it coffee or carrots. If there is no alternative employment, these diminishing returns will eventually cause real wages to fall. The more a country specializes in the production of raw materials, the poorer it will become.

The old English classical economists understood the principle of diminishing returns well. It was, in fact, this very principle that led the poet, writer and philosopher Thomas Carlyle to proclaim economics the 'dismal science'. Sooner or later, humankind's activities would run into a wall in the form of a natural resource that was no longer available in the same quantity as before. This was, admittedly, a flexible wall that could be bent a bit and which varied from year to year, but sooner or later society would meet the very real wall of overpopulation.

This fundamentally pessimistic English economic science can quickly be made optimistic if one incorporates technological change and increasing returns. If costs fall with increasing volume, this is good news. A network becomes more useful as more people are added to it; a technology becomes cheaper for the single user the more diffused it is. Malthus's dismal population theory is in fact reversed by such increasing returns or economies of scale: the more people live in a country, the cheaper their goods can be produced and delivered. Alternatively, human society can be perceived as proceeding by forever pushing forward a neverending frontier of new knowledge and new technology. With this vision, economics becomes super-optimistic. The more people the better; the more potential customers we have, the more we can research and the more diverse goods we can supply. This was a vision of the world already prevalent at the time of the mercantilists, before pessimism came to reign with Malthus in 1798. As we have seen, before Malthus, the goal was to attract as many inhabitants as possible to a country, preferably to the cities. The mercantilists wanted industry, and then simultaneously had to find the largest possible markets, domestically and abroad. Economies of scale were therefore vital to their theories and policies.

A country with no industry, however, must still obey the iron laws of diminishing returns. Even if technological change can move the flexible wall, it remains none the less. This is the main difference between the economic structures of developed and developing countries.

In his *Principles of Political Economy* (1848), the textbook that was to dominate English economics for the rest of the century, John Stuart Mill flags the crucial importance of diminishing returns:

> I apprehend [the elimination of Diminishing Returns] to be not only an error, but the most serious one, to be found in the whole field of political economy. The question is more important and fundamental than any other; it involves the

whole subject of the causes of poverty; ... and unless this matter be thoroughly understood, it is to no purpose proceeding any further in our inquiry.[24]

The next textbook to take over the English scene and dominate the field until Keynes was Alfred Marshall's *Principles of Economics* (1890). In the spirit of his predecessor Mill, Marshall argued that all major migrations in history resulted from diminishing returns. Doing research for my doctoral dissertation in 1980, I attempted to check out the theoretical edifice from Antonio Serra to Alfred Marshall that associated poverty with diminishing returns. My thesis revealed that the main export items of Peru (cotton), Bolivia (tin) and Ecuador (bananas) during the twentieth century were all produced under a large degree of diminishing returns. When production fell, productivity increased, which was the exact opposite of what happens in the industrial sector. Figure 13 shows the change in the productivity of bananas in Ecuador between 1961 and 1977, when a quick fall in productivity was triggered by

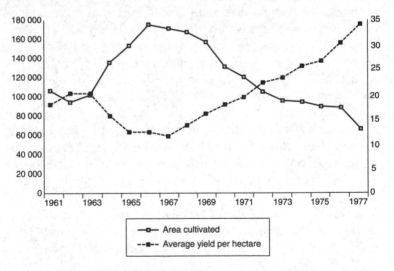

Source: Erik Reinert, *International Trade and the Economic Mechanisms of Underdevelopment*, Ph. D. thesis, Cornell University, 1980

Figure 13   Ecuador: Increased Production and Diminishing Returns in Banana Production, 1961–77

events that, at first sight, should have been an advantage. A closer look at this case will shed light on what Gunnar Myrdal called 'perverse backwash effects' in developing countries.

In the early 1960s, banana plantations in Central America were attacked by Sigatoka disease. Ecuador, at the time a relatively small producer, was spared an outbreak, and saw its chance to gain market share. Between 1962 and 1966 Ecuador increased its area under banana cultivation by 75 per cent. Sweating over piles of documents in the heat of Guayaquil in Ecuador some years later, I found that during the same period productivity per acre fell by 40 per cent, from 19 tons per acre to less than 12 tons. As always, more than one factor was at play in such developments, but the main reason for this decline in productivity was that production had to move from the prime banana-producing area of Provincia el Oro into more marginal areas. What originally seemed to be an enormous chance to improve Ecuador's position, in reality led to a fall in productivity, and falling wages for its banana producers. This will come as no surprise to any agricultural economist; the problem is that the consequences of this at the macro level are so poorly understood. The main point here, that cannot be emphasized enough, is that the exact opposite would have happened in industry: an increase in production would as a general rule have reduced costs. In manufacturing, the next machine one starts up will not be less effective than the previous one, rather the opposite; the next hour worked will reduce fixed costs per unit of production. In manufacturing, increasing production leads to falling unit costs. In manufacturing, increasing market share gives you the opportunity to get ahead in the race down the learning curve; in agriculture it drives you into the wall of diminishing returns.

The 1994 Rwanda genocide is generally presented to us as evil men promoting ethnic hatred, while the rest of the world stood by and watched. However, this drama can only be understood in the light of the law of diminishing returns, created, in this case, by increasing population pressure on arable land with almost no alternative opportunities for employment outside of the primary sector. In such a situation, where opportunities for increasing returns are entirely absent, Malthusian pessimism is entirely justified. Increasing populations create crises. The population density in Rwanda is 281 inhabitants per square kilometre. This is not particularly high compared to the population density in some industrial nations – Japan has 335 inhabitants and the Netherlands 477 inhabitants per square kilometre – but for a poor agricultural country the number is enormous. In comparison, rich Denmark has 125 inhabitants, Tanzania 20, South Africa 36, Namibia 2 and Norway 14 inhabitants per square kilometre.

Two large studies have been conducted on Rwanda's genocide, one by the World Bank in 1997 and one by UNDP, the United Nations Development Program, in 1999. What is truly remarkable about these studies is that they do not consider the role played by diminishing returns in the Rwandan drama: the effects of falling marginal productivity in agriculture with an increasing population. The contemporary world, at least as it manifests itself in our policies towards the Third World, no longer grasps the differences between economic activities. We no longer look for what would once have been fairly obvious, i.e. for links between a genocide and the lack of opportunities for employment outside of an agricultural sector suffering from diminishing returns. Rwandan agriculture is, of course, not particularly efficient, but attempts to render agriculture more effective without also diversifying the economy of a country go against all the teachings of history. Only industrialization can create an effective agricultural sector. In fact, all the world's failed states share the fact that they experience frequent problems of food supply and have weak industrial sectors. Once, economists understood such structural connections. Today, we study failed states and famines as if they were entirely distinct phenomena, divorced from an economic structure, whereas in reality they are complementary effects of the same basic set of problems. The result of this is that the global community generally seeks to remedy the symptoms, rather than the causes, of world misery and poverty.

In his book *Collapse* (2005)[25], biologist Jared Diamond brilliantly does what others investigating the Rwanda affair have not managed; in the tradition of Robert Malthus, John Stuart Mill and Alfred Marshall, he links the problem of genocide to diminishing returns. During a period before the genocide, Rwanda suffered a decline in per capita food production because of diminishing returns, drought and overworked soil that in turn led to massive deforestation. The upshot was dramatically rising levels of theft and violence perpetrated by landless and hungry young men. Diamond quotes a French scholar on East Africa, Gerard Prunier: 'The decision to kill was of course made by politicians, for political reasons. But at least part of the reason why it was carried out so thoroughly by the ordinary rank-and-file peasants ... was feeling that there were too many people on too little land, and that with a reduction in their numbers, there would be more for the survivors.'

Australia has traditionally been all too aware of the dangers of specializing in producing raw materials. Had Australia followed traditional trade theory and specialized in supplying the world with raw wool, Australian economists realized, the first consequence would be overproduction and a rapid fall in the price of wool. Second, if no alternative source of employment existed, sheep herding and the production of wool would spread to areas which were unsuitable for such activities.

This was why Australia insisted on establishing its own manufacturing sector, even though it never would be able to compete with English and American industry. This is the attitude needed in order to create middle-income countries. The Australians reasoned that a national manufacturing sector would create an alternative wage level that would prevent the producers of raw materials from moving production on to marginal lands. The wage level created by the presence of industry would signal that this would not be profitable. An industrial sector – which by definition produces under increasing returns – would also help mechanize the production of wool. This very same logic, based on the dichotomy between increasing returns in industry and diminishing returns in agriculture, had been a principal argument for European and American industrialization throughout the nineteenth century.

The great cyclical swings in productivity resulting from the whims of nature form another problem in agriculture. Unlike manufacturing, agriculture is unable to stop production or store semi-manufactured goods once Nature has begun the process of production. Nor do farmers have the economic clout that industry has to hold back production in order to keep prices up. Since demand does not move in sync with production, agricultural commodities often experience huge price fluctuations. At times fluctuations can be so large that the total value of the crop in a year with bad harvests can be higher than the total value in a good year. When the underlying economic business cycle also changes, the consequences can be severe. Agriculture, in fact, is usually the first sector to enter into a downward business cycle and the last to come out of it. In the old days in Norway the saying was that 'when the farmer is wealthy, everybody is wealthy'. Following the depression of the 1930s, the Western world attempted to solve the problems of the agricultural sector by making agriculture more like industry. Both in the United States and Europe, farmers were allowed to form marketing monopolies. To this day, the agricultural sector is exempt from anti-trust legislation in the USA, and we buy our almonds and raisins from the United States from legal monopolies.

In agriculture it is unthinkable to double wages as Henry Ford did with his employees. Not only that, there are good reasons not to increase wages at all. The production of raw materials usually requires unskilled labour, the supply of which is unlimited in poor countries. While Henry Ford's productivity gains were permanent, farmers' gains from higher prices are reversible. The cyclicality makes a big difference. If wages were increased during good years, the producer would have to reduce them again during subsequent bad times that are bound to follow. At the same time, the production of agricultural commodities does not necessarily give the right incentives to increase effectiveness through investments in new technology. Success in such industries often depends more on the timing of sales and financial muscle than on cost efficiency in production.

To sum up, the producers of raw materials live in an entirely different world from that inhabited by industrial producers. Prices fluctuate widely and sometimes unpredictably. While Bill Gates establishes the prices of his own products, producers of raw materials have to read the newspaper every day to see what the market is willing to pay them. Producers of raw materials inhabit a world close to that described by standard economic theory, with its perfect competition and with low barriers to entry. From Figure 12, we can see that poor countries generally specialize in Malthusian activities, where a perfect competition forces producers to give away their productivity increases to their customers in the form of lower prices. The fact that increases in productivity are extracted differently in industry than in agriculture was the most important point made by the English economist Hans Singer in his seminal 1950 paper.[26] Singer, by the way, was a student of Joseph Schumpeter.

Like the rest of Latin America, Peru embarked on an ambitious programme of industrialization some time after the Second World War. Through tariffs on imported industrial goods numerous industries were established, creating a number of new jobs where the wage levels gradually rose. As we can observe from Figure 14, the endeavour was successful. In essence, their strategy differed little from that begun in England by Henry VII in 1485, and which all industrialized nations have been through. Towards the end of the 1970s, however, the World Bank and the International Monetary Fund began their 'structural adjustment programmes' for the developing world. Peru was forced to open its economy, its industry died, and wage levels fell dramatically across the entire nation, as can be seen in Figure 14.

The German economist Friedrich List theorized about the timing of tariffs and free trade. The sequence goes like this: (1) all nations first needed a period of free trade to change the patterns of consumption and thus to create a demand for industrial goods. Then followed a period (2) when small states protected and built their own industries (i.e. activities subject to increasing returns, including advanced services) and synergies. Once this was done, List suggested (3) a period where ever larger geographical areas would be integrated economically. The tariff barriers that once protected each of more than thirty German states around 1830 needed to be lifted and established around an economically united Germany. Subsequently, when all countries had established their own competitive industrial sectors, it was (4) in everyone's mutual interest to open for global free trade. It is important to understand that List was both a protectionist and a free trader, depending on the stage of development of a nation.

From a Listian perspective, countries like Peru made the mistake of attempting to jump from stage 2 to stage 4. Although planned, the

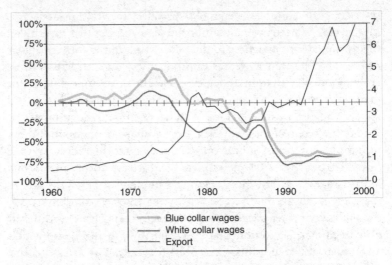

━━━ Blue collar wages
───── White collar wages
───── Export

This graph shows how real wages in Peru peaked when the country did everything 'wrong' according to the Washington institutions. Although not competitive at a world level, the presence of a manufacturing sector produced real wages twice as high as the present ones. The post-Cold War era produced a world economic order that maximizes world trade rather than human welfare.

The export figures are in current US dollars, exaggerating somewhat the visual effect.

Sources: Real wages: Santiago Roca and Luis Simabuco, 'Natural Resources, Industrialisation and Fluctuating Standards of Living in Peru, 1950–1997: A Case Study of Activity-Specific Economic Growth' in Erik S. Reinert, *Globalization, Economic Development and Inequality: An Alternative Perspective*, Cheltenham, 2004. Exports: Richard Webb and Graciela Fernández Baca, *Perú en Números*, Lima, 2001

Figure 14   Peru, 1960–2000: Diverging Paths of Real Wages and Exports

stage between national protectionism and global free trade, the Latin American Free Trade Association (LAFTA or ALALC), never became operational. The industrial entrepreneurs of the relatively small countries were too well off with their near monopolies to accept free trade with their neighbours. Moving directly from List's stage 2 to his stage 4 had the same effect on Latin American manufacturing as if suddenly subjecting a greenhouse plant to a cold climate. Manufacturing industry largely died out, and the lack of demand from the manufacturing sector prevented these economies from upgrading their knowledge-intensive service sector in the way it happened in the rich countries. Very similar synergies exist between manufacturing and knowledge-intensive service sectors as those between manufacturing and agriculture. It is clear that Latin American standards of living would have been much higher today if List's advice and his sequencing of globalization had been followed, allowing a much bigger manufacturing sector to survive.

This, however, brings us to an important point understood by economists for centuries, but which seems entirely incomprehensible to many of today's economists: a country with an inefficient industrial sector is far better off than one with no industrial sector at all. Figure 14 shows the extent to which real wages in Peru sank dramatically with deindustrialization, and it is clear that we have produced a world economic order that maximizes world trade rather than world income. The argument used by the World Bank, and the economic theory that drives it, is that Peruvian industry was 'inefficient' and 'not competitive'. My point is that this 'inefficient' industrial sector none the less created a wage level that was about twice as high as what today's globalized economy is able to deliver in Peru. This shows up much more clearly in the wage statistics than in the statistics for gross domestic product. As wages fell, the mix of the financial sector, insurance and real estate (the FIRE sector: Financial, Insurance, Real Estate) has increased its share of total GDP considerably. Consequently the fall in people's standard of living is much higher than it appears from looking at GDP figures.

If the world had taken Friedrich List's path to economic integration and globalization, as Europe did with its internal market, globalization would have been a positive-sum game for all countries. The problem with globalization as it is practised today is that real wages fall drastically in the countries that are left behind, deindustrialized, in its wake. In fact, wages peaked in most Latin American countries around the same time they did in Peru. These countries, in fact, were richest when, according to the World Bank, they did everything wrong and protected their ineffective industries. Many countries in Asia, like Mongolia, did the same, and so did most of the countries in the former Second World, including Russia itself. There is little desire to discuss this, but the fact remains that the notoriously inefficient industries of the centrally planned economies in most cases created a far higher standard of living than capitalism does in the same countries today. Even when Estonia, portrayed as one of the big success stories, joined the EU in 2005, a worker producing mobile phones was paid an hourly wage of 1 Euro, less than one tenth of the income of someone sweeping the streets of Frankfurt or Paris. Having employed the same economic theories as those of globalization, Europe has created its own internal tensions similar to those present in the global economy.

The mechanisms we can observe in Peru, and which we shall later examine more closely in the case of Mongolia, make it extremely difficult to create middle-income countries. A national economy is either so strong that its industrial sector survives and it remains in the club of rich countries, or it is deindustrialized and ends up in the group racing to the bottom. The phenomenon is comparable to the problems facing national airlines today. As in many industries, you are either very big, or you specialize. Medium-sized airlines have a hard time. An airline either grows to a network big enough to feed into its hub or hubs profitably, or – if it falls below a certain occupancy level – it either goes bankrupt or becomes a regional airline flying passengers to the hubs of the surviving larger airlines. The airlines Swissair and Swiss are examples of these mechanisms at work, as are most European airlines. In the same way that medium-sized airlines have problems surviving as global players in a deregulated market, small and middle-sized industrial economies cannot survive sudden free trade. In both cases – nations and airlines – minimum efficient sizes exist below which it is impossible to survive profitably. In both cases the alternative to surviving or going bankrupt is integrating with neighbours. If we had allowed these middling industrial economies – like Peru and Mongolia – to develop their industries through protection, gradually integrating them with their neighbours, some day they could have become strong enough to compete in a global free market. Instead, neo-classical economic theory has figuratively bombed Mongolia 'back to the Stone Age', to use an American expression from the Vietnam War. Robert McNamara, former president of the World Bank, has been accused of coining this term while he was Secretary of State for Defense, but the expression seems to have originated among the career military. As we shall see, far subtler ways exist of returning countries to the Stone Age than carpet-bombing and napalm.

5

Globalization and Primitivization: How the Poor Get Even Poorer

That all Negroes shall be prohibited from weaving either Linnen or Woollen, or spinning or combing of Wooll, or working at any Manufacture of Iron, further than making it into Pig or Bar iron: That they be also prohibited from manufacturing of Hats, Stockings, or Leather of any Kind... Indeed, if they set up Manufactures, and the Government afterwards shall be under a Necessity of stopping their Progress, we must not expect that it will be done with the same Ease that now it may.

Joshua Gee,
Trade and Navigation of Great Britain Considered, 1729

Colonies and poverty

While unpleasant, the above quotation is sadly indicative of hundreds of years of economic policy. Not only any economic policy, however, but *the* policy pursued by Europe as it took off economically in the early modern period. From today's perspective it none the less appears striking primarily because of its honesty, because it so openly admits that the goal of the policy is to keep the colonies as pure suppliers of raw materials. Traditionally, colonies have always been forcedly barred from establishing manufacturing in order to concentrate on supplying raw materials, but while the term itself may have become politically incorrect, the practice definitely continues.

In the previous chapter we argued with Werner Sombart that industrialization is at the core of capitalism itself, so barring colonies from industrialization was therefore tantamount to condemning them to poverty. This section of the book discusses how deindustrialization can lead to the opposite of development, to retrogression and economic primitivization. One of the mechanisms contributing to this is the Vanek-Reinert effect,[1] which causes the most advanced economic sectors in the least advanced trading nation to be the first casualties of instant free trade. As the virtuous circles based on increasing returns are put in reverse, the world periphery experiences a sequence of deindustrialization, deagriculturization, and depopulation, mechanisms that can be observed today from southern Mexico to Moldova. Migration to the areas of the world dominated by increasing returns activities appears as the only option for survival.

At the time of Joshua Gee, economic writers also had advice for what to do if the inhabitants of the colonies began to suspect the link between the ban on their industry and their own poverty. The solution was to confuse them by allowing them to export agricultural produce freely:

> Because People in the Plantations, being tempted with a free Market for their Growths all over *Europe,* will all betake themselves to raise them, to answer the prodigious Demand of that extensive Free Trade, and their Heads be quite taken off from Manufactures, the only thing which our Interest can clash with theirs... (Mathew Decker, *An Essay on the Causes of the Decline of the Foreign Trade*, 1744)

The parallel to today's situation is telling. Deindustrialized developing countries are tempted with free export of agricultural products to the EU and the US, and so forget their desire to industrialize. Yet no country has ever become rich by exporting foodstuffs without also having an industrial sector. The risk is that the rich countries become dependent on food produced by people so poor they can barely afford to eat it themselves.

Spain, which, as we have seen, had been deindustrialized by the flows of gold and silver it extracted from the New World, had managed to develop some industries again in the early eighteenth century. However, she had to reduce her tariff levels during the peace negotiations with the Netherlands in Utrecht in 1713 following the War of Spanish Succession, and again became a victim of deindustrialization and increasing poverty among the general population. When the consequences of deindustrialization showed themselves to be catastrophic, the Spaniards burned many of those deemed responsible for free trade concessions. The luckiest ones were executed before being burned.[2]

Around 1750 German economist Johann Heinrich Gottlob von Justi was therefore able to take for granted that all countries forced to produce only raw materials would soon understand that they were being kept 'artificially' poor. Justi could not predict, however, that Adam Smith and the English classical economists would soon create an economic theory which for the first time made colonization morally defensible. Not that Smith's moral and economic works were in favour of colonies per se, but the theoretical abstractions he propagated made it possible to argue righteously that some countries should be manufacturers while others were delegated to producing raw materials. Since labour now became the measuring rod – and all kinds of labour could be measured in hours of work – there was simply no need for the latter countries to industrialize, as there was no benefit.

According to Adam Smith and the English classical economists, the American colonies and the rest of Europe would be making a big mistake in trying to follow England's example of industrialization. Much like today's zealots of globalization, Smith and his followers argued that an era of world economic harmony would automatically be created as soon as the forces of the market were given free reign. England would then be able to import raw materials from the four corners of the world and export its manufactured goods in return. No European power followed this advice, and in Norway even nineteenth-century economists who were normally considered 'burning liberals,' – such as Anton Martin Schweigaard (1808–70), agreed that the country had to industrialize through active policy. The ideological debate in nineteenth-century continental Europe was not whether the rest of Europe should follow England's path to industrialization – virtually everyone agreed on that – the point of discussion was the balance between state and private activity.

Looking at how the USA today leads in the rhetoric of globalization, the similarity to the role played by England in the nineteenth century is striking. It is particularly interesting to note that the United States then fought long and hard against the economic theories and policies that today they vehemently support. The first American Secretary of the Treasury, Alexander Hamilton (1757–1804), was an important theorist with regard to the importance of industrialization. For more than ten years I have brought along images of dollar bills to my lectures that depicted American politicians whose economic strategies were not accepted by the Washington institutions: Benjamin Franklin, George Washington, Alexander Hamilton, Ulysses S. Grant and Abraham Lincoln. All wanted to industrialize the United States under the protection of tariffs – in clear opposition to the advice of English economists and a continuous flow of sarcastic remarks by English politicians and economists over a period of 150 years. The nineteenth-century saying in the USA was 'Don't do as the English tell you to do, do as the English did'. As already indicated in Chapter 2, today's best advice to Third World countries is 'Don't do as the Americans tell you to do, do as the Americans did'.

The American turnaround from defender of the rights of poor countries to classic imperial power is relatively recent. When in 1941 Winston Churchill used all his charm to convince President Franklin D. Roosevelt to enter the war, Roosevelt took the opportunity to vent his frustration over the historical injustice of English economic policy. Here Roosevelt's son, Elliot, tells the story of the historic meeting on a battleship off the coast of Newfoundland:

> Churchill shifted in his armchair. 'The British Empire trade agreements,' he began heavily, 'are –'

> Father broke in. 'Yes. Those Empire trade agreements are a case in point. It's because of them that the people of India and

Africa, of all the colonial Near East and Far East, are still as backward as they are.'

Churchill's neck reddened and he crouched forward. 'Mr President, England does not propose for a moment to lose its favoured position among the British Dominions. The trade that has made England great shall continue, and under conditions prescribed by England's ministers.'

'You see,' said Father slowly, 'it is along in here somewhere that there is likely to be some disagreement between you, Winston, and me. I am firmly of the belief that if we are to arrive at a stable peace it must involve the development of backward countries. Backward peoples. How can this be done? It can't be done, obviously, by eighteenth-century methods. Now –'

'Who is talking about eighteenth-century methods?'
'Whichever of your ministers recommends a policy which takes wealth in raw materials out of a colonial country, but which returns nothing to the people of that country in consideration. Twentieth-century methods involve bringing industry to these colonies. Twentieth-century methods include increasing the wealth of a people by increasing their standard of living, by educating them, by bringing them sanitation – by making sure that they get a return for the raw wealth of their community.'[3]

Thus, only sixty-odd years ago, we find the US using all its power to contest the economic theory that all countries could become wealthy no matter what they produced. The more cynical of my Latin American friends would claim that this was part of an American plot to take over Britain's position as global hegemon. I think the Marshall Plan shows there was more to it than that. From 1776 to the end of the Second World War, American economic practice in fact constituted a prolonged war against the economic theories which they today force on the developing world. The Americans, however, were not at all alone in this. As we have seen, an uninterrupted continuity in this type of thinking exists – the fundamental idea that only certain economic activities produce wealth – from the late fifteenth century to Roosevelt's attack on Churchill. In fact, in light of a longer historical perspective, faith in the market's ability to automatically create harmony is limited to a few, quickly overcome historical parentheses.

One of these parentheses occurred when Adam Smith's trade theory first crossed the line from theory into practice in the 1840s, but it did not last long. In 1904, Cambridge economist W. Cunningham could thus unapologetically write a book entitled *The Rise and Decline of the Free Trade Movement*. For the sake of the poor of this world, we may hope to see this title published again soon. It is, however, interesting to note that earlier waves of globalization came to an end because the hegemon itself was hurt. Globalization then destroyed English agriculture in much the same way it perhaps destroys American manufacturing now.

From 1990 onwards we again began to experience one of these historical parentheses. Unlike today, however, nineteenth-century English trade theory had been ceaselessly pummelled by a balancing theoretical tradition, successfully practised in the US and in continental Europe, and so its damage was largely limited to the Third World. A looming threat in today's situation is that the alternative, production-focused theories have been almost entirely extinguished. The neo-classical paradigm and its successors have acquired a monopoly on what is considered acceptable economic theory. This is the reason why the conditions of the poor will probably have to deteriorate even further before things can change for the better. We may have to await something akin to the global version of the 1848 revolutions. World hegemons have twice given up their insistence on 'free trade' and ideological liberalism and allowing poor laggard countries to catch up though late industrialization. On both occasions – after 1848 and after 1947 – this happened as a result of communist threats to the entire world economic system. What the results of today's religious fundamentalism will be remains to be seen.

Primitivization as an economic phenomenon and how it works

The idea of progress that emerged during the Renaissance also contains within it the possibility of its opposite – retrogression. In fact, the idea of the Re-naissance, re-birth, was inspired by seeing sheep grazing among the fabulous ruins of ancient Rome and by the rediscovery of ancient texts. Rise and decline were inexorably intertwined. Progress and modernization – as development was often referred to in the 1960s – in reverse become retrogression and primitivization. Economic activities, technologies and whole economic systems may fall back into modes of production and technologies that have been past history for some time. Systems based on increasing returns, synergies and systemic effects all require a critical mass; the need for scale and volume creates a 'minimum efficient size'. When the process of expansion is put in reverse and the necessary mass and scale disappears the system will collapse. After 1980, national economic systems subject to shock therapy collapsed like the airline network that loses 50 per cent of its passengers overnight. The sudden loss of volume caused by the shock therapy killed scale-based activities, shielding only activities subject to constant and diminishing returns (the traditional service sector and agriculture). This interconnectedness of factors explains why experience-based economic theorists, from James Steuart (1713–80) to Friedrich List stress the importance of gradualism in matters of free trade.

About ten years ago I was external examiner in a very interesting Ph.D. thesis defence that raised the problem of primitivization.[4] The thesis showed that the depletion of fish resources in South-East Asia made it increasingly unprofitable to use such modern technology as outboard engines. The fishermen returned to less capital-intensive and more 'primitive' methods. At its core, the normal form of primitivization as an economic phenomenon is tied to diminishing returns: where one factor of production has been produced by an act of God, and is available only in increasingly inferior qualities. Under such conditions, the technologies offered by the modern economy become unprofitable, and – if they have nowhere else to go – increasingly impoverished human beings struggle with increasingly primitive tools in order to produce at falling rates of productivity. Today the miners in the Bolivian city of Potosí – once the second largest city in the world after London – struggle with pickaxes to lure ore out of a material that has already been smelted at least once.

German economist Johann Heinrich von Thünen (1783–1850) drew a map of civilized society, with four concentric circles around a core of increasing returns activities – the city. Moving outwards from the city core, the use of capital gradually decreased and the use of nature gradually increased. Near the city the most perishable products are produced; dairy products, vegetables and fruit, and grain for bread is produced further out, and in the periphery there is hunting in the wilderness. Economists today have rediscovered von Thünen's approach to economic geography, but some totally miss the crucial point he stresses, that the increasing returns city activities needed tariff protection in order to get the entire system to function.[5]

Von Thünen drew the stage theories we have already discussed on to a map where the most 'modern' sector, manufacturing, formed the city core, and the most 'backward' sector, hunting and gathering, furthest from the city, formed the periphery; moving away from the city, the use of nature increases and the use of capital decreases. Only the city has authentic increasing returns, free from Nature's flimsy supply of resources of different qualities. As one moves outwards from the city, man-made comparative advantage gradually diminishes and nature-made comparative advantage increases.

Primitivization occurs when a labour market no longer has the core city activities, and human beings are forced back into the diminishing return activities we have previously discussed. They confront 'the flexible wall of diminishing returns', as John Stuart Mill calls it. Diminishing returns constitute 'a highly elastic and extensible band, which is hardly ever so violently stretched that it could not possibly be stretched any more, yet the pressure of which is felt long before the final limit is reached, and felt more severely the nearer that limit is approached'.[6]

As manufacturing industries die out, the systemic effects also retrogress. In his study of the Mexican National Innovation System, Mario Cimoli[7] shows how the NAFTA integration between the Mexican and the US economy affected the National Innovation System in Mexico. From a position of relative independence, the Mexican system developed into a core–periphery relationship between North American owners and Mexican subsidiaries. This recalls the centre–periphery dependence theories of classical development economics. Killing the core of von Thünen's system – the city activities – thus primitivizes the whole system. Von Thünen and his contemporaries in continental Europe and the United States understood this, but his contemporary David Ricardo and his descendants did not. They had removed the tools necessary for this kind of reasoning from their toolbox. That's why the Washington institutions could do what they did in Mongolia.

The loss of increasing returns and plummeting real wages – the case of Mongolia

In Mongolia's capital of Ulaanbaatar the situation was dire in March 2000. As the only non-Asian participant I was part of a conference held in the country's parliament, the purpose of which was to set out a strategic course for Mongolia's economy. In the wake of the Cold War, the country's previously considerable industrial sector had been virtually eradicated. Statistics showed that, one by one, all of the country's various industries had disappeared, beginning with the most advanced. Even the production of goods where imports had not supplanted local production was down drastically. Statistics showed that the production of bread was down by 71 per cent, and the production of books and newspapers by 79 per cent, without the population having diminished. Mongolians, in other words, probably ate and read less than before. In only a few years, real wages had been almost halved and unemployment was rampant. The country's imports exceeded the value of exports by a factor of two, and the real interest rate, corrected for inflation, was 35 per cent.[8]

The only sectors that, according to the national industrial statistics, were expanding, were the production of alcohol, which showed a minimal growth, and the collection and preparation of 'combed down' from birds (to the extent this can be defined as an industry), which had more than doubled since the fall of the Berlin Wall. Closing down the country's steel mills and newspapers and sending its population out to collect bird down cannot be considered anything but a primitivization of the economy. The more I studied Mongolia in the months that followed, the clearer it became that this nation, vanquished in the Cold War, was, for all practical purposes, being subjected to a Morgenthau Plan.

During the fifty years preceding the reforms of 1991, Mongolia had slowly but successfully built a diversified industrial sector. The share of agriculture in the national product had declined steadily from 60 per cent in 1940 to about 16 per cent in the mid-1980s. However, the de facto Morgenthau Plan proved exceedingly successful in deindustrializing Mongolia. Half a century of industry-building in Mongolia was virtually annihilated over a period of only four years, from 1991 to 1995. In most industrial sectors, production was down by more than 90 per cent in physical volume since the country had opened up to the rest of the world, almost overnight, in 1991.

Meanwhile, in March 2000, not far from my meeting in the capital, between two and three million herding animals were dead or dying from the lack of pasture. To the extent that the global media reported this event, it was blamed on global warming. Studying the data that had been made available to me, however, it gradually became clear that what had killed these animals was not global warming, but the global economy. The way in which Mongolia had been integrated into the global economy had resurrected an ancient economic mechanism: diminishing returns to scale on land resources. Years ago, when I taught economics at American universities, this law was one of the first things we taught our first-year undergraduates.

The combination of deindustrialization and deconstruction of the state had created large-scale unemployment in Mongolia. Many people had been forced to return to their ancestral way of living: nomadic pastoralism. Space was not really the issue. Mongolia is as large as France, Great Britain and Austria put together, but has only 2.5 million inhabitants. The climate, however, is subarctic and fragile, a landscape where tractor-tracks can remain for hundreds of years. July is the only month without frost, and the many herds of animals graze on mounds of what looks like freeze-dried grass. In 1990, before the fall of the Berlin Wall, Mongolians shared their lands with 21 million herding animals – sheep, cows, goats and camels. Losing their jobs in industry and government a large number of Mongolians turned back to herding, the mode of production of their forefathers. As a consequence of this, the number of grazing animals had risen by 12 million to 33 million in ten years. After a few mild years, a normal winter followed, and the two to three million animals that died that year represented only a few years' worth of growth to the animal population. Mongolia was thus welcomed into the twenty-first century by a mechanism already proclaimed in the Book of Genesis, but no longer at work in the industrialized world: 'The Land could not Bear them All'.

As the dust settled around the remains of the Berlin Wall, Mongolia quickly rose to become the World Bank's 'star student' of the former Second World. Mongolia opened its economy entirely almost overnight, and faithfully followed the advice given by the Washington institutions, the World Bank and the International Monetary Fund, to minimize the state and let the market take control. Mongolia was supposed to find its place in the global economy by specializing where its comparative advantage lay. The result was that the Mongolian economy was driven back from the age of industry to that of pastoralism. The nomadic economy, however, was unable to sustain the same population density as the industrial system, and the outcome was a combined ecological, economic and human catastrophe.

The warnings against such devolution did not only exist in the Bible and in the forgotten works of non-canonical economists. Some of the loudest caveats were uttered by the very same English economists proudly claimed as ancestors by the economists advising Mongolia through the Washington institutions. As we have seen, men like John Stuart Mill and Alfred Marshall were all too aware of the crucial importance of increasing and diminishing returns to scale for understanding the economic mechanisms of civilization.

During our meeting in Parliament at Ulaanbaatar, the local employees of the World Bank presented three possible scenarios for the country's future development: Mongolia could either grow by 3 per cent per annum, by 5 per cent per annum, or by 7 per cent per annum. The curve representing 7 per cent cumulative growth per annum naturally had a tendency to go through the roof. But they only spoke of hypothetical yearly growth; no attempt was made to present an explanation of how the rapid decline of the economy could be stopped, nor was it discussed how new industries could develop with a real interest rate of 35 per cent. Instead, the local representatives of USAID presented us with a complaint over Mongolia's lacking culture of entrepreneurship. I remember finding this argument somewhat absurd, for few entrepreneurs are able to make money with the real interest rate of 35 per cent. The interest rate was kept high to prevent a local version of the Asian financial crisis, with the usual result that the real economy is sacrificed in order to save banks and the financial sector.

The meeting in Ulaanbaatar gradually became more and more surreal. The well-paid consultants from the World Bank had brought documents and models that had precious little to do with the Mongolian reality. They were standardized studies which all developing countries, no matter their particular situation, were offered. Later my Western colleagues, closer to the World Bank, explained to me how it works. All countries receive a standardized presentation, where practically the only change of the analytical part in each case is the country's name. Because the theory itself is not sensitive to contexts, this approach is logical. The only problem appears when a representative fails to use the 'Find and Replace' function in his word-processing program properly, and all appearances of the word 'Ecuador', for example, are not replaced by the word 'Mongolia'. Embarrassed government officials then have to ignore the scattered appearances of the wrong country's name in the reports on their own long-term development. If the members of the Mongolian Parliament had known what was going on it could have been awkward, but they did not.

The situation was reminiscent of Franz Kafka's *The Trial*. Much like Joseph K, the hero and victim in Kafka's work, the Mongolians are overwhelmed by decisions made on the basis of a reality that does not exist, and which anyway has nothing to do with them. If they only open their borders to the global economy, their country will automatically plug into a growth curve of 3, 5, or 7 per cent per annum. The 'Court', though, here represented by the Washington institutions, does not even use its own theories correctly, becoming nothing but the pretext for a headless and unadulterated ideology. In the logic of this ideology, there is nothing that would have prevented Bill Gates from having built the same fortune he has today from goat-herding in Mongolia. Unless all economic activities are qualitatively alike as carriers of economic development, standard textbook economics tends to collapse.

Only a few months later the level of surrealism increased when American economist Jeffrey D. Sachs, a man who must bear his part of the responsibility for the economic policies which halved Mongolia's real wages, suggested in the pages of *The Economist* that the country should specialize in producing computer software. Since the theories proposed by the World Bank happily live in a realm where contextual concerns do not matter, Sachs could, with the best of intentions, propose this brilliant strategy without considering the tiny detail that only 4 per cent of Mongolia's inhabitants outside of the capital have access to electricity. Not to mention that they obviously lacked resources for computers and the education necessary to harness them.

Only in that strange world of economics textbooks can nomadic yak-herders without telephones and electricity suddenly compete with and supply Silicon Valley. Only in economic theory does it take the same amount of time to grow a tree as to cut it down, namely the same nanosecond. The invented story of Marie Antoinette, supposedly asking why the people didn't eat cake when they lacked bread, was once the object of ridicule and fuel for the most powerful revolution of modern history. Now, the stories are sadly not invented, as Sachs in fact *asks* why Mongolians don't specialize in advanced technology when they lack the most basic of infrastructure and industries. An important cause of this seeming absurdity is embedded in the structure of economic science as practised in most academic institutions. Professional status and prestige is gained by publishing papers in journals reviewed by like-minded peers, and not by studying the real world. As in Kafka's case there is no connection between the reality reported by the authorities and the one observable in the field. As with Kafka's main protagonist, the Mongolian economy was destroyed by powers the people were not meant to understand. The industrial statistics for Mongolia supplied by the Washington institutions only begin after most of the industry had already disappeared. The one statistic they *do* have is identical to the one made available to me in Mongolia for the corresponding period, so it is not that the data is missing. This strategic cancellation of history completes the Kafka metaphor. According to the official statistics of the World Bank and the International Monetary Fund, Mongolia's industry never existed. Orwell's 'Ministry of Truth' is not far away.

Such experiences began to form a pattern for me, which stretched back to the observations I first made while living in Lima at the end of the 1970s, when the results of the policies proposed by the Washington institutions were becoming clear to the naked eye. Abrupt free trade caused industrial death – and the key increasing returns activities were killed off. Massive unemployment, falling real wages (see Figure 14) and mounting malnutrition naturally went hand in hand with a dogmatic faith in what was called 'free trade' and 'market forces', but which really was that oxymoron 'managed free trade', that caused increased poverty and human suffering. There was no Schumpeterian 'creative destruction' where new and better opportunities would replace the old.

Large volumes of fresh milk were then being poured into Peru's rivers, while milk of a much lower quality – produced with subsidized European powdered milk – filled the supermarkets in Lima, further weighing down an already overburdened trade balance. European farmers drove Peruvian farmers from their own markets. But 'the market' did not cause this. Political power did, by creating prices both for powdered milk and for the transportation of fresh milk that were far from what would have resulted from a free market. Europe exported its surplus milk – produced by farmers who were unable to compete on the world market – at subsidized prices to countries like Peru, and probably, as is the case with similar US exports, got it accepted as foreign aid. Simultaneously, the World Bank and the International Monetary Fund forced Peru to raise its gasoline prices. They were, in other words, no longer allowed to use the national market price for their own gasoline, from their own oil. The price of gas had to rise. In the name of the market, Peru's national production of milk was outperformed by European prices through artificial prices – artificially low on milk and artificially high on gasoline – forced upon them from outside. Simultaneously, Europeans felt good for helping starving children.

At the time, this was an observation of a single absurdity – that power politics had perverse consequences which hurt developing economies. Later, it became clear that it was part of a broader pattern, of a process of development and modernization put into reverse gear. As American economist James K. Galbraith has pointed out, perhaps the most incredible part of this situation is that the economists responsible for the failed economic policies in the Second and Third Worlds today are still hailed as the greatest authorities on the matter. We have in a sense put Attila the Hun in charge of the reconstruction of Rome, with the predictable result that there is no discussion of the damage caused and how it could have been avoided. One of them, Jeffrey Sachs, has become a great champion of *palliative economics*, of giving aid to soothe the poverty and suffering his own economic policies helped create.

Globalization as a Morgenthau Plan for the Third World

Two major economic experiments took place in the late 1940s, from which the world at the time learned a lot. In many ways, the Americans, and the world, were taught not only that Roosevelt had been right in his accusations against Churchill and England's imperial economic policy, but also that the consequences of deindustrializing a country were so powerful and far-reaching, so devastating, that the experiment had to be aborted after only two years. The hard-won lessons of the Morgenthau and Marshall Plans, however, are being forgotten.

Politicians today abuse the concept of a Marshall Plan by using it to describe any large transfers of resources to poor countries. It cannot be emphasized strongly enough that the kernel of Marshall's plan was *re*industrialization; the demand and supply of capital was per se entirely secondary to the principal strategy of developing the industrial life of a nation. The Marshall Plan was implemented with heavy tariff protection of national industries and strict rules of currency transactions. It was fully acknowledged that jobs needed long-term protection, and that foreign exchange was a scarce resource. In my own country Norway, for example, this resulted in a total prohibition on the import of clothing until 1956, combined with severe restrictions on the transfer of funds abroad. Importing cars for private use was prohibited until 1960.

In my view, the process of globalization that has taken place since the mid-1980s – but particularly since the fall of the Berlin Wall – has taken the form of a Morgenthau Plan. Weak industrial economies in the Second and Third Worlds – metaphorically 'in transition' – have been subject to shock therapies, converting them literally overnight in some cases into untrammelled free trade. A nation like Mongolia had around 90 per cent of its substantial industry destroyed in the course of only two to three years; in countries like Russia and Peru, half of all industrial jobs were lost in a few, frantic years which also saw real wages halved. The correlation between such losses in employment and in real wages is not incidental. Globalization has become the new process of 'colonization' through what is a de facto Morgenthau Plan: a colony, now as five centuries ago, is fundamentally a country that is only allowed to produce raw materials.

The problem facing us today, however, is that *re*industrialization is far more difficult than it used to be. Even though the most extreme ideology sooner or later will have to succumb to horror at the economic crimes perpetrated in the name of globalization in the world's economic peripheries, the reversal of this process will be much harder than it was in 1947. In the twentieth century, poor countries could catch up with the rich through 'reverse engineering', through, for example, dismantling an American car and producing a national brand from a slightly different blueprint. In a situation where ever larger numbers of knowledge-intensive industries are protected by patents, this has become almost impossible. Industry is also becoming ever more 'weightless' and harder to nurture in specific geographic areas than before. Simultaneously, new service industries – where the

ITCs are the businesses that resemble traditional industries the most – have occupied the role of industry. Advanced service industries, however, are dependent on the demand of the old industrial sectors. They simply do not appear in nations of goat-farmers, because such nations lack the purchasing power required to demand the necessary goods and services. At the same time, such industries are hard to protect because they are, as previously mentioned, weightless and footloose. As always, cumulative causations are behind both development and underdevelopment, creating 'virtuous' and 'vicious' circles.

Deindustrialization and winner-killing effect of free trade

The *Rybczynski Theorem* of standard trade theory predicts that international trade will reinforce a nation's specialization in the factor – either capital or labour – that is used most intensively in its exports. 'For instance, when only labour grows, the output of the labour-intensive commodity expands, and the output of the capital-intensive commodity contracts. On the other hand, when only capital grows, the output of the capital-intensive commodity expands and the output of the labour-intensive commodity contracts.'[9]

An extension of this is what I have referred to as the Vanek-Reinert effect, or the winner-killing effect of international trade. When, following a situation of relative autarky, free trade suddenly opens up between a relatively advanced and a relatively backward nation, the most advanced and knowledge-intensive industry in the least advanced country will tend to die out. The most advanced sectors are the ones most subject to increasing returns and consequently the most sensitive to the drop in volume caused by sudden competition from abroad. This Vanek-Reinert effect was evident after the nineteenth-century unification of Italy and, in the 1990s, the first casualties of free trade were the Czech and Brazilian computer industries. In extreme cases, nations become almost completely deindustrialized – as in the case of Mongolia during the 1990s.

As international value chains become 'chopped up' through outsourcing, the most advanced nations specialize in capital- and innovation-intensive goods, where scale and increasing returns are key elements. The less advanced countries come to specialize in maquila-type (assembly plant) low-technology goods, bereft of scale effects at the assembly stage. A frequent effect of this is that free trade destroys more than it contributes in terms of national wealth. As an example, Mexican real wages dropped drastically as the NAFTA agreement slowly decimated traditional 'complete industries' while increasing the simple assembly (maquila) activities. The increasing returns industries died out in order to give birth to constant return activities, thus 'primitivizing' the national production system. Thus we experience cases of 'destructive destruction' – destruction where no regenerative activities take place.

A second-round effect of deindustrialization is its impact on the nation's Terms of Trade. The Terms of Trade refer to the relationship between the price of a country's export commodities and the price of its import commodities. If the price of a country's exports increases relative to imports, the country gets richer. With the opposite effect, it gets poorer.

Changes in Terms of Trade are a complex issue, but it is remarkable that the terms of trade in some small Latin American nations peaked during the period of highest industrial development, in the 1970s. As industry collapsed, so did the prices for the raw materials the countries exported. Figure 15 shows this phenomenon in the case of Peru. Deindustrialization and falling terms of trade seem to be connected in such a way that nations may be hit simultaneously by two negative economic shocks. The connection can be explained by a combination of two factors: the collapse of trade union power and the loss of industrial employment removed the floor of the labour market, creating falling wages. The pressures of the international commodity markets could then press down both the relative price of the commodity and of national wages. With no alternative employment for the workforce, commodity production could also spread into the areas of diminishing returns, reducing the marginal productivity of labour.[10] A self-reinforcing vicious circle has been created, and can only be stopped by reintroducing increasing returns activities to the nation.

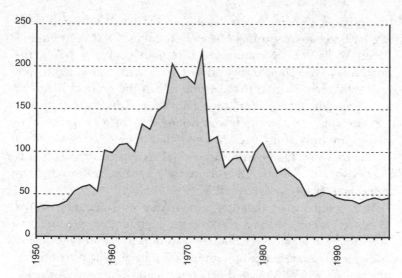

Although the development of the Terms of Trade (export prices as they relate to prices of imports) is a complex phenomenon – influenced, for example, by the oil shock of the 1970s – we can observe a surprising degree of improvement of the Terms of Trade as Peru industrialized, while deindustrialization brought the opposite effect.

Source: Santiago Roca and Luis Simabuco, 'Natural Resources, Industrialization and Fluctuating Standards of Living in Peru, 1950–1997' A Case Study of Activity-Specific Economic Growth' in Erik Reinert (ed.), *Globalization, Economic Development and Inequality: An Alternative Perspective*, Cheltenham, 2004

Figure 15 Peru's Terms of Trade 1950–2000

The early twentieth-century Australian argument for the creation of an industrial sector, albeit not internationally competitive, was designed to prevent exactly this chain of events from taking place. The existence of an alternative labour market in the manufacturing sector would prevent wool production from going into marginal areas by creating a 'wage floor', under which wages would not move, not even in the commodity sector.[11]

In some cases, typically that of Mexico, deindustrialization is followed by a specialization in the technological dead-end products, bereft of increasing return effects. The product lifecycle theories in international trade that we have already referred to in the preceding chapter were created in the late 1960s and early 1970s by Harvard Business School economists Ray Vernon and Louis Wells.[12] They maintained that poor countries will automatically have a comparative advantage in mature products (those using old technologies) towards the end of the product lifecycle, thus impeding their potential for innovation. This is the argument already alluded to in the Introduction, that the globalized value chains are broken up in such a way that poor countries tend to specialize in technological dead-ends. This type of production is farmed out to the poor world precisely because the production appears to be labour-intensive.

If a comparative advantage in mature and unsophisticated products can be used as a platform for continuous upgrading – as it has been in Japan and China – this is only a transitory problem. However, the experience of nations in the geographic proximity of the United States – squeezed between US and Chinese industries – indicates that the comparative advantage in innovationless activities may become a permanent feature. As I have previously argued, the understanding of lifecycles both of products and of technologies is an important factor which must be considered in order to understand 'Schumpeterian underdevelopment'.[13]

The perils of the 'commodity lottery'

Economic historians have recently introduced the term 'commodity lottery' when discussing economic development. This is a useful term, since the characteristics of different commodities will influence national economies in many ways: the 'commodity lottery' will in many ways shape the national economy and determine the potential for cultivating innovations and imperfect competition.

Some natural resources produce greater linkages to knowledge-intensive sectors than others. In the early twentieth century waterfalls for the production of electricity were perfect examples of this kind of 'enforced linkages': the loss of energy was, at the time, so high per kilometre travelled that the new industrial centres dependent on electricity had to be built directly under the waterfall. The impossibility of transporting Norway's raw material

– hydroelectric power – over large distances caused Norway's economic periphery to be industrialized rather than transporting the raw material to the European Continent where both markets and investors were located. In contrast, the smelting of Bolivian zinc was done in England for the longest time.

One particularly interesting example is given by Cuban social scientist Fernando Ortiz, in his 1940 book *Cuban Counterpoint*.[14] From an economic point of view, Cuba had an absolute advantage in two tropical crops, sugar and tobacco. In Cuban society tobacco was the hero, sugar the villain. Tobacco – predominantly grown on the western part of the island – created a middle class, a free bourgeoisie. Sugar – grown on the rest of the island – created two classes of people: masters and slaves. The cultivation and picking of tobacco created a demand for specialized skills: tobacco leaves were harvested individually, and the market price of the product depended on the skill of the picker. Growing tobacco bred skills, individuality and modest wealth. 'Sugar was an anonymous industry, the mass of labour of slaves or gangs of hired workmen, under the supervision of capital's overseers.' Tobacco created national ownership, sugar the dependence of foreign multinationals.

Where tobacco required skills, care and judgement, sugar only required brute force in cutting the commodity. Cuban tobacco carries its origins with the imperfect competition that comes with a brand name – like the expensive cigars 'Partagas' or 'Upmann' – while sugar is a commodity that 'comes to the world without a last name, like a slave', as Ortiz puts it. Tobacco means stable prices; sugar means wildly fluctuating prices. A skilled tobacco selector can distinguish seventy or eighty different shades of tobacco; whereas, for the cutting of cane, timing is not important. Tobacco is delicately cut leaf by leaf with a small sharp knife, making sure that the rest of the plant survives; the sugar plant is brutally slashed with a big machete. Working with sugar is a trade; working with tobacco an art. The origins of the wealth of western Cuba and the poverty of the eastern part of the island were 'activity-specific': the economic and social outcomes were inherent to the crop itself.

As the Renaissance and Enlightenment students of the Dutch Republic and Venice claimed – and today one might add those of

Japan and Switzerland – the best draw in the commodity lottery was to have no commodity. This forced the nation directly into a man-made, rather than a nature-based comparative advantage, subject to increasing rather than diminishing returns. As the great Montesquieu (1689–1755) noted:

> The barrenness of the earth renders men industrious, sober, inured to hardship, courageous, and fit for war; they are obliged to procure by labour what the earth refuses to bestow spontaneously.[15]

Technological change: central vs. peripheral effects

We have already observed the importance of waves of new technologies that periodically change our technological environment. However, these techno-economic paradigms affect the centre and periphery differently. Carlota Perez treats their cyclical aspects in terms of income distribution, and also looks at the geographical aspects of financial crises between the core and periphery nations.[16]

Nations specialized in the *production* of new technologies generally experience very different effects from the consuming nations or the nations supplying the raw materials needed for that same technology. In the nineteenth century, the experience of cotton-growing states in the south of the United States was very different from that of the cotton-spinning states in the north, and in fact the friction between these two groups of states – and the north's effort to industrialize and spin cotton – was an important element leading up to the American Civil War. In the Fordist technological revolution the increased demand for rubber had some very negative welfare effects in the rubber-producing countries. A particularly ugly case – the so-called Putumayo Affair – involving the mistreatment, slavery and brutality towards the Amazon Indian rubber collectors, created a major scandal in England and Europe in 1912–13. The sheer volume of the official English documents on the affair indicates its importance at the time.[17] The north entered a new Fordist techno-economic paradigm, but the effects in the roadless Amazon periphery were mainly negative. The opera house in the Amazon town of Manaos still testifies to the profits made in the trading, rather than in the physical production, of natural rubber.

The differing geographical impact of technical change – creation at the core and destruction in the periphery – brings us to the concept of the *dual economy* which was identified by early development economists as being a key characteristic of underdeveloped countries. A modern export sector – an economic enclave – was not integrated in the rest of the economy. With increasing import substitution, industrialization and a more diversified industrial sector, this gap between the 'modern' and 'backward' sectors of the national economy was greatly reduced.

Concomitant with deindustrialization and falling protection in the late 1980s, many small and medium-sized poor nations saw the diversity of their productive sector being whittled away. They were once again moving towards an enclave economy: economic monoculture based on the export of raw materials. At the same time the rolling back of the state made it more difficult to monitor the (mostly foreign-owned) enclaves. A recent example of this is the large number of Chilean-owned mines in Peru that imports all the necessities, including food and drink, by air from Chile, bypassing any Peruvian customs. In Africa the growth of private armies, seen as necessary today to protect mining companies, is another example of 'retrogression' to the early days of colonialism when private armies held sway. Thus many Third World countries are now in danger of losing the development gains they achieved in the post-Second World War era.

Another aspect of technological change is that new technologies may be used both to upgrade and to downgrade the skills of labour, a phenomenon which takes place in all countries, both those of the centre and those of the periphery. New technology can be used in order to produce Burger King cashier terminals with symbols which eliminate the need for operators to be able to read and write. Such developments, however, are much more serious in developing countries, where the lack of qualified jobs – often the extreme shortage of job possibilities for university graduates – is a serious problem. Not only are these countries not using their own resources (they produce far from their 'production possibility frontiers'), perhaps only 20–30 per cent of the economically active have what in the north would be defined as a 'job', but innovations may also come in a guise which reduces the numbers of qualified jobs.

In a paper, two economists from the UN Economic Commission for Latin America and the Caribbean (ECLAC/CEPAL), Mario Cimoli and Jorge Katz, demonstrate these 'deskilling' effects in Argentine automotive production on the employment of engineers.[18] They argue that these developments are pushing Latin American economies into a trap, and show how the region may be locked into a low-growth pattern that reinforces the technology gap between the rich and poor countries. In other words, the poor specialize in being poor.

Strategies formulated around the ideas of National Systems of Innovation are also finding their way to the Third World. Such visions of 'innovation-based societies' are, however, normally based on an insufficient qualitative understanding of the different ways innovations affect wages in different businesses. For example, information technology (IT) creates very different results around Microsoft's headquarters in Seattle compared to the hotel industry. In the hotel business as well as in the used book business across Europe, the use of IT has led to falling margins and increased downward pressures on wages and profits. Using the standard definition of 'competitiveness' – an ability to create higher real wages – in these industries in isolation, IT-based innovations have resulted in *decreased* rather than *increased* competitiveness.

Innovations are generally divided into two categories. Microsoft products provide *product innovations*, produced under huge increasing returns, huge barriers to entry, huge profits, and an ability to pay very high wages. This same innovation hits the hotel industry in Venice as a *process innovation*, affecting how people book hotels. More perfect information available on the net increases price competition among hotels in Venice and puts pressure on profit margins and the ability to pay high wages. The same process innovation in the airline industry produces similar results. While IT increases wages around Microsoft's headquarters, the same technology puts downward pressures on the wages of air hostesses in Europe.

Although it is well known in innovation economics that product innovations and process innovations often have different effects on employment, not enough emphasis has been given to the fact that innovations may actually reduce value added in certain industries and geographic areas.

'The death of distance': implications for the periphery

Geography and distance have always been viewed as economic factors that promote the spread of production across the world. Using an idea presented by German economist Franz Oppenheimer (1864–1943), we can imagine, as a starting point, a world devoid of the costs, frictions and lags created by geography and time. To this a factor representing these costs, frictions and lags of time and geography in the real world would have to be added. The importance of geography as an economic factor is combined and compounded with the factor time: what Alfred Chandler calls 'economies of speed'. Oppenheimer calls this factor '*Transportwiderstand*', 'transport resistance', or 'resistance caused by time and geography'. Historically, Australia's geographic isolation gave the country a higher transport resistance than that of Ireland. Time and distance, in other words, provided natural protection for the country's manufacturing industry.

One key feature of technological change during the last century has been the decrease of this transport resistance – sometimes called 'the death of distance'. This has clearly made catching up – getting the national economies into increasing return activities – in peripheral countries more difficult. We would argue that the extreme transport resistance present in traditional service industries which, including public administration, provide a large percentage of First World jobs, combined with the non-globalization of the labour market, together form the main reason why the world does not experience a strong trend towards factor–price equalization downwards. Only teleporting – as seen in science fiction movies – would have totally eliminated transport resistance, opening up international trade in traditional service industries.

A transport and time resistance of virtually zero makes protection meaningless in many new industries. At the same time, those with ideas that could previously be profitably developed within a national innovation system may often have to travel to the parts of the world where the innovative *milieu* and necessary venture capital can be found. While attending the annual convention of the Association of University Research Parks (AURP) in Madison, Wisconsin, a few years ago, I was struck by remarks from representatives from universities in the American Midwest who complained that all those with good research ideas left the Midwest to go either to the East or the West Coast where the industrial *milieux* and the venture capital was located. These forces are clearly at work – even more strongly so – in the Third World. We therefore run the risk that the good ideas produced by a peripheral National Innovation System will be sucked into the global economy in the First World. That innovations frequently will take place in the centre, although the invention took place in the periphery, is another dimension of what we could call Schumpeterian development geography.

Destructive destruction and Schumpeterian development geography

Creative destruction is an important term in Schumpeterian economics, a term that originated with Friedrich Nietzsche.[19] Like Schumpeter, Nietzsche saw the process of creative destruction as a positive one. The eminent Renaissance historian Jacob Burckhardt (1818–97), Nietzsche's friend and colleague at the University of Basle, was, however, of a different opinion. In his view 'there are (or at any rate there seem to be) absolutely destructive forces under whose hoofs no grass grows'.[20] Destruction and creativity may take place in entirely different parts of the globe, for example when the textile mills of Manchester replaced the weavers of Bengal. In order to illustrate this dramatic effect, Marx quoted the English Governor-General, who wrote home to London that 'The misery hardly finds a parallel in the history of commerce. The bones of the cotton-weavers are bleaching the plains of India.'

The fact that the labour market itself is not globalized in our increasingly globalized economy leads directly to this type of 'destructive destruction' – sometimes with very serious consequences, as in the case of Mongolia. In addition, the fact that an increasing number of traded products are subject to copyrights and patents will only increase the tendency for creation to be concentrated in a few geographic areas. The previous techno-economic paradigm – Fordist mass production – made development thorough reverse engineering a viable option. This seems to be much less feasible in the future. The huge implications of the patent and copyright issues for global inequality is an issue which we are only now beginning to confront.

In my view, this collection of primitivization mechanisms works to create formidable barriers to economic development in the Third World. Together they produce what Gunnar Myrdal called 'perverse backwashes': more skilled labour and more capital tend to flow from the poor world to the rich world rather than the other way around.

Native peoples: a case of primitivization through government policy

For native peoples, globalization, if anything, increases the strong economic pressures they were already subject to under the nation-states. Like the Jews, aboriginal peoples became obstacles to the eighteenth-century project of building nation-states. As in Spain, until the fall of Franco, any minority language was seen as a threat to national unity. The difference between a dialect and a language, the old European saying goes, is that a language is essentially a dialect with its own army.

The Nordic welfare states also have their native peoples, Inuits in Greenland (a self-governed Danish territory) and Saami in Norway, Sweden and Finland. In Norway, until very recently, the Saami were prohibited from speaking their own language at school, and the account below of the Saami reindeer herders there shows how even an admired welfare state managed to 'primitivize' its own aboriginal culture. The case is all the more interesting because, compared to the majority of native cultures, this aboriginal group is in a uniquely favourable situation: in Norway the Saami possess a national monopoly to herd reindeer, and reindeer meat is considered a delicacy, frequently served at royal dinners both in Norway and as far away as the Court of the Principality of Monaco. Nevertheless, during the 1990s, their economic situation had deteriorated rapidly. The reason is a tale of governmental mismanagement over a period of twenty-five years where policies rooted in the planning paradigm made the Saami herders retrogress economically into a colonial-type situation.

In 1999 I found myself on the vast plateau of Finnmark, way beyond the Arctic Circle in northernmost Norway, with a brief from the Ministry of Agriculture in Oslo to find out why the Saami herders, in spite of their monopoly in producing a national luxury product, were getting poorer and poorer. I later clocked up 6,100 km in one car trip, visiting all the herders' organizations, covering the whole wide-stretched upper half of Norway, and probably visited more reindeer abattoirs old and new than any other living person. My subsequent reports were to make me a *persona non grata* in the same ministry.[21]

My first find was a strange anomaly in the local market for reindeer meat. The majority of herders in Finnmark were selling their animals on hoof to a few big slaughterhouses – 'listed slaughterhouses' in the government parlance – for what amounted to about 40 kroner (5 Euro) per kilo. However, a few herders who slaughtered locally and sold on the 'street market' managed to get a price per kilo, after taking into account the cost of slaughtering, that was more than 50 per cent higher. Observing widely different prices for identical goods at the same location is a strange phenomenon. My surprise was even greater when I found that in this supposed welfare state, only the wealthiest herders were selling at the high price. How had such a system arisen?

The economic decline of the Saami started in 1976, when reindeer herding – previously totally unregulated – was brought into the 'planned economy' through an annually negotiated 'Reindeer Agreement' between the Saami and the Norwegian government. A key item to be negotiated was the price the Saami were to receive for their meat. The official figures show that while a kilo of reindeer meat brought the Saami 68 kroner in 1976, in 1990 they only received 32 kroner for the same meat (in constant value kroner of 1990 (i.e. adjusted for inflation), so the numbers are directly comparable). From an impressive profit margin of 48 kroner a kilo in 1976, in 1990 the Saami households were operating at a loss.

The falling margins were a result of imposing a rigid price structure on a very cyclical production. Although not as extreme as the fluctuation in lemmings, the North Atlantic Oscillation (NAO) – similar to the *El niño* phenomenon on the west coast of the American continent – produces a wide fluctuation in the number of reindeer that can be sustained in the Arctic. The twentieth century brought four cyclical waves, where reindeer population peaked at about twice as many animals as during the trough.

The 1980s brought a huge increase in the reindeer population and the production of meat, and prices fell. In order to improve marketing, the Ministry of Agriculture named the Farmers' Meat Monopoly (Norsk Kjøtt) – at the time exercising a virtual monopoly of meat production in the closed Norwegian market – as 'market maker' and 'price regulator' for reindeer meat. The government gave the marketing rights of the aboriginal herders' products to their biggest competitor.

In the 1990s the sharp fall in prices was followed by a sharp fall in the volume of production, adding to the economic squeeze of the reindeer herders. Reindeer meat disappeared from the market, but prices failed to rise because the Ministry of Agriculture failed to increase the official 'target price'. The farmers' monopoly, Norsk Kjøtt, refused to recommend price increases for reindeer meat. During the 1980s, the herders had first experienced a halving of the prices for their goods – albeit with an increasing volume – and now the volume of production fell cyclically by half, virtually without any increase in the price per kilo. This meant effectively that the income of the herders fell by 50 per cent.

As the reindeer herders started losing money, the Norwegian government started handing out social welfare through a government grant for every kilo of meat produced. However, in order for the government to control this scheme, the Saami were forced to sell to a very few 'listed' slaughterhouses on a government shortlist. While an unofficial street market paid close to the old price, these 'listed slaughterhouses' only paid the low 'target price'. Thus, in order to receive welfare payments, the Saami herders were forced to sell at an artificially low price, while the few relatively well off could sell at a much higher price close to the old market price.

The government had created a monopsony – a monopoly on purchasing – the same mechanism used by the English government when the Indian competitors to the Manchester cotton producers were put out of business. In India, one company with one fixed low non-negotiable purchasing price produced an even more devastating effect than that on the reindeer herders (see page 190).

Parallel to this, new and much stricter sanitary rules were enforced, applying the same regime to the slaughtering and processing of animals at 20 degrees below zero on the new snow as in downtown Athens at 40 degrees above zero. Mandatory cockroach traps at 20 degrees below zero is one of the true stories the Saami tell about what killed their profitable aboriginal industry. Slaughtering, processing, and marketing had been the cultural and economic centre of their culture: now the economic activity of the herders stopped when their animals were herded on to the truck taking them to be slaughtered at a non-Saami abattoir and to be marketed by their competitors. The Saami in Norway had been reduced to providers of raw materials only, in a case of internal colonialism.

The Norwegian Association of Saami Reindeer Herders was under extreme pressure at the time, not only because of their members' deteriorating economic situation, but also because the effects of the cyclical variation of climate – and thus Nature's change in carrying capacity or sustainability – were blamed on herders' overgrazing. The Ministry's mental models came from the stability of the barns at the Agricultural University in Southern Norway, and climate was expressly excluded from their analyses. In addition – in contrast to the Ministries of Agriculture in Sweden and Finland – the Norwegian Ministry saw it as their mission to 'improve' the millennial practices of the herders with 'modern science'. Instead of seeing cyclical production as a result of cycles in climate, the Norwegian Ministry of Agriculture came very close to declaring the cyclical irresponsibility of aboriginal herders as the driving force. Indeed, Norway for a long time practised a kind of 'domestic orientalism' towards its aboriginals.

For several years I was an adviser to the Saami herders in their annual negotiations with the Norwegian government. The reindeer herders are only a small group within the Saami minority, where the majority of Saami have been integrated into 'Norwegian' professions. The setting was unequal. On one side of the table were representatives of all the many ministries involved and the Saami Parliament (as part of the 'government'), and on the other side the tiny aboriginal organization, having one and a half employees at the time, and myself. This was the first time in my life I was deeply ashamed to be a Norwegian. Refusing to see the dismal economic situation as a result of their own policy of fixed prices to a widely fluctuating production, the government – suffering from any lack of doubt in its own wisdom – was slowly making every herder dependent on social welfare. The same type of process in the Canadian Arctic was dubbed 'welfare colonialism' by anthropologist Robert Paine. This was a rare situation in which a 'free market' would actually greatly help to increase the income of a raw material producer. Only a few years earlier the aboriginal association had been thrown out of the negotiations, given the choice of either leaving through the window or through the door.

After heavy rounds of negotiations, the situation of the Saami herders has improved somewhat today. Herders' income more than doubled between 1999 and 2003. Those interested in the whole story are referred to the journal article in note 21. I think this story is interesting for a couple of reasons, one general and one very Scandinavian. The general one is this: at the same time this blatant mismanagement of the economy of the Norwegian aboriginals was carrying on, Norway had a high international profile – towards the World Bank for example – of protecting aboriginals elsewhere, e.g. in Brazil. Everywhere, both in Brazil and Norway, aboriginals of other nations tend to be seen as fascinating and exotic, while one's own aboriginals are somehow in the way. The biblical principle that you see the mote in your neighbour's eye, but you fail to see the beam in your own is clearly part of the problem.

The second – and Scandinavian – reason why this case study is important is because it foreshadows our discussion on the Millennium Goals in Chapter 7. I had studied aboriginal production in the Andes, but until 1999 my knowledge of reindeer herding was extremely limited. When I started my work with the herders, I therefore asked two of my colleagues at work – both previous vice-ministers on different sides of the right–left divide – how they thought the problem of the herders could be resolved. Their reaction was immediate and fully synchronized: this problem is so messy that the only way to solve it is to throw money at it. And this is exactly what the Norwegian government had been doing. In 1999 government subsidies to Norway's Saami reindeer herders equalled the value of the herders' net sales. The industry itself added no value over and above the government subsidies.

Meanwhile I have created a label for this attitude: 'the Scandinavian Fallacy' is a frame of mind where complex problems of poverty, rather than being attacked from the inside by improving the system of production, are solved by throwing money after them from the outside. This attitude has its origins in a collective Scandinavian understanding that their wealth is created above all because of their willingness to distribute income in an equitable way. Politically, however, the Scandinavian collective memory has wiped out the extreme economic interventions – heavy industrial policy including protection and subsidies – that has characterized their economic policy in waves from eighteenth-century Cameralism to twentieth-century Marshall Plan and its equivalents.

This focus on distribution rather than growth began in the late 1960s. When I first went to Peru, the attitude in Scandinavia was that Peru's problem was that the rich did not want to share with the poor. This may also be true, but it did not change the fact that average GDP per capita in Peru at the time was around 300 dollars annually. The typically skewed distribution of wealth in pre-industrial countries was taken as an explanation for the low average per capita income.

Economists' gradual loss of interest in production over the last decades has only reinforced this distribution-based view of poverty. As the 1990s advanced it became increasingly clear that the neo-liberal agenda was a failure in most small and poor states. This carried the Scandinavian Fallacy to the global level in the form of the Millennium Goals. The weakness of this approach is that it addresses poverty – that of the Saami and that of Africa – not by improving the ability of the poor to create wealth of their own, but by reallocating income created elsewhere. The Scandinavian Fallacy attacks the symptoms of poverty rather than its causes. The Saami reindeer herders were economically 'primitivized' by having the increasing returns activities that add value to their raw materials taken away from them, subsequently to be put 'on the dole'. Such internal welfare colonialism in Norway has its parallels on a huge scale on the African continent.

Primitivization and the Cold War heritage

'Economists work for the applause of their own peers.'

Paul Samuelson, *New York Times*, 1974

How can these mechanisms of economic retrogression and primitivization be so totally disregarded by today's economists? The rhetoric of globalization today is based on the trinity of 'free markets, democracy and liberty'. There are very few attempts to problematize the interdependence of these three factors, and even more importantly, to establish the prerequisites that have proved themselves necessary for such historical rarities as democracy and individual rights to develop. It seems to me that today's collective understanding of reality has got stuck in economic delusions created by the Cold War. Two economic theories of that time – with common roots in the illusory system of David Ricardo – painted two different utopias: the utopia of the planned economy and the utopia of the free market. Four important legacies of this Cold War mentality, in particular, keep us from appreciating why the way in which we globalize forces large parts of the world's population to specialize in modes of production of the past. This brings us back to the 'dual economies' described by early development economists.

Four elements are inexorably intertwined: 1) trade theory; 2) the lack of will to discuss the assumptions of economic theory on the basis of common sense; 3) faith in the ability of the market to produce 'spontaneous order'; and 4) the lack of prestige in studying reality.

When the communists promised 'from each according to his abilities, to each according to his need', neo-classical economics responded with Samuelson's trade theory – published at the time of the Berlin Blockade – proving that, given the standard theoretical assumptions, global free trade would produce factor–price equalization. The price, in other words, of labour and capital would become the same in the entire world.[22] The market would work even better than communism, and everyone would become equally rich if only the invisible hand was given free reign. This theory was for a long time considered so counter-intuitive that it was not used in actual policy practice. Although far more sophisticated discussions of trade theory exist in the neo-classical tradition, this parody of a theory none the less laid the groundwork for the work of the Washington institutions in the Second and Third Worlds. The result was nothing less than catastrophic for many developing economies, yet the same gurus and the same theories are still in power. The fact that non-Ricardian Other Canon economics today is as good as dead must again be emphasized as a major contributing factor.

A key problem with trade theory, as previously mentioned, results from its insistence on drawing its metaphors, and particularly the foundational one of 'equilibrium', from the science of physics. This choice was first exercised in the 1880s and displaced the reigning metaphor of the body politic – with its differentiated functions based on mutual dependence – which had served jurists and social scientists since the time of Aristotle, if not before. The choice of metaphor carried with it a need to build certain assumptions into the science of economics, and the conclusions of trade theory – that free trade will benefit everybody by making them all equally rich – is built into its very assumptions: perfect information, perfect competition, no increasing returns to scale, etc. To paraphrase Nobel Laureate in Economics James Buchanan, under these assumptions there is no reason why any trade should develop at all. If everybody knew the same things and there were no fixed costs (which allow for economies of scale), every single human being would have functioned like a self-sustained microcosmos of production, and there would have been no trade except in raw materials. The assumptions necessary for trade theory to deliver on its promises to the poor, would, by logical consequence, have eliminated all trade that was not in primary products. In 1953, during McCarthy's witch-hunt for leftists in American society, Milton Friedman (1912–2006) effectively buried all debate over the assumptions of economic theory: do not look at what trade theory assumes, but look at what it does for the United States.[23]

During the Cold War, the 'spontaneous order' of the market became the response of economists to the planned economy. Somalia, Afghanistan and Iraq give us the counter-example of 'spontaneous chaos' when a nation's productive system lacks the increasing return activities and the synergies that are the prerequisites for an integrated nation-state rather than tribal societies. These activities do not appear spontaneously. History abundantly shows that functioning markets, and indeed civilization itself, has been created by a conscious focus on national production and strong policies that sometimes 'got the prices wrong' in order to increase public welfare. German economist Johann Gottfried Hoffman put it well in 1840:

> As the grown man has long since forgotten the pains it cost him to learn to speak, so have the peoples, in the days of their mature growth of the State, forgotten what was required in order to free them from their primitive brutal savagery.[24]

Europe was built again from the ruins of the Second World War by very heavy-handed policies just before the illusion of 'spontaneous order' was formulated. The chasm that separates American policy in post-war Europe and Japan from American policy in today's Iraq is almost incomprehensible. The devastating the assumptions that the removal of 'bad guys' and the introduction of free trade would create 'spontaneous order' and growth, Iraq may indeed represent the closing chapter of the Cold War and the illusions it created.

Perhaps our most influential living economist, Paul Samuelson, remarked several years ago in the *New York Times* that economists were opportunists. On Monday, Wednesday and Friday they can work on one kind of model, while on Tuesdays and Thursdays they can work on models with entirely different assumptions. Given this attitude, which I have previously labelled 'assumption-juggling', research projects can prove very dangerous. The assumptions used and conclusions drawn can all too quickly be derived from the exigencies of the project. This, of course, carries with it the advantage that one can find economic models that prove practically everything. One problem is that the choice of economic theory to implement in developing countries in the end becomes a simple matter of power – of might makes right. Since economists at the best universities in Africa make around $100 a month, while the World Bank may offer them $300 a day as consultants for the true faith, it should come as no surprise that so few economists in the developing world make their voices heard in opposition. An application for funds for economic research *outside* of the accepted theoretical toolbox has equally predictable results – as if Martin Luther had applied for funds from the Vatican.

A science that seemingly represents a solid block of wisdom in the end shows itself to be a mixture of bits and pieces of various theories that can be used to 'prove' almost anything. Upon closer scrutiny, orthodox economics is not unlike the curious taxonomy or classification system for animals that Argentine author Jorge Luis Borges created in an imaginary Chinese dictionary: 'animals are divided into (a) those that belong to the Emperor, (b) embalmed ones, (c) those that are trained, (d) suckling pigs, (e) mermaids, (f) fabulous ones, (g) stray dogs, (h) those that are included in this classification, (i) those that tremble as if they were mad, (j) innumerable ones, (k) those drawn with a very fine camel's hair brush, (l) others, (m) those that have just broken a flower vase, (n) those that resemble flies from a distance.'[25] Borges' classification system has been used by Michel Foucault for the same reason I am using it here: to sow seeds of doubt regarding scientific dogmatism. To the eyes of a layman, however, the arbitrariness of Borges' imaginary dictionary is far easier to identify than that of economics, encircled, as it is, by bulwarks of mathematics not penetrable by the man on the street.

As Keynes said, 'practical men, who believe themselves to be quite exempt from any intellectual influences, are usually the slaves of some defunct economist. Madmen in authority, who hear voices in the air, are distilling their frenzy from some academic scribbler of a few years back. I am sure that the power of vested interests is vastly exaggerated compared with the gradual encroachment of ideas ... But, soon or late, it is ideas, not vested interests, which are dangerous for good or evil ...'[26]

This book presents a new set of long dead economists, many of them mentioned in Figure 3 and Appendix II, some of whom are even longer dead than those who have enslaved modern practitioners of the science. Compared to today's heroes, like Adam Smith, the selection here has the advantage of having had clear ideas about why some countries become rich and others poor. If one takes the time to consult the evidence amassed in the lab-oratory of the international economy over the past five hundred years, one will even find that history has vindicated them. But the point is not to substitute one set of dogmas for another. Rather, one must come to accept the incredible wealth and diversity of economic theory and practice, and subsequently appreciate the need for a much, much larger toolkit of economic policy. The policies that will benefit Great Britain are probably not exactly the same as those that will benefit Switzerland, and even less probably the same as those that will benefit Equatorial Guinea, Myanmar, or Vanuatu. History, in the end, can be our only guide in navigating these tumultuous waters and new contexts.

6

Explaining Away Failure:
Red Herrings at the End of History

Believe me, do not fear crooks or evil people, fear the honest person who is wrong. That person is in good faith, he wishes everyone well, and everyone has his confidence: but unfortunately his methods fail to get out the good in humans.

Ferdinando Galiani, Italian economist, 1770

And whatever harm the evil may do, the harm done by the good is the most harmful harm.

Friedrich Nietzsche, 1885

When being good makes us evil

Arusha, Tanzania, May 2003. While I was absentmindedly flipping through the notes for my upcoming lecture, the Tanzanian general and Member of Parliament came up to the rostrum. 'I have read your paper, and I only have one question,' he said earnestly. 'Do they underdevelop us on purpose?'

I was just about to present my views on globalization and free trade to members of the East African Parliament (the joint parliament of Kenya, Uganda and Tanzania), who were representing countries where globalization had led to primitivization rather than modernization in many areas. The burly and humorous general had gained my respect as an efficient chairman of that morning's session. The meeting took place in a big tent on an old coffee plantation made 'uncompetitive' by falling coffee prices, even with the minuscule wages paid. Most of the few industries in the region that had developed after independence had been killed off by consistent 'structural adjustment' by the Washington institutions. Unemployment and poverty surrounded us.

'There appear to be only two alternatives,' I replied to the general. 'They either do it out of ignorance, or they do it out of evil. A combination of these two factors is of course also possible. Perhaps you can also say it's the system that makes them do it.' 'Thank you,' he replied, 'I was just wondering.' I could have added that, after the Nuremberg trials of Nazi war criminals, 'the system made me do it' is no longer considered an acceptable excuse.

The set of policies producing the effects the Tanzanian general referred to was the so-called 'Washington Consensus'. These policies appeared on the scene in 1990, immediately after the fall of the Berlin Wall, and are associated with American economist John Williamson. As a set of commandments the Washington Consensus required, among other things, trade liberalization, liberalization of inflows of foreign direct investments, deregulation and privatization. Although this may not have been Williamson's original intention, the Washington Consensus reforms as they were carried out became virtually synonymous with neo-liberalism and 'market fundamentalism'.

The Washington Consensus Mark 1 has often been summarized as 'getting the prices right': its unambiguous promise was that poor countries would achieve sustained high growth rates if state intervention was removed and the market left to rule. Regardless of a nation's economic structure, growth would be the 'default position' of the market system if left to itself. This chapter looks at how mainstream rhetoric has evolved from its most triumphalist moment – Mark 1 – in 1990 until 2007. The mainstream 'consensus' has continually added new features and factors – new 'commandments' – to the original 'getting the prices right': if we just 'get the prices right' plus this or that factor, poor countries will achieve growth. The key point here is that these new 'commandments' never detract or amend the core features of the original 1990 commandments; they therefore fail to modify to any important extent the policies actually carried out.

When it comes to practical policy recommendations, then, the original commandments are still applied. The plethora of theoretical models showing the importance of increasing returns, for example, has not resulted in any recommendation that poor countries should target or nourish such activities. 'Comparative advantage' and the original 1990 policy prescriptions prevail. This is what I have referred to as the Krugmanian vice (in chapter 2): having models that show why the poor stay poor, but refusing to use them in practical policy. Having found a medicine is a goal in itself, but using it to help patients is another matter.

From 1990, years passed under Washington Consensus rules, but growth – particularly increasing real wages – failed to materialize in many countries. One initial reaction to this was the same as that observed when huge social problems emanated from the liberalization of the 1760s and 1840s: 'We just don't have enough market, when the last impediments are gone, *laissez-faire* will show its su-periority.'[1] But the worsening conditions in the poor periphery became increasingly difficult to overlook, and so did the global protest movements. Both were difficult to keep at bay. Another reaction was to retreat to the caves of pure theory: 'No reality please, we are economists,' as UK economist Edward Fulbrook put it, paraphrasing the musical *No Sex Please, We're British*. The successes of China and India were not easy to use in defence of Washington Consensus policies. For more than fifty years both these countries had followed a protectionist industry-building strategy – probably too protectionist – and were now ready to 'graduate' to the international marketplace in order to reap the benefits from freer trade.

Rhetoric also became important. Italian premier Silvio Berlusconi's strategy of labelling anyone who disagreed with him a 'communist' was, for example, surprisingly effective. My fellow student at Harvard Business School in the mid-1970s, George W. Bush, successfully used a similar strategy for a long time: either you are with us or you are with the Taliban. At the economic level this works out as 'either you are in favour of globalization in its present form, or you are in favour of a planned economy'. Using the same type of strategy, Martin Wolf of the *Financial Times* rids himself of Werner Sombart in one sentence, by accusing him of being both fascist and communist. This was the rhetoric of 'the end of history' interlude, the low end of public debate as it clung desperately to the Cold War economic axis. It was as if the fall of the Soviet sphere had provided proof not only that a market economy was intrinsically more efficient than a planned economy, but also that if untouched by human hands the market economy would provide utopian universal harmony. The fall of the Berlin Wall was, as Francis Fukuyama put it, 'the end of history'.

What made the 'end of history' interlude possible was, of course, an economic theory that 'scientifically' backed up the view that the market – if left to itself – is a harmony-producing institution. Some well-known model-builders in economics, such as Frank Hahn of Cambridge, willingly admit that their models have precious little to do with reality. Had more economists openly admitted to this, it would have been possible to establish the study of economic reality as a separate academic subject. As it is now, this is extremely difficult.

Other economists, such as former World Bank senior research economist William Easterly, readily and admirably admit the failure of the more than $2.3 trillion[2] of development assistance over five decades to actually create development. It is not clear, however, that Easterly is able to offer alternative strategies despite observing early on that something was fundamentally wrong in a period when the common attitude was that the poor needed 'more of the same thing'. The move to explain what had gone wrong developed into a search that did not even question the catallactic (barter-centred) core of standard textbook economics – its fundamental failure to understand the world productive system which, by its very nature, produces uneven economic development. Apart from the initial denial and the recommendation of 'more of the same thing', the path of enquiry followed a string of red herrings, of false starts. The real core of the problem, the activity-specific nature of economic development, as it had been understood from the late 1400s until the Marshall Plan in 1947, is still not recognized.

The Tanzanian general's question raises two further issues. One is the relationship between good intentions and kindness on the one hand and economic development on the other. How, for example, could so much generous giving to Africa not have created wealth? The second question is how 500 years of wisdom about the links between wealth, civilization and 'city activities' – so well expressed by George Marshall when he announced the Marshall Plan in June 1947 – could be discarded so unanimously, virtually by the whole world? You don't have to be a historian to understand this; many people in power today were born at the time of the Marshall Plan. We shall deal with these questions separately.

Capitalism and the paradox of intentions

Capitalism and successful market economies can only be properly understood if one understands its paradoxes. As Adam Smith explains, we do not get our daily bread through the kindness of the baker, but rather because the baker needs to make money. Our own interest in eating bread is satisfied through the greed of another person. Clearly a paradox. Adam Smith's insight was part of an important eighteenth-century debate, begun by Bernard Mandeville in 1705, when he claimed that private vices could turn into public benefits. By the time Adam Smith published *The Wealth of Nations* in 1776 the debate had been virtually concluded. However, both Adam Smith's rendering of the debate – and particularly our contemporary interpretation of Adam Smith today – have hidden very important qualifications from Mandeville's principle in its crudest form.

In my own country, in 1757, the editor of *Denmark and Norway's Economic Magazine* expressed a common reaction to Mandeville's assertion that public welfare was caused by private vices. The editor, Erik Pontoppidan, had formerly been the Bishop of Bergen, which partly explains his moral indignation: if vice was the moving force of welfare, someone who sets fire to the four corners of London would be a hero because of all the employment and wealth thus created, from loggers to saw mills and carpenters. The formula for solving this problem and consolidating the theory of the market economy was well expressed by Milanese economist Pietro Verri in 1771: 'the private interest of each individual, *when it coincides with the public interests*, is always the safest guarantor of public happiness' [my italics].[3] At the time it was obvious that these interests were not always in perfect harmony in a market economy. The role of the legislator was seen as creating the policies that made sure that individual interests coincided with the public ones.

Today's economic theory builds on an interpretation of Mandeville and Smith which differs from that of eighteenth-century continental European consensus in three important areas.

- First of all, it cannot be assumed that self-interest is the *only* moving force of society. Private virtues rarely turn into anything but virtues, public or private. As we shall see below, however, public virtues could turn into private vices. Other and nobler sentiments than greed and merciless profit-maximizing are harder to model.
- Secondly, because of factors well known to economists before Adam Smith – synergies, increasing and diminishing returns, and qualitative differences in entrepreneurship, leadership, knowledge and between economic activities – the market economy, left alone, will often tend to increase rather than decrease economic inequalities. What we call economic development is an 'unintended' consequence of economic activities only in the presence of factors such as increasing returns, a large division of labour, dynamic imperfect competition, and windows of opportunity for innovation. Consequently, economic development became a fairly intended consequence of certain economic policies. Being poor became a consequence of being a colony, because the above factors were absent. This, as we have emphasized again and again, is a blind spot in standard economics because it generally and implicitly assumes that all economic activities are alike.[4]
- Thirdly, it is entirely possible to make money in ways that are contrary to the public interest. Money can be made at the expense of destroying economies, as exemplified by George Soros and by the case provided by Mr Pontoppidan. American

economist William Baumol distinguishes between *productive, unproductive* and *destructive* entrepreneurship. Standard economics has problems in incorporating this because 'methodological individualism' has defined away the national public interest as a category: 'there is no such thing as society' as Margaret Thatcher so eloquently put it. In contrast to English economics, continental European economics has generally kept the national interest as a separate category.

While unintended consequences are often construed into an argument for laissez-faire, in the mainstream continental economic traditions understanding such consequences became an instrument for an enlightened economic policy. It may be argued that Henry VII's successful industrialization policy in England, starting in 1485, was partly a result of the growth of woollen industries that had followed as an unintended effect of the duties imposed – for revenue reasons – by his early predecessor Edward III. The second time around, what was an unintended consequence becomes the key objective of the policy. Indeed, the fortuitous double effect of duties – providing tax income while building industry – was extremely important through the ages. This was also the case in the United States, and still is, particularly in small states.

In the early twentieth century continental economists continued to understand economic development as the result of unintended consequences of intentions that were far from noble. Even in the sixteenth century innovations and technological change were largely related to government demand in two areas: war (gunpowder, metal for swords and cannons, warships and their equipment) and luxury (silk, porcelain, glass objects, paper). In 1913 Werner Sombart published two books (see Chapter 3) describing these elements as the driving forces of capitalism, *War and Capitalism* and *Luxury and Capitalism*, a work that only in a later edition was daringly retitled *Love, Luxury and Capitalism*, the original title intended by the author. King Christian V of Denmark and Norway (1670–99) describes his 'main passions' in a way that fitted Sombart's scheme as 'hunting, love life, war and naval affairs'. Prudent financial management tended to be put aside in the interests of both warfare and royal mistresses.

Once capitalism has been understood as a system of imperfect competition and unintended consequences rather than as a system of perfect markets, it is then possible to use this insight to craft wise economic policies. Towards the end of the fifteenth century – just about the time when Columbus reached the Americas – the Venetians had turned the understanding of progress as a by-product of warfare and public expenditure into a new institution: patents. Giving an inventor a monopoly period for seven years – the normal period for a craftsman's apprenticeship – would enable inventors to appropriate the benefits of new knowledge hitherto mainly found as by-products of huge targeted public outlays. Progress was created through dynamic imperfect competition. A twin institution to patents, consciously created at about the same time, was tariff protection, set up to enable the inventions to take root in new geographic areas.

The mechanism private vices – public benefits can also work in reverse: public vices – private benefits. Government vices – excessive nationalism and warmongery – often lead indirectly to private benefits in the long run. Many new inventions important to civilian life originate as by-products of war: canned goods (Napoleonic War), mass production with standardized pieces (arms during the American Civil War), the ballpoint pen (US Air Force during the Second World War), burglar alarms (Vietnam War), and mobile satellite communication (the 'Star Wars' programme). If this is properly understood, it becomes possible to create economic progress avoiding the roundabout way. If we come to accept that a main factor in economic development is resources demanding performance at the border of what is technologically possible, we can throw more money directly at, for example, the health sector, and bypass war completely.

The third alternative – public virtues – private vices – can also be observed: what in the first instance appears as public virtues may in fact develop into systemic vices. As we shall see in the next chapter, systematic development aid can turn into 'welfare colonialism', which is a vehicle for 'governing at a distance' through the exercise of a particularly subtle, non-demonstrative and dependency-generating form of neo-colonial social control. The

Millennium Goals are a case in point. Regardless of the initial intention of generous support – in the case of Ethiopia – when a recipient government falls out of favour, the donor countries are left with the decision whether or not to turn off the food supply to the poor nation. Whether intended or not, the virtue of aiding the poor – while keeping them out of production capitalism – has created a system that can feed private vices of corruption and warmongery. Welfare colonialism pre-empts local autonomy through well-intentioned and generous – but ultimately morally wrong – policies. It creates paralysing dependencies on the centre in a peripheral population, a centre exerting control through incentives that create total economic dependency, thus preventing political mobilization and autonomy.

Five hundred years of wisdom lost

The second question we raised above is how it was possible for the end-of-history euphoria to so completely disregard 500 years of experience in building welfare. Early in this book we discussed how the Cold War had reduced economics to a civil war between two factions of Ricardian economics, crowding out a previous qualitative understanding of production systems. Still, it is difficult to understand how a choir of contemporary economists, singing almost in unison, can fail to bring to the policy level the age-old understanding of national economic growth as an interplay between the increasing returns activities in the cities and the diminishing returns activities in the countryside. Only sixty years ago, when he launched the Marshall Plan, US Secretary of State George Marshall hailed this interplay as the very basis for Western civilization.

When it was important to build a defence line to protect Asia and Europe from the communist threat, the United States understood that the way to create wealth was to industrialize the nations bordering communism – from Norway and Germany to Korea and Japan – and to support this project wholeheartedly economically, politically and militarily. Once the communist threat had dissolved, the developed countries rapidly started applying a policy that had the opposite effect in poor countries, a type of economic policy that resembled old British colonial policy at its worst. It was against this policy of premature free trade that the US itself had industrialized, and it was against this policy Roosevelt, with great moral authority, stood up to Churchill and his colonial policy during the Second World War.

During the 1950s and 1960s, when the nations bordering communism were so successfully industrialized, the United States knew very well how to make poor nations rich: they employed their own nineteenth-century strategy. How come the United States no longer understands the link between industrialization and 'civilization' perceived so clearly from George Washington to George Marshall? How come the West, instead of contributing to produce world welfare – as the USA did after the Second World War – now stages terrible carnage in futile attempts to bomb pre-industrial nations into democracy? Gunnar Myrdal's term 'opportunistic ignorance' comes to mind as nations fail to recognize anything that goes against their own immediate interest. In this setting, the old definition of a liberal (in the European sense) as 'someone whose interests are not threatened at the moment' becomes increasingly appropriate.

'It is remarkable how economic theories survive long after their scientific bases have disappeared' commented American economist Simon N. Patten in 1904. He was referring to the same equilibrium economics that still survives today. What kinds of mechanisms protect theories that are so blatantly inadequate? Vested interest is obviously one important factor. Some nations have a short-term interest in free trade with desperately poor nations, yet it is hardly in the interest of capitalism as a system that roughly half of the world's population has virtually no purchasing power. So even the economic vested interests are extremely short-sighted.

An additional factor is that the ruling theory seems to be protected by human nature itself. Rather than questioning one's own pet theory, explanations are sought outside the theory itself. The core of the Washington Consensus is not amended at the policy level. The logic goes something like this: since *my* theory in its mathematical elegance is perfect (which is proved by the fall of the Berlin Wall) the explanation must lie somewhere outside my theoretical framework. Today this leads economists into areas where they are often at best amateurs, like geography, climate and disease. There is an interesting parallel here from the aftermath of the first wave of globalization that ended early in the twentieth century. Anthropologist Eric Ross points to the relationship between economics and eugenics (racial hygiene) as it developed at that time.[5] This first globalization wave created poor colonies, bereft of industry, technological change, increasing returns, advanced division of labour and synergies between economic activities. Since the problem could not lie with economic theory, factors outside economics itself had to be found. The most influential American economist at the time, Irving Fisher (1867–1947) was also the most influential person in the US eugenics movement. John Maynard Keynes (1883–1946) was vice-president of the English Eugenics Society. Race was convenient for explaining poverty in the colonies, thus exonerating the colonial prohibition of industrial production from blame and leaving Ricardian trade theory unblemished. Africans were not poor because they had not been allowed to industrialize, they were poor because they were black. Today when we emphasize the role of corruption in creating poverty, we are a little bit more politically correct. Africans are no longer poor because they are black, they are poor because blacks are corrupt. In the final analysis the difference is marginal.

Explaining away failure: the red herrings

It is the year 1989. It is clear that the communist system, with its disdain for markets, is about to collapse. Imagine you are an economist and are given the task of explaining the difference in wealth between the by now obvious wealth potential in Silicon Valley on the one hand and the poverty of rural Africa, say among the Masai, on the other. Since you are an economist, however, you are professionally trained to disregard certain aspects:

1.   You are not allowed to claim that any qualitative differences exist between economic activities, i.e. that it is better for a group of people to produce platforms for software than to

herd animals. If left alone, the market will take care of evening out such differences.

2. As a consequence of the above, you are not allowed to recommend any change in specialization. Every nation should specialize according to its comparative advantage, be it herding animals or producing software, which will produce factor–price equalization.

3. Your tools prevent you from observing any synergies. You may not say that people who herd animals but live among people who produce software are wealthier than herders living only among other herders.[6]

4. You are not allowed to refer to history. History and the future have both been collapsed into 'the here and now'. Consequently the argument that the country where Silicon Valley is located did, for 150 years or so, follow a strategy subsidizing and protecting itself away from rural activities into the mechanical arts and high-tech is not valid. With reference to points 1 to 3 it is obvious that the United States grew rich in spite of, not because of these policies.[7]

5. You are no longer allowed to use unemployment and underemployment – factors that were important after the Second World War – as arguments for policy. Factoring in unemployment would require using something called 'shadow prices' which are very messy and would, anyway, lead to market-unfriendly policies. The Washington institutions assume full employment in their economic models.[8]

6. You are not allowed to claim any arrows of causality running from the structure of the economy to the political structure. Parliamentary democracy, or any other institution for that matter, is as likely to appear in a hunting and gathering tribe as under feudalism or in an urban society.

To give an example: you observe a poor part of town inhabited by people making their living by washing dishes in restaurants and shining shoes, and a rich part of the same town inhabited by stockbrokers and lawyers. Your task is to explain the differences in income, within the logic of international trade theory, which means that you are not allowed to make reference to the fact that the source of the income gap between the two parts of the city is a direct result of the differences in earnings potential of the professions involved. The toolbox of that theory hardly contains any instruments with which you can observe qualitative differences between economic activities.[9] Barred from saying that differences in earning between shoe-shiners and stockbrokers are a direct result of inherent differences between the two professions, economists therefore come up with explanations that tend to be secondary effects of the main cause: the poor do not have enough education (ignoring the fact that you cannot profitably invest in education that improves your income as shoe-shiner or dish-washer), the poor have not saved enough (without seeing that their low income prevents them from saving), the poor have not innovated enough (without noticing that the opportunities for innovation in shoe-shining are more limited than in other fields), etc. etc.

As was so obvious to American economists around 1820, a nation – just as a person – still cannot break such vicious circles without changing professions. In the case of a nation, that meant the industrialization project that for a century was referred to as the American System of Manufactures.[10] However, having unlearned the successful strategies of the past, the economics profession at present shows a singular ability to focus on and attack the symptoms of poverty rather than its root causes. Experiments with the loosening of assumptions are usually done by letting go of one at a time, and have so far failed to influence our policies towards the poor.

The above approximates the brief of the Washington institutions at the start of the end of history in 1989 – the unconscious brief that the professionals brought with them to work every day, deeply embedded in their conviction of how the world actually works. This brief was a product of the implicit and explicit assumptions of standard textbook economics. Such a world-view consistently prohibits the observation of any qualitative differences, other than differences in the capital–labour ratios in firms. The risk of deviation from the above principles was minimized by not recruiting professionals who had any experience in working in rich countries and, as Joseph Stiglitz has pointed out, by recruiting weak students from the best universities. This approach was summed up by a poem – 'Our dream is a world free of poverty' – put up by World Bank director James Wolfensohn in the lobby of the World Bank headquarters. The poem was eloquently written and no doubt well intentioned on Wolfensohn's part, but indicated clearly that several key factors producing uneven development – poverty on the one hand and wealth on the other – had been eliminated from the analytical toolbox used by Mr Wolfensohn's employees.

Barred from broaching the fundamental causes of uneven development as they had been researched over the last 500 years, we shall see how the study of poverty proceeded through the period of the 'end of history' as a series of what are basically red herrings and false starts, sometimes secondary and ancillary effects. Prevented from challenging the six interlocking assumptions listed above, the Washington Consensus developed along the following path, so that each discovery tended to be celebrated as if it had provided the final solution to poverty:[11]

1. 'get the prices right'
2. 'get the property rights right'
3. 'get the institutions right'
4. 'get the governance right'
5. 'get the competitiveness right'
6. 'get the innovations right'
7. 'get the entrepreneurship right'
8. 'get the education right'
9. 'get the climate right'
10. 'get the diseases right'.

In my view this string of arguments results, subconsciously, from an attempt to save standard textbook economics and its core assumptions. Their sequential appearance constitutes what Robert Wade of the London School of Economics calls 'the art of paradigm maintenance', and attempts to add features outside the standard economic model in order to save the core of the theory.[12] While the factors are indeed relevant, they fail to address the core of the development process: 'get the economic activities right'. If the models fail to include, simultaneously, the factors repeatedly referred to in this book that create diversity – increasing and diminishing returns, degrees of imperfect competition, synergies and structural connections, and the hugely varying windows of opportunity for innovation – this type of list simply serves to divert attention from more important issues. Above all, this sequence of simplistic explanations takes the focus away from a holistic and into a piecemeal understanding of the process of development. Diverting attention from the real issues and creating what prove to be false paths towards a solution is the key characteristic of a 'red herring'.

While the Washington institutions continue to produce what are essentially academic red herrings, well-intentioned national governments proceed to jump on the bandwagon and fund projects. The result of this is a sequence of what Michael Porter of the Harvard Business School calls 'single issue management': the world of development economics goes through periods extremely focused on one issue at a time; and researching whatever is 'the flavour of the month' is what makes it possible to survive as an academic. The international funding of this sequence of fashionable issues inhibits a necessary diversity in economic approaches.

1 Get the prices right

As already mentioned, the Washington Consensus Mark 1, as it was defined in 1990, amounted to little more than 'getting the prices right'. In May of that same year my friend Santiago Roca became chief economic advisor to the Peruvian president-elect, Alberto Fujimori. To a much greater degree than his opponent Mario Vargas Llosa, Fujimori had stressed the need to protect the poor in the upcoming fight against rampant inflation. At the time Santiago had built the only existing econometric model of the Peruvian economy, and could show how the traditional policies that were bound to be brought in would crush the poor. I called my friend in Peru to congratulate him on his new task, and was promptly invited to Lima to assist in the development of the programme of Fujimori's party, Cambio 90.[13]

Eastern Europe at the time was in political ferment with the creation of new political party structures out of nothing. The situation in Peru was similar, with the two main candidates' parties being established with no organizational structure in place. Vargas Llosa had the support of some wealthy individuals, but Fujimori's Cambio 90 was a poor organization. The Cambio 90 headquarters was in a small office abandoned by an ophthalmologist who, like so many other Peruvian professionals, had set off for Miami in search of clients who were better able to pay for his services. The office, on the Avenida Arequipa, leading from down-town to the old traditional suburbs of Lima, had no electricity and no running water, but a telephone line. The economic team sketched its plans for the nation on the prescription pads left behind by the good doctor, and there were no funds bar for the absolutely necessary.

The lack of funds was compensated for by a great deal of idealism and enthusiasm. Many people put in their work for free; Santiago and I contacted our former professors at Cornell who were experts on Latin America. In the evenings, the team often met at Santiago's house, where – to the consternation of his wife Teresa – Fujimori's team raided her refrigerator and conspicuously placed their firearms on her highly polished furniture – not exactly normal occurrences in the lives of Peruvian academics. When serious threats against Santiago and his family started coming in, a group of volunteers eagerly organized a programme of watching the house. Later a bomb hit their home, preventing Santiago from attending an Other Canon conference in Oslo, but fortunately without hurting anyone.

In July 1990, before he was to be installed as the new President of Peru on 28 July, Alberto Fujimori went to Washington. He came back a completely different person: gone were the social concerns. We jokingly asked ourselves what kind of arm-twisting he had been subject to. Fujimori had been told that if he removed all government interventions in the economy, shrank the public sector and essentially 'got the prices right', the rest would take care of itself. However, in the case of Peru there were two serious impediments to letting the markets do their job: inflation and the guerrillas. Fujimori's marching order was to get rid of the two, and in the end he delivered the bacon: inflation fell from 7469 per cent in 1990 to 6.5 per cent in 1997 and the guerrillas virtually disappeared. As can be seen from Figure 14, by 1990 deindustrialization

had already taken its toll of 50 per cent of the real wage level of
the average Peruvian, and there was an obvious link between the
increased poverty and high levels of terrorism. In terms of social
and human rights the cost of Fujimori's victories had been high, but
compared to the wealth which would now come to the impoverished people of Peru, it is understandable that the benefits could be
seen as outweighing the costs.

The problem was that after the dramatic success of reducing
inflation and killing the guerrillas, nothing happened. Getting rid of
industries had brought down the real wages, much as David Ricardo
had foreseen, to close to subsistence level. Wages did not go up and
the poor farmers did not get better paid for their produce; in fact it
became an important political goal to keep both wages and prices
down in order to halt inflation. The small increases in GDP that
followed did not result in higher real wages; the benefits went to
the financial sector and to profits. Economic orthodoxy had begun
in Peru back in the 1970s and had had a very high cost: reducing
the average person's income by half. Dismayed at the social costs of
the policies which – contrary to campaign promises – were implemented by Fujimori, Santiago Roca refused the job as Director of
the Central Bank that had informally been offered to him. He had
worked hard and for free, even risking the lives of his family, and
nothing came out of it. 'Getting the prices right' was not enough, it
just established a new and lower plateau of poverty.

The story of the Roca family also helps to explain the difficulties
of being an intellectual in the Third World. The risks are high and
combining idealism – Veblen's 'parental bent' – with the goal of
maintaining a family is extremely hard. A former student of mine,
who works at Makerere University, the best university in Uganda,
makes 100 dollars a month. If he would take a job with any of the
Washington institutions, he would be paid several hundred dollars
a day. The price and risks of virtue are overwhelming.

2 Get the property rights right

As it became increasingly obvious that – contrary to prevailing
theory – the market alone did not provide equalization of world
incomes, the search continued for new explanations that did not

violate the assumptions of standard textbook economics. Capitalism obviously needed property rights in order to function, and since property could be observed as being less developed in poor countries than in rich ones, the lack of property rights was conveniently flagged as a major cause of underdevelopment. Capitalism was not a reason for poverty in the periphery, this reasoning went, poor countries were just not capitalistic enough.

The reasoning ran that the Masai are poor and stuck in subsistence agriculture because they lack property rights. I would argue that, although economic development involves many cases of arrows of causality moving simultaneously in both directions (co-evolution), it is more likely that the Masai lack property rights because they are poor and stuck in subsistence agriculture. In other words, the problem lies in their mode of production – subsistence agriculture rather than, say, manufacturing – and *not* narrowly in an institutional arrangement in a restricted sense. An institution that suits one production system may not suit another. It can, for example, be argued that the sequential usufruct of land found in pastoral societies[14] is much better suited to that particular mode of production than are capitalist property rights.

These attempts to isolate single features of market economies without seeing the whole – exercises in single-issue management – tend to obfuscate rather than illuminate. In the Republic of Venice, property rights and their titles were well developed almost one thousand years ago. The first cadastral register, creating a public record of land ownership, had already been established in Venice in the years 1148 to 1156. The mode of production of the Venetians – in contrast to the mode of production of hunters and gatherers – brought with it the need for the regulation of property rights. Property rights per se were not responsible for either capitalism or economic growth; it was an institution created by a certain production system in order to make it function better.

Hernando de Soto, another Peruvian economist, achieved his fame by arguing for state protection of property rights in a formal recorded system. De Soto is no doubt right when he claims that the slow bureaucracy in poor Latin American countries represents an obstacle to development, and he is also right that the poor's lack of property rights hinders them in using their homes as collateral for loans. But as several studies in Latin America have shown, giving property rights to the poor may very well lead them to sell their houses in order to buy food or healthcare. They also easily fall victims to fraud in this new and unfamiliar situation. Property rights without economic development may actually make things worse than they were in pre-capitalist societies. In such societies, the absence of property rights made it possible for everyone to build his house on communal land. Property rights, while necessary in a developed economy, may create in poor countries a larger number of social outcasts and higher barriers for the poor to establish homes than in the pre-capitalist world from which city migrants come.

3 Get the institutions right

After the emphasis on property rights, Mark II of the Washington Consensus broadened the discussion to include other forms of institutions.[15] The Institutional School of economics which dominated American economics from the end of the eighteenth century until the Second World War was a school in opposition to the English type of neo-classical theory. The New Institutional School that arose during the age of the 'end of history' was explicitly based on neo-classical economics, with institutions added in order to explain what could not be explained by standard textbook economics.

The term 'institutions' is a very wide one, covering human arrangements from morality and the celebration of Christmas or Ramadan to the establishment of parliaments or constitutions. Using the definition provided by Ha-Joon Chang and Peter Evans: 'Institutions are systematic patterns of shared expectations, taken-for-granted assumptions, accepted norms and routines of inter-action that have robust effects on shaping the motivations and behaviour of sets of interconnected social actors. In modern societies, they are usually embodied in authoritatively coordinated organizations with formal rules and the capacity to impose coercive sanctions, such as the government or firms'.[16]

Just as in the case of property rights, other institutions per se, divorced from the structural changes that prompt the demand for such institutions, cannot be seen as promoters of economic development. Long-distance trade in camel caravans or on the high seas led to the creation of insurance as an institution. Introducing insurance among hunting and gathering tribes will not have the same effect as for long-distance traders: The fundamental key to understanding development lies in appreciating the increases in knowledge and productivity created by new technologies and new 'modes of production'. The institutional changes necessitated by these changing forms of production are surely important, but they are ancillary. Institutions, just like capital, have no intrinsic value per se. Just like capital, they provide the scaffolding that keeps up the productive structure of a nation.

The social sciences started using the concept of an 'institution' very early. 'It is not sufficient to enquire whether an institution of the state is attested to have been founded by our ancestors. Rather it is necessary that we understand and explain *why* it was instituted. For it is by knowing the *cause* that we gain knowledge of a thing.' This statement on methodology is found in an analysis of the Florentine Constitution written in 1413 at the request of Emperor Sigismund of the Holy Roman Empire. The author, Leonardo Bruni (1369–1444), represents what has become known as the school of *civic humanism*, the ideology of the successful Italian city-states of the Renaissance.[17]

Also, the fact that the mode of production moulds and determines institutions – more than the other way around – has long been recognized. In 1620 Francis Bacon formulated a view that was to dominate in the social sciences for almost the next two centuries: there is a startling difference 'between the life of men in the most civilized province of Europe, and in the wildest and most barbarous districts of New India ... And this difference comes not from the soil, not from climate, not from race, but from the *arts*' [my italics].[18] Francis Bacon is crystal clear on the causality in question: man's activities – his mode of production – determine his institutions. Thorstein Veblen, one of the founders of the old institutional school, also emphasized the arrow of causality from daily activities to institutions.

Precisely because institutions and the mode of production of a society evolved together, institutions cannot be usefully studied separately from a technological system which needed and created them. Today, one side of the equation – institutions in isolation as instruments favouring development – has been over-emphasized, thus skewing our understanding of economic and institutional development.

In his 1882 novel *De lycksaligas ö* ('The island of the blissful') Swedish playwright August Strindberg discusses the relationship between modes of production and economic institutions. In this novel a group of eighteenth-century Swedish convicts, including two young students who had insulted the king, experience a sequence of Robinson Crusoe-type shipwrecks on their way to a faraway colony that they never reach. Led by the students, the convicts – by now free from any authority – establish their own society and consciously discuss the abolition or establishment of the institutions they are used to at home. While at the most tropical of the islands, they decide to abolish most of the known institutions. You need no inheritance law if you walk around naked and harvest the fruits of the earth, they argue. When, after a second shipwreck, they reach an island with a more temperate climate, they discover that their new lifestyle requires the reintroduction of institutions that they had previously abandoned as useless. August Strindberg reaffirms Francis Bacon's point: institutions are moulded and determined by the mode of production more than the other way around, and it is not really constructive to attempt to reverse the arrows of causality.

Having lost a qualitative type of understanding which can only be achieved by understanding production – rather than just barter and trade – neo-classical economics has also relinquished this connection between production and institutions: the activity-specific element of institutional development which for centuries was commonly known to social scientists.[19] This loss is much to the detriment of many developing countries today. Thus we would argue that the problem of 'failed states' and their institutional failures cannot meaningfully be discussed independently of the kind of economic activities in which these states engage.

4 Get the governance right

During the triumphalist years following 1990, 'rolling back the state' was an integral part of the Washington Consensus. 'State' and 'government' became negatively loaded words. Later in the 1990s, however, state and government were brought back again under the guise of 'governance'. The World Bank defines 'governance' as *'the exercise of political authority and the use of institutional resources to manage society's problems and affairs'*, in other words fairly close to what the terms 'state' and 'government' used to cover.

At the global level the most serious problem of 'governance' is failed states. According to the *Financial Times*, the World Bank keeps a list of forty-eight nation-states that risk collapsing into failed states. If one looks at the economic structure of failed states, even a relatively superficial analysis reveals that there is a strong relationship between a particular type of national economic production structure and the propensity of a nation-state to fail. The failed states have common economic factors that distinguish them from, for example, Germany, Canada or Norway. Any policy aiming at preventing nation-states from failing, should, in order to avoid treating mere symptoms rather than causes, include an analysis of how to bring the productive structures of failing states closer to the structure of those states that work satisfactorily and democratically.

Common economic characteristics of failing states are, among others: very few if any urban increasing returns industries, very little division of labour (i.e. monoculture), no urban middle class bringing political stability, no artisan class that is economically independent, commodity competition in export activities, a comparative advantage in supplying cheap labour to the world markets, a low demand for educated labour combined with very low level of education, and brain-drain. In nations with this type of economic structure a particular kind of regionalism tends to evolve, which in Latin America is referred to as *caudillismo* and in Somalia and Afghanistan as the rule of 'war lords'. The economic structures that provide the 'glue' for a functioning nation-state are weak or absent.

The first wealthy states with some kind of republican rule were often islands, like Venice, or maritime countries with little arable land, like Genoa and the Dutch Republic. The lack of arable land meant the absence of a feudal structure and contributed to the creation of a diversified economic structure including activities subject to increasing returns. This makes Florence, which traditionally had an important landowning class, so interesting. There the *corporazioni* (guilds) and the burghers fought for power among themselves, but very early on (in the twelfth and thirteenth centuries) they had banned the families who owned the land around from participating in politics. These families continued to trouble Florence for centuries through alliances with other cities.

In this book we have already noted the connection between the economic structures and political structures of a nation. Early democracies were states where artisan and manufacturing classes achieved political influence over the nobility. In Giovanni Botero (*c.* 1544–1617), and the German *Staatsraison* ('reason of state') tradition there are clear links between economic structure and the viability and governability of states. Botero's *Ragion di Stato* (Reason of State) and *Sulle grandezze delle Città* (On the Wealth of Cities) are parts of the same work,[20] linking states, cities and their economic structures. This tradition was continued by eighteenth-century social scientists, including Montesquieu.

We have also looked at the work of Veit Ludwig von Seckendorff (1626–92) (see Chapter 3), who found that Germany did not have the economic basis to create a society like the one observed and so admired in the Dutch Republic. Seckendorff's approach to making the state function better was intimately tied to changing the economic basis of the state itself, its mix of professions and industries and their geographical relocation within the realm. In the tradition started by Seckendorff, the *Fürsten* (Princes) were turned into modernizers by arguing that their *Recht* (right) to govern was accompanied by a *Pflicht* (duty) to modernize and, in effect, in the long term to create the conditions where the *Fürsten* would eventually be obsolete and the conditions needed for a functioning democracy would have been created. A successful Principality carried with it the seeds of its own destruction and the birth of democracy, but the road to democracy was created by diversifying the economy away from the production of raw materials.[21] Today, 'the strong correlation between advanced industrialization and democracy' is also recognized by Francis Fukuyama,[22] but what is *not* recognized is a) that the most important arrow of causality runs from the economic structure (urban artisanal and industrial activities) to the political structure, not the other way around; and b) that, with virtually no exception, such industrial activities have not been created other than by conscious targeting, nurturing and protection of industrial activity. Creating and protecting industry is creating and protecting democracy.

5 Get the competitiveness right

The term 'competitiveness' is also a product of end-of-history economics, coming into fashion in the early 1990s.[23] At first the term was highly contested. 'National competitiveness', wrote Robert Reich in 1990, 'is one of those rare terms of public discourse to have gone directly from obscurity to meaninglessness without any intervening period of coherence.' Later Reich, a professor at Harvard's John F. Kennedy School of Government, was to become US Secretary of Labor under President Bill Clinton. Here he championed the idea that the United States should move into high-value sectors of the economy (a view consistent with our quality index of economic activities). In a paper published a couple of years later, MIT's Paul Krugman twice referred to Reich as a 'pop internationalist' and somewhat unacademically condemned his Harvard colleague's notion of 'high-value sectors' as 'a silly concept'. But in the same paper Krugman also had a go at the term 'competitiveness': 'if we can teach undergrads to wince when they hear someone talk about "competitiveness", we will have done our nation a great service'. To Krugman the key insights were still those of David Ricardo.

Although the two opposing camps in US industrial and trade policy – those of Reich and Krugman – both disliked use of the term 'competitiveness' it continued to grow in popularity. In my view, two reasons for its success are the opacity and the malleability of the term. You can convincingly say both to an individual beggar and to a whole nation that 'you are not competitive enough' – it says it all yet it says very little. As we shall see, the term is also very flexible in that it may denote exactly opposite phenomena: both higher wages, *and* lower wages according to the circumstances.

At the level of the firm, the term 'competitiveness' is fairly straightforward. It refers to the capacity of a firm to compete, grow and be profitable in the marketplace. In his book *The Competitive Advantage of Nations* Michael Porter comments that there is no accepted definition of competitiveness, but later adds 'the only meaningful concept of competitiveness at the national level is national productivity'.[24] This is not a very enlightening definition. As we have seen in the examples of baseballs and golf balls, the key factor is what a nation chooses to be productive in, not productivity per se. Bruce Scott of Harvard Business School was to provide the definition that was later adopted by the OECD in their Technology and Economy Programme: 'Competitiveness may be defined as the degree to which, under open market conditions, a country can produce goods and services that meet the test of foreign competition *while simultaneously maintaining and expanding domestic real income* [my italics].[25]

By this definition, competitiveness can be seen as a process where real wages and national income are jacked up by a system of imperfect competition, producing a 'rent' to the nation. This is probably the reason why neo-classical economists opposed the term. This perspective, however, is compatible with our Other Canon view of how the rich countries got rich. Traditionally, when this development was not possible under market conditions, tariffs were established to protect the areas that experienced the most technological change, while competition was maintained. The more backward the nation, the higher the tariffs had to be in order to produce the desired effects.

Competitiveness, then, denotes a process that makes people and nations richer by increasing real wages and income. And yet, while visiting Uganda a few years ago, I experienced at first-hand how the term was used in order to argue for the opposite, for *lower* wages. The textile plants attracted to Uganda by the African Growth and Opportunity Act (AGOA) – a maquila-type set-up between the USA and Africa – could no longer compete internationally, and President Museveni argued that in order for Uganda to achieve 'competitiveness', workers' wages had to come down.

So competitiveness is a wonderfully flexible term, fitting a confused age of muddy thoughts and a need to explain away the utter failure of key economic theories. It can be used to describe a mechanism which makes everyone richer (the OECD definition), but it can also be used as a term describing the opposite, to convince workers that they must accept more poverty (Museveni's definition). The sad thing in Europe is that the term competitiveness is increasingly used in the Ugandan sense, coupled with 'labour market flexibility' (which invariable means flexibility downwards). In order to be 'competitive' we must lower our standards of living.

6 Get the innovations right

In the course of several speeches in 2000 and 2001 Alan Greenspan assimilated Joseph Schumpeter into the economic mainstream: only Schumpeter's theories could explain the combination of fast economic growth and low inflation experienced in the US at the time. As the phenomena surrounding the 'New Economy' temporarily seemed to have cancelled the normal laws of economic gravity, Greenspan heralded Schumpeter as the theoretician and prophet of the events. At the core of the phenomenon was the process of creative destruction that had become associated with the name of Schumpeter. This concept seemed tailor-made to describe the process by which information and communication technology destroyed previous technological solutions and laid waste old companies in order to make room for the new.

Here was another opportunity to explain why the Third World is poor: they do not innovate in the same way as they do in Silicon Valley. Again, however, in the context of standard textbook economics, some important aspects were missed. Several mechanisms are at work to cause such periods of rapid technological change to lead to increasing, rather than diminishing, economic differences.

First of all, as we have described in the section on techno-economic paradigms (see Chapter 4), the gales of creative destruction focus around a specific cluster of industries. These industries are located in geographical space – be it Manchester, Detroit or Silicon Valley – where a Klondike effect spreads. The increase in profits and real wages creates so much purchasing power that money is easily made in a whole array of businesses that would not be feasible elsewhere. These core innovations are activity-specific; they are found in some industries and not in others. Put in a different way, the windows of opportunity for innovations vary enormously from activity to activity. We can all intuitively understand that if Bill Gates had been in the business of herding goats in Mongolia, he could not have achieved what he has achieved with Microsoft. This common sense, however, does not necessarily transmit easily to standard economic theory.

Secondly, two different types of innovations spread in fundamentally diverse ways. Product innovations, such as those of Microsoft now or Henry Ford in another era, tend to spread in the economy in the form of higher profits and higher wages.[26] The utilization of new technology in other industries, as process innovations, has a tendency to spread much more in terms of lowered prices. While aircraft are largely as they were twenty-five years ago, the use of new technology in the airline business has caused a precipitous fall in the prices of air travel (much to the benefit of everyone as a consumer). As we explained in the previous chapter, in some areas innovations produce a downward pressure on wage levels (innovation punishing the producers); while the hotels in Venice or on Spain's Costa del Sol have not changed very much in themselves, bookings via the internet have caused hotel prices and business margins to fall in both places.

Schumpeter's student Hans Singer made an important contribution to development economics by showing that innovations in the raw materials sector of the Third World tended to spread as lower prices to the First World, while innovations (essentially product innovations) in the First World tended to be converted into higher wages in the First World itself.[27] Even when poor countries innovate, they are very often not able to harvest the benefits.

We have previously seen how poor nations from Mexico to Haiti have specialized in economic activities that are essentially technological dead-ends, bereft of any possibilities for innovation or for economies of scale. These are activities – as our example of baseball production demonstrated – where all the capital and all the engineers of the United States did not manage to create further innovations or productivity improvements. What we find, then, is that nations are forced to specialize in economic activities where there are no possibilities for innovation, only to be accused later of not innovating enough. These are countries that have specialized in being poor within the international division of labour.

7 Get the entrepreneurship right

Entrepreneurship – and human initiative in general – as an economic factor generally exists in isolation outside mainstream economics. However, the lack of entrepreneurship has recently been raised as a reason for poverty. This seems a particularly ill-advised explanation. While most inhabitants of wealthy countries have jobs to go to, the poor of this world depend on their daily entrepreneurship to survive. What vary so enormously are the windows of opportunity for successful entrepreneurship in poor countries. The lack of demand, the lack of supply, the lack of capital, and the type of competition found in commodity markets, lock poor countries into a situation where entrepreneurial success is extremely difficult. An increasing number of poor, very logically therefore, direct their entrepreneurial initiative into leaving their own countries to get into the rich countries that – thanks to wise policies now outlawed – have historically managed to get on to the virtuous circles of increasing returns, synergies and imperfect competition.

8 Get the education right

The fundamental moving forces of capitalism are human wit and will – in other words, new knowledge and entrepreneurship. Superficially it may therefore appear that what poor countries need above all are better educated people. This is of course also true, but successful cases of economic development prove the importance of *simultaneously* providing not only a flow of better educated people, but also jobs where their skills are demanded. Such a coordinated effort, matching both the supply and the demand of educated people, is the hallmark of successful development policies from nineteenth-century America to post-Second

World War Korea to Ireland after 1980. Such strategies have always required massive departures from laissez-faire policies.

Nations that only address the supply side of educated people end up educating for migration. The flow of educated people from the poor to the rich nations parallels the flow of capital going in the same direction, as one of Gunnar Myrdal's 'perverse back-washes' of the world economy. In many poor countries the most important export item is, sadly, the country's own people, whose remittances in some cases constitute the main item on the balance of payments. It also seems that these remittances are mainly used for consumption rather than for investment, and that, in some cases, they discourage rather than encourage efforts at home. Why work for 50 cents an hour in Haiti if your brother gets a minimum hourly wage of US $6.40 in Florida and sends money home?

9 Get the climate right

One important response of today's mainstream economics to the utter failure of their policies in the poor world is to bring back early themes of development economics that had justly been relegated to the periphery of the science. Climate, geography and disease are back at the core of mainstream development economics, and these factors are now incorporated in the rewriting of history with a neo-colonial/neo-imperial twist.[28] These factors are clearly not without impact, but their main effect lies in the way they influence human settlements and the vested interests of the settlers. The principal explanatory variable of development is the type of economic structure of a nation, and the type of structure is highly dependent on the vested interests of the ruling elites.

Settlements in the tropics were essentially established in order to produce raw materials,[29] and this production – whether in agriculture or mining – needed slave labour. While Europe slowly got rid of its feudalism, the economic and social structures of the tropics settled into the social divisions between master and slave. Also, outside the export sector land tenure tended to be feudal. For centuries the temperate zones without raw materials were not desirable property. The Dutch rejoiced in 1667 when the Peace of Breda gave them Surinam (later Dutch Guyana) in exchange for New York.

Settlements in the temperate zones tended to be qualitatively very different. They attracted people who came to farm themselves, not through use of slaves, and the local governments tended to distribute land in equal pieces to each farmer.[30] When institutions were slowly set up, the financing of a school system was very different in the slave and feudal societies compared to countries with independent farmers. Everyone knew that a slave who could read and write was a useless slave – he would try to escape. In the temperate zones the farmers set up school systems to educate their own and their neighbours' children, which they had good reason to promote. The tropical slave colonies earned foreign exchange to pay for imported manufactured goods, and the poverty of the aboriginals and the slaves provided no market for local manufacturing. The temperate colonies had few sources of foreign exchange, and with time they attracted a growing white population with European habits of consumption and increasing purchasing power. The industrialization strategy on which the temperate colonies embarked slowly created the kind of urban conglomerations also found in the wealthy parts of Europe. The cities of the tropics continued as administrative and trading centres.

An anonymously published book by 'A New Zealand Colonist' describes the logic applied by temperate zone settlers in 1897. The New Zealand settler refuses to see cheap imports as a boon, because accepting them would prevent his country from becoming industrialized.

An even more marked deviation from the creed of the Individualist is quickly seen. The British colonist is scarcely seated in the saddle when he begins a furious tilt against one of its most cherished articles. He discards all theories of free trade with the outer world and levies high import duties on every product which his colony is capable of supplying in adequate quantity for its own needs. He levies these duties even on the products of the country under whose flag he lives. He believes that only in this way can his new land be made a prosperous field for emigration from the old, and that prosperity so large as this aim implies will not be attainable while subject to unrestricted competition with the great Capital, the power of giving unlimited credit, and the more poorly paid labour of older lands. Their surplus stocks are dumped upon his own market to be sold at any price in order to prevent a fall in the far greater quantity which the exporter sells at home. When the colonist is told that to obtain these goods so cheaply is a boon, he refuses to recognise the right of any man to receive such boons at the cost of suffering to his own people.

In addition to these incentives to a policy of protection, the colonist desires that the children growing up around him may have opportunities of acquiring mechanical skill, and so saved from becoming mere hewers of wood and drawers of water for richer nations. He regards mechanical skill and the great products of that skill as the buttress of a people's strength and safety. He is firmly convinced that without a variety in industries no single industry can thrive, and that without a local ready market for a variety of agricultural products the proper rural settlement of his new country is impossible. These are the considerations which make nearly every British colonist, who is not a trader in imported commodities, strongly protectionist in policy. He does not regard immediate results. His eye is on the future and on the children growing up around him. The great risk, in his view, is that protection may make fortunes for a few employers while doing little for the employed. To this he is fully alive, but trusts to widespread education and to perfect freedom for arming alike the people of all classes and enabling them to find a suitable remedy when the need for such remedy shall come. Let what may happen his new policy is full of hope, and is strengthened by the conviction that it cannot breed more harm or be more injurious, under any circumstances, than the individualist form of free trade which it has replaced.[31]

This settler in a latecoming country, New Zealand, here sums up centuries of wisdom that I hope have also come across in this volume. As in the continental economic tradition, the settlers' economic theory requires simultaneous consideration of both the view of the individual and of society. The colonist's perspective goes far beyond limited profit-maximizing, extending to what Thorstein Veblen a little later was to call 'the parental bent', the care for future generations, be they one's own children or those of others. With its methodological individualism present-day economics misses that dimension (it is assumed that the market automatically provides harmony), just as it tends to overlook geography, time and ignorance. The colony attempts to protect 'every product which his colony is capable of supplying'. Here the size of the market will be a key factor determining what the colony will be able to supply. Small island colonies or colonies (as those in the tropical zones) with few white settlers will not have large enough markets to achieve this.

So today we find the colonist observing that rich countries dump their surplus products in the poor countries, and poor countries refuse to see cheap goods as a boon. In the hierarchy of nations a country that did not protect its industry would be doomed to the biblical curse of being bonded as 'hewers of wood and drawers of water' (Joshua 9:23).[32] This phrase was commonly used also in the United States as part of the string of arguments for protecting manufacturing industries. The Bible thus recognizes a hierarchy of skills – similar to our Quality Index of Economic Activities (Appendix VI) – where hewers of wood and drawers of water are located at the bottom. This view is incompatible with the core philosophy of international trade theory.

Our New Zealand colonist understood the importance of the mechanical skills needed for industry, and he also understood the synergy argument dating back to Antonio Serra in 1613: an industry does not survive in isolation. He also sees the potential problem of rent-seeking that so worries the Washington Consensus today. But if people are educated and wealthy, a democracy will form that can deal with this problem. We can add that this problem is infinitely more easy to deal with if the wealthy employer is abroad than if he is a national. In any case, this problem of internal income distribution is much better than the alternative, of being stuck as a raw-material producer where the farmers do not have a sufficient national market for their goods.

The most important effect of climate on economic development therefore comes about in a roundabout way – as a result of different modes of production, different settlement patterns, and different vested interests of the settlers. Singapore – one of the richest countries in the world – is located just one degree above the Equator. Singapore's wealth is not a result of being in some strange 'pocket' of a temperate climate at the Equator, but is attributable to an imported population (Asian and white) which is large enough to establish industries and to pursue an enlightened industrial policy. Malaysia's tropical success story is no doubt largely influenced by the successful policies of Singapore, which seceded from Malaysia in 1965.

It has been well known since the 1500s that geography and climate influence the location of industry, but it was equally acknowledged that the disadvantages of geography and climate not only could be, but had to be compensated by economic policy in order to build a manufacturing sector. The larger the geographical and climatic handicap, the larger the protective barriers had to be. Distance and transportation costs, however, provided 'natural protection'. The real problem started to appear with 'structural adjustment', which prematurely removed all policy tools from the countries whose manufacturing industries (no doubt also partly due to 'wrong' policies) had not yet reached the level of being competitive on the world market. Geography and climate are now being brought back towards the centre of development economics, in an attempt to find excuses for the misery caused by a premature removal of industrial policy tools.

10 Get the diseases right

Crippling diseases in the tropics have now also entered mainstream discourse as a key factor in explaining the failure of poor countries to develop.[33] Focus has been particularly on malaria. I shall argue that, yet again, mainstream economics is focusing on the effects of poverty rather than on its root causes.

Malaria was endemic in Europe for centuries, and the fight against this disease is already documented from the times of the Roman Empire. Historically, malaria was present in areas no one today would associate with the disease: Swiss Alpine valleys as high as 1400 metres above sea level were infested with malaria in the Middle Ages, and the disease has been found as far· north as the Kola Peninsula in northwestern Russia, beyond the Polar Circle. Europe got rid of its malaria through industrialization and development. More advanced and intensive agriculture caused swamps to be drained, and irrigation canals – even hydro-electric power plants – meant that the type of stagnating water where malaria thrives was incompatible with economic development. Huge public health works and eradication systems also freed Europe from malaria. The same type of development, over time, enabled European states to honour the debts they had contracted.

In the place of this economic development that made Europe rich and malaria-free, Africa gets to keep a colonial economic structure, exporting raw materials with an underdeveloped industrial sector. Instead of development enabling the continent to service debt, Africa gets debt cancellations. Instead of development that eradicates malaria, Africa gets mosquito nets. The structural problems underlying Africa's situation are not addressed, just the symptoms of these problems. This is an argument we shall deal with in more depth in the next chapter.

By stressing geography, climate and disease as economic factors, focus is moved away from the massive policy failures of the Washington Consensus during the last decades. We should therefore not be surprised that key proponents of past failed policies – like Jeffrey Sachs – are now the key proponents of the theories that bring in this new focus. When the invisible hand fails to deliver growth, economics seems to degenerate into a rather primitive belief that the misery of this world is caused by fate, providence and nature – geography, climate and disease – not by mankind. The Renaissance brought an understanding of the factors that create national wealth on the one hand and cause national poverty on the other. The Enlightenment and later the nineteenth century reinforced this understanding and fine-tuned the policy measures of the past. The United States was a prime example of the resounding success of the 'high wage strategy', as it was called at the time. The countries that did not change their economic structures into increasing returns activities before the Enlightenment's policy tools were outlawed by the Washington Consensus are now at the mercy of Nature's whims in a 'natural' equilibrium of poverty. As David Ricardo pointed out, the 'natural' wage is the one sufficient for physical subsistence.

The invisible hand of the market keeps a large number of the world's inhabitants at subsistence level. The proponents of the geography, climate and disease school of development economics do not seem to realize that these factors now create a trap because they themselves have removed the tools that historically made it possible for countries to escape the same trap. By keeping the theoretical focus away from the key issue – the need to change the economic structures of poor countries – these economists create a system that exemplifies Nietzsche's point that 'the harm done by the good is the most harmful harm'.

7

Palliative Economics: Why the Millennium Goals are a Bad Idea

Just as we may avoid widespread physical desolation by rightly turning a stream near its source, so a timely dialectic in the fundamental ideas of social philosophy may spare us untold social wreckage and suffering.

Herbert S. Foxwell, English economist, 1899

In parallel with the theoretical dead-ends and red herrings described in the previous chapter, the end of history project triggered an attempt to eradicate poverty – or rather to eliminate the symptoms of poverty – in the form of the huge and ambitious Millennium Development Goals (MDGs). At first sight the MDGs appeared to be noble goals for a world in sore need of urgent action to solve pressing social problems. They included worthy targets like reducing by half the number of people living on less than a dollar a day and the proportion of people who suffer from hunger, reducing diseases and child mortality, as well as educational and environmental goals. Nevertheless, the MDGs rest upon completely new principles with long-term effects that are neither well thought through nor well understood. In this chapter I shall attempt to explain why the focus on poverty reduction is erroneous and why the MDGs do not represent good social policy in the long run. The chapter echoes a presentation made at a meeting on the MDGs organized by the UN Department of Economic and Social Affairs in New York in 2005.[1]

One novelty of the MDGs' approach lies in the emphasis on foreign financing of domestic social and redistribution policies, rather than on domestic financing by the developing countries themselves. Disaster relief, which used to be of a temporary nature, now finds a more permanent form in the MDGs. In countries with more than 50 per cent of the government budget financed by foreign aid, huge additional resource transfers are being planned. This raises the question of the extent to which this approach will put a large number of nations permanently 'on the dole' – a system similar to 'welfare colonialism'.

The pursuit of the MDGs seems to indicate that the United Nations institutions, following several failed development decades, have abandoned the effort to treat the causes of poverty, and have instead concentrated on attacking the symptoms of poverty. In many ways the plight of Africa resembles a gigantic version of the case of the Saami reindeer herders discussed in Chapter 5. Just like the herders, Africans have been prevented from entering into the parts of the business that create processing, manufacturing, employment and development. Just like the herders, the Africans are being subject to what I have dubbed 'the Scandinavian fallacy' (because it seems to have originated there): instead of attacking the sources of poverty from the inside through the production system – which is what development economics used to be about – the symptoms are addressed by throwing money at them from the outside.

In this chapter, I shall argue that this palliative economics has, to a considerable extent, taken the place of development economics. Indeed, the balance between development economics (i.e. radically changing the productive structures of poor countries) and palliative economics (i.e. easing the pains of economic misery) is key to avoiding long-term negative effects. It is important to note that this change for the worse has happened while, at the same time, responsibility for world development has been shifted from the UN organizations to the Washington institutions.

How development problems were dealt with in the past

As we saw in the previous chapter, a stark contrast has emerged between the type of economic understanding underlying the Marshall Plan and the type of economic theory behind today's multilateral development discourse and the Washington institutions. The Marshall Plan grew out of recognition of the flaws of its predecessor, the Morgenthau Plan. While the goal of the Morgenthau Plan was to deindustrialize Germany, the goal of the Marshall Plan was not only to reindustrialize Germany, but also to establish a *cordon sanitaire* of wealthy nations along the borders of the Communist Bloc in Europe and Asia, from Norway to Japan. The self-reinforcing mechanisms that maintain the virtuous circles of a Marshall Plan are outlined in Figure 16, while the vicious circles of a Morgenthau Plan are outlined in Figure 17.

Judging from the number of nations lifted out of poverty, this reindustrialization plan was probably the most successful development project in human history. The fundamental insight behind the Marshall Plan was that the economic activities in the countryside and those in the cities are qualitatively different. The Marshall Plan thus recognized the relevance of the cameralist and mercantilist economic policies of previous centuries. In his famous June 1947 speech at Harvard, US Secretary of State George Marshall (who was later to be awarded the Nobel Peace Price) stressed that 'the farmer has always produced the foodstuffs to exchange with the city dweller for the other necessities of life'. 'This division of labour', i.e. between increasing returns activities in the cities and the diminishing returns activities in the countryside, '*is the basis of modern civilization*', said Marshall, adding that at the time it was threatened with breakdown.

Civilization requires increasing returns activities, something that economists and politicians from Antonio Serra (1613) to Alexander Hamilton, Abraham Lincoln and Friedrich List had been saying for a long time. Friedrich List particularly insisted on the links between city activities and political freedom. 'City air makes free' goes the old German saying. Figure 12 contrasts the Schumpeterian activities that are typical city activities with the Malthusian activities that are typical rural activities. Trying to

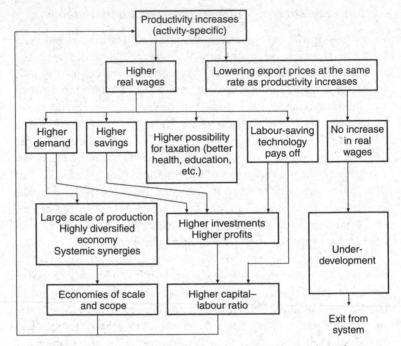

Note: In a closed system, with constant employment rate, the only way GNP per capita can grow is through the 'Virtuous Circle'. However, the system can be cut off at any one point; for example, if higher demand goes to foreign goods alone, the circle will break.

Source: Erik Reinert, *International Trade and the Economic Mechanisms of Underdevelopment*, Ph. D. thesis, Cornell University, 1980 (text slightly modified)

Figure 16   The Virtuous Circles of Economic Development – Marshall Plans

impose our 'civilization' and democracy on nations in the absence of a critical mass of Schumpeterian activities leads to 'failed states' and to the carnages and quagmires of Iraq and Afghanistan.

As we have seen in Chapter 2, the principles behind the toolbox used by nations moving from poverty to wealth through the creation of 'city activities' have been surprisingly stable from the time they were first employed by Henry VII of England in 1485 until their use in Korea in the 1970s. Schumpeterian activities and their productivity explosions (the principle illustrated in figure 6)

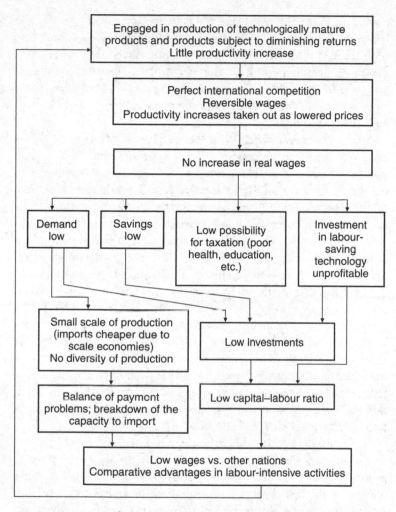

Note: It is futile to attack the system at any one point; for example, increasing investment when wages are still low and demand is absent. An instance of this is poor capital utilization and excess capacity in Latin American LDCs.

Source: Erik Reinert, *International Trade and the Economic Mechanisms of Underdevelopment*, Ph. D. thesis, Cornell University, 1980 (text slightly modified)

Figure 17   The Vicious Circles of Poverty – Morgenthau Plans

have catapulted the real wage levels in Ireland and Finland – the last European nations to be free from colonialism – over the last few decades. On the other hand, I claim that many of today's problems are as a result of the Washington institutions classifying the tools needed to create increasing returns activities – tools employed by all countries that developed after Venice and Holland – as 'illegal activities'.

After the Second World War, these general principles did not produce the same success in every country. Some of the most successful countries (for example, South Korea) temporarily protected new technologies for the world market, while some of the least successful ones permanently protected mature technologies, often for small home markets, by limiting competition (for example with the small countries of Latin America). (See Appendix IV which compares 'good' and bad' protectionist practices.) However, in many countries, real wages were considerably higher when this inefficient industrial sector was in place than they are today with a much weakened industrial sector, as seen in the example of Peru (figure 14). For centuries, it was understood that having an industrial sector – even if this sector was less efficient than those of the richest nations – produced higher real wages than having no industrial sector at all. So, if inefficient, the industrial sector ought to be made more efficient, rather than be closed down. This is probably the most important single element that was unlearned with the 1989 'end of history'.

In its simplest form, this argument is born out of the role of increasing and diminishing returns in trade theory as the starting points for virtuous and vicious circles of growth or poverty. As we saw in the last chapter, ignoring these mechanisms may cause factor–price polarization rather than factor–price equalization. In 1613 Serra first established increasing returns, virtuous circles and large economic diversity as necessary elements for wealth creation. This principle was used almost continuously – with brief interruptions – until it was abandoned with the emergence of the Washington Consensus. Since the 1980s, 'structural adjustment' has deindustrialized many poor peripheral countries and produced falling real wages.[2] Mainstream theory has long claimed that deindustrialization does not matter. On the contrary, according to the first WTO Director General Renato Ruggiero, free trade would unleash 'the borderless economy's potential to equalize relations between countries and regions'.

In the 1930s, maintaining the gold standard and balancing the budget were viewed as economic fundamentals, which locked the world into a sub-optimal equilibrium and prevented Keynes's policies from being carried out. Similarly, having free trade as the ideological centrepiece of development policies since the 1980s' debt crises has locked the less industrialized countries into a sub-optimal equilibrium.

Rather than continuing to pursue policies based on the most simplistic version of mainstream trade theory, the conflict between free trade and real wages in non-industrialized countries must be considered seriously. Specialization in activities with diminishing returns in the face of increasing population pressures also has serious environmental consequences.[3] Poverty in many Third World and former Second World countries is not caused by transitory problems, but rather by the permanent features of nations having different economic structures. When the US started industrializing, its leaders merely wanted to create a (less efficient) version of the production structure in England, a process requiring tariffs. Successful industrialization under protection, however, carries the seeds of its own destruction. By the 1880s, American economists – invoking the same arguments based on scale and technology that were used to protect American industries in the 1820s – argued for free trade. The same tariff that had helped to create manufacturing industry was now hurting the industry.[4] This is why Friedrich List, a prominent protectionist, was only in favour of global free trade after all countries had achieved their comparative advantage outside the diminishing returns sector.[5] In other words, he disagreed not over the principle of free trade as such, but rather over its timing.

If one reads what Adam Smith, an icon of free trade and laissez-faire, says about economic development in its early stages, one finds his views are very much in line with those of classical development economists who advocate industrialization. In his early work, *The Theory of Moral Sentiments*,[6] Smith interestingly argued that new manufactures are not to be promoted to help suppliers or consumers, but in order to improve the 'great system of government'.

As discussed in Chapter 4, it is also entirely possible to argue that Adam Smith was a misunderstood mercantilist, who strongly supported the mercantilist policies of the past, but argued that they were no longer necessary for England. He praised the Navigation Acts protecting English manufacturing and shipping against Holland, arguing 'they are as wise ... as if they had all been dictated by the most deliberate wisdom' and holding them to be 'perhaps, the wisest of all the commercial regulations of England'.[7] All in all, Smith described a development that had become self-sustaining – a kind of snowballing effect – originating in the protectionist measures of the past. Only once did Smith use the term 'invisible hand' in *The Wealth of Nations* – when it sustained the key import substitution goal of mercantilist policies and when the consumer preferred domestic industry to foreign industry.[8] This could only happen when 'the market' had taken over the role previously played by protective measures, and national manufacturing no longer needed such protection.

The praxis of economic development has been to emulate and produce less efficient 'copies' of the economic structure of wealthy nations. The key features of these economic structures – significant division of labour (amongst a large number of different industries and professions) and a sector with increasing returns (industry and knowledge-intensive services) – were codified by economists such as Antonio Serra (1613), James Steuart (1767), Alexander Hamilton (1791) and Friedrich List (1841). As we saw in chapter 1, these principles have, at times been *un*learned: in France in the 1760s, Europe in the 1840s, and the world in the 1990s.

Nevertheless, these periods ultimately came to an end because of their great social costs. Physiocracy in France created shortages and scarcity of bread, contributing to the onset of the French Revolution.[9] The free trade euphoria of the 1840s met its backlash in 1848, with revolutions in all large European countries except England and Russia. David Ricardo's trade theory was proved wrong every time it was applied asymmetrically to increasing and diminishing return industries.[10] At the same time, however, Ricardo's argument that the 'natural' wage level is subsistence has proved correct. As we saw in chapter 5, the free trade euphoria of the 1990s has again created increased poverty in several peripheral countries, but this time our response was wrong: we are still focusing too much on the symptoms – rather than the causes – of the problem.

How development problems are dealt with now

Standard economics tends to see development as a process largely driven by accumulation of investments in physical and human capital.[11] As we have seen, standard economic theory underlying today's development policies is generally unable to recognize qualitative differences between economic activities. None of today's failed or failing states could pass George Marshall's test for what creates modern civilization, as they have very weak manufacturing sectors and are unable to generate the virtuous exchange between city and rural activities. They also have very little diversity in their economic bases, a limited division of labour, and they specialize in activities subject to diminishing returns and/or commodity competition (where they have no power over prices and where technological change tends to reduce prices to the foreign consumers rather than raising their wages).

Historically, modern democracy began in nations where this civilizing trade between urban and rural areas had already been established, for example, in the Italian city-states. In the most successful city-states – including those with a scarcity of arable land such as Venice and the Dutch Republic – power did not lie with the landowning class. This enabled Schumpeterian 'cronyism', with political and economic interests 'colluding' in ways to create widespread wealth. Dependency on raw materials encouraged feudalism and colonialism, neither of which leads to political freedom. Similarly, the American Civil War was essentially between Southern landowners with vested interests in agriculture and cheap labour and the North with vested interests in industrialization. The history of Latin America, in many ways, has been similar to the history of the USA, but as if the South had won the Civil War.

In the alternative Other Canon economic paradigms – combining the historical and evolutionary schools – the process of development is driven by emulation and assimilation: learning from more advanced countries by 'copying' both their economic structures and their institutions. Key elements in this emulation and assimilation strategy are institutions such as patent protection, scientific academies and universities. In this model, economic growth tends to be activity-specific, tied to 'clusters' of economic activities characterized by increasing returns, dynamic imperfect competition and rapid technological progress. In addition to capital, the process requires the transferring and mastering of skills and, above all, the creation of a viable market for activities with increasing returns where the absence of purchasing power and massive unemployment tend to go hand in hand. By generally using models assuming full employment, the Washington institutions avoid a key issue that locks nations in poverty – the lack of formal employment. Since Holland and Venice in the sixteenth century, only nations with healthy manufacturing sectors have achieved anything close to full employment without massive rural underemployment.

The dominant economic theory today represents what Schumpeter called 'the pedestrian view that it is capital per se that propels the capitalist engine': development is seen as largely driven by the accumulation of capital – physical or human. 'The premise of neo-classical theory is that, if the investments are made, the acquisition and mastery of new ways of doing things is relatively easy, even automatic,' as Richard Nelson says.[12] More importantly, a core assumption of standard economics that is seldom acknowledged is that economic structure is irrelevant, as capital per se will lead to economic development, regardless of the economic structure within which investment is made. In the alternative Other Canon theory, economic activities have very different windows of opportunity as carriers of economic growth. In other words, we have to get rid of what James Buchanan calls 'the equality assumption' in economic theory, probably its most important, but least discussed premise. At its core, the Enlightenment project was one of ordering the world by creating taxonomies or classification systems, of which Linnaeus's is the best known. Neo-classical economics is pre-Enlightenment in that it achieves its analytical precision precisely by lacking any taxonomy: everything is qualitatively alike. Therefore its conclusions, like factor–price equalization, are essentially already built into its assumptions. The ability, at any time, to absorb innovation and knowledge – and consequently to attract investments – varies enormously from one economic activity to another.

Viewing capital per se as the key to growth, loans are given to poor nations with productive/industrial structures that are unable to absorb such capital profitably. Interest payments often exceed the rate of return on investments made. 'Finance for Development' may therefore take on the characteristics of a pyramid scheme, with the only ones to gain being those who started the scheme and are close to the door.[13] Similarly, investments in human capital, made without corresponding changes in the productive structure to create demand for the skills acquired, will tend to promote emigration. In both cases, Gunnar Myrdal's 'perverse backwashes' of economic development will be the result: more capital – both monetary and human – will flow from the poor to the rich countries. One explanation for this lies in the type of economic structure that characterizes poor nations: a vicious circle resulting from the lack of supply and demand, and the absence of increasing returns. US industrial policy from 1820 to 1900 is probably the best example for Third World countries to follow today until these nations are ready to benefit from international trade.

What to do about it

As with the Marshall Plan, funds must be matched by the establishment of industrial and service sectors that can absorb the physical and human investments. Diversifying from raw material production is necessary for creating a basis for democratic stability and increased welfare, even if the new sectors will initially be unable to survive world market competition. This incipient industrialization will need special treatment of the kind the Marshall Plan afforded, and requires interpreting the Bretton Woods agreement in the same way as was done in the immediate post-Second World War era.

The neo-classical economists' poor understanding of how businesses operate also contributes to the problem. At the core of their economic theory of capitalism is perfect competition and equilibrium, a situation which produces very little profit. Any successful and profitable business enterprise rests, almost by definition, on some kind of rent-seeking. The poverty-stricken Third World corresponds most closely to conditions of diminishing returns and perfect competition, while the rich countries, whose exports are produced under conditions of Schumpeterian-dynamic imperfect competition, are 'rent-seekers' whose rents lead to higher wages and a higher tax base. This failure to understand development as Schumpeterian imperfect competition is at the heart of the arguments against industrial policy. Anything that causes imperfect competition tends to be seen as contributing to 'cronyism'.

Keynes saw investments resulting from what he called 'animal spirits'. Without 'animal spirits' – the will to invest in uncertain conditions – capital is sterile, both in the worlds of Joseph Schumpeter and Karl Marx. The motivating force behind 'animal spirits' is the desire to maximize profits, thus upsetting the equilibrium of perfect competition. From a businessman's point of view poor countries often suffer from low investments because of a lack of profitable investment opportunities, largely due to low purchasing power and high unemployment. Subsistence farmers are not profitable customers for most producers of goods and services. Tariffs can create incentives to move production to the labour markets of the poor. Historically this has been seen as a conscious trade-off between the interest of man-as-a-wage-earner and man-as-a-producer. The idea that industrialization would rapidly increase employment and wages – which would more than offset the temporarily higher cost of manufactured goods – was at the core of Latin America's import-substitution industrialization which was very successful for a long time – and also of American economic theory around 1820.[14]

The idea that greater 'openness' would improve the lot of the poor countries is both counter-intuitive and contrary to historical experience. In many cases, suddenly 'opening' a backward economy killed off the little manufacturing activity that existed, thus exacerbating the situation. The wise development theorists of old – James Steuart and Friedrich List – stressed the need to open trade slowly in order to give the productive sector of the poor trading partner time to adjust. This was also the European Union's approach to the successful integration of Spain into the EU in the 1980s. With the triumphalism following 1989 all this was unlearned: 'shock therapy' became the name of the game.

From the unification of Italy in the nineteenth century to the integration of Mongolia and Peru in the 1990s, historical experience has shown that free trade between nations at very different levels of development tends to destroy the most efficient industries in the least efficient countries. I have referred to this common phenomenon as the Vanek-Reinert effect. It was seen in France after the Napoleonic War, during the Unification of Italy and – during the end of history – both in the Second and Third World. The first thing to die is advanced manufacturing, the last thing to die out is subsistence agriculture, the least advanced. The sequence is 1) deindustrialization, 2) deagriculturalization, 3) depopulation. This phenomenon can be observed in many countries, for example in the south of Mexico and in Moldova in the European periphery, where only the population over sixty and under fourteen stay behind while those in the working age bracket are working abroad.

In Peru and Mongolia, as in many other countries, real wages peaked during the period of 'inefficient' import substitution. What mainstream economics fails to see is that the ports, airports, roads, power stations, schools, hospitals and service industries created by this 'inefficient' industrial sector were real and could not have been created without the demand for labour and infrastructure that this sector generated.[15] This is really no different from what England created after 1485, what Germany created after 1650, what the United States created after 1820, and Korea after 1960. These countries all started building wealth by creating what at the time were 'inefficient' national industrial sectors.

National efficiency needs a preliminary stage of what to small minds (but not to Adam Smith) may appear as relative inefficiency. This strategy has been a mandatory rite of passage for all presently wealthy nations, a strategy which has now been outlawed by the Washington institutions.

The only difference between the currently rich countries on the one hand and Peru and Mongolia on the other, is that the latter countries never made it to the point where their industries were internationally competitive. The explanation for this is mixed; partly their type of protectionism was of the wrong and less dynamic type (see Appendix IV), but certainly one important negative factor was the speed of opening up of the economy. In the former communist countries many firms went bankrupt even before they had an accounting system in place that made them understand their own costs. The shock therapy of the end of history will, given a bit more perspective, come across as sheer folly.

As I have previously argued, the timing of the opening up of an economy is crucial. Opening up too late can seriously hamper growth, while opening up too early will result in deindustrialization, falling wages[16] and increasing social problems. That large numbers of subsistence farmers should be made 'uncompetitive' by subsidized First World agriculture is a relatively new, but alarming trend that may persist even after the First World remove their export subsidies on food. Mexican farmers' lack of 'competitiveness' compared to American producers of maize and wheat – subsidized and not – is a key factor in the migration from southern Mexico. In India there are around 650 million farmers, with a large proportion of them as 'uncompetitive' as their Mexican colleagues who produce maize and wheat today. 'Uncompetitive' Mexican farmers can seek work in the United States, but where do we move the 650 million Indian farmers who will be placed in the same position by 'free trade'?

In the poorest countries today, a trade-off exists between maximizing international trade – what present policies achieve – and maximizing human welfare. This is exactly the problem eighteenth-century French economist Simon Linguet pointed to as the result of the Physiocratic policies of the time. This important trade-off between freedom to trade and freedom from hunger needs to be addressed in a different way today, not merely by compensating the losses (and increasing the dependency) of the poor countries through increased aid.

History has shown that the vicious circles of poverty and underdevelopment can be effectively attacked only by qualitatively changing the productive structures of poor and failing states. A successful strategy implies increasing diversification away from sectors with diminishing returns (traditional raw materials and agriculture) to sectors with increasing returns (technology, intensive manufacturing and services), creating a complex division of labour and new social structures in the process. In addition to breaking away from subsistence agriculture, this will create an urban market for goods, which will induce specialization and innovation, bring in new technologies, create both alternative employment and the economic synergies that unite a nation-state. The key to coherent development is interplay between sectors with increasing and diminishing returns in the same labour market.

Understanding Malthusian vs. Schumpeterian cronyism

Among economists 'mercantilist' is about the worst imaginable insult. This is in spite of the fact that the twentieth century's two most famous economists – John Maynard Keynes and Joseph Schumpeter – both defended mercantilism and pre-Smithian economics in its context. Someone who is of the opinion that some economic activities better promote economic growth and welfare than others are often called 'mercantilists'. Mercantilists tilted the economic playing field in order to promote increasing return activities. Lately, when voices are again being raised in favour of industrializing poor countries, a new set of arguments has developed: industrial policy will create 'rent-seeking' and 'cronyism'.

In chapter 4 I argued that rent-seeking is the basic driving force of capitalism. The question is whether this rent spreads through society in general – in the form of higher profits, higher wages and higher taxable income – or not. The theoretical goal of 'perfect competition' is a situation that does not create wealth for the producers. To this rent-seeking argument is now added the related argument that industrial policy creates 'cronyism', that money is being made through favouritism shown to friends and associates.

With reference to the two types of economic activities – Malthusian and Schumpeterian – described in figure 12, we also need to separate the two types of cronyism. Consider these examples:

2005: A Filipino sugar producer uses his political influence to get import protection for his products.

2000: Major Daley in Chicago (ignoring the advice of University of Chicago economists) provides subsidies to already wealthy high-tech investors through an incubator.

1950s and 1960s: Swedish industrialist Marcus Wallenberg uses his close contacts with Labour Party Minister of Finance Gunnar Sträng, to win political support to carry out his plans for Swedish companies, Volvo and Electrolux.

1877: Steel producers in the United States use their political clout to impose 100 per cent duty on steel rails.[17]

1485: Woolworkers use their connections to King Henry VII to influence the state to give them subsidies and to impose an export duty on raw wool to increase raw material prices for their competitors on the Continent, slowly strangulating the wool industry elsewhere, for example in Florence.

The above examples all involve crony capitalism and rent-seeking behaviour which mainstream economic theory tends to abhor. However, a crucial difference separates the first example from the rest. The Filipino crony differs from the other cronies in that he gets subsidies for a raw material with diminishing returns that competes in a world market facing perfect competition. In other words, he is a Malthusian crony, leading his country down the path of diminishing returns (in spite of technological change which counteracts this) in an activity where technical change fails to raise real wages. The others are Schumpeterian cronies, producing under what Schumpeter called historical increasing returns (a combination of both increasing returns and fast technological change). If we couple this with new trade theory, we see that the tilted playing fields of Schumpeterian cronyism produce vastly different results from those of the Filipino crony.

Keynes once said, 'the worse the situation, the less laissez-faire works'. If we insist on abandoning industrial policy because moving away from perfect competition will cause some cronies to get rich, we have totally misunderstood the nature of capitalism. After all, capitalism *is* about getting away from perfect competition. The most important thing good business schools teach is how to escape from the situation of perfect competition that economists tend to assume.

Economic development is caused by structural changes which break the equilibrium creating rents. Insisting on the absence of rents is the same as demanding a steady and stationary state. However, there is still a need to choose which activities to protect, which in turn creates cronies. Abraham Lincoln protected the steel cronies – by paying a little more for steel[18] the US created a huge steel industry with many high-paying jobs that also provided a base for government taxation. The triple rent structure we referred to in chapter 3 in place in Venice, the Dutch Republic and England had also been recreated in the United States. Economic development is about aligning the public interests of the nation with the private vested interests of the capitalists. The failure of standard economics to understand the dynamics of the business world has led to a failure to understand the economic essence of colonialism. By preventing colonies from having their own manufacturing industries, economic activities with high growth potential and mechanization remained in the metropolis, whereas activities with diminishing returns went to the colonies.

The immense transfers that accompany the MDG process will also necessarily lead to cronyism. Through this initiative, some will get wealthy, since crony-free economics only exists in neoclassical models. By opting for Schumpeterian cronyism, instead of aid-based cronyism, it would be possible for poor countries to extricate themselves from economic dependency. Schumpeterian cronyism increases the size of the national and world economic pie. Aid-based cronyism adds nothing, but creates an incentive system that moves attention away from creating national values and deeper into foreign dependency.

We seem to have unlearned the logic behind policy tools for economic development. Patents and modern tariffs came into being at about the same time, in the late 1400s. These rent-seeking institutions were created using the very same understanding of the process of economic development in order to protect knowledge (in the case of patents) and to produce in new geographic areas (in the case of tariffs). Both patents and tariffs represent legalized rent-seeking to promote goals not achievable under perfect competition.

Yet why are the rent-seeking and cronyism arguments not applied to patents, but only used against tariffs and other policy instruments employed in poor countries? With some justification, it can be said that the wealthy countries are establishing rules that legalize constructive rent-seeking in their own countries, but prohibit similar ones in the poor countries.

Diversity as a precondition for development

Another blind spot in economics is its inability to understand the importance of diversity for economic growth. Diversity is a key factor in development for a variety of reasons. First, a diversity of activities with increasing returns – maximizing the number of professions in an economy – is the basis for the synergy effects which lead to economic development. This was understood from the 1600s. Secondly, modern evolutionary economics points to the importance of diversity as a basis for selection between technologies, products and organizational solutions, which are all key elements in an evolving market economy.[19] Thirdly, diversity has been an important explanation for European 'exceptionalism', where a large number of nation-states in competition with one another created tolerance and a demand for diversity. A scholar, whose views were not popular with a particular king or ruler, could find employment in a different nation, thus creating a greater diversity of ideas.

A fourth reason – religious diversity – was emphasized by Johann Friedrich von Pfeiffer (1718–87), one of the most influential German economists of the eighteenth century. While some economists believe that more rapid economic growth is promoted by some religions rather than by others,[20] Richard Tawney (1880–1962),[21] the famous English historian, emphasized the declining importance of religion in propelling capitalism. About 150 years earlier, Pfeiffer had argued that when a diversity of 'competing' religions exists within a state, religion as an institution will lose much of its power over the inhabitants. The existence of alternative beliefs will remove fear and other factors that contribute to fanaticism, and a new tolerance will open up for a desirable diversity of its population and skills).[22] As a visiting professor at the University of Malaya in Kuala Lumpur on two occasions, I have had the opportunity to observe Muslim religion as it is practised in an industrialized country, among a multitude of other religions. In my mind, Tawney and Pfeiffer both got it right, which strongly indicates that we are attacking the security problems of the West from completely the wrong angle.

We live in an age of great ignorance today, when established qualitative arguments exploring the process of economic development have been abandoned. The importance of diversity is just one. The banality of today's explanations about poverty being a result of climate and corruption amply testifies to this ignorance, fortified by the absence of historical knowledge and interest in proven principles that have brought nation after nation from poverty to wealth over five centuries. In a similar situation to the one we are in now, an enlightened group of nineteenth-century German economists caught the ear of Chancellor Otto von Bismarck, and were allowed to design Germany's developmental and welfare state. Similarly, just after the Second World War, the world understood that economic development was the result of synergies and increasing returns. Combined with the political threat of communism, this understanding made it possible to overrule the free trade ideologies in Washington, and reindustrialize Europe and industrialize parts of Asia. In order to restart growth, it is necessary to reinvent this type of economic theory.

Restoring a more comprehensive theory

Following the fall of the Berlin Wall, variations of neo-classical economics became the only game in town. However, neo-classical economics was, using Nicholas Kaldor's term, an untested theory. Although neo-classical theory had provided an effective ideological shield during the Cold War, no nation had ever been built on this theoretical framework. By 1990, policy recommendations were formulated around Samuelson's 'law' of factor–price equalization, and neglected other important theoretical contributions. Three key insights by the founding father of neo-classical economics, Alfred Marshall, were lost as theory gravitated away from Marshall's qualitative understanding of industrial production to the mathematics found in the appendices to his *Principles of Economics* (1890). Marshall had not only described taxes on activities with diminishing returns in order to subsidize activities with increasing returns as good development policy, but had also emphasized the importance for a nation to produce in sectors where most technical progress is to be found, and the role of synergies (industrial districts).

This sequence of policy fads described in chapter 6 failed to address several fundamental blindspots in neo-classical economics:

a)   its inability to register qualitative differences, including the different potentials of economic activities as contributors to economic growth;
b)   its inability to acknowledge synergies and linkages, and
c)   its inability to cope with innovations and novelties, and how these are differently distributed among economic activities.

Together, these blindspots of contemporary mainstream economics prevent many poor countries from developing. China and India – probably today's most successful developing countries – have for about fifty years followed the recommendations of the Marshall Plan rather than those of the Washington Consensus.

The accuracy and the irrelevance of mainstream economics are both products of the same process whereby relevant factors have been increasingly excluded, thus creating blindspots of increasing magnitude. The guiding insight of French philosopher Jacques

Derrida's deconstruction theory is highly relevant to economics: every structure, be it literary, psychological, social, economic, political or religious, that organizes our experience is constituted and maintained through such acts of exclusion. In the process of creating something, something else inevitably gets left out. These exclusive structures can become repressive – and repression comes with consequences. In a manner reminiscent of Freud, Derrida insists that what is repressed does not disappear, but always returns to unsettle every construction, no matter how secure it seems. Standard textbook economics as applied by the Washington institutions has repressed qualitative differences between economic activities. But, as Derrida would have suspected, these differences – those creating the qualitative gaps between the Afghan economy and that of Silicon Valley – come back to haunt us as we try in vain to mould Afghanistan into our image of what a nation-state should be like. The war in Iraq was based on Cold War economic models of a frictionless and harmony-creating kind where markets and free trade would create 'spontaneous order'. There is a direct link between the repression of relevant economic factors and what an increasing number of Afghans and Iraqis today perceive as repression. A 'new and improved' development economics must consciously keep Derrida's caveat in mind. Rather than theorizing by exclusion, we must again theorize by inclusion, as was the hallmark of the historical schools of economics.

Recently, innovation has been reintroduced as an economic factor, but this is not sufficient. While learning and innovation are key elements in development, they may also be passed on in the economy as falling prices to foreign consumers. The key insight by Schumpeter's student Hans Singer was that learning and technological change in the production of raw materials, particularly in the absence of a manufacturing sector, tend to lower export prices, rather than increase the standard of living in the raw material-producing nation.[23] Learning tends to create wealth for producers only when they are part of a close network once called 'industrialism' – a dynamic system of economic activities subject to increasing productivity through technical change and a complex division of labour. The absence of increasing returns, dynamic imperfect competition and synergies in raw material-producing countries are all part of the mechanisms that perpetuate poverty.

Figure 18 summarizes the arguments that have been made historically to explain why some economic activities are better than others, why a nation that only produces raw materials cannot lift itself out of poverty. Cold War economics and 1989 triumphalism excluded them all from the Washington Consensus policy toolbox. These differences are presented as two 'ideal types'. The production and marketing of flower bulbs in the Netherlands – although technically agriculture – share many of the characteristics listed under 'manufacturing'. Maquila type manufacturing, on the other hand, shares many of the characteristics of 'agriculture'.[24] In the tradition of Charles King[25] that dominated Enlightenment economic thinking, the left column lists 'good' economic' activities, the right column 'bad' economic activities. It is important that this list is considered in its totality, including the cumulative synergy, positive and negative interplay, between the different factors.

Just one of these factors is enough to block economic development. If the farmers' customers are abroad, rather than being part of the same labour market in a nearby city, the crucial synergetic and 'civilizing' links that George Marshall referred to in 1947 will fail to appear. The plans to develop Africa through the export of food to the First World is therefore doomed to fail as a result of this factor alone, not to mention all the others in figure 17.

Since the Second World War, acts of exclusion left the above factors outside the toolbox that influences Washington Consensus policies. As a result, those nations that had not yet reached the threshold above which free trade is beneficial, were falling further behind in terms of real wage levels. As we discussed in chapter 6, instead of reintroducing these economic factors, since the 1990s huge resources have been increasingly employed by well-intentioned governments along a relatively sterile path of increasingly non-economic factors ('red herrings'). Simultaneously 'aid' was increased, creating an international social policy that covered up the lack of real progress. However, the best social policy is to create development, though not by the rich creating subsidized reservations

'Manufacturing'	'Agriculture'
Generalized wealth only found in cities with artisans and manufacturing, and explained as a systemic effect: *il ben comune* (Florence, 1200s).	Traditionally very little systemic effects, no *ben comune* (common weal)
The experience of Spain in the 1500s: the real gold mines are the manufacturing industries, because the gold from the Americas ends up in the manufacturing cities outside Spain (generalized knowledge, 1600s).	The experience of Spain in the 1500s: deindustrialization and return to agriculture creates increased poverty: a nation is better off with a relatively ineffective manufacturing sector than with none. (See Figure 14 for a parallel to Latin America today.)
Windows of opportunity for innovation concentrated in few activities (all urban: Botero, 1590) (Perez and Soete, 1988)	Few windows of opportunity for innovation (until very recent history).
Generalized wealth caused by a large diversity/large division of labour/ maximizing the number of professions (Serra, 1613). Division of labour simultaneous.	Traditionally only a minimum of diversity. Very little division of labour (Adam Smith). Division of labour sequential over the seasons, from ploughing to harvesting.
International specialization leads to increasing returns/economies of scale, producing falling costs, barriers to entry and higher profits (Serra, 1613).	Specialization will meet the flexible wall of diminishing returns and increasing costs/falling productivity (from Genesis to Ricardo and John Stuart Mill).
Increased population a necessity in order to create scale/markets for manufactures (European pre-Malthusian population theory).	Increased population a problem because of diminishing returns and no new land (Malthus).
Important synergies between city and countryside: only farmers near manufacturing cities produce efficiently (Europe in the 1700s to George Marshall, 1947).	Only farmers who share a labour market with manufacturing activities are wealthy: market for products, market for excess labour, access to technology (US/Europe in the 1800s).
Export of manufactured goods and import of raw materials, but also exchanging manufactures for other manufactures, is 'good trade' for a nation (King, 1721). [26]	Export of raw materials and import of manufactured goods is 'bad trade' for a nation (King, 1721).
Dynamic imperfect competition	Perfect competition (*commodity competition*).

continued overleaf

Figure 18   The Qualitative Differences between Manufacturing and Agriculture (raw material production) as Perceived Over Time as *Ideal Types* or *Stylized Facts*

'Manufacturing'	'Agriculture'
Activities with high growth in demand as income grows/Verdoorn's Law ties increase in demand to increase in productivity.	Activities with low-income elasticity of demand (when people get richer, they tend not to use more of these products).
Subject to 'productivity explosions' since the 1400s.	Slow growth in productivity until after Second World War.
Stable production that can be fine-tuned to demand. Overproduction avoided by storing raw materials and semi-manufactures.	Cyclical production/overproduction (no possibility of storing semi-manufactures).
Stable prices.	Large price fluctuations. Timing of sales often more important for income than production skills.
Creates a middle class and conditions for democracy ('City air makes free').	Generally creates a feudal class structure.
Creates bargaining power for labour and irreversible wages: 'stickiness' of wages in money.	Reversible wages and payment in kind.
Dominated by product innovations which, when products mature, turn to process innovations.	Dominated by process innovations, product innovations for agriculture are made outside the agricultural sector (Ford's tractors, Monsanto's seeds, biotechnology).
Technological change leads to higher wages, profits and taxes in the producing countries ('a Fordist wage regime').	Technological change leads mainly to lower prices in the consuming countries (Singer, 1950).
Terms of Trade tend to improve over time compared to agriculture.	Terms of Trade tend to deteriorate over time compared to industrial products.
Creates large synergies (linkages, clusters).	Creates few synergies.

Figure 18   continued

where the poor are kept, largely underemployed and 'underproductive'. The Indian reservations in North America are a sad example of policies that subsidize without changing productive structures. Similarly, the MDGs are far too biased towards palliative economics rather than structural change, towards treating the symptoms of poverty rather than its causes. While such policies may be needed under currently critical conditions, they will remain poor social policies in the longer term unless the deeper roots of the problem are confronted. Towards the end of the last chapter we contrasted the eradication of malaria – endemic in Europe at least since Roman times – with the handing out of mosquito nets that is presented as the solution in Africa today.

Creating 'welfare colonialism'

Current policies risk inadvertently undermining the development potential of aid with its palliative effects. What we may be creating is a system that could be described as 'welfare colonialism', a term coined by anthropologist Robert Paine to describe the economic integration of the native population in Northern Canada.[27] The essential features of welfare colonialism are:

1. a reversal of the colonial drain of the old days, with the net flow of funds to the colony, rather than to the mother country;
2. integration of the native population in ways that radically undermine their previous livelihoods; and
3. the native population is put on what are essentially unemployment benefits.

In Paine's view, welfare becomes the vehicle for a stable 'governing at a distance' through the exercise of a particularly subtle, 'non-demonstrative' and dependency-generating form of neo-colonial social control that pre-empts local autonomy through well-intentioned and generous, but ultimately morally wrong, policies. Welfare colonialism creates paralysing dependencies on the 'centre' in a peripheral population, a centre exerting control through incentives that create total economic dependency, thus preventing political mobilization and autonomy. The social conditions in which the native inhabitants of North American reservations find themselves today show us that, in their case, the final effect of massive transfer payments has been to create a dystopia, rather than a utopia.

We also see aid and other transfers creating passivity and disincentives to work in poor nations. Haitian observers point to family transfer payments from the United States creating disincentives to work for a going rate of 30 US cents an hour. Brazilian research on the highly laudable Zero Hunger project, carried out at different government levels (national, state and local) through various programmes targeted to fight hunger, concludes that these projects are, to a large extent, ineffective since they treat the symptoms of poverty by distributing food or subsidizing food prices, rather than by creating situations where the poor can become breadwinners.[28]

Recent events illustrate the kind of dilemmas which will necessarily accompany welfare colonialism. It has been discussed whether or not aid to Ethiopia should be cut off as a sanction against the Ethiopian government. Regardless of possible noble intentions that may have created the initial move to aid the poor, welfare colonialism will develop into a system where the rich countries will always be able to cut off aid, food and livelihood sources from the poor countries if they disapprove of their national policies. As long as 'development aid' remains palliative, rather than truly developmental, seemingly generous and well-intentioned development aid will inevitably become extremely powerful mechanisms by which rich countries end up controlling poor countries. Rather than promoting global democracy, such policies will lead towards global plutocracy. This is feudalism with a new geographical twist: feudal lords still have total political control over the poor masses producing the raw materials, but the feudal lords and the masses now live in different countries.

The political situations that develop from economic dependency and welfare colonialism are evident. Elections in Palestine and Iraq have made it clear that the West essentially approves of democracy only as long as the poor elect the politicians approved by the West. The democratically elected leader of Bolivia has nowhere to turn for advice or funds that may present an alternative to the Washington Consensus, and therefore gravitates back into a Cold War-type alliance with Cuba. The absence of alternative economic theories creates political dead-ends, in which economic dead-ends continue to repeat themselves.

The political aspects of welfare colonialism are grim. In an expanding world economy, where many raw materials are rapidly becoming strategic commodities, the poor 'stand in the way' of access to these raw materials, not unlike the native American Indians being a hindrance to the settlers' use of land. For some American conservatives, placing the poor on 'reservations' is an option to be seriously considered. Only about a decade ago, two American authors recommended the establishment of a custodial state in a much publicized book: 'by custodial state, we have in mind a high-tech and more lavish version of the Indian reservation for some substantial minority of the nation's population, while the rest of America tries to go about its business'.[29] The MDGs are uncomfortably close to combining the consumption-based view of poverty with the idea of establishing reservations where the basic needs of the poor are taken care of, while the rest of the world get on with their business. The defiant stances found in the Muslim world can be understood as a reaction to this situation, where it is obvious that world capitalism is failing them and merely offering a 'custodial state' as the only alternative.

From the point of view of economic theory, the MDGs can be seen as a system where nations producing under increasing returns (industrialized nations) pay annual compensation to nations producing under constant or diminishing returns (raw material producers) for their losses (see Appendix III). This idea is not a new one, and has been present in American college textbooks since the 1970s.[30] Until the victory of the Washington Consensus over the UN development institutions, the favoured option was to indus-trialize the poor countries, even if it meant that their industries would not be competitive in the world market for a long time. Making free trade the linchpin of the world economic system – one to which all other considerations must yield – has made welfare colonialism appear as the only option. The alternative option of developing the poor world is currently absent because many do not wish to abolish free trade as the core of the world economic order.

Twice the political pressure created by the spectre of communism has resulted in successful development practices. Both after the almost continuous European revolutions from 1848 to 1871 and during the Cold War and with the Marshall Plan in 1947, capitalism was able to adjust in order to solve pressing social problems. In 1947 the free traders in Washington had to yield to the political need for protectionist development policies encircling the Communist Bloc, which led to the astonishing success of the Marshall Plan in Europe, and the East Asian miracle. It is perhaps a faint hope that Osama bin Laden and today's terrorist threat may play the same role as Karl Marx did on those two occasions. It does seem, however, that the poverty created by market fundamentalism needs crises, like the social upheaval that brought down Physiocracy, the German *Verein für Sozialpolitik* that created the modern welfare state out of the 1848 to 1871 revolutions, and the enlightened policies of the Marshall Plan which created the wealth that stopped communism. What all these events have in common is that free trade was temporarily abandoned in order to promote development as a political, rather than as a social, goal. A social goal, such as the MDGs, is clearly not sufficient. In the long run, the political consequences of the economic and social dependency created by the MDGs will become completely intolerable to the poor.

Increasing inequality within Europe

As we have seen, our present failure to understand why so many countries stay poor is intimately tied to a number of blindspots that make it extremely difficult, if not impossible, to create a theory of uneven economic development. Any long-term solution for Africa and other poor regions will have to rest on a theory of uneven development, which today is poorly developed. This theory, which enabled successful economic policies for 500 years – from Henry VII's England in 1485 to the integration of Spain and Portugal into the European Union in 1986 – is now virtually extinct.

The present approach to the poor is heavily tilted in favour of palliative economics, in other words to ease the pains of poverty rather than to eradicate it permanently through economic development. In addition, the current approach makes it possible to continue and even extend (as in the WTO negotiations) present practices without investigating the problems with globalization in the periphery. The same myths – based on ideology, rather than experience – and the same policies are still in place. Unfortunately, having the same people and the same theories that brought in the neo-classical shock-therapy measures in charge of the MDGs was clearly a big mistake and responsible for much of the present mess. This virtually guarantees that we do not engage in a fundamental discussion of *what went wrong* at the 'end of history'. Instead, what is needed is a theory that explains why economic development, by its very nature, is such an uneven process. Only then can the appropriate policy measures be put in place.

In 2005 the process of European integration had reached a serious crisis. The rejection of the European Constitution by the French and Dutch voters indicates a strong distrust of the way the integration was proceeding. A survey conducted recently for the Polish *Rzeczpospolita* newspaper found widespread admiration for the achievements of winning freedom of speech and leading the country into NATO and the EU, but 85 per cent of those polled blamed the Solidarity movement for setting in motion the liberalization that has put many Poles out of work. Those in the old member states of the European Union feel betrayed because their welfare is being eroded, while those in the new member states feel betrayed because their welfare is not improving as fast as they expected. Not surprisingly, this unexpected situation has caused many to question what went wrong. The fact that this change of mood has surfaced after merely a year after the euphoric celebrations of the enlargement of the Union makes it even more surprising.

The problems created by the currently dominant economic theory are not limited to the Third World countries. In the case of the European Union, most developed nations have experienced increasing internal economic inequalities. The same problems are thus experienced on three levels: globally, within the European Union, and within most developed nations. The causes are essentially the same: theories that worked for centuries which have now been abandoned.

Although German economist Friedrich List (1789–1846) is hardly mentioned in today's economics textbooks, his economic principles not only industrialized Continental Europe in the nineteenth century, but also facilitated European integration from the early 1950s until, and including, the successful integration of Spain and Portugal into the EU in 1986. Not until the 1997 Stability and

Growth Pact were List's principles abandoned in favour of the kind of economics that now dominate the Washington Consensus. The result has been increasing unemployment and poverty in the old core countries, inflaming the debate that resulted in rejection of the proposed new European Constitution.[31] Below are three of List's key principles contrasted with standard textbook economics.

- *Listian principle*: A nation first industrializes and is then gradually integrated economically with nations at the same level of development.
- *Neo-classical principle*: Free trade is the goal per se, even before the required stage of industrialization is achieved. The 2004 EU enlargement went directly against Listian principles. First, the former communist countries in Eastern Europe (with the exception of Hungary) suffered dramatic deindustrialization, unemployment and underemployment. These countries were then abruptly integrated into the EU, creating enormous economic and social tensions. From the point of view of Western Europe, the factor–price equalization promised by international trade theory proved to be an equalization *downwards*.

- *Listian principle*: The preconditions for wealth, democracy and political freedom are all the same: a diversified manufacturing sector subject to increasing returns[32] (which would historically mean manufacturing, but also includes knowledge-intensive services). This was the principle promoted by the first US Secretary of the Treasury, Alexander Hamilton,[33] upon which the United States economy was built, and which was rediscovered by George Marshall in 1947.
- *Neo-classical principle*: all economic activities are qualitatively alike, so what is produced does not matter. The ideology is based on 'comparative advantage' without recognizing that it is actually possible for a nation to specialize in being poor and ignorant, engage in economic activities that require little knowledge, and operate under perfect competition and diminishing returns, and/ or bereft of any scale economies and technological change.

- *Listian principle*: Economic welfare is a result of synergy. The thirteenth-century Florentine Chancellor Brunetto Latini

(1210–94) explained the wealth of cities as a common weal (*'un ben comune'*).
- *Neo-classical principle*: 'There is no such thing as society' (Margaret Thatcher, 1987).

In order to develop Africa and other poor countries, the present neo-classical economic principles must be abandoned in favour of the old Listian principles. Understanding List requires recognizing qualitative differences between economic activities, diversity, innovations, synergies and historical sequencing of processes – all apparent blindspots in standard economics.

Working with economic tools that prevent them from understanding List's points, today's mainstream economists grope for explanations of continued poverty. They return to factors that have been studied and discarded, like race and climate: theoretically the movement is down the slippery slope of red herrings listed in chapter 6, and in practice the movement is towards 'welfare colonialism'.

Quoting Nietzsche is a risky business, particularly after his sister Elisabeth Förster Nietzsche systematically misappropriated his work for political reasons. With the Millennium Development Goals, however, the temptation is overwhelming. Having embraced an economic theory that has left out the main driving forces of human progress – what Nietzsche calls *Geist- und Willens-Kapital,* the human 'wit and will' that include all forces of change: new knowledge, technical change and entrepreneurship – Nietzsche's unhealthy preserver types, 'the good and the just', enter the scene. Unable to change Africa's economic structure and create wealth, their solution is – to a considerable extent – to put the poor parts of Africa 'on the dole'.

'The good and the just' are back in the pre-Renaissance zero-sum game mood we described early in the book: economics is about allocation of already created wealth rather than the creation of new wealth. Not understanding the connection between colonial economic structure and poverty, the only solution that 'the good and the just' can envisage is to distribute the wealth created in the rich countries among the poor countries. To Nietzsche, 'the good and the just' is merely the prelude to the worst of all human specimens, the 'most despicable man', and the embodiment of decline: the '*letzte Mensch*' (the Last Man), or the dull post-human remains that litter the earth at the end of time. 'What is creation?... asks the last man, and he blinks.'[34] This quasi-human is Nietzsche's bleak projection of the decadent human animal of modernity, the ultimate outcome of the historical process whereby humanity condemns itself to stagnation and decline by embracing the comfortable mediocrity of the status quo, rather than in creating anything new. The Last Man personifies the final extinction of human will and creativity, the bartering man *homo economicus neoclassicus*.

8

'Get the economic activities right', or, the Lost Art of Creating Middle-Income Countries

...economists are interested in growth. The trouble is, that even by their standards, they have been terribly ignorant about it. The depth of the ignorance has long been their best-kept secret.

The Economist, 4 January, 1992

Perhaps some of you are thinking 'If we are already ignorant of 90 per cent of the sources of per capita growth, how much worse can it be? Can it be worse than 100 per cent?' In a sense it can ...'It ain't what we don't know that bothers me so much, it's all the things we do know that ain't so.' That is really the nub of the matter.

Moses Abramovitz, 'The Search for the Sources of Growth: Areas of Ignorance, Old and New', *The Journal of Economic History*, June 1993

When the Great Depression was at its worst, during the summer of 1934, two young economics students from Columbia University spent six weeks together in the wilderness of northern

Ontario in Canada. They were alone, and their only means of transportation was a canoe. For Moses Abramovitz (1912–2000) and Milton Friedman (1912–2006) this was the beginning of a lifelong friendship.

They both became distinguished economists, one at Stanford and the other at Chicago. Both received the honour of being elected president of the American Economic Association. Apart from that, their approaches to economics were remarkably different. Milton Friedman became the spokesman for what I see as Cold War economics, for 'the magic of the market' and the idea that distance from reality strengthens the science of economics. In his 1953 book, Friedman says: 'Truly important and significant hypotheses will be found to have "assumptions" that are wildly inaccurate descriptive representations of reality, and, in general, the more significant the theory, the more unrealistic the assumptions'.[1] Friedman established a negative re-lationship between science and reality, in a profession where unrealistic assumptions added scientific prestige. To Friedman, 'the market' supplied the answer to most questions; he suffered from a lack of doubt. As seen from the epigraph above, Moses Abramovitz, on the other hand was fascinated by our level of ignorance about what creates economic growth. Of the two, Friedman was the most convincing orator. 'I have won many debates against Milton', Moses Abramovitz told me, 'but never when he has been present.'

Only once, some time in the late 1970s, did I attend a lecture by Milton Friedman. He was defending the 'free market' against the accusation that it creates monopolies. The only lasting monopoly, he said, was the diamond monopoly. In terms of understanding Third World poverty, however, this is not the point. In several books, another president of the American Economic Association, John Kenneth Galbraith (1908–2006) described what separates the economic structures of rich countries from that of poor countries: rich countries build oligopolistic competitions in manufacturing industry where power and rents are divided between the 'countervailing powers' of big business, big labour and an activist government.[2] Economics, however, continued to model the reality of poor countries – that of the powerless individual Third World farmer facing the world market – at its very core.

Throughout my professional life, I have experienced the gap between the free market rhetoric of people like Milton Friedman and the actual economic policies carried out. I have observed a reality where active economic policies have consistently attempted to build the kind of structures described by Galbraith. My first academic position was as a research assistant at the Latin American Institute at the Hochschule St Gallen in Switzerland. In the early 1970s, as a very young man, this took me to many South American countries in the service of the Swiss Technical Cooperation and UNCTAD, and I worked in Chile under both President Salvador Allende and President Augusto Pinochet. That Pinochet simply unleashed 'the magic of the market' is a myth. First of all, Chile had been a regional economic and industrial powerhouse – a 'branch office of the empire' – ever since its victory over its northern neighbours in the War of the Pacific (1879–83). Secondly, it is not that after 1973 Chile did not have an industrial policy, rather that it shifted to a more aggressive, outward-looking and sophisticated type of policy. The conscious shift of wine exports from bulk to bottles, probably against the WTO rules, is one example. That Pinochet did not reprivatize Chile's biggest export earner, the copper company CODELCO, but kept it in government hands, is another case where reality does not correspond to the free market rhetoric. Chile's restrictions on inter-national capital flows are yet another example.

In chapter 3 I summarized my experience with Irish industrial policy in 1980. In 1983 I moved with my family from Italy to Finland in order to set up a manufacturing firm there. Both Ireland and Finland had followed an import substitution policy similar to that of Latin America.[3] One reason I wanted to establish production in Finland was the tariff protection granted there to national producers. As a would-be foreign investor in Finnish manufacturing, however, I needed permission from the Ministry of Industry. Only after having consulted with my potential customers in Finland, the three big paint producers, did the Finnish Ministry of Industry grant permission, which then specifically prohibited my company from entering into activities where I would compete with existing Finnish companies. Establishing a factory outside the areas of economic pressure in Finland, I was granted the same type of incentives given to manufacturing firms establishing themselves in Ireland at the time. Typically, this package of subsidies provided ownership of the factory building virtually for free, and a subsidy towards the wage bill of 30 per cent in year one, 20 per cent in year two, and 10 per cent in year three. Today, an army of well-paid economists explain to the world that the success of Ireland and Finland was just the result of 'the magic of the market'.

This type of policy was not limited to the periphery of Europe. When, in the 1990s, I was engaged as a consultant to the General Secretariats of the European Union in charge of innovation and regional affairs, I noticed a huge map of the European Union, coded in numerous colours not necessarily representing national borders, in a prominent position in many offices. The curious thing about the map was that some very small areas, around the biggest European cities like London, Paris and Frankfurt, had no colour code. These tiny spots on the map were the only areas not subject to any type of economic incentives; in contrast, 95 per cent of European Union territory was subject to some kind of 'subsidy'. The policy tools I encountered in Finland in the mid-1980s were the very same ones employed by Henry VII in England exactly 500 years earlier: tariffs and bounties in order to attract manufacturing industries.

Moses Abramovitz's work helps us to understand why this 500 years' cult of manufacturing has been a mandatory passage point to economic development. In the mid-1950s, armed with the statistics of the American economy from 1870 to 1950, he decided to measure what percentage of economic growth could be attributed to the variables that traditionally have explained growth: capital and labour. To his great surprise he found that the two factors combined could only explain 15 per cent of growth during this eighty-year period. Traditional factors of economic growth left a 'residual' of 85 per cent unexplained, a 'measurement of our level of ignorance', as Abramovitz appropriately put it.

Other economists, among them later Nobel Laureate Robert M. Solow, picked up this challenge, attacking the problem from different angles and with different methodologies. Surprisingly enough, they all ended up with an unexplained residual of around 85 per cent.[4] In the United States this led to a prolonged project of 'growth accounting'; of trying to split up and attribute this residual to different factors, under headings like education, research and development (R&D), technological change, etc.

At the time Richard Nelson placed the emphasis on the synergy between the different inputs. Education and R&D together make innovation and technical change possible, but if a nation does not have any innovation, neither capital nor education per se will solve any problems. The whole process that explains the 'residual' of 85 per cent is a systemic one, what English economist Christopher Freeman would later name a 'national innovation system'. In a sense we are back to Florentine chancellor Brunetto Latini's thirteenth-century explanation of wealth as a synergic *ben commune* (common weal) discussed in chapter 3. Abramovitz himself emphasized the difference between what he called the 'immediate' sources of growth, and the causes at a deeper level. In his view, the advance of physical and human capital, total factor productivity, and the variables used in growth accounting were the 'immediate' sources of economic growth. The deeper question is what lies behind these variables.

The abstract of my Ph.D. thesis, written in 1978–9,[5] starts out with a reference to Abramovitz's 1956 article where he discovered the 'residual'. The thesis itself starts with a quote from Antonio Serra, who in 1613 explained the wealth of Venice as being a result of synergy among a large number of different economic activities (a large division of labour) all subject to increasing returns. On the other hand, the poverty of Serra's home town Naples, so rich in natural resources, was essentially due to the lack of economic diversity and increasing returns.

As time went by I was increasingly convinced that Antonio Serra's and Moses Abramovitz's insights – although 340 years apart – were somehow intimately connected. The 'residual' and economic growth itself were 'activity-specific'; the 'residual' would be huge with the type of activities and the conditions Serra described in Venice, and minimal under the conditions he described in Naples. Sustained growth and a huge 'residual' require diversity and increasing returns that feed the self-reinforcing mechanisms of economic growth: a system where innovations would 'jump' from one sector of the economy to another as visitors to Delft would observe in 1650 (see Figure 5 in chapter 3) and those to Silicon Valley and London in 2000. Only under such circumstances would the wage of the common people – like the barbers – increase significantly.

My first meeting with Moses Abramovitz and his wife Carrie was at a small international conference that I helped to organize outside Oslo in May 1993, the same year he had revisited the 'residual' argument in the quote above. As is clear from his article, in his view understanding had not advanced very much since 1956. The conference theme was, in Abramovitz's terminology, nations 'Catching Up, Forging Ahead and Falling Behind'. This was just two years after I had sold my business and was trying to get back into academic life. I was convinced that of all the blindspots of standard economics, the most important of all its assumptions was 'the equality assumption': that all economic activities were qualitatively alike as carriers of economic development.

In my conference paper I attempted to address the Third World's problems using Abramovitz's terminology.[6] I had produced what I called a quality index of economic activities (see Appendix VI): people and nations engaged in economic activities with the high-quality characteristics would be wealthy, the ones producing under low-quality characteristics would be poor. This was an attempt to bring together a number of factors that tend to be correlated. The index would explain why – in spite of both industries representing world best practice – the world's most efficient producers of golf-balls would have a nominal wage level about forty times that of the world's most efficient producers of baseballs. In other words, being a high-income nation, just like being a high-income individual, was only possible with activities of a certain kind. 'Catching up' was climbing in this hierarchy of skills; 'falling behind' was sliding down.

I was fully aware that such a proposition was completely incompatible with standard economic theory. I had discussed the idea with my former professor in international trade theory, Jaroslav

Vanek, who envisioned my quality dimension as being a third dimension in the traditional graphical representations of trade theory. Ricardo's trade theory, the foundation of the world economic order, was based on bartering labour hours devoid of any qualities or skills, in activities that were qualitatively alike, in a world without capital. Introducing a quality index of economic activities would be like entering into an international chess competition with the intention of changing the basic rules of the game.

Not unexpectedly, the youngest among the approximately twenty economists present burst out in a loud laugh at the idea of ranging economic activities by 'quality'. But I happened to be sitting next to Abramovitz around the horseshoe-shaped table, and when I got back from the presentation and sat down he said, 'A very good paper'. My surprise was such that I thought my hearing had failed me, but he repeated it.

Getting to know Moses Abramovitz was akin to getting to know an old-fashioned and extremely generous academic culture, generous with time and advice and in sharing knowledge. To me, the historical record of all successful wealth-creation – from England's Henry VII in 1485 through all the centuries up to and including the 1947 launch of the Marshall Plan – was based on the basic and fundamental premise that a nation could only get rich if it harboured economic activities of a certain kind within its borders. As I saw it, economic growth, particularly in its fragile early stages, was 'activity-specific': intimately tied to particular types of economic activities and structures. In a letter dated 16 August 1996,[7] commenting on one of my papers, Abramovitz wrote: 'I agree with much of what you say. I agree in particular that the "residual" and growth in general are industry-specific.' To which he added that this is something everyone knew in the 1930s. The activity-specific nature of economic growth – which is the core idea of my book – makes Ricardian trade theory an extremely dangerous policy guide for poor countries.

This book has associated economic growth and development with the mechanisms of the Marshall Plan (adding increasing returns activities) and underdevelopment and primitivization with the opposite mechanism, the Morgenthau Plan (removing the increasing return activities). In 1945, when Secretary of the Treasury Henry Morgenthau's plan to deindustrialize the German economy was to take effect, the same Moses Abramovitz was employed as economic adviser to the United States representative on the Allied Reparations Commission. A team headed by Moe wrote a memorandum arguing that this plan would destroy Germany's capacity to export, leaving it unable to pay for food and other essential imports, and with mass unemployment. The memorandum predicted that, if carried out, the Morgenthau Plan would bring post-war Germany's average income down to a level well below the miserable standard of pre-war Poland. Morgenthau was outraged and called the group to a meeting. After Abramovitz, as head of the team, had admitted his responsibility for the conclusions, Morgenthau withdrew with a severe migraine headache. Nowadays, the Washington Consensus has created a new Morgenthau Plan in the world periphery, and it is again time to turn it into a Marshall Plan, promoting increasing return activities, as was done in 1947.

Needless to say, in 1945 the Morgenthau Plan was implemented. Just as Abramovitz's team had predicted, it caused severe hardship, huge unemployment and plummeting standards of living in Germany. Not until early 1947 – in an astonishing mental and political turnaround – did the United States ditch it. Former President of the United States Herbert Hoover had been sent to Germany to investigate the reports on deepening poverty, and reported back in March 1947: 'There is the illusion that the New Germany left after the annexations can be reduced to a "pastoral state". It cannot be done unless we exterminate or move 25,000,000 out of it.'[8] Less than three months later, during a speech at Harvard on 5 June 1947, Secretary of State George Marshall announced the Marshall Plan, which had precisely the opposite objective of that of the Morgenthau Plan: to reindustrialize.

Herbert Hoover makes a key point here about the connection between industrial activity and a nation's carrying capacity in terms of population. In a deindustrialized Germany, there were suddenly 25 million superfluous people. Today's pattern of mass migration is away from areas without manufacturing industry and without 'residual' to economic areas with huge increasing returns sectors, both in manufacturing and services, producing a huge residual. Hannah Arendt at one point refers to 'the combination of superfluous wealth and superfluous men'. This is also a good description of the world today. Structural adjustment and premature globalization at first created a lot of superfluous machinery in deindustrialized areas of the world, cemeteries of rusting machine parks from Lima to Ulaanbaatar, and the superfluous people from these areas are now moving to where the superfluous wealth is located.

The father of neo-classical economics, Alfred Marshall, correctly points to the fact that diminishing returns is 'the cause of most migrations of which history tells'.[9] Today we can refine this statement slightly by saying that today's migration is from areas with diminishing returns activities to areas with increasing returns activities. In the same first textbook of neo-classical economics, Marshall also outlines a policy prescription for this situation. A nation could tax the economic activities subject to diminishing returns (raw materials) and pay a bounty (subsidy) to the economic activities subject to increasing returns. This has also been the successful strategy for creating middle-income nations ever since Henry VII took over the impoverished kingdom of England in 1485 and started taxing the export of raw wool in order to subsidize the manufacture of woollen textiles. This is also the logical consequence of Paul Krugman's New Trade Theory that emerged in the 1980s, but is a policy recommendation that he and his colleagues failed to make.

Middle-income nations are created through this type of policies, making it possible for poor countries to emulate the economic structures of rich countries, bringing in the activities subject to the productivity explosions illustrated in figure 6. The key is to achieve the diversity and increasing returns that create the synergetic 'residual', even if this sector is only 'regional champion' and not 'world-class'. A nation needs a 'world-class' champion to furnish foreign exchange. For a long time, the Australian development strategy was based on a diminishing returns sector (wool) as provider of foreign exchange, but the presence of a manufacturing sector, although not 'world-class', created the necessary productivity explosions and industry/labour union balance of power that raised overall real wages. This was also the early development strategy of the United States, and in principle it works as well today as it did then.

As proved by Europe under the Marshall Plan, the wages, jobs, schools, ports and hospitals created around a sub-scale and often relatively inefficient manufacturing sector (compared to the 'world champion' US at the time) are real – as long as the process is dynamic. In Europe, tariffs and other barriers were slowly scaled down, and integration achieved. The European Union followed this gradual practice until and including the integration with Spain in the 1980s, thereby ensuring that key Spanish industries were saved.

Scale is still important, and Schumpeter's term 'historical increasing returns' usefully describes the combination of technical change and increasing returns that is at the core of economic growth; separable in theory but inseparable in practice. Neither Ford's car plant nor the Microsoft empire exist in small versions that can be studied, so it is impossible to know how much of the productivity increase is relatable to technical change and how much to scale. Scale means that market size matters, and at the core of poverty lie the vicious circles of lack of purchasing power and consequently also of demand and scale of production. As previously mentioned, trade among nations at roughly the same levels of development is always beneficial. Because of the huge diversity of production that comes with increased wealth, small rich countries – like Sweden and Norway – have a lot to sell to each other. In spite of its market of 4.5 million people, Norway is Sweden's third largest export market, not far behind Germany and the US. These are the kind of trading relationships that should also be created among the countries that are presently poor, but often have little to sell to each other. Just like the WTO negotiations, integration has been like a train going in the wrong direction. The best thing that can happen in the short run is that it stops.

Instead of regional integration, what we see in Latin America and Africa is the opposite. Through bilateral trade agreements with the United States, the smaller Latin American nations are cementing their position at the low end of the world wage hierarchy as monoculture economies, be it in raw materials or in technological dead-ends. Through at least twelve different trading arrangements and as a result of competition between the European Union and the United States, the African economy is being split up. Instead of experiencing the needed regional integration, Africa is being economically carved up today as it was politically carved up by the European powers during the 1884–5 Berlin conference. The result is what Africans descriptively call 'the spaghetti bowl'; if drawn on paper the pattern of overlapping trading relationships between African nations has so many lines it looks like a bowl of spaghetti. Instead of increasing regional integration, intercontinental trade is prematurely replacing regional trade: the European Union is pressing for Egypt to buy their apples, replacing Lebanon which has been Egypt's supplier for centuries. The globalization orchestrated by the Washington Consensus hit the periphery prematurely and asymmetrically, and is therefore doomed to create a group of nations that specialize in being poor within the world division of labour. Schumpeter's 'creative destruction' is frequently geographically divided so that creation and destruction take place in different parts of the world: this is the core of Schumpeterian development economics.

This book has pointed to a number of factors and mechanisms that determine wealth and poverty, beyond those factors Abramovitz labelled 'immediate', i.e. capital, labour or total factor productivity. I have also argued that obvious and essential elements in the process – such as education and institutions – in and of themselves will not solve the problem. The extremely focused and uneven advances of technological progress that we have referred to as 'productivity explosions' create 'historical increasing returns', dynamic imperfect competition and enormous barriers to entry for laggard nations. Increasing and diminishing returns create vicious and virtuous circles described by the classical development economists, and Antonio Serra's observation that the larger the number of different professions, the richer the city is still valid.

These are mechanisms that may pull a nation further into poverty as well as out of it, and they need to be addressed by economic policies. Abramovitz referred to the whole set of problems as a nation's 'organizational capabilities'. That poor nations, particularly those where the absence of increasing returns creates zero-sum economic games, also have the lowest organizational capabilities, is an important part of the interlocking system of vicious circles. As a general rule, the worse the situation the less likely it is that the winds of the market are blowing your way.

My argument in this book is that historically the only way such vicious circles can be broken, is by attacking the problem by first changing the productive structure itself. This sometimes requires heavy-handed policy measures, and the Third World needs to bring back the type of economic debate that dominated nineteenth-century Europe from Italy to Norway. The debate was not whether or not the European continent should follow England's path to industrialization – the answer was an obvious 'yes' – but the division of responsibility between the state and the private sector in this process.

In his work of 1613 Antonio Serra devoted a whole chapter to economic policy, describing in a poetic way the difficulties of formulating such a policy when the same policy will affect different industries in very different ways: 'As the sun hardens clay but softens wax, as the same whistle will calm the horse, but excite the dog.' No policies are therefore 'neutral'. Having a technology policy to support research and development (R&D) is accepted. However, this policy will greatly assist the national pharmaceutical industry which innovates through R&D, but it will relatively punish the printing industry that does no R&D on its own, but innovates by purchasing machinery that incorporates the machine-producers' R&D. There are also other traps. As is increasingly found in the new EU member states, national R&D may have very loose, or non-existent, ties to the national productive structure; by investing in R&D a nation may simply be subsidizing other nations' productive sectors. This is a situation similar to that described by Hans Singer, quoted earlier: if all your national productivity increases are given away to your customers abroad, innovations do not make you wealthier.

In the historical school and the Other Canon approach the mechanisms described are elements that return in new combinations and in different contexts. The key is to employ mechanisms that have been observed in the past in their new contexts. This is also the principle behind the case-method at Harvard Business School: the cases provide an 'artificial experience' from which you draw in new contexts. While other business school deans do not rank Harvard Business School at the very top of the academic hierarchy, the labour market generally does by rewarding their graduates with the highest starting salaries. Experience is more rewarded in business than in academia. This book claims that Cold War Economics created an extreme case of this: we have lived through a period when reality economics had no prestige at all.

Experience also means utilizing international economic fads in ways that relate intelligently to your own national context. In the 1990s, Michael E. Porter's *The Competitive Advantage of Nations* created a focus on 'national clusters'. Keeping in mind that Porter's main frame of reference was the United States, if your responsibility is towards the industrial sector in a small nation like San Marino (it has industry, I had a customer there) you wish to downplay the 'national' element. If you fail to perceive that underlying the goal of 'national clusters' are innovations, you may have ended up supporting Norway's successful cluster of exporting ice blocks: frozen lakes, sawdust for insulation, and international shipping. That cluster died, however, with the invention of the refrigerator.

Finland provided an example of an extremely intelligent adaptation of Porter's book. At the time, in the early 1990s, Nokia was a small company getting out of the production of rubber boots and cement for tiles and into electronics. It was 'national', but definitely no 'cluster'. If you followed Porter, you would not support it. When formulating the strategy for Finnish industrial policy in the early 1990s, ETLA (The Research Institute of the Finnish Economy), under the direction of Pekka Ylä-Anttila, solved the problem by adding a new theoretical category: the 'lone star', which could also be acceptable even if it was not a cluster. That creativity saved the policy that supported Nokia.

Nationalism has, for all its horrible excesses, indeed been a mandatory passage point – parallel to that of industrialization – for economic development:[10] the wish for one's country and one's descendants to do well was the main motivating force in Europe's stride for emulation over the centuries. Also economists were nationalists. Like everyone else, economists' views are coloured by their setting, and the person in Silicon Valley in the 1990s who was against international free trade should have had his head examined. Seen from Kampala, Uganda, however, the perspective might be different. An insurmountable problem is then created by the fact that economic theory and its recommendations are context-free, and its practitioners take pride in economic theories that are undisturbed by facts, as noted by trade theorist Victor Norman.

I would never have dared to formulate an accusation of nationalism against Adam Smith and David Ricardo as strongly as did English economist Lionel Robbins (1898–1984), who was made a life peer for his work at the London School of Economics: 'We get our picture wrong if we suppose that the English classical economists would have recommended, because it was good for the World at large, a measure which they thought would be harmful to their own community.'[11] For this reason, it has always been important that economists are also homegrown in the poor periphery. Indeed, in nineteenth-century Europe we find that those who wanted their country to stay as a raw material producer tended to be relatively few, and could form an alliance of 'feudal' agricultural sector and foreign powers. Typically following this pattern, England supported the 'free trade' and slaveholding South in the American Civil War against the industry-building and anti-slavery North. The earliest such political fight between an urban artisan and industrial sector against the old regime was the 1521–2 Revolt of the Comuneros in Spain, where the traditional sectors (the 'South') won, leading to an early case of deindustrialization in Segovia.

If we continue to follow this nationalist pattern, we find that the early English free traders (in the modern sense of the word) tended to be either Dutch, like Gerard de Malynes, whose real name was Geraart van Mechelen (1586–1641),[12] or had studied there, like Nicolas Barbon (c.1640–1698).[13] Typically, two hundred years later, the leader of the German free-trade movement was named John Prince-Smith (1809–74). He was the son of a bankrupt previous Governor of British Guyana, and came to Germany as an

English teacher ending up as a member of the Reichstag. Today, in the globalized world, many national elites identify more with a global elite than with their own country, and they successfully play the role John Prince-Smith tried, unsuccessfully, to play in Germany.

The truly great nationalists – such as Friedrich List (1789–1846) in Germany and Giuseppe Mazzini (1805–72) in Italy – were also very early proponents of a 'United States of Europe'. At the time Germany and Italy were both laggards, each comprising an out-dated collection of small city-states. Both List and Mazzini saw the uniting of Germany and Italy into nation-states as a necessary step towards a United Europe, and – in the view of List – in the end also towards global free trade. A United Europe, created between the industrial powers of Europe on the one hand and industrially weak collections of small city-states on the other, would have deindustrialized Germany and Italy. Nationalism required industrialization and political unification, but this nationalism was, both for List and Mazzini, just one step towards European unification. It was an indispensable step, however.

List argued for the formation of an intermediate continental free trade area before globalization. This is the step that Latin America never took: the Latin American Free Trade Association (LAFTA or ALALC) was a failure. Latin America's import substitution strategy was initially very successful – even the small central American countries achieved growth around 10 per cent for a long time – but it degenerated into superficial industrialization and monopolistic competition (the 'bad' protectionism in Appendix IV) that Friedrich List derogatively called '*Kleinstaaterei*', the problem of a state being below a minimum efficient size. When the industrial systems of the small Latin American nations went directly and instantly from this '*Kleinstaaterei*' to the global economy, deindustrialization caused the same type of problems Hoover described in Germany in 1947.

Here is where we get back to the relationship between theories of history and the timing of globalization. Towards the end of the nineteenth century economists tended to view history in terms of qualitatively different periods or 'stages',[14] in which the evolution of human societies in terms of economic activities, geographic settlements and political structures were all structurally connected. In the long term the economic basis for human existence moved from hunting and gathering on to the taming and herding of animals, to agriculture, to an increasing division of labour in artisan and industrial activities. In a parallel process, human settlements developed from nomadic tribal societies to villages, to city-states, and then to nation-states. As early as 1826 Johann Heinrich von Thünen (1783–1850)[15] had pictured all these types of economic activities as forming concentric circles around the city, with the most 'primitive' economic activity – hunting – in the furthest periphery, then herding a bit closer to the city, and agriculture even closer, etc.

At the core of von Thünen's isolated state was the city, and for him, if the city activities were too weak to survive they needed targeting, nourishing and protection. Going back to Abramovitz and Serra, the qualitative differences between the city activities and those in the concentric circles around it were the glue that created the common weal of the nation. To reiterate George Marshall announcing the Marshall Plan in 1947 (see chapter 7): the exchange between the countryside and the city 'is the basis of modern civilization'.

Some historical stages may be skipped. Korea did not have to go through the age of steam power. It is entirely possible that nations may go directly to mobile telephony, skipping wires. But taking a nation from a hunting and gathering tribe directly into a modern service economy is not feasible. The synergies between the sectors are crucial. The growth of the city activities depended on the rural markets just as much as the rural market depended on the purchasing power, labour market and technologies of the city in order to raise its wage level. In the same way, today's modern service sector depends on the demand from the manufacturing sector. It is theoretically possible for Mongolian pastoralists to use high-tech 'electronic shepherds' combined with global positioning systems (GPS), if they only had electricity and if the cost of the equipment had not exceeded what is probably the lifetime income of a shepherd. In industrialized countries, on the other hand, the price of meat is so high that it pays to use 'electronic shepherds'.

Historically, the only successful formula for escaping such vicious circles of low productivity and low purchasing power – to lift a poor country up to become a middle-income country – is by inserting an increasing returns sector of a certain minimum size and diversity into the national labour market.

Even more important are the structural links between the economic and the political structures. For example, a planned Soviet-type economy is not compatible with democracy.[16] Democracy appeared in city-states where, as we saw particularly in the case of Florence, the class with economic interests vested in landholding had to be kept out of politics by force. Nation-states grew out of collections of city-states, and Friedrich List and Giuseppe Mazzini saw these nation-states as necessary stepping stones towards successful supranational political systems.

Through the 'shock therapies' that ruined the core city activities that produced synergies and 'residual' in the Third World periphery, the Washington Consensus formula for globalization dismantled von Thünen's idealized state. Many nations were left without the cities which housed the increasing return activities that create 'residual'. Simply pumping money into these countries will not help unless a critical mass in an increasing returns sector is created. Even in the century preceding von Thünen's book, economists had distinguished between what we could call 'parasite administrative cities', that only housed administration, and 'productive manufacturing cities'; they also noticed the differing impact on the surrounding agriculture. Two hundred and fifty years ago Ferdinando Galiani[17] commented on the backward agricultural practices surrounding Madrid, an administrative city, compared to the flourishing agriculture surrounding the industrial city of Milan.

Today's parallel economic and political approaches – the Washington Consensus policies and the 'War on Terror' – are bound to fail for the same reason: they both disregard the historical experiences – we could almost call them historical laws – that created both wealth and democracy. Countries like Somalia and Afghanistan have pre-increasing returns economic structures where the synergic *ben comune* – common weal – is missing. Here the zero-sum game situation that we described at the beginning of chapter 3 still reigns. The natural political structures are tribal, with leaders we tend to call 'war-lords'. Controlling the capital city means controlling the rents from the countryside, but the capital does not give anything back in the form of production under increasing returns. It is a 'parasitic' capital. The more natural wealth, for example in the form of oil, present in the country, the larger the spoils from controlling the capital. The fact that the colonial powers drew their borders disregarding old tribal borders makes this situation even worse.

Muslim historian and philosopher Ibn Khaldun (1332–1406) described society's development, from the nomadic tribes of the desert, organized in clans originating in blood relationships, to agriculturalists and ultimately into town-dwellers.[18] The town-dwellers become extravagant, and as their wants increase, the city must resort to constantly increasing taxation. Resenting the claims of their clansmen to equality they rely for aid on foreign supporters, who become necessary because of the decline of clansmen as warriors. Thus the state grows decrepit and over time becomes the prey of a fresh group of nomads, who undergo the same experience. In Ibn Khaldun's pre-industrial setting, history logically becomes a cyclical sequence of tribal wars – with foreign supporters – fighting over the static and non-productive rents that accrue to the capital. This was also the history of Norway for centuries.

Pre-increasing returns and pre-common-weal productive systems specializing in raw materials create a type of feudal political structure. But even where there is no real feudalism involved, as in some African agriculture, the state seems to continue the extraction of economic surplus, characteristic of colonialism, and gives very little back. Under such conditions pre-capitalist production structures and political structures are very durable, and probably for some good reasons. One adviser to Tanzanian President Julius Nyerere, the Swede Göran Hydén, talks about Africa's 'uncaptured peasantry'. Similarly, NATO and the West today face an 'uncaptured peasantry' in Afghanistan. My suggestion is that Nyerere's African socialism failed for the very same reason NATO and the West are failing in Afghanistan and in the Middle East in general: 'It's the economic structure, stupid.'

The development that broke the Ibn Khaldunian circle of rent-seeking tribal violence was described in chapter 3 as the simultaneous development of a large division of labour and growth of increasing returns industries. With these activities, the capital became an asset to the countryside and vice versa: the nation-state was no longer a zero-sum game. The formula for the construction of nation-states – from the time of Jean-Baptiste Colbert (1619–83) in France – was to industrialize, invest heavily in infrastructure and create free trade within national borders. Once that was done, the next larger regional steps could be taken.

A few months ago the Norwegian Institute of Strategic Studies brought Edward Luttwak, known as a hawkish and conservative Washington Republican, to a small seminar in Lillehammer, the 1992 Olympic town. To everyone's surprise Luttwak had come out against the war in Iraq even before it started. 'You know what,' he said to me, 'an official of the Department of Defense, in 2003, just before the Iraq War, called me a racist because I said I did not believe removing Saddam would bring forth democracy in Iraq.'

Luttwak, knowing his history extremely well, would essentially align himself with people as diverse as Francis Bacon and Karl Marx on this issue: the question is not race, but economic structure. Yet the fact that the Europeans forbade manufacturing industries in their colonies with few whites – whereas the colonies with many whites industrialized and got independence – makes development appear like a racial issue. On my second day in Peru in 1967, during the visit to the presidential palace referred to in chapter 1, President Belaúnde had just come back from a trip to an isolated part of the Peruvian forests, only accessible by helicopter, populated by German settlers who had arrived after the First World War. They, while often pale and blue-eyed, now lived just like other Peruvian settlers in the jungle. Many years later, I visited the southern Brazilian state of Rio Grande do Sul, where a larger number of German settlers had created manufacturing and welfare. To quote Francis Bacon again: 'There is a startling difference between the life of men in the most civilized province of Europe, and in the wildest and most barbarous districts of New India. This difference comes not from the soil, not from climate, not from race, but from the arts (i.e. from the professions exercised).'

There are reasons to be optimistic. Mentalities and institutions change relatively rapidly when the structure of economic activities changes. English travellers to Norway in the early nineteenth century saw small possibilities for development in this backward nation of drunken farmers. But fifty years later much was changed. David Landes of Harvard uses a quote from the *Japan Herald* in 1881 to make the same point: 'Wealthy we do not at all think (Japan) will ever become: the advantages conferred by nature, with the exception of climate, and the love of indolence and pleasure of the people themselves, forbid it. The Japanese are a happy race, and being content with little, are not likely to achieve much.'[19] The basic direction of development's arrow of causality is that described by Johann Jacob Meyen in 1769: 'It is known that primitive nations do not improve their customs and habits, later to find useful industries, but the other way around.' The change of mentality occurs with the change of mode of production.

There are also reasons to be pessimistic, and this pessimism is related to what Moses Abramovitz referred to as the changing 'factor bias' of technological change. Technologies have different characteristics. For example, information technology made it possible for relatively small companies to develop 'killer applications' and make a lot of money fast. The biotechnology business, on the other hand, develops very slowly, and the whole business has, cumulatively, lost money. There are many reasons to believe that this is a result of more than just different stages of technological maturity. Some years ago I was external examiner for a Ph.D. thesis at the University of Cambridge, where a young American woman made the point that while information technology had brought world economic power back to the United States, the different nature of biotechnology might be better suited for the Japanese economic structure with large conglomerates: they could use and learn from the same biotechnology in many areas from fermenting beer to creating new medicines. To adopt Abramovitz's terminology, we are facing technological systems with different 'biases' towards scale: a plausible idea with important implications for explaining uneven development.

One reason to be pessimistic about such qualitative changes between technological periods is namely that the Fordist nation-based paradigm may have embodied unique elements that are difficult to replicate under the present conditions. The mechanisms that made it possible to capture so much 'residual' in the national labour markets may be weakened or no longer there. One sign is that wages not only peaked in most Latin American countries in the 1970s, in 1973 real wages also peaked in the United States. In the US this is a problem that can largely be solved politically by increasing the minimum wage. In a poor country the solution is much more complex and involves radically changing the productive structure of the nation.

The combination of Fordist mass production and a primarily nation-based manufacturing sector created unique conditions for increasing real wages. This has to do with a factor economists are very poor at handling: economic and political power. In the analysis that follows we should keep in mind that for the developed world the first wave of globalization was primarily one of raw materials. To use Keynes's term, manufactured goods tended to be 'homespun'.

Economists of the American Institutional School, throughout its existence – from John Commons (1862–1945) to John Kenneth Galbraith (1908–2006) – were aware of the role of power. To them economic growth required a balance of countervailing power between business and labour. A key element in wealth creation after 1848 was labour power, that assured what we have called the collusive spread of economic growth: people of the rich countries got richer by taking out productivity improvements in the form of higher wages, rather than in the form of lower prices which would have been the case under 'perfect competition'. The barbers got rich by raising the price of haircuts parallel with the increasing productivity of the industrial workers, and consequently also with their increasing wages. The 'Terms of Trade' – the number of hours exchanged when industrial workers bought a haircut – were stable. In that way First World barbers saw their income rise enormously compared to that of their equally productive colleagues in the Third World. The barbers shared in a national industry-based rent (an income above normal).

There are several reasons why this path for a nation to grow rich is much less feasible now than before. The changes are partly due to process innovations that were made possible by information technology. While product innovations (new products) tend to create imperfect competition and higher wages, process innovations (new ways to produce old products) will often tend to create price competition and wage pressures. At Microsoft, information technology as a product innovation creates high wages and high profits. When the same technology is employed in the hotel and airline industries, the results are falling margins for hotels in Venice and the Costa del Sol and lower real wages for air hostesses.

In the twentieth-century nation-based world system, the main paradigm-carrying industry was the automotive industry. The car industry was widely spread, there were more than twenty car producers in Japan by the 1920s and even a relatively small country like Sweden had two. The twentieth century also saw the rise of emulation through reverse engineering: the Japanese could buy an American car, pull it apart and make a better one. These two elements together, the fact that every nation of any size had a) a national source of product innovations in the paradigm-carrying industry, and b) had the possibility to emulate through reverse engineering, are key features of early twentieth-century economic growth that are very difficult to replicate today.

Microsoft is a global supplier, and is protected internationally by patents and copyrights, making reverse engineering impossible. Replicating small Microsofts in every nation – as was done with car factories – not only produces extreme inefficiencies, it is also illegal. Products protected by patents, copyright and royalties account for a rapidly increasing percentage of world trade. Such intellectual property protection will increase the economic gap between nations as only a handful of nations have a positive balance of trade in such products. The increasing percentage of copyrighted and patented goods in world trade will inevitably widen the gap between rich and poor countries.

Four other parallel changes in the 'bias' of technological change
have contributed to the breakdown of the traditional ways in
which rich countries got rich – until now.

1. There is a trend away from single-plant economies of scale –
    huge plants that bring many workers together in the same spot
    – towards multi-location economies of scope.
2. At the same time employment is decreasing in manufacturing
    and increasing in services, partly because manufacturing
    increases its degree of automation in a way the service sector
    cannot.[20]
3. Traditional services lack the bargaining power created by the
    skill level of traditional specialized industrial workers. They
    are more easily substituted by people taken in 'from the street'.
4. Decentralized franchising instead of centralized ownership
    also waters down workers' power because there are so many
    different employers to deal with.

All these factors together make it more difficult for today's
employees at McDonald's to achieve the bargaining power that
workers at Ford used to be able to take for granted. Lack of
political will to adjust minimum wages also contributes to this
development. In the United States, in a period of high productivity
growth such as now, a higher minimum wage is to a large degree a
matter of political will. In Africa, much more than a local political
decision is needed, it requires a change in the basic rules of the
global economy.

Compared to the nation-based system, the relationship between
industrialist and employee is completely changed in a global
economy. Any capitalist worth his salt understands that having
to give a wage increase is not a big problem as long as he is sure
that all his competitors will also have to put up wages. Really
enlightened capitalists understand that a generalized wage level
will also increase the demand, and thus the potential profit, for his
own products. In 1914 Henry Ford famously doubled the wages
of his workers, announcing the five-dollar day. The argument was
that his production capacity was such that he needed people like
his own workers to be able to afford automobiles.[21]

Such a relationship – 'my worker is also my customer' or 'the kind of people I employ are also the kind of people who are my customers' – has broken down in yet another way that separates the twenty-first-century mode of production from that of the Fordist twentieth century. Countries like China and Vietnam enter the world market for manufactured goods by paying extremely low wages. Never before has a country upgraded technologically as fast as China, accompanied by such small increases in real wages. This creates downward wage pressures everywhere, from Mexico to Italy. For consumers in the rich countries this is great news because it brings lower prices. As long as their own wages are not also sliding downwards, that is. Eight years ago I received a letter from a prominent American economic historian, quoted in this book, with a perceptive PS: 'If we ever get factor–price equalization, who says it will be upwards?'

Strategies that successfully produce high wages in the First World may fail to do so in a Third World context. For raw material producers, particularly farmers, in the developed world, a good strategy is to concentrate on high-quality niches; Italy's Parmesan cheese and Parma ham are the best-known examples. It is also possible to do well in agricultural products. However, these successful raw material products are deeply embedded in successful industrial economies. The cheese and ham just mentioned are products of the same Italian region – Emilia Romagna – which also produces cars like Ferrari, Lamborghini, Bugatti and Maserati. It is very unlikely that poor countries – even if they manage to produce the best raw materials in the world, even in niche markets – will be able to raise wages that way. Historically, rapidly increasing wages have been tied to labour union power, a countervailing oligopoly power that could only be created in the presence of an even more oligopolistic power in industry itself. The niche strategy will not work because the labour power that leads the successful pressure for higher real wages is absent. Perhaps the most efficient producer in the world of the best broccoli for export, in Ecuador, is not able to pay his workers a decent wage. What we call 'economic development' is at its very core a 'rent' created by countervailing oligopoly powers of industry and labour.

Still, the nations that manage to capture the productivity explosions today – like Ireland with information technology and Finland with mobile phones – create a catapult effect of real wage growth. Europe as a whole has created a problem for itself by first deindustrializing Eastern Europe and then instantly integrating with the same countries, thus creating a local version of the Third World army of unemployed and underemployed in their own backyard. The big problem, however, is faced by the nations that still have not passed the critical mass threshold of increasing return activities, that is, large parts of Africa, Latin America and also Asia.

The very low transportation costs and 'death of distance' also contribute to the problems for laggard nations to get rich the way it was done from 1850 to the 1970s. Taking a short-cut into the high-end 'service economy' is hardly an option. Poor people who get richer still demand manufactured goods first. An advanced service economy is not created from hunting and gathering societies; the synergies from an advanced manufacturing sector are needed. This is what makes the perhaps irreversible deindustrialization – the killing of the increasing returns sector – of the periphery under the management of the Washington institutions into a crime against a considerable percentage of humanity. Now also, economists of the Washington institutions produce models that explain why they were wrong. As long as no change in policy recommendations accompanies these studies, they simply lift what we have called the Krugmanian Vice – having medicines that cure but denying their use – on to a higher institutional and supranational level.

When Argentina tried to recover from its massive economic disaster a few years ago, the saying was 'would those who created this mess please do us the favour of keeping quiet'. On the global level, we now have to do the same thing. The economists and institutions whose ideologies – more than economic science – created a shambles in the world periphery, should also step down. Instead, what has actually happened is that institutions and individuals who have made their inability to create wealth so abundantly clear are put in charge of the gigantic project of redistributing wealth that has been created elsewhere to poor countries that are even less able to create it themselves than they once were. These Millennium

Goals are a historical dead-end. I feel forced to repeat: the individuals and the institutions that created the problems should now step down.

For all their problems, the alternative institutions – those of the United Nations system – have for decades made considerable contributions to our understanding of wealth and poverty. The latest UNCTAD report on the least developed countries[22] points in the right direction: towards a re-emphasis on production and knowledge, and away from trade and investment per se. This renewed emphasis on production will automatically refocus the problem of Third World poverty away from the role of the poor as consumers ('we have to transfer purchasing power to the poor through aid') to their role as producers ('Third World unemployment and underemployment is a gigantic waste of human resources, we have to create employment').

This brings us back to the spirit reigning after the Second World War, when the looming experiences of the 1930s gave impetus to a development strategy that produced some decades of healthy growth in the Third World, from Peru to Mongolia. The problems of the Third World today are very similar to those of the United States and Europe in the 1930s: huge underemployment and unemployment and a techno-economic paradigm (then Fordist mass production) that had been stopped by under-consumption long before reaching its full potential. Joseph Alois Schumpeter had an explanation for the problems of the 1930s, based on a clustering of innovations in time, while John Maynard Keynes had the solution: deficit spending. Today, through the Millennium Goals, we are making the very temporary solutions of the 1930s – aid through soup kitchens and shelters for the homeless – into permanent solutions to the problems of the Third World.

The permanent solutions to the problems of the Third World still lie within the theoretical realms of Schumpeter and Keynes. The Third World, from the maquilas of Central America to the women in Uganda employed by AGOA-companies (African Growth and Development Act), need to get out of technological dead-end products, they need to get Schumpeterian competition in their national production systems. Moving Schumpeterian effects

across borders requires resurrecting past policies which globalization has removed. If poor countries participate in technological
development only as consumers, their wage level and purchasing
power will not be lifted. Achieving this requires reviving – in a new
setting – the toolboxes of economic policy that move production
across borders. Globalization has also dulled the Keynesian tools.
Through deficit spending, national governments used to be able
to lever their national economies up by increasing the demand for
local goods and services. In deindustrialized small open economies,
such traditional Keynesian policies, rather than invigorating local
production, mainly suck in imports. Thus previously efficient tools
are either outlawed or have lost their force.

I am confident that it *is* practically possible to create middle-
income countries in the future, but that new contexts may require
both different and stronger policy tools than in the past. If we
look to history, some shock therapies – but of the opposite kind
than those of the Washington Consensus – have actually proved
beneficial. I am referring to economic boycotts, which, under some
circumstances, by blocking imports of manufactured goods may
create Marshall Plan-type growth of the manufacturing sector.
With Alexander Hamilton's 1791 'Report on Manufactures',
the United States had received both a theory and a toolbox for
industrialization. But industry only mushroomed when the United
States was virtually cut off from trade with Europe as a result of
Napoleon's continental blockade and the 1812 war with England.
Only then had a sufficient critical mass been created to establish
the American System of Manufactures, a blueprint for a successful
national development strategy. The Second World War had a similar
effect in Latin America. The war effort diverted goods from Latin
America, which, combined with high prices for Latin American raw
ma-terials, gave an impetus to local industrialization. A student of
mine wrote his MA thesis on Rhodesia/Zimbabwe, and discovered
that the international boycott of the white regime resulted in industrialization and very rapidly increasing real wages for all.

So, tongue in cheek, a mild form of apartheid – for example,
placing pale people with blue eyes at the back of all buses – may
be a national strategy to get the 'policy space' needed to create the

economic 'residual' formed by synergies of increasing return activities. Once the venerable economic strategy of creating a critical mass of increasing return activities – following the successful blueprints of the US development strategy and the Marshall Plan – has been understood again, when, to paraphrase Nietzsche, even the memory of the shadow of Cold War economics is finally dead, such policies may be permitted in a less roundabout way. In the spirit of Friedrich List, such a policy would be one of symmetrical economic integration, of gradually creating larger and larger areas of free trade where the free flow of goods and ideas will make everyone better off. Only by understanding the causes can one begin to search for the remedy: only by understanding the mechanisms that make trade unfair in the first place can we create 'fair trade' without creating a system of welfare colonialism.

The present period represents a juncture where much can happen. First of all, a major financial crisis is increasingly likely, and Keynesianism shall have to be re-invented in a new and global context. 'Free trade' as the centrepiece of the present world economic order is likely to delay the solution to future problems in much the same way as a stubborn belief in the 'gold standard' delayed Keynesianism in the 1930s. Secondly, as Christopher Freeman has pointed out, the increasing economic inequality experienced since the 1980s – as with similar surges of inequality in the 1820s, 1870s, and 1920s – was associated with the techno-economic shifts discussed in Chapter 4: they brought major structural changes, demand for new skills, exceptionally high profits in new industries, and a stock market boom.

It is possible, then, to associate cycles of ideology to technological cycles. Initially, strongly pro-business governments tend to aggravate the growing inequality, but ultimately, this leads to a political revulsion against the hardships which these policies produce. An American economist, Brian Berry, mentions President Jackson's policies in the 1830s, for the 'farmers and mechanics of the country' over the 'rich and well born' (later formalised in the Homestead Act of 1862, anti-trust legislation and other reforms in the 1890s, and the New Deal in the 1930s and 1940s), as examples of redistributive policies following the periods of growing inequality mentioned above. The huge difference between the US minimum wage debate in 1996, when the economics profession was massively against any increase, and the little debated and almost unanimous Senate approval of an increased minimum wage in 2007, is one important sign that the ideological winds are turning. Once again human needs are ranked as being more important than letting the market forces run their course freely. But, as usual, pragmatism will win at home first, while ideological orthodoxy linger on much longer in our attitude to faraway places like Africa.

But even if the present policies continue, even if we should forever forbid poor countries from emulating the economic structures of rich countries, and even if we succeed in turning Africa's poor nations into reservations of unemployed poor on the dole, this book will hopefully still have fulfilled its initial objective, formulated on top of the Lima garbage dump in 1967. We at least understand better why the Third World man and woman in the street, in spite of being just as productive as their First World counterparts, are so much poorer.

Appendix I

David Ricardo's Theory of Comparative Advantage in International Trade

In his 1817 book, *Principles of Political Economy and Taxation*, David Ricardo laid the foundation for our present world economic order with his theory of comparative advantage. As an example he used the trade in wine and cloth between England and Portugal and, being the gentleman he was, he allowed Portugal to be more efficient than England in the production of both wine and cloth. Ricardo attempted to prove that it could still be mutually beneficial for both countries to specialize and trade if each country specialized where it was relatively most efficient (or less inefficient) compared to the other country.

In addition to the standard assumptions stated at the end of this appendix, one problem with this theory is that it does not allow for the possibility that after specialization one country's production may get caught in the spiral of diminishing returns and rising production costs (as would wine production) while another country might find its production costs falling as production increased due to increasing returns (as would cloth production). Using American economist Frank Graham's 1923 example, Appendix III shows how this would make one nation (the industrial country) specialize in being rich and the other (the agricultural country) specialize in being poor.

It is important to understand that this theory represents the world economy as a process of bartering of labour hours which are devoid of any skills or other characteristics. A labour hour in Silicon Valley equals a labour hour in a refugee camp in Darfur in the Sudan. Ironically, capitalist trade theory in its purest form does not consider the role of capital; instead it is based on the labour theory of value. Therefore it does not consider that one country's production process might potentially absorb much knowledge and capital (like Microsoft's products) while the other country's production process might remain highly labour-intensive, in processes where capital cannot profitably be employed (as in the baseball example mentioned in Chapter 4).

The example below demonstrates Ricardo's logic, but I have also included a qualitative, technological, and developmental element by using 'industrial goods' and 'stone-age goods' instead of cloth and wine. The example shows an initial situation where Portugal is more efficient than England both in stone-age goods and industrial goods, but in the end specializes in stone-age technology.

Table 1

Country	Industrial goods Cost per unit in man-hours	Stone-age goods Cost per unit in man-hours
England	15	30
Portugal	10	15

In Table 1, a unit of stone-age goods in England costs the same amount to produce as 2 units of industrial goods. Production of an extra unit of stone-age goods means foregoing production of 2 units of industrial goods (economists would say that the opportunity cost of a unit of stone-age goods is 2 units of industrial goods). In Portugal, a unit of stone-age goods costs 1.5 units of industrial goods to produce (i.e. the opportunity cost of a unit of stone-age goods is 1.5 units of industrial goods in Portugal).

Because relative or comparative costs differ, it will still be mutually advantageous for both countries to trade even though Portugal has an absolute advantage in both commodities.

Portugal is relatively better at producing stone-age goods than industrial goods: so Portugal has a comparative advantage in the production of stone-age goods. England is relatively better at producing industrial goods than stone-age goods: so England is said to have a comparative advantage in the production of industrial goods.

Table 2 shows how trade might be advantageous. Costs of production are as set out in Table 1. England is assumed to have 270 man-hours available for production. Before trade takes place it produces and consumes 8 units of industrial goods and 5 units of stone-age goods. Portugal has fewer labour resources with 180 man-hours of labour available for production. Before trade takes place it produces and consumes 9 units of industrial goods and 6 units of stone-age goods. Total production between the two economies is 17 units of industrial goods and 11 units of stone-age goods.

Table 2

| | Production | | | |
| | Before trade | | After trade | |
Country	Industrial goods	Stone-age goods	Industrial goods	Stone-age goods
England	8	5	18	0
Portugal	9	6	0	12
Total	17	11	18	12

If both countries now specialize – with Portugal producing only stone-age goods and England producing only industrial goods – total production is 18 units of industrial goods and 12 units of stone-age goods. By keeping Portugal in the stone-age, free trade and specialization have made the world as a whole richer: world production has increased by 1 unit of industrial goods and 1 unit of stone-age goods. However, in this book I argue that there are other and much better arguments for free trade than Ricardo's comparative advantage, and that the theory of comparative advantage actually may lock poor countries into a poverty trap, into primitivization: specializing in being poor.

As we saw in Chapter 5, the core economic policy at the time of Ricardo was the prohibition of manufacturing in the colonies. The main consequence of his theory of comparative advantage was that for the first time colonialism was made morally defensible. Before Smith and Ricardo most economists understood that colonies were kept poor on purpose, and many therefore predicted they would rebel in order to industrialize as did the United States in 1776. During the nineteenth century all presently rich countries understood that it was not in their interest to follow Ricardo's theory of comparative advantage until they had industrialized themselves. In Chapter 5 we observed how, after 1989, free trade deindustrialized Mongolia and created a situation where the only 'industrial' growth sector was the collection of bird feathers, 'combed down' as it is called in the trade statistics. Mongolia's development after 1989 was indeed tantamount to specializing in stone-age activities rather than in industrial activities.

The theory of comparative advantage outlined above makes other important assumptions:

- there are no transport costs
- there are only two economies producing two goods
- that traded goods are homogeneous (i.e. identical)
- factors of production are perfectly mobile
- there are no tariffs or other trade barriers
- there is perfect knowledge, so that all buyers and sellers know where the cheapest goods can be found internationally.

Appendix II

Two Different Ways of Understanding the Economic World and the Wealth and Poverty of Nations

Starting point for the Standard Canon:	Starting point for the 'Other Canon':
Equilibrium under perfect information and perfect foresight	Learning and decision-making under uncertainty (Schumpeter, Keynes, George Shackle)
High level of abstraction	Level of abstraction chosen according to problem to be resolved
Man's wit and will absent	Moving force: *Geist- und Willens-Kapital*: Man's wit and will, entrepreneurship
Not able to handle novelty as an endogenous phenomenon	Novelty as a central moving force

Starting point for the Standard Canon:	Starting point for the 'Other Canon':
Moving force: 'capital per se propels the capitalist engine'	Moving force: new knowledge which creates a demand for capital to be provided from the financial sector
Metaphors from the realm of physics	Metaphors from the realm of biology
Mode of understanding: mechanistic (*begreifen*)	Mode of understanding: qualitative (*verstehen*), a type of understanding irreducible only to numbers and symbols
Matter	*Geist* precedes matter
Focused on *Man the Consumer* Adam Smith 'Men are animals which have learned to barter'	Focused on *Man the Innovator and Producer*. Abraham Lincoln 'Men are animals which not only work, but innovate'
Focused on static/comparative static	Focused on change
Not cumulative/history absent	Cumulative causations/'history matters'/backwash effects (Myrdal, Kaldor, Schumpeter, German Historical School)
Increasing returns to scale and its absence a non-essential feature	Increasing returns and its absence essential to explaining differences in income between firms, regions and nations (Kaldor)
Very precise ('would rather be accurately wrong than approximately correct')	Aiming at relevance over precision, recognizes the trade-off between relevance and precision as a core issue in the profession

Starting point for the Standard Canon:	Starting point for the 'Other Canon':
'Perfect competition' (commodity competition/ price competition) as an ideal situation = a goal for society	Innovation- and knowledge-driven Schumpeterian competition as engine of both progress and ideal situation. With perfect competition, with equilibrium and no innovation, capital becomes worthless (Schumpeter, Hayek)
The market as a mechanism for setting prices	The market also as an arena for rivalry and as a mechanism for selecting between different products and different solutions (Schumpeter, Nelson & Winter)
Equality Assumption I: no diversity	Diversity as a key factor (Schumpeter, Shackle)
Equality Assumption II: all economic activities are alike and of equal quality as carriers of economic growth and welfare	Growth and welfare are activity-specific – different economic activities present widely different potentials for absorbing new knowledge
Both theory and policy recommendations tend to be independent of context ('one medicine cures all')	Both theory and policy recommendations highly context-dependent
The economy largely independent from society	The economy as firmly embedded in society
Technology as a free good, as 'manna from heaven'	Knowledge and technology are produced, have costs and are protected. This production is based on incentives of the system, including law, institutions and policies

Starting point for the Standard Canon:	Starting point for the 'Other Canon':
Equilibrating forces at the core of the system and of the theory	Cumulative forces are more important than equilibrating ones, and should therefore be at the core of the system
Economics as *Harmonielehre*: the economy as a self-regulating system seeking equilibrium and harmony	Economics as an inherently unstable and conflict-rich discipline. Achieving stability is based on man's policy measures (Carey, Polanyi, Weber, Keynes)
Postulates the representative firm	No 'representative firm'. All firms are unique (Edith Penrose)
Static optimum. Perfect rationality	Dynamic optimization under uncertainty. Bounded rationality
No distinction made between real economy and financial economy	Conflicts between real economy and financial economy are normal and must be regulated (Hyman Minsky, Keynes)
Saving caused by refraining from consumption and a cause of growth	Saving largely results from profits (Schumpeter) and saving per se is not useful or desirable for growth (Keynes)

Appendix III

Frank Graham's
Theory of Uneven Development

Increasing and diminishing returns in international trade: a numerical example

STAGE 1: World income and its distribution before trade

Product	Country A			Country B		
	Man-days	Output per man-day	Total	Man-days	Output per man-day	Total
Wheat	200	4	800	200	4	800
Watches	200	4	800	200	3	600

World production: 1,600 wheat + 1,400 watches. In wheat equivalents: 3,200
Country A's income in wheat equivalents: 1,714 wheat
Country B's income in wheat equivalents: 1,486 wheat
Price: 4 wheat = 3.5 watches

STAGE 2: World income and its distribution after each country specializes according to its comparative advantage

	Country A			Country B		
Product	Man-days	Output per man-day	Total	Man-days	Output per man-day	Total
Wheat	100	4.5	450	300	3.5	1050
Watches	300	4.5	1350	100	2	200

World production with trade: 1,500 wheat + 1,550 watches. In wheat equivalents: 3,271
Country A's income in wheat equivalents: 1,993 wheat
Country B's income in wheat equivalents: 1,278 wheat

My 1980 thesis set out to verify this model empirically – that specializing in raw materials could make a country poorer. I showed that the main twentieth-century export activities in three Andean countries – Bolivia (tin mining), Ecuador (bananas) and Peru (cotton) – all produced well into an area of diminishing returns. For the very reasons emphasized by English nineteenth-century economists, when national production increased production costs also increased, while production costs fell every time national production fell. This is the opposite of what happens in manufacturing industry.

As Hans Singer showed in his 1950 paper, technological change does not solve the income problems in the raw materials sector because productivity increases tend to cause lower export prices rather than higher income. Figure 14 shows how Peru got out of this trap by creating a manufacturing sector, but fell into it again when the Washington institutions started their deindustrialization policies.

Appendix IV

Two Ideal Types of Protectionism Compared

East Asian: 'Good'	Latin American: 'Bad'
Temporary protection of new industries/products for the world market	Permanent protection of mature industries/products for the home market (often very small)
Very steep learning curves compared to the rest of the world	Learning that lags behind the rest of the world
Based on a dynamic Schumpeterian view of the world – market-driven 'creative destruction'	Based on a more static view of the world – planned economy
Domestic competition maintained	Little domestic competition
Core technology locally controlled	Core technology generally imported from abroad/assembly of imported parts/'superficial' industrialization

East Asian: 'Good'	*Latin American: 'Bad'*
Massive investment in education/industrial policy created a huge demand for education. Supply of educated people matched demand from industry.	Less emphasis on education/type of industries created did not lead to huge (East Asian) demand for education. Investment in education therefore tends to feed emigration
Meritocracy – capital, jobs and privileges distributed according to qualifications	Nepotism in the distribution of capital, jobs and privileges
Equality of land distribution (Korea)	Mixed record on land distribution
Even income distribution increased home market for advanced industrial goods	Uneven income distribution restricted scale of home market and decreased competitiveness of local industry
Profits created through dynamic 'Schumpeterian' rent-seeking	Profits created through static rent-seeking
Intense co-operation between producers and local suppliers	Confrontation between producers and local suppliers
Regulation of technology transfer-oriented towards maximizing knowledge transferred	Regulation of technology transfer-oriented towards avoiding 'traps'

Appendix V

Philipp von Hörnigk's Nine Points on How to Emulate the Rich Countries (1684)

First, to inspect the country's soil with the greatest care, and not to leave the agricultural possibilities of a single corner or clod of earth unconsidered. Every useful form of *plant* under the sun should be experimented with, to see whether it is adapted to the country, for the distance or nearness of the sun is not all that counts. Above all, no trouble or expense should be spared to discover gold and silver.

Second, all commodities found in a country, which cannot be used in their natural state, should be worked up within the country; since the payment for *manufacturing* generally exceeds the value of the raw material by two, three, ten, twenty, and even a hundred-fold, and the neglect of this is an abomination to prudent managers.

Third, for carrying out the above two rules, there will be need of people, both for producing and cultivating the raw materials and for working them up. Therefore, attention should be given to the population, that it may be as large as the country can support, this being a well-ordered state's most important concern, but, unfortunately, one that is often neglected. And the people should be turned by all possible means from idleness to remunerative *professions*;

instructed and encouraged in all kinds of *inventions*, arts and trades; and, if necessary, instructors should be brought in from foreign countries for this.

Fourth, gold and silver once in the country, whether from its own mines or obtained by *industry* from foreign countries, are under no circumstances to be taken out for any purpose, so far as possible, or be allowed to be buried in chests or coffers, but must always remain in *circulation*; nor should much be permitted in uses where they are at once *destroyed* and cannot be utilized again. For under these conditions, it will be impossible for a country that has once acquired a considerable supply of cash, especially one that possesses gold and silver mines, ever to sink into poverty; indeed, it is impossible that it should not continually increase in wealth and property. Therefore,

Fifth, the inhabitants of the country should make every effort to get along with their domestic products, to confine their luxury to these alone, and to do without foreign products as far as possible (except where great need leaves no alternative, or if not need, widespread, unavoidable abuse, of which the Indian spices are an example). And so on,

Sixth, in case the said purchases were indispensable because of necessity or *irremediable* abuse, they should be obtained from these foreigners at first hand, so far as possible, and not for gold or silver, but in exchange for other domestic wares.

Seventh, such foreign commodities should in this case be imported in unfinished form, and worked up within the country, thus earning the wages of *manufacturing there*.

Eighth, opportunities should be sought night and day for selling the country's superfluous goods to these foreigners in manufactured form, so far as this is necessary, and for gold and silver; and to this end, *consumption*, so to speak, must be sought in the farthest ends of the earth, and developed in every possible way.

Ninth, except for important considerations, no importation should be allowed under any circumstances of commodities of which there is a sufficient supply of suitable quality at home; and in this matter neither sympathy nor compassion should be shown foreigners, be they friends, kinsfolk, *allies* or enemies. For all friendship ceases, when it involves my own weakness and ruin. And this holds good, even if the domestic commodities are of poorer quality, or even higher priced. For it would be better to pay for an article two dollars which remain in the country than only one which goes out, however strange this may seem to the ill-informed.

(Translated by Arthur Eli Monroe in *Early Economic Thought, Selection from Economic Literature prior to Adam Smith*, Cambridge, Mass., 1930)

Hörnigk's book *Österreich über alles* was published just one year after the last Turkish siege of Vienna. Outlining an economic strategy for Austria, the book went through sixteen editions, remaining continuously in print for more than one hundred years. In the nine points above, Hörnigk summarizes the strategy. On its hundredth anniversary in 1784 the book was republished by Benedikt Hermann with his added comment that the great increase in wealth experienced in Austria over the past hundred years was a result of Hörnigk's strategy.

Hörnigk's nine points provide several theoretical insights. In this book we claim that the 'cult of manufacturing' has continuously been the key factor for success in European development from Henry VII in England in the 1480s to Ireland's and Finland's industrial policies in the 1980s, 500 years later. Hörnigk's points are a typical example of this kind of strategy, which is often thought to have discriminated against agriculture. Yet his first point observes the need for innovation in agriculture through the introduction of new plants. In point three we find the population-friendly policies that emanate from the need for scale of production and increased division of labour. The same point underlines the need for foreign skills, rather than foreign capital – a useful insight for today. The skills of foreigners also played an important part in the economic strategy of Tudor England from 1485.

In point two we find perhaps the most important theoretical insight, which we could call 'the manufacturing multiplier': that 'the payment for *manufacturing* generally exceeds the value of the raw material by two, three, ten, twenty, and even a hundred-fold'. In Chapter 3 I quote Spain's Minister of Finance describing the same multiplier more than one hundred years earlier, in 1558. A few years ago I found the 'manufacturing multiplier' myself while working with the Saami reindeer herders in northern Norway. The herders sell their reindeer skins to tanneries in Sweden for 50 kroner, and buy back the same skin as leather for 500 kroner, a 'manufacturing multiplier' of 10.

As in Africa today, the levels of unemployment and under-employment in Spain in 1558 and in Austria in 1683 were considerable. Between the value of the raw material and that of the manufactured product lie much employment, stable profits under increasing returns and much taxable income for the government. The benefits from manufacturing spread as 'triple rents': 1) to the entrepreneur in the form of profit; 2) to the employee in terms of employment; and 3) through the government in terms of increased taxes.

Appendix VI

The Quality Index of Economic Activities

Innovations
New technologies

Dynamic imperfect competition (high-quality activity)

Characteristics of high-quality activities
- new knowledge with high market value
- steep learning curves
- high growth in output
- rapid technological progress
- high R&D content
- necessitates and generates learning by doing
- imperfect information
- investments come in large chunks/are indivisible (drugs)

Shoes (1850–1900)
- imperfect, but dynamic, competition
- high wage level
- possibilities for important economies of scale and scope

Golf balls
- high industry concentration
- high stakes: high barriers to entry and exit
- branded product

Automotive paint
- produce linkages and synergies
- product innovations
- standard neo-classical assumptions irrelevant

Characteristics of low-quality activities
- old knowledge with low market value
- flat learning curves
- low growth in output
- little technological progress
- low R&D content
- little personal or institutional learning required
- perfect information
- divisible investment (tools for a baseball factory)

House paint
- perfect competition

Shoes (2000)
- low wage level
- little or no economic of scale/risk of diminishing returns

Baseballs
- fragmented industry
- low stakes: low barriers to entry and exit
- commodity
- produce few linkages and synergies
- process innovations, if any

Perfect competition (low-quality activity)
- neo-classical assumptions are reasonable proxy

Appendix VII

The Quality Index Expressed in Real US Data (1899–1937)

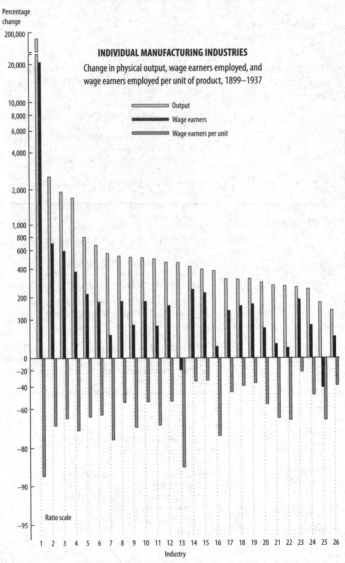

Graph source: Fabricant, Solomon (1942), *Employment in Manufacturing, 1899–1939: An Analysis of its Relation to the Volume of Production*, New York, National Bureau of Economic Research, pp. 90–91.

Industry
1 Automobiles, incl. bodies and parts
2 Chemicals, industrial, incl. compressed gases and rayon
3 Petroleum refining
4 Beet sugar
5 Fruits and vegetables, canned
6 Ice
7 Glass
8 Paper and pulp
9 Silk and rayon goods
10 Knit goods
11 Printing and publishing, total
12 Butter, cheese, and canned milk
13 Cigars
14 Rice
15 Paints and varnishes
16 Coke-oven products
17 Zinc
18 Liquors, distilled
19 Steel–mill products
20 Tanning and dye materials
21 Copper
22 Explosives
23 Wood–distillation products
24 Fertilizers
25 Blast–furnace products
26 Jute goods

Industry
27 Cotton goods
28 Hats, wool–felt
29 Shoes, leather
30 Cane sugar
31 Salt
32 Meat packing
33 Cottonseed products
34 Leather
35 Woolen and worsted goods
36 Liquors, malt
37 Shoes, rubber
38 Carpets and rugs, wool
39 Lead
40 Cordage and twine
41 Gloves, leather
42 Hats, fur–felt
43 Chewing and smoking tobacco
44 Flour
45 Ships and boats
46 Cars, railroad
47 Lumber-mill products
48 Turpentine and rosin
49 Linen goods
50 Locomotives
51 Carriages, wagons, and sleighs

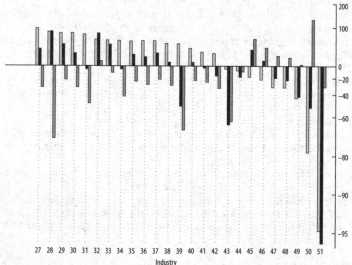

Notes

Introduction to the 2019 Edition

1. Erik Reinert, 'Neo-classical economics: A trail of economic destruction since the 1970s', *Real-World Economics Review*, no. 60, 20 June 2012, pp. 2–17, <http://www.paecon.net/PAEReview/issue60/Reinert60.pdf>
2. This term indicates that financial assets – financial instruments such as bonds and shares and real estate – appreciate in value. In many European countries the value of apartments goes up, while the salaries of the people wanting to buy apartments go down.
3. John Kenneth Galbraith, *American Capitalism – The Concept of Countervailing Power*, Boston: Houghton-Mifflin, 1972.
4. Chapter 5 in this book shows the fall of real wages and the diminishing percentage of wages to GDP in Peru. A recent report shows similar trends in the United States: higher profits, lower wages, and a falling share of wages. Bridgewater Associates, *Peak Profit Margins? A US Perspective*, Westport, CT, 2019.
5. Justin Yifu Lin, *New Structural Economics: A Framework for Rethinking Development and Policy*, Washington, DC: World Bank Publications, 2012, p. 350.
6. <http://bilbo.economicoutlook.net/blog/?p=42041>
7. Francis Fukuyama, *The End of History and the Last Man* (1992), expanded on his 1989 essay "The *End of History*?", published in the international affairs journal *The National Interest*.
8. Kenichi Ohmae, *The End of the Nation-State: the Rise of Regional Economies*. New York: Simon and Schuster, 1995.
9. The important effect of this was to make bread cheaper in England. Since bread was a main staple for workers' diets, the Repeal of the Corn Laws made UK manufacturing more competitive. The interest of UK farmers

(tariffs on important grains) was thus sacrificed in the interest of the manufacturers.

10. Marx saw the destructive power of free trade: "But, in general, the protective system of our day is conservative, while the free trade system is destructive. It breaks up old nationalities and pushes the antagonism of the proletariat and the bourgeoisie to the extreme point. In a word, the free trade system hastens the social revolution. It is in this revolutionary sense alone, gentlemen, that I vote in favor of free trade." Karl Marx, *On the Question of Free Trade* (1848).

11. Friedrich von Hayek, *The Counterrevolution of Science: Studies on the Abuse of Reason*, Glencoe, IL: The Free Press, 1952.

12. Harold Innis, *The Bias of Communication*, Toronto: University of Toronto Press, 1951.

13. For a discussion of this, see Erik S. Reinert, 'Mechanisms of Financial Crises in Growth and Collapse: Hammurabi, Schumpeter, Perez, and Minsky', *The Other Canon Foundation and Tallinn University of Technology Working Papers in Technology Governance and Economic Dynamics*, no. 39, 2012. Downloadable at <http://hum.ttu.ee/tg>

14. For an extensive bibliography of the relationship between financial capital and the real economy, see Erik S. Reinert and Arno Daastøl, 'Production Capitalism vs. Financial Capitalism – Symbiosis and Parasitism. An Evolutionary Perspective and Bibliography', *The Other Canon Foundation and Tallinn University of Technology Working Papers in Technology Governance and Economic Dynamics*, no. 36, 2011. Downloadable at <http://hum.ttu.ee/tg>

15. See, e.g., George Dangerfield, *The Strange Death of Liberal England 1910–1914*, New York: Putnam, 1961 [1935].

16. In the United States the vision behind this policy was formulated by Eisenhower's science advisor Vannevar Bush in his 1945 report to the President: *Science: The Endless Frontier.*

17. My book *Spontaneous Chaos* was published in Norwegian in 2009 and has, tellingly, been translated into Russian and Serbian.

18. Erik Reinert and Rainer Kattel, 'Modernizing Russia: Round III. Russia and the other BRIC Countries: Forging Ahead, Catching Up or Falling Behind?', *The Other Canon Foundation and Tallinn University of Technology Working Papers in Technology Governance and Economic Dynamics*, no. 32, 2010, <http://technologygovernance.eu/eng/the_core_faculty/working_papers>

19. The term *Knechtschaft* is the same used by Friedrich von Hayek in the title of his 1944 book, *The Road to Serfdom (Der Weg zur Knechtschaft)*.

20. Data from former World Bank economist Branco Milanovic.

21. This point is made here: <https://oecd-development-matters.org/2018/10/19/africa-time-to-rediscover-the-economics-of-population-density-and-development>

22. Reprinted in John Maynard Keynes, *The Collected Writings*, Macmillan / Cambridge University Press, vol. XXI, pp. 233–246, 1982.

23. In the case of Germany today that would mean leaving the Euro and facing a highly revalued German Mark, which would also save many of the problems of the Euro nations in the European periphery.

24. India is clearly the exception here.
25. See Erik Reinert and Arno Daastøl, 'The Other Canon: The History of Renaissance Economics. Its Role as an Immaterial and Production-based Canon in the History of Economic Thought and in the History of Economic Policy'. In Erik Reinert (ed.), *Globalization, Economic Development and Inequality: An Alternative Perspective*, Cheltenham: Edward Elgar, 2004, pp. 21–70. We have argued that the key to European exceptionalism lies in the Renaissance *duty to invent*, which contrasts the *inertia of status quo* typical of traditional societies: Erik Reinert and Arno Daastøl, 'Exploring the Genesis of Economic Innovations: The Religious Gestalt-Switch and the *Duty to Invent* as Preconditions for Economic Growth' in *European Journal of Law and Economics*, vol. 4, no. 2/3, 1997, pp. 233–283, and in *Christian Wolff. Gesammelte Werke*, IIIrd series, vol. 45, Hildesheim: Georg Olms Verlag, 1998. The implications of this for government policy is outlined in my 'The Role of the State in Economic Growth.' in *Journal of Economic Studies*, vol. 26, no. 4/5, 1999, pp. 268–232. On the very different canon that emerges when one takes the book history of economics seriously, see Erik Reinert, Kenneth Carpenter, Fernanda Reinert, and Sophus Reinert, '80 Economic Bestsellers before 1850: A Fresh Look at the History of Economic Thought', *The Other Canon Foundation and Tallinn University of Technology Working Papers in Technology Governance and Economic Dynamics*, no. 74, 2017. Downloadable at <http://technologygovernance. eu/eng/the_core_faculty/working_papers>
26. A more detailed argument on the subject of taxonomies is found in my paper 'The Terrible Simplifiers: Common Origins of Financial Crises and Persistent Poverty in Economic Theory and the new "1848 Moment"', United Nations DESA Working Paper No. 88, December 2009.
27. Readers who are interested in further information on alternative theories to today's mainstream economics are referred to three other works by this author: Erik Reinert, , Jayati Ghosh, and Rainer Kattel (eds.) *Handbook of Alternative Theories of Economic Development*, Cheltenham: Edward Elgar, 2016; Erik Reinert, *The Visionary Realism of German Economics. From the Thirty Years' War to the Cold War*, London: Anthem, 2019; and Erik Reinert and Fernanda Reinert, "33 Economic Bestsellers published before 1750", in *The European Journal of the History of Economic Thought*, vol. 25, 2018, pp. 1206–1263.

Introduction to the 2007 Edition

1. David Ricardo (1772–1823) was an English political economist who advocated international trade based on 'comparative advantage'; a nation ought to specialize where it is relatively most efficient (least inefficient) compared to its trading partner. His *Principles of Political Economy and Taxation* appeared in 1817.
2. For the importance of emulation, see Istvan Hont, *Jealousy of Trade: International Competition and the Nation-State in Historical Perspective*, Cambridge, Mass., 2005.

3. As it originated with Thorstein Veblen (1857–1929) and Joseph Schumpeter (1883–1950), and in its modern version with Richard Nelson and Sidney Winter, *An Evolutionary Theory of Economic Change*, Cambridge, Mass., 1982 and Giovanni Dosi et al. (eds), *Technical Change and Economic Theory*, London, 1988.

4. Joseph Alois Schumpeter, *History of Economic Analysis*, New York, 1954, p. 473.

1 Discovering Types of Economic Theories

1. See Herbert Heaton, *A Scholar in Action – Edwin F. Gay*, Cambridge, Mass., 1952; Jeffrey Cruikshank, *A Delicate Experiment. The Harvard Business School 1908–1945*, Boston, 1987; and Erik Reinert, 'Schumpeter in the Context of Two Canons of Economic Thought' in *Industry and Innovation*, 2002.

2. 'Intellectual Innovation at the Harvard Business School. A Strategy', Division of Research, Harvard Business School, 1991, p. viii.

3. This is Paul Krugman's expression.

4. Antonio Serra, *Breve trattato delle cause che possono far abbondare l'oro e l'argento dove non sono miniere*, Naples, 1613. The Other Canon Foundation has financed an English translation which will be published shortly.

5. The account on Henry VII in this book is based on an earlier work (Reinert 1994) which relied heavily on Daniel Defoe's *Plan of English Commerce* (1728). Other sources indicate that these policies started before 1485. The key point is of course the policies carried out, not who started them.

6. In 1848 Marx actually argued in favour of free trade because it would hasten the revolution (by making poor countries poorer).

7. Kenneth Carpenter, *The Economic Bestsellers Before 1850*, Kress Library of Business and Economics, Boston, 1975, downloadable at <http://www.othercanon.org>

8. Many professional librarians in the US are worried about this development.

9. *Grundriss der Staatswirtschaft zur Belehrung und Warnung angehender Staatswirte*, Frankfurt, 1782.

10. Unbound books of less than ninety pages.

11. This means that the United States was destined to grow wealthy in spite of making such 'mistakes' as promoting industrialization.

12. Early overview articles on this are published as my articles 'Catching-up From Way Behind – A Third World Perspective on First World History' in Jan Fagerberg, Bart Verspagen and Nick von Tunzelmann (eds), *The Dynamics of Technology, Trade, and Growth*, Aldershot, 1994; 'Competitiveness and Its Predecessors – a 500-Year Cross-National Perspective' in *Structural Change and Economic Dynamics*, vol. 6, 1995; and 'The Role of the State in Economic Growth' in *Journal of Economic Studies*, 1999. Some of these points were elaborated by my colleague Ha-Joon Chang in his *Kicking Away the Ladder: Development Strategy in Historical Perspective*, London, 2002.

13. Smithies also wrote Schumpeter's obituary in the *Quarterly Journal of Economics*.

14. This would not exclude Marx's understanding of economic dynamics. My approach to Marx developed into what I later discovered was the consensus of most German economists a hundred years ago: 'great analysis, poor policy prescriptions'. In his Foreword to the Japanese edition of the *Theory of Economic Development*, the very conservative Schumpeter makes the point that his analysis is very similar to that of Marx.

15. Quoted in Niccolò Machiavelli, *Tutte le opere storiche e letterarie*, Florence, 1929.

16. John Hobson, *The Eastern Origins of Western Civilisation*, Cambridge, 2004; Martin Bernal, *Black Athena: The Afroasiatic Roots of Classical Civilization*, New Brunswick, NJ, 1991.

17. Kenneth Pommeranz, *The Great Divergence: China, Europe, and the Making of the Modern World Economy*, Princeton, 2000.

18. Edward Said, *Orientalism*, New York, 1978.

19. Jared Diamond, *Guns, Germs, and Steel: The Fates of Human Societies*, New York, 1997.

20. These issues are discussed in Patrick O'Brien, 'Historiographical Traditions and Modern Imperatives for the Restoration of Global History' in *Journal of Global History*, vol. 1, issue 1, 2006.

21. On the importance of geographical and climatic diversity for the development of the Andean civilizations, see John Murra, *La organización económica del estado inca*, México, 1978 and subsequent works.

22. My son Sophus brought the word *emulation* into the family. It is the essence of the Ph.D. thesis he is writing on the history of economic thought and policy at the University of Cambridge. It describes much better what I previously had labelled 'bench-marking'.

23. Istvan Hont, *Jealousy of Trade: International Competition and the Nation State in Historical Perspective*, Cambridge, Mass., 2005.

24. Christian Wolff, *The Real Happiness of a People under a Philosophical King Demonstrated; Not only from the Nature of Things, but from the undoubted Experience of the Chinese under their first Founder Fohi, and his Illustrious Successors, Hoam Ti, and Xin Num*, London, 1750 and Johann Heinrich Gottlob von Justi, *Vergleichungen der Europäischen mit den Asiatischen und andern vermeintlich Barbarischen Regierungen*, Berlin, 1762.

25. Gold and silver coins were the currencies at the time, and the lack of currency – also because it disappeared out of circulation through hoarding – was seen as a considerable problem.

26. Ferdinando Galiani, *Dialogues sur le Commerce des Bleds*, Milan, 1770/1959.

27. This point is well made in Mario Cimoli, Giovanni Dosi, Richard Nelson and Joseph Stiglitz, *Institutions and Policies Shaping Industrial Development: An Introductory Note*, Working Paper, Initiative for Policy Dialogue, Columbia University, 2006.

28. This refers to the prototype colonial economic policies. Occasionally territories that are political colonies are treated in unconventional ways which attempt to induce economic development. Examples are Norway's nineteenth-century 'colonial' experience and that of Puerto Rico starting with the political leader Luis Muños Marin and Governor Rexford Tugwell (1941–6).

29. Paul Krugman, 'Ricardo's Difficult Idea. Why Intellectuals Don't Understand Comparative Advantage' in Gary Cook (ed.), *The Economics and Politics of International Trade*, vol. 2, *Freedom and Trade*, London, 1998, pp. 22–36.

2 The Evolution of the Two Different Approaches

1. William Ashworth, *Customs and Excise. Trade, Production and Consumption in England 1640–1845*, Oxford, 2003, p. 382.
2. Reported in 'Let States be Entrepreneurs', *Newsweek* 13 March 2006, p. 72.
3. Krugman quoted in Melvin Reder, *Economics. The Culture of a Controversial Science*, Chicago, 1999.
4. Antonio Genovesi, *Storia del commercio della Gran Brettagna*, 3 vols, Naples, 1757–58, vol. 1, p. 249.
5. It is worth noting that virtually all economics before Adam Smith was based on metaphors from biology. For a discussion on metaphors in economics see Philip Mirowski, *More Heat Than Light: Economics as Social Physics, Physics as Nature's Economics, Historical Perspectives on Modern Economics*, Cambridge, 1989; Neil de Marchi (ed.), *Non-Natural Social Science: Reflecting on the Enterprise of More Heat than Light*, Durham, 1993; and Sophus Reinert, 'Darwin and the Body Politic: Schäffle, Veblen, and the Shift of Biological Metaphor in Economics, *The Other Canon Foundation and Tallinn University of Technology Working Papers in Technology Governance and Economic Dynamics*, No. 82, 2006. Downloadable on <http://hum.ttu.ee/tg/>
6. Richard Jones, *An Essay on the Distribution of Wealth*, London, 1831.
7. John Rae, *Statement of Some New Principles on the Subject of Political Economy, Exposing the Fallacies of the System of Free Trade, and of Some Other Doctrines Maintained in the 'Wealth of Nations'*, Boston, 1834.
8. Alfred Marshall was the founder of neo-classical economics, the origin of today's standard textbook economics.
9. The Other Canon is intended as a reference point for 'reality economics', and is also a network of economists.
10. Of course Marxist economics also included much more, particularly a sophisticated analysis of technical change and economic dynamics. Turning the societal pyramid upside down, however, proved too simple a solution for the societal ills described by Marx. It can also be argued that what is seriously wrong in Marx is what he got from David Ricardo; see Herbert Foxwell, Foreword to Anton Menger, *The Right of the Whole Produce of Labour*, London, 1899.
11. At the end of the Second World War the two dominant Other Canon traditions were institutional economics in the United States and the various historical schools, most prominently the German one, in Europe.
12. Interview in the daily newspaper, *Dagens Næringsliv*, 31 December 1994, p. 21.
13. Quoted in John M. Ferguson, *Landmarks of Economic Thought*, New York, 1939, p. 142.

14. For a discussion of economics as becoming a religion, see Robert H. Nelson's *Economics as Religion: From Samuelson to Chicago and Beyond*, University Park, 2001.
15. It can be argued that diminishing returns is the only fact-based element in standard economics. It will be shown later, however, how the neglect of this fundamental mechanism caused an economic disaster in Mongolia.
16. It may be argued that standard economics differentiates between economic activities in the sense that they may be more or less capital-intensive. Had this insight been carried over to international trade theory, it could have been shown that nations specializing in economic activities that are less able to absorb capital would stay poorer (assuming that capital is a main source of growth). However, this is not possible, because international trade theory is based on the labour theory of value, and does not consider capital investments. This juggling between different sets of assumptions for different parts of the theory is a core feature of textbook economics. What is presented as a coherent set of theories is in reality a hotchpotch of different approaches.
17. This point I owe to a conference at the University of Notre Dame in 1991.
18. One exception being Robert Lucas, 'On the Mechanics of Economic Development' in *Journal of Monetary Economics*, vol. 22, 1988, pp. 3–42.
19. Joseph Schumpeter, *History of Economic Analysis*, New York, 1954, p. 195.
20. Ernst Ludwig Carl, *Traité de la Richesse des Princes, et de leurs Etats: et des Moyens Simples et Naturels Pur y Parvenir*, Paris, 1722–3.
21. See particularly Alfred Marshall, *Principles of Economics*, London, 1890, p. 201, for a policy statement.
22. Jagdish Bhagwati, *Free Trade Today*, Princeton, 2002, p. 22.
23. See David Warsh, *Knowledge and the Wealth of Nations. A Story of Economic Discovery*, New York, 2006, for one particularly celebrative version of the story.
24. Charles Babbage, *On the Economy of Machinery and Manufactures*, London, 1832, p. 84.
25. Frederick Lane, *Profits from Power. Readings in Protection-Rent and Violence-Controlling Enterprises*, Albany, 1979.
26. Charles Tilly, *Coercion, Capital and European States AD 990–1992*, Cambridge, 1990.
27. Nicholas Kaldor, 'Alternative Theories of Distribution' in *Review of Economic Studies*, vol. XXIII, no. 2, 1955–6. Reprinted in *Essays on Value and Distribution*, Glencoe, Ill., 1960, p. 211.
28. This point is very well expressed by Herbert Foxwell, a Cambridge economist, in the work already quoted. See also Keynes's obituary of Foxwell in the *Economic Journal* in 1936. For a German statement of the same anti-Ricardian *Zeitgeist*, see Gustav Schmoller's inaugural speech as Rector of the University of Berlin, *Wechselnde Theorien und feststehende Wahrheiten im Gebiete der Staats- und Socialwissenschaftlichen und die heutige deutsche Volkswirtschaftslehre*, 1897.
29. See Philip Mirowski, *Machine Dreams: Economics becomes a Cyborg Science*, Cambridge, 2001, for an account of this, and for the role of the Cowles Commission. See Geoffrey Hodgson, *How Economics Forgot History: The*

Problem of Historical Specificity in Social Science, London, 2001, for the loss of the historical dimension and Yuvoal Yonay, *The Struggle over the Soul of Economics*, Princeton, 1998, for the demise of American institutional economics.

30. Quoted in Erik Reinert, *International Trade and the Economic Mechanisms of Underdevelopment*, Ph.D. thesis, Cornell University, 1980.

31. This discussion is based on Wolfgang Drechsler, 'Natural versus Social Sciences: on Understanding in Economics' in Erik Reinert (ed.), *Globalization, Economic Development and Inequality: An Alternative Perspective*, Cheltenham, 2004, pp. 71–87.

32. <http://www.peacon.net> This very informative site is run by Edward Fulbrook.

33. Mark Blaug, 'The Problem with Formalism: An Interview with Mark Blaug' in *Challenge*, May/June 1998, <http://www.btinternet.com/-pae_news/Blaug1.htm>

34. This is discussed in Erik Reinert, 'Full Circle: Economics from Scholasticism through Innovation and back into Mathematical Scholasticism. Reflections around a 1769 Price Essay: "Why is it that Economics so Far has Gained so Few Advantages from Physics and Mathematics?"' in *Journal of Economic Studies*, vol. 27, no. 4/5, 2000, pp. 364–76.

35. Paula Tubaro, 'Un'esperienza peculiare del Settecento italiano: "la scuola milanese" di economia matematica' in *Studi Settecenteschi*, vol. 20, 2000, p. 215.

36. Paul Samuelson, 'International Trade and the Equalisation of Factor Prices' in *Economic Journal*, vol. 58, 1948, pp. 163–84, and his 'International Factor–Price Equalisation Once Again' in *Economic Journal*, vol. 59, 1949, pp. 181–97. As with David Ricardo's theories, the most important thing is not necessarily what Samuelson claims in these papers, but how his theories were used to construct a world view in which instant free trade would benefit everyone.

37. Karl Polanyi, *The Great Transformation*, New York, 1944, p. 44.

38. Thorstein Veblen, 'Why is Economics not an Evolutionary Science' in *Quarterly Journal of Economics*, vol. XII, July 1898, pp. 373–97.

39. Adam Smith, *The Theory of Moral Sentiments* in *Collected Works*, London, 1759/1812, pp. 318–19.

40. Anthony Giddens, *The Third Way. The Renewal of Social Democracy*, Cambridge, 1998, p. 111.

41. This analysis is based on Carlota Perez, *Technological Revolutions and Financial Capital. The Dynamics of Bubbles and Golden Ages*, Cheltenham, 2002, and her 'Technological Revolutions, Paradigm Shift and Socio-Institutional Change' in Erik Reinert (ed.), *Globalization, Economic Development and Inequality: An Alternative Perspective*, Cheltenham, 2004.

42. This effect is observed if China and India – countries that have consistently followed a strategy of industrial protection for more than fifty years and were not subjected to shock therapies – are removed from the group of poor countries. As a group, the rest of the poor countries got poorer.

43. This has precipitated an internal banana war within the European Union, where Germany is the main nation siding with Ecuador.

44. Sixto Durán Ballén, *A mi manera: Los años de Carondelet*, Quito, 2005.

45. For a broader discussion of stage theories, see Erik Reinert, 'Karl Bücher and the Geographical Dimensions of Techno-Economic Change' in Jürgen Backhaus (ed.), *Karl Bücher: Theory – History – Anthropology – Non-Market Economies*, Marburg, 2000, pp. 177–222.

46. Ronald Meek, *Social Science and the Ignoble Savage*, Cambridge, 1976, p. 219. Emphasis in original.

47. Ibid., p. 12.

48. *The Works of Francis Bacon*, quoted in Meek, op. cit., p. 13.

49. July/August 2005, p. 21.

50. For a discussion of this, see Polanyi, op. cit.

51. This very useful term was to my knowledge introduced by Carlota Perez.

52. Johan Åkerman, *Politik och Ekonomi i Atomålderns Värld*, Stockholm, 1954, pp. 26–27.

53. UNCTAD, United Nations Conference on Trade and Development (2006), *The Least Developed Countries Report 2006. Developing Productive Capacities*, Geneva, <http://www.unctad.org/en/docs/ldc2006_en.pdf>

3 Emulation: How Rich Countries Got Rich

1. The works of Jane Jacobs (1916–2006) document the importance of the cities in world history.

2. John Hales, *A Compendious or Briefe Examination of Certayn Ordinary Complaints of Divers of Our Countrymen in These Our Dayes: Which Although ... in Some Parte Unjust and Frivolous, Yet Are All, by Way of Dialogue, Thoroughly Debated and Discussed*, London, 1561/1751.

3. See Charles Emil Stangeland, *Pre-Malthusian Doctrines of Population. A Study in the History of Economic Theory*, New York, 1904/1966, for a good discussion.

4. See Erik Reinert and Arno Daastøl, 'Exploring the Genesis of Economic Innovations: The Religious Gestalt-Switch and the *Duty to Invent* as Preconditions for Economic Growth' in *European Journal of Law and Economics*, vol. 4, no. 2/3, 1997, pp. 233–83.

5. Alexandre Koyré, *From the Closed World to the Infinite Universe*, Baltimore, 1957.

6. For a good brief introduction to the mercantile system, see Gustav Schmoller, *The Mercantile System and its Historical Significance*, New York, 1967.

7. This is first described in Erik Reinert, 'Catching-up From Way Behind – A Third World Perspective on First World History' in Jan Fagerberg, Bart Verspagen and Nick von Tunzelmann (eds), *The Dynamics of Technology, Trade, and Growth*, Aldershot, 1994, pp. 168–97.

8. This statement by John Cary was first published in 1696. The quote is from the third edition of *A Discourse on Trade and Other Matters Relative to it*, London, 1745, p. 84.

9. Anonymous, *Relazione di una scorsa per varie provincie d'Europa del M. M ... a Madama G ... in Parigi*, Pavia, 1786.

10. I make the standard assumption that in countries that have been settled for centuries the best land is already in use, forcing an expansion of production into inferior land and/or climates.

11. These were the main mining cities, in present-day Bolivia and Mexico respectively. At one point Potosi, 4,000 metres above sea level, was the second largest city in the world.

12. See Giovanni Botero's 1589 work in English translation, *The Reason of State*, New Haven, 1956, p. 152. The material on Italy is heavily influenced by Sophus Reinert, 'The Italian Tradition of Political Economy. Theories and Policies of Development in the Semi-Periphery of the Enlightenment' in Jomo K. S. and Erik S. Reinert (eds), *Origins of Development Economics*, London and New Delhi, 2005, pp. 24–47.

13. Anders Berch, *Innledning til Almänna Hushålningen, innefattande Grunden til Politie, Oeconomie och Cameral Wetenskaparne*, Stockholm, 1747, p. 217.

14. For this argument, see Albert Hirschman, *The Passions and the Interests. Political Arguments for Capitalism before its Triumph*, Princeton, 1977.

15. Ferdinando Galiani, *Dialogues sur le Commerce des Bleds*, Milan, 1770/1959, p. 116.

16. Alexis de Tocqueville, *Democracy in America*, Chicago, 1855/2000, p. 515.

17. Earl Hamilton, 'Spanish Mercantilism before 1700' in Edwin Francis Gay, *Facts and Factors in Economic History – Articles by Former Students*, Cambridge, Mass., 1932, p. 237.

18. Luis Ortiz, 'Memorandum to the King to Prevent Money from Leaving the Kingdom', Madrid, 1558. Quoted in Earl Hamilton, op. cit., pp. 230–31.

19. For this very influential theory, see Charles King, *The British Merchant; or, Commerce Preserv'd*, 3 vols, London, 1721.

20. Friedrich List, *The National System of Political Economy*, Kelly, New Jersey, 1991. Original German edition published 1841.

21. This is documented in Erik Reinert, 'Benchmarking Success: The Dutch Republic (1500–1750) as seen by Contemporary European Economists' in *How Rich Nations Got Rich. Essays in the History of Economic Policy*, Oslo, 2004, pp. 1–24. <http://www.sum.uio.no/publications> forthcoming in Oscar Gelderblom (ed.), *The Political Economy of the Dutch Republic*, Aldershot, 2007.

22. For anyone interested in books, it is important to know that at the time libraries were often held for ransom, much as human beings can be today. The Swedes had particularly developed the art of holding libraries to ransom, see a two-volume study on the subject: Otto Walde, *Storhetstidens litterära krigsbyten. En kulturhistorisk-bibliografisk studie*, Uppsala, 1920.

23. Werner Sombart, *Krieg und Kapitalismus*, Munich and Leipzig, 1913.

24. Werner Sombart, *Luxus und Kapitalismus*, Munich and Leipzig, 1913.

25. *Girl with a Pearl Earring* (2003).

26. Again, see John Murra *La organización económica del estado inca*, México, 1978, and his subsequent work on the important role of geographic and climatic diversity in the creation of Andean civilizations and the Inca Empire.

27. Giovanni Botero, *Le Relationi Universali, diviso in sette* parti,Venice, 1622, p. 48.

28. Joshua Child, *A Treatise Concerning the East-India Trade*, London, 1681, p. 90.

29. Iceland, counting parliamentary traditions back to AD 930, shows that independent farmers – in the absence of feudalism – could also develop democracies.

30. See Erik Reinert, 'A Brief Introduction to Veit Ludwig von Seckendorff (1626–1692)' in *European Journal of Law and Economics*, 19, 2005, pp. 221–30.

31. Telesis was a spin-off of the Boston Consulting Group, and among our tools were those measuring learning and experience that are used in the next chapter.

4 Globalization:
the Arguments in Favour are also the Arguments Against

1. Schumpeter therefore created the term 'historical increasing returns' in order to cover both phenomena.

2. For a good explanation of this, see Gustav Schmoller, *The Mercantile System and its Historical Significance*, New York, 1967; see also Erik Reinert and Sophus Reinert, 'Mercantilism and Economic Development: Schumpeterian Dynamics, Institution Building and International Benchmarking' in Jomo K. S. and Erik S. Reinert (eds), *Origins of Development Economics*, London and New Delhi, 2005, pp. 1–23.

3. See the chapter 'Equality as Fact and Norm' in James Buchanan, *What Should Economists Do?*, Indianapolis, 1979, pp. 231 ff.

4. Exceptions to this can be found in what the League of Nations called 'areas of recent settlement'. In the United States, East Coast land, which, it was later discovered, was not the best, was used first. In Brazil, the same thing happened to coffee plantations, the land that was first being used later proved not to be the best suited. The general point of diminishing returns remains, however.

5. James Buchanan, *What Should Economists Do?*, Indianapolis, 1979, p. 236.

6. François Quesnay, *Traité des Effets et de l'Usage de la Saignée*, Paris, 1750.

7. Werner Sombart's key work on capitalism is *Der moderne Kapitalismus*, Munich and Leipzig, 1st edition in two volumes, 1902, last edition in six volumes, 1928. See the bibliography for French, Italian and Spanish trans-lations of the last two volumes. Prof. Jürgen Backhaus of Erfurt University and this author have engaged in an attempt to publish the English translation of this work, made before the Second World War for Princeton University Press but never published. Prof. Backhaus is now completing the project. For a good overview of the last volumes, see Wesley Claire Mitchell, 'Sombart's Hochkapitalismus' in *The Quarterly Journal of Economics*, vol. 43, no. 2, 1929, pp. 303–23.

8. This transition is well explained in Mary S. Morgan and Malcolm Rutherford (eds), *From Interwar Pluralism to Postwar Neoclassicism*, Durham, 1998.

9. 'Report on the Commission on Graduate Education in Economics' in *Journal of Economic Literature*, September 1991, pp. 1044–5.

10. I am not implying that such people are limited to economics, 'the world is full of high-IQ morons' writes anthropologist Clifford Geertz, quoting Saul Bellow (in Geertz, *Local Knowledge. Further Essays in Interpretive Anthropology*, Basic Books, New York, 1983, p. 76). The point is that only economics has an incentive and reward system, where factual knowledge has extremely low prestige.

11. Martin Wolf, *Why Globalization Works*, New Haven, 2004, p. 125.

12. Jan Kregel, 'External Financing for Development and International Financial Stability', Geneva, 2004.

13. Friedrich Nietzsche, *Werke*, Digitale Bibliothek, Berlin, 2000, p. 4708. For Nietzsche's influence on Schumpeterian economics via Werner Sombart, see Erik Reinert and Hugo Reinert, 'Creative Destruction in Economics: Nietzsche, Sombart, Schumpeter' in Jürgen Backhaus and Wolfgang Drechsler (eds), *Friedrich Nietzsche 1844–2000: Economy and Society*, Boston, 2006.

14. See Carlota Perez, *Technological Revolutions and Financial Capital. The Dynamics of Bubbles and Golden Ages*, Cheltenham, 2002, and her chapter 'Technological Revolutions, Paradigm Shift and Socio-Institutional Change' in Erik Reinert (ed.), *Globalization, Economic Development and Inequality: An Alternative Perspective*, Cheltenham, 2004.

15. For a more complete discussion of how the fruits of technical change spread in the economy, see Erik Reinert, 'Catching-up From Way Behind – A Third World Perspective on First World History' in Jan Fagerberg, Bart Verspagen and Nick von Tunzelmann (eds), *The Dynamics of Technology, Trade, and Growth*, Aldershot, 1994, pp. 168–97.

16. This is often also referred to as 'path dependency', see e.g. W. Brian Arthur, *Increasing Returns and Path Dependency in the Economy*, Ann Arbor, 1994. However, we shall see later, diminishing returns also creates path dependency, in the form of the vicious circles of classical development economics.

17. See the bibliography for works of Daniel Raymond and Mathew Carey, and the work of Schutz (1887) for Henry Clay. For the similarities of arguments favouring industrialization used on both sides of the Atlantic, see Charles Patrick Neill, *Daniel Raymond. An Early Chapter in the History of Economic Theory in the United States*, Baltimore, 1897.

18. Raymond Vernon, 'International Investment and International Trade in the Product Cycle' in *Quarterly Journal of Economics*, May 1966, and Louis T. Wells (ed.), *A Product Life Cycle for International Trade?*, Boston, 1972.

19. The first introduction of the idea in the West was Kaname Akamatsu's article 'A Theory of Unbalanced Growth in the World Economy', in *Weltwirtschaftliches Archiv*, no. 86, 1961, pp. 196–217.

20. The system was referred to as the *scala mobile*, or escalator.

21. John Kenneth Galbraith, *The World Economy Since the Wars*, London, 1995, p. 83.

22. Henry Morgenthau Jr., *Germany is Our Problem. A Plan for Germany*, New York, 1945.

23. Nicholas Balabkins, *Germany Under Direct Controls. Economic Aspects of Industrial Disarmament 1945–1948*, New Brunswick, 1964.

24. John Stuart Mill, *Principles of Political Economy*, London, 1848/1909, p. 176.

25. Jared Diamond, *Collapse*, New York, 2005.

26. Hans Singer, 'The Distribution of Gains between Investing and Borrowing Countries' in *American Economic Review*, 40, 1950, pp. 473–85.

5 Globalization and Primitivization: How the Poor Get Even Poorer

1. My 1980 thesis, *International Trade and the Economic Mechanisms of Underdevelopment*, describes this as the winner-killing effect of asymmetrical

international trade. Jaroslav Vanek's analyses inspired the description of this effect. The most advanced sectors are those operating under increasing returns and large investments in technology. Competitors from foreign higher-volume markets will tend to have a cost advantage, and a shrinking sales volume will easily bankrupt the few manufacturing firms that exist in each industry. In other sectors, a shrinking demand will have different effects than in manufacturing. A house painter will paint fewer houses, but house painting will survive as a profession. As was shown in my 1980 thesis, a shrinking demand in the production of raw materials will cause a nation's unit production costs to fall, as marginal land and marginal mines are left unused. Lowering production volume will therefore lower unit costs. This is the opposite effect of that experienced in manufacturing, where increasing returns and a large 'minimum efficient size' often make sudden free trade cause the sudden death of a whole economic sector.

2. See Reyes Fernández Duran, *Jerónimo de Uztáriz (1670–1732). Una Política Económica para Felipe V*, Madrid, 1999, pp. 230–33.
3. Quoted from Elliot Roosevelt, *As He Saw It*, New York, 1946.
4. Sylvi Endresen, *Modernization Reversed? Technological Change in Four Asian Fishing Villages*, Ph.D. thesis, University of Oslo, 1994.
5. Johann Heinrich von Thünen, *Der isolierte Staat in Beziehung auf Landwirtschaft und Nationalökonomie, oder Untersuchungen über den Einfluss, den die Getreidepreise, der Reichtum des Bodens und die Abgaben auf den Ackerbau ausüben*, Hamburg, 1826.
6. John Stuart Mill, *Principles of Political Economy*, London, 1848/1909, p. 177.
7. Mario Cimoli (ed.), *Developing Innovation Systems: Mexico in a Global Context*, London, 2000.
8. For a more extensive account of the deindustrialization of Mongolia, see Erik Reinert, 'Globalization in the Periphery as a Morgenthau Plan: The Underdevelopment of Mongolia in the 1990s' in Reinert (ed.), *Globalization, Economic Development and Inequality: An Alternative Perspective*, Cheltenham, 2004, pp. 115–56.
9. Miltiades Chacholiades, *International Trade Theory and Policy*, New York, 1978, p. 343.
10. My 1980 thesis, *International Trade and the Economic Mechanisms of Underdevelopment*, documents several cases of this.
11. This is also extensively discussed in Reinert, *International Trade*.
12. The works of Raymond Vernon and Louis Wells are referred to in the previous chapter: Raymond Vernon, 'International Investment and International Trade in the Product Cycle' in *Quarterly Journal of Economics*, vol. 80, May 1966, pp. 190–207 and Louis Wells, *The Product Life Cycle and International Trade*, Boston, 1972. This issue, together with the Marxist debates on 'unequal exchange', are also extensively discussed in Reinert, *International Trade*.
13. Erik Reinert, 'The Role of Technology in the Creation of Rich and Poor Nations: Underdevelopment in a Schumpeterian System' in Derek Aldcroft and Ross Catterall (eds), *Rich Nations – Poor Nations. The Long Run Perspective*, Aldershot, 1996, pp. 161–88.

14. Fernando Ortiz, *Cuban Counterpoint. Tobacco and Sugar*, New York, 1947. The Spanish original was published in Havana in 1940.
15. Charles-Louis de Secondat, Baron de Montesquieu, *The Spirit of the Laws*, New York, 1949, p. 273.
16. Carlota Perez, *Technological Revolutions and Financial Capital. The Dynamics of Bubbles and Golden Ages*, Cheltenham, 2002.
17. See *Report by His Majesty's Consul at Iquitos on his Tour in the Putumayo District, Presented to both Houses of Parliament by Command of His Majesty*, London, 1913. The *Index and Digest of Evidence to the Report and Special Report from the Select Committee on Putumayo* (London, 1913) indicates that the total number of pages in the collected reports exceed 13,000. The index itself is 90 pages folio size. There is an extensive bibliography of the events.
18. Mario Cimoli and Jorge Katz, 'Structural Reforms, Technological Gaps and Economic Development: a Latin American Perspective' in *Industrial and Corporate Change*, vol. 12, no. 2, 2003, pp. 387 ff.
19. Erik Reinert and Hugo Reinert, 'Creative Destruction in Economics: Nietzsche, Sombart, Schumpeter' in Jürgen Backhaus and Wolfgang Drechsler (eds), *Friedrich Nietzsche 1844–2000: Economy and Society*, Boston, 2006.
20. Jacob Burckhardt, *Reflections on History*, London, 1943, p. 214.
21. A resumé in English is found in my 'The Economics of Reindeer Herding: Saami Entrepreneurship between Cyclical Sustainability and the Powers of State and Oligopolies' in *British Food Journal*, vol. 108, no. 7, 2006, pp. 522–40.
22. Whatever David Ricardo and Paul Samuelson may have intended, this is the way their theories have been interpreted, compare the quote from the WTO's director already referred to.
23. Milton Friedman, 'The Methodology of Positive Economics' in his *Essays in Positive Economics*, Chicago, 1953.
24. Quoted in Erik Reinert, 'The Role of the State in Economic Growth' in *Journal of Economic Studies*, vol. 26 (4/5), 1999.
25. Originally published in Jorge Luis Borges, *Otras Inquisiciones*, Buenos Aires, 1952.
26. The final words in John Maynard Keynes, *The General Theory of Employment, Interest and Money*, London, 1936.

6 Explaining Away Failure:
Red Herrings at the End of History

1. At the 1872 founding meeting of the Verein für Sozialpolitik, the organization that created the European welfare state, Gustav Schmoller described the challenge in this way: 'The deep cleavage in our society separating entrepreneurs and workers, owning and not owning classes, represents a threat of a social revolution. This threat has drawn closer. In wide circles there have been serious doubts whether the economic doctrines which dominate in today's market – and which were expressed at the Economic Congress – forever will keep their dominance. Will the introduction of the free right to carry

on business (*Gewerbefreiheit*) and the elimination of all medieval legislation on guilds really create the perfect economic conditions that the hotheads (*Heißsporne*) of that tradition predict?', in Verein für Socialpolitik (*sic*), *Verhandlungen der Eisenacher Versammlung zur Besprechung der Sozialen Frage am 6. und 7. October 1872*, Leipzig, 1873, p. 3.

2. William Easterly, *The Elusive Quest for Growth: Economists' Adventure and Misadventure in the Tropics*, Cambridge, Mass., 2001 and *The White Man's Burden: Why the West's Efforts to aid the Rest have done so much Ill and so little Good*, New York, 2006. The figure is from Easterly's website <http://www.nyu.edu/fas/institute/dri/Easterly/>

3. Pietro Verri, *Mediazioni sulla Economia Politica*, Genoa, 1771, p. 42. Emphasis added.

4. Whenever differences are introduced systematically – like increasing and diminishing returns as in Paul Krugman's New Trade Theory – the result becomes a system producing development on the one hand and underdevelopment on the other, as is claimed here.

5. Eric Ross, *The Malthus Factor: Poverty, Politics and Population in Capitalist Development*, London, 1998.

6. As the importance of Michael Porter's clusters grew, a neo-classical version of clusters developed that allowed knowledge to spill over among businesses, but did not create synergies among different economic activities.

7. In historiography this is called the 'Manifest Destiny' theory of history, which raises its head every time the US enters an imperialist cycle: the move for the annexation of the whole of Mexico (1840s), the annexation of Cuba, Puerto Rico and the Philippines (1898 to the First World War) and the im-perialism of the 'end of history'.

8. My colleagues in Haiti, where a maximum of 30 per cent of the adult population has a job, claim with justification that this point alone is enough to disqualify the Washington institutions.

9. Different economic activities may differ in capital intensity. If adding capital to labour is what creates growth, poor nations would benefit from protecting those economic activities that absorb most capital. However, the international economy is in effect ruled by the most simplistic version of trade theory, where capital is absent and the argument is based essentially only on the bartering of labour hours.

10. Wikipedia has an informative entry on 'The American System'.

11. It is also worth while to notice how extremely different this brief is from the type of understanding that brought forward the Marshall Plan in 1947. As a result of the disasters of the 1930s – and the expectation of the usual post-war depression – all of the six points above were an integral part of the analysis.

12. As I see it, 'New Growth Theory' involves an exercise in saving core assumptions. This book argues for the need to get rid of the 'equality assumption': reducing the level of abstraction by introducing the activity-specific nature of technical change, of increasing returns and of economic growth in general.

13. As will be obvious from what follows, the invitation came with no funds.

14. 'Sequential usufruct' means that, rooted in traditional usage, different groups use the same land at different times of the year. Property rights in

the capitalist sense do not exist. The system can best be compared to 'time-sharing' of apartments as practised in many holiday resorts today.

15. This section is discussed in detail in my paper 'Institutionalism Ancient, Old and New: a Historical Perspective on Institutions and Uneven Development', Research Paper No. 2006/77, United Nations University, Helsinki, 2006.

16. Ha-Joon Chang and Peter Evans, 'The Role of Institutions in Economic Change', in Silvana de Paula and Gary Dymski (eds), *Reimagining Growth*, London, 2005, p. 99; downloadable on <http:www.othercanon.org>

17. Hans Baron, *The Crisis of the Early Italian Renaissance*, Princeton, 1966, p. 207.

18. Francis Bacon, *Novum Organum*, Book 1, Section CXXIX; available on <"http://www.constitution.org/bacon/nov_org.htm>

19. Carlota Perez convincingly shows how technological change influences institutional 'common sense' in her chapter 'Technological Revolutions, Paradigm Shift and Socio-Institutional Change' in Erik Reinert (ed.), *Globalization, Economic Development and Inequality: An Alternative Perspective*, Cheltenham, 2004.

20. Giovanni Botero, *Della ragione di stato. Libri dieci*, also containing *Delle cause della grandezza delle città, libri tre*, Rome, 1590; English edition, New Haven, 1956.

21. For the notable continuity of German development theory over time, see Erik Reinert, 'German Economics as Development Economics: From the Thirty Years War to World War II' in Jomo K. S. and Erik Reinert (eds), *Origins of Development Economics*, London and New Delhi, 2005, pp. 48–68.

22. Francis Fukuyama, *The End of History and the Last Man*, New York, 1992, p. 223.

23. This section is based on my paper 'Competitiveness and Its Predecessors – a 500 Year Cross-National Perspective' in *Structural Change and Economic Dynamics*, vol. 6, 1995, pp. 23–42, 1995, where sources for the quotes are found.

24. Michael Porter, *The Competitive Advantage of Nations*, New York, 1990, p. 6.

25. Also quoted in my 'Competitiveness and Its Predecessors – a 500 Year Cross-National Perspective' in *Structural Change and Economic Dynamics*, vol. 6, 1995, pp. 23–42.

26. Of course prices also fall, but the key point here is that wages are also rising.

27. Hans Singer, 'The Distribution of Gains between Investing and Borrowing Countries' in *American Economic Review*, vol. 40, 1950, pp. 473–85.

28. Niall Fergusson, *Colossus. The Rise and Fall of the American Empire*, London, 2005, pp. 174–81.

29. An empirical survey showing that countries richly endowed with natural resources grow less than countries specializing in tradable manufactured products was presented by Jeffrey Sachs and Andrew Warner, 'Natural Resource Abundance and Economic Growth', National Bureau of Economic Research Working Papers, 5398, 1995. Yet the authors failed to explain the reasons underlying those differences and they then argue that free trade is beneficial for all parties involved.

30. This section is inspired by discussions with Prof. Bruce Scott of Harvard Business School.

31. 'A New Zealand Colonist' (F. J. Moss), *Notes on Political Economy from the Colonial Point of View*, London, 1897, pp. 41–4.
32. 'Now therefore ye are cursed, and there shall never fail to be of you bondmen, both hewers of wood and drawers of water for the house of my God.' (Joshua 9: 23).
33. Jeffrey Sachs, *The End of Poverty: Economic Possibilities for Our Time*, New York, 2005.

7 Palliative Economics: Why the Millennium Goals are a Bad Idea

1. Erik Reinert, 'Development and Social Goals: Balancing Aid and Development to Prevent "Welfare Colonialism"', United Nations Department of Economic and Social Affairs, DESA Working Paper No. 14, 2006; downloadable at <http://www.un.org/esa/desa/papers/>
2. This analysis is complicated by the fact that the wages and incomes of the self-employed as a percentage of GDP are falling in most countries, whereas wages for those working in the FIRE (finance, insurance, real estate) sector are increasing. This wage/self-employed share of GDP has been close to 70 per cent in Norway and around 23 per cent in Peru.
3. See Erik Reinert, 'Diminishing Returns and Economic Sustainability: The Dilemma of Resource-Based Economies Under a Free Trade Regime' in Stein Hansen, Jan Hesselberg and Helge Hveem (eds), *International Trade Regulation, National Development Strategies and the Environment: Towards Sustainable Development?*, Oslo, 1996, and Jared Diamond's chapter on Rwanda in his *Collapse*, New York, 2005.
4. Jacob Schoenhof, *The Destructive Influence of the Tariff Upon Manufacture and Commerce and the Figures and Facts Relating Thereto*, New York, 1883.
5. Erik Reinert, 'Raw Materials in the History of Economic Policy; or, Why List (the Protectionist) and Cobden (the Free Trader) Both Agreed on Free Trade in Corn' in Gary Cook (ed.), *The Economics and Politics of International Trade*, vol. 2, *Freedom and Trade*, London, 1998.
6. Adam Smith, *The Theory of Moral Sentiments* in *Collected Works*, London, 1759/1812.
7. Adam Smith, *An Inquiry into the Nature and Causes of the Wealth of Nations*, Chicago, 1776/1976, vol. I, pp. 486–7.
8. Ibid., p. 477.
9. See, for example, Steven Kaplan, *Bread, Politics and Political Economy in the Reign of Louis XV*, The Hague, 1976.
10. This asymmetry is the core of the argument in Frank Graham's 1923 article (Appendix III), quoted by Paul Krugman in his 'New Trade Theory', *Rethinking International Trade*, Cambridge, Mass., 1990.
11. Richard R. Nelson, 'Economic Development from the Perspective of Evolutionary Economic Theory' in *The Other Canon Foundation and Tallinn University of Technology Working Papers in Technology Governance and Economic Dynamics*, no. 2, 2006; downloadable on <http://hum.ttu.ee/tg/>

12. Ibid.
13. Jan Kregel, 'External Financing for Development and International Financial Stability', Discussion Paper Series, no. 32, UNCTAD, Geneva, 2004.
14. See, for example, the works of Daniel Raymond and Mathew Carey referred to earlier in this book.
15. I am grateful to Carlota Perez for having formulated this insight.
16. But not necessarily falling GDP per capita. See note 2 in this chapter.
17. This tariff level can be calculated from Frank Taussig, *The Tariff History of the United States*, New York, 1897, p. 222.
18. That the steel tariff later got as high as 100 per cent was a result of technological change and rapidly falling prices in a situation where the tariff was not based on value, but on weight (dollars per ton).
19. Richard R. Nelson and Sidney G. Winter, *An Evolutionary Theory of Economic Change*, Cambridge, Mass., 1982.
20. Werner Sombart emphasized the role of Judaism and Max Weber the role of Protestantism.
21. Richard Tawney, *Religion and the Rise of Capitalism. A Historical Study*, London, 1926.
22. Johann Friedrich von Pfeiffer, *Vermischte Verbesserungsvorschläge und freie Gedanken*, vol. 2, Frankfurt, 1778.
23. Hans W. Singer, 'The Distribution of Gains between Investing and Borrowing Countries' in *American Economic Review*, 40, 1950, pp. 473–85.
24. With the exception that they are subject to constant rather than diminishing returns to scale, much as the case of the house painter discussed in chapter 3.
25. Charles King, *The British Merchant; or, Commerce Preserv'd*, London, 1721, 3 volumes.
26. If we assume that manufactures are produced under increasing returns and raw materials under diminishing returns this is perfectly compatible with Krugman's New Trade Theory (see Krugman, *Rethinking International Trade*, 1990).
27. Robert Paine (ed.), *The White Arctic. Anthropological Essays on Tutelage and Ethnicity*, St Johns, Newfoundland, 1977.
28. Lena Lavinas and Eduardo Henrique Garcia, *Programas Sociais de Combate à Fome. O legado dos anos de estabilização econômica*, Rio de Janeiro, 2004.
29. Richard Herrnstein and Charles Murray, *The Bell Curve: Intelligence and Class Structure in American Life*, New York, 1994, p. 526.
30. 'Thus the country which eventually specializes completely in the production of X (that is, the commodity whose production function is characterized by increasing returns to scale) might agree to make an income transfer (annually) to the other country, which agrees to specialize completely in Y (that is, the commodity whose production function is characterized by constant returns to scale)', Miltiades Chacholiades, *International Trade Theory and Policy*, New York, 1978, p. 199; see also Reinert, *International Trade*.
31. This negative development in Europe is discussed in Erik Reinert and Rainer Kattel, 'The Qualitative Shift in European Integration: Towards Permanent Wage Pressures and a "Latin-Americanization" of Europe?', Working Paper no. 17, Praxis Foundation, Estonia, 2004; downloadable at

<http://www.praxis.ee/data/WP_17_2004.pdf>; and Erik Reinert, 'European Integration, Innovations and Uneven Economic Growth: Challenges and Problems of EU 2005' in Ramón Compañó et al. (eds), *The Future of the Information Society in Europe: Contributions to the Debate*, Seville, 2006, pp. 124–52; downloadable as Working Paper No. 5 at <http: //hum.ttu.ee/tg/>

32. The works of Jane Jacobs on the role of the cities arrive at the same conclusion as List from a different starting point.

33. In his 1791 *Report on the Subject of Manufactures*.

34. Friedrich Nietzsche, *Thus spoke Zarathustra*, London, 1968, p. 17.

8 'Get the economic activities right', or, the Lost Art of Creating Middle-Income Countries

1. Milton Friedman, *Essays in Positive Economics*, Chicago, 1953, p. 14.

2. The first of these books was *American Capitalism: The concept of counter-vailing power*, published in 1952.

3. Independent Ireland's industrial policy had followed Keynes' recommen-dations in a 1933 speech at University College, Dublin, later published as 'National Self-Sufficiency' (see Bibliography). In this speech Keynes explains how and why he came to change his view on the wisdom of free trade under all circumstances. Finland had followed an import substitution policy starting in the 1850s, see Heimer Björkqvist, *Den Nationalekonomiska Vetenskapens Utveckling i Finland intill år 1918*, Åbo (Turku), 1986, particularly pp. 156 ff.

4. For a discussion, see Nathan Rosenberg, 'Innovation and Economic Growth' at <http://www.oecd.org/dataoecd/55/49/34267902.pdf>

5. My thesis was never published. Just before it was defended at Cornell University in April 1980, my committee chairman unofficially presented good news and bad news in a typically American way. The good news was that I had made an important and original contribution to economics; the bad news was that, in his opinion, I would never get a job as an economist at a university. My message was not compatible with what would be acceptable to the academic community. With a Harvard MBA I would probably be able to make a living anyway, was his fair comment. The thesis was actually accepted for publication by the Norwegian University Press (Universitetsforlaget) in 1980, on the condition that I toned downed my criticism of the economics profession. I was criticizing elements from David Ricardo cherished both by the political right and the political left and found myself in the world depicted in Figure 2: anything not going back to David Ricardo had been refined out as not belonging to mainstream economics. Temporarily fed up with economics, I refused to change anything, and for the next eleven years went back to running my business and collecting books written by long defunct economists sharing my non-Ricardian perspectives.

6. Published as 'Catching-up From Way Behind – A Third World Perspective on First World History' in Jan Fagerberg, Bart Verspagen and Nick von Tunzelmann (eds), *The Dynamics of Technology, Trade, and Growth*, Aldershot, 1994, pp. 168–97.

7. Quoted with permission.
8. Hoover's report no. 3, 18 March 1947, quoted in Erik Reinert, 'Globalisation in the Periphery as a Morgenthau Plan: The Underdevelopment of Mongolia in the 1990s' in Erik Reinert (ed.), *Globalization, Economic Development and Inequality: An Alternative Perspective*, Cheltenham, 2004.
9. Alfred Marshall, *Principles of Economics*, London, 1890, p. 201.
10. This subject is well dealt with in Liah Greenfield, *The Spirit of Capitalism, Nationalism and Economic Growth*, Cambridge, Mass., 2001.
11. Lionel Robbins, *The Theory of Economic Policy in English Classical Economics*, London, 1952, pp. 10–11.
12. Mechelen is a town in Belgium.
13. These were typically economists who tended to look for solutions on the monetary side of the economy. During the early 1600s ink flowed like blood between these monetarists and their opponents emphasizing the role of production and the real economy. In a 1622–3 debate, Malynes and his opponent Edward Misselden insulted each other in seven languages. Antonio Serra's book was written a decade earlier as part of the same type of debate against monetarist Marc'Antonio de Santis.
14. I discuss these periodizations in 'Karl Bücher and the Geographical Dimensions of Techno-Economic Change' in Jürgen Backhaus (ed.), *Karl Bücher: Theory – History – Anthropology – Non-Market Economies*, Marburg, 2000.
15. Johann Heinrich von Thünen, *Der isolierte Staat in Beziehung auf Landwirtschaft und Nationalökonomie, oder Untersuchungen über den Einfluss, den die Getreidepreise, der Reichtum des Bodens und die Abgaben auf den Ackerbau ausüben*, Hamburg, 1826.
16. For a comment on today's discussion of the relationship between democracy and development, see James Galbraith, 'Development's Discontents. How to explain the link between economics and democracy – and how not to' in *Democracy. A Journal of Ideas*, Issue 2, Fall 2006, pp. 108–15.
17. In Ferdinando Galiani, *Dialogues sur le commerce des bleds*, Milan, 1770/1959.
18. I discuss this in the paper referred to in note 14 above.
19. David Landes, *The Wealth and Poverty of Nations*, New York, 1988, p. 350.
20. Economists refer to this as Baumol's Law. It is difficult for a symphony orchestra or a nurse to increase their efficiency without sacrificing quality. The same problem does not apply to the production of cars. This means that even if the consumption pattern between manufacturing and traditional services stays the same, the percentage of service workers in the economy will grow at the expense of the manufacturing sector.
21. The background was much more complex, including the unwillingness of workers to do the monotonous assembly line work.
22. UNCTAD, United Nations Conference on Trade and Development, *The Least Developed Countries Report 2006. Developing Productive Capacities*, Geneva, 2006; downloadable at <http://www.unctad.org/en/docs/ldc2006_en.pdf>

Bibliography

Abramovitz, Moses, 'Resource and Output Trends in the United States since 1870' in *American Economic Review*, vol. 46, no. 2, 1956, pp. 5–23

Abramovitz, Moses, 'The Search for the Sources of Growth: Areas of Ignorance, Old and New' in *The Journal of Economic History*, vol. 53, no. 2, 1993, pp. 217–43

Akamatsu, Kaname, 'A Theory of Unbalanced Growth in the World Economy' in *Weltwirtschaftliches Archiv*, no. 86, 1961, pp. 196–217

Åkerman, Johan, *Politik och Ekonomi i Atomålderns Värld*, Natur och Kultur, Stockholm, 1954

Amsden, Alice, *Asia's Next Giant: South Korea and Late Industrialization*, Oxford University Press, New York, 1989

A New Zealand Colonist, 1897 (F. J. Moss), *Notes on Political Economy from the Colonial Point of View. By a New Zealand Colonist*, Macmillan, London, 1897

Anonymous, *Relazione di una scorsa per varie provincie d'Europa del M. M.... a Madama G in Parigi*, Monastero di S. Salvatore, Pavia, 1786

Arthur, W. Brian, 'Competing technologies, increasing returns and lock-in by historical events' in *Economic Journal*, 99, pp. 116–31, 1989

Arthur, W. Brian, *Increasing Returns and Path Dependency in the Economy*, University of Michigan Press, Ann Arbor, 1994

Ashworth, William J., *Customs and Excise. Trade, Production and Consumption in England 1640–1845*, Oxford University Press, Oxford, 2003

Babbage, Charles, *On the Economy of Machinery and Manufactures*, Charles Knight, London, 1832

Bacon, Francis, *The Advancement of Learning*, Clarendon Press, Oxford, 1605/1974

Bacon, Francis, *Novum Organum*, Joannem Billium, Typographum Regium, London, 1620

Balabkins, Nicholas, *Germany Under Direct Controls. Economic Aspects of Industrial Disarmament 1945–1948*, Rutgers University Press, New Brunswick, 1964

Baron, Hans, *The Crisis of the Early Italian Renaissance*, Princeton University Press, Princeton, 1966

Berch, Anders, *Innledning til Almänna Hushålningen, innefattande Grunden til Politie, Oeconomie och Cameral Wetenskaparne*, Lars Salvius, Stockholm, 1747

Bernal, Martin, *Black Athena: The Afroasiatic Roots of Classical Civilization*, Rutgers University Press, New Brunswick, NJ, 1991

Bhagwati, Jagdish, *Free Trade Today*, Princeton University Press, Princeton, 2002

Biernacki, Richard, *The Fabrication of Labour: Germany and Britain, 1640–1914*, University of California Press, Berkeley, 1995

Björkqvist, Heimer, *Den Nationalekonomiska Vetenskapens Utveckling i Finland intill år 1918*, Åbo Akademi, Åbo (Turku), 1986

Blaug, Mark, 'The Problem with Formalism: An Interview with Mark Blaug' in *Challenge*, May/June 1998; downloadable at <http://www.btinternet.com/~pae_news/Blaug1.htm>

Borges, Jorge Luis, *Otras Inquisiciones*, Emecé Editores, Buenos Aires, 1952

Botero, Giovanni, *Della ragione di stato. Libri dieci*; this work also contains *Delle cause della grandezza delle città, libri tre*, Vicenzio Pellagallo, Rome, 1590; English translation, *The Reason of State*, Yale University Press, New Haven, 1956

Botero, Giovanni, *Le Relationi Universali, diviso in sette parti*, Alessandro Vecchi, Venice, 1622

Buchanan, James, *What Should Economists Do?*, Liberty Press, Indianapolis, 1979

Burckhardt, Jacob, *Reflections on History*, Allen & Unwin, London, 1943

Campanella, Tommaso, *The City of the Sun*, University of California Press, Berkeley, 1602/1981

Carey, Mathew, *Essays on Political Economy; or, the Most Certain Means of Promoting the Wealth, Power, Resources and Happiness of Nations: Applied Particularly to the United States*, H. C. Carey & I. Lea, Philadelphia, 1822

Carey, Mathew, *Displaying the Rise and Progress of the Tariff System of the United States: the Various Efforts Made from the Year 1819, to Establish the Protecting System; Its Final Triumph in the Tariff of 1824*, Thomas B. Town, Philadelphia, 1833

Carey, Henry C., *Commerce, Christianity and Civilization versus British Free Trade. Letters in Reply to the London Times*, Collins, Philadelphia, 1876

Carl, Ernst Ludwig, *Traité de la Richesse des Princes, et de leurs Etats: et des Moyens Simples et Naturels Pur y Parvenir*, 3 volumes, Theodore Legras, Paris, 1722–3

Carpenter, Kenneth, *The Economic Bestsellers Before 1850*, Bulletin No. 11, May 1975, of the Kress Library of Business and Economics, Harvard Business School, Boston, 1975. Downloadable at <http://www.othercanon.org>

Cary, John, *An Essay on the State of England in Relation to its Trade, its Poor, and its Taxes, for Carrying on the Present War against France*, W. Bonny, for the author, Bristol, 1695

Cary, John, *A Discourse on Trade and Other Matters Relative to it*, T. Osborne, London, 1745

Chacholiades, Miltiades, *International Trade Theory and Policy*, McGraw-Hill, New York, 1978

Chang, Ha-Joon, *Kicking Away the Ladder: Development Strategy in Historical Perspective*, Anthem, London, 2002

Chang, Ha-Joon (ed.), *Rethinking Development Economics*, Anthem, London, 2003

Chang, Ha-Joon and Peter Evans, 'The Role of Institutions in Economic Change' in Silvana de Paula and Gary Dymski (eds), *Reimagining Growth*, Zed, London, 2005, pp. 99–140

Child, Joshua, *Brief Observations Concerning Trade and Interest of Money*, Elizabeth Calvert and Henry Mortlock, London, 1668

Child, Joshua, *A Treatise Concerning the East-India Trade*, printed for the Honourable the East India Company, London, 1681

Cimoli, Mario (ed.), *Developing Innovation Systems. Mexico in a Global Context*, Continuum, London, 2000

Cimoli, Mario and Jorge Katz, 'Structural Reforms, Technological Gaps and Economic Development: a Latin American Perspective' in *Industrial and Corporate Change*, vol. 12, issue 2, 2003, pp. 387–411

Cimoli, Mario, Giovanni Dosi, Richard Nelson and Joseph Stiglitz, *Institutions and Policies Shaping Industrial Development: An Introductory Note*, Working Paper, Initiative for Policy Dialogue, Columbia University, 2006

Clark, Colin, *The Conditions of Economic Progress*, Macmillan, London, 1940

Cruikshank, Jeffrey L., *A Delicate Experiment. The Harvard Business School 1908–1945*, Harvard Business School Press, Boston, 1987

Cunningham, William, *The Rise and Decline of the Free Trade Movement*, Cambridge University Press, Cambridge, 1905

de Marchi, Neil (ed.), *Non-Natural Social Science: Reflecting on the Enterprise of More Heat than Light*, Duke University Press, Durham, 1993

Decker, Mathew, *An Essay on the Causes of the Decline of the Foreign Trade*, George Faulkner, Dublin, 1744

Diamond, Jared, *Guns, Germs, and Steel: The Fates of Human Societies*, Norton, New York, 1997

Diamond, Jared, *Collapse*, Viking, New York, 2005

Dosi, Giovanni et al. (eds), *Technical Change and Economic Theory*, Pinter, London, 1988

Drechsler, Wolfgang, 'Christian Wolff (1679–1754): A Biographical Essay' in *European Journal of Law and Economics*, vol. 4, nos. 2–3, Summer/Fall 1997, pp. 111–128

Drechsler, Wolfgang, 'On the Possibility of Quantitative-Mathematical Social Science, Chiefly Economics' in *Journal of Economic Studies*, 27: 4/5, 2000, pp. 246–59

Drechsler, Wolfgang, 'Natural versus Social sciences: on Understanding in Economics' in Erik S. Reinert (ed.), *Globalization, Economic Development and Inequality: An Alternative Perspective*, Edward Elgar, Cheltenham, 2004, pp. 71–87

Duran Ballén, Sixto, *A mi manera: Los años de Carondelet*, Editorial Universidad Andina Simón Bolívar, Quito, 2005

Easterly, William, *The Elusive Quest for Growth: Economists' Adventure and Misadventure in the Tropics*, MIT Press, Cambridge, Mass., 2001

Easterly, William, *The White Man's Burden: Why the West's Efforts to aid the Rest have done so much Ill and so little Good*, Penguin, New York, 2006

Ellerman, David, *From the World Bank to an Alternative Philosophy of Development Assistance*, University of Michigan Press, Ann Arbor, 2005

Endresen, Sylvi, *Modernization Reversed? Technological Change in Four Asian Fishing Villages*, Ph.D. Thesis, Department of Human Geography, University of Oslo, 1994

Evans, Peter, *Embedded Autonomy*, Princeton University Press, Princeton, 1995

Ferguson, John, *Landmarks of Economic Thought*, Longmans, Green and Co., New York, 1938

Fergusson, Niall, *Colossus. The Rise and Fall of the American Empire*, Penguin, London, 2005

Fernández Duran, Reyes, *Jerónimo de Uztáriz (1670–1732). Una Política Económica para Felipe V*, Minerva, Madrid, 1999

Foxwell, Herbert S., Foreword to Anton Menger, *The Right of the Whole Produce of Labour*, Macmillan, London, 1899

Frank, Robert and Philip Cook, *The Winner-Take-All Society*, Free Press, New York, 1995

Freeman, Christopher and Francisco Louçã, *As Time Goes By. From the Industrial Revolutions to the Information Revolution*, Oxford University Press, Oxford, 2001

Friedman, Milton, *Essays in Positive Economics*, University of Chicago Press, Chicago, 1953

Fukuyama, Francis, *The End of History and the Last Man*, Free Press, New York, 1992

Fukuyama, Francis, *After the Neocons. America at the Crossroads*, Profile Books, London, 2006

Galbraith, James, 'Development's Discontents. How to Explain the Link between Economics and Democracy – and how not to' in *Democracy. A Journal of Ideas*, Issue 2, Fall 2006, pp. 108–15

Galbraith, John Kenneth, *American Capitalism: The concept of countervailing power*, Houghton Mifflin, Boston, 1952

Galbraith, John Kenneth, *The World Economy Since the Wars*, Mandarin, London, 1995

Galiani, Ferdinando, *Dialogues sur le Commerce des Bleds*, Ricciardi, Milan, 1770/1959

Gasser, Simon Peter, *Einleitung zu den Oeconomischen, Politischen und Cameral-Wissenschaften*, in Verlegung des Waysenhauses, Halle, 1729

Gee, Joshua, *Trade and Navigation of Great Britain Considered*, Bettesworth & Hitch, London, 1729

Geertz, Clifford, *Local Knowledge. Further Essays in Interpretive Anthropology*, Basic Books, New York, 1983

Genovesi, Antonio, *Storia del commercio della Gran Brettagna*, 3 volumes, Benedetto Gessari, Naples, 1757–8

Giddens, Anthony, *The Third Way. The Renewal of Social Democracy*, Polity Press, Cambridge, 1998

Graham, Frank, 'Some Aspects of Protection Further Considered' in *Quarterly Journal of Economics*, vol. 37, 1923, pp. 199–227

Greenfield, Liah, *The Spirit of Capitalism, Nationalism and Economic Growth*, Harvard University Press, Cambridge, Mass., 2001

Hales, John, *A Compendious or Briefe Examination of Certayn Ordinary Complaints of Divers of Our Countrymen in These Our Dayes: Which Although ... in Some Parte Unjust and Frivolous, Yet Are All, by Way of Dialogue, Thoroughly Debated and Discussed*, Charles Marsh, London, 1561/1751

Hamilton, Alexander, 'Report on the Subject of Manufactures' (1791), reprinted in Frank Taussig (ed.), *State Papers and Speeches on the Tariff*, Harvard University, Cambridge, Mass., 1893

Hamilton, Earl J., 'Spanish Mercantilism before 1700' in Edwin Francis Gay, *Facts and Factors in Economic History – Articles by former Students*, Harvard University Press, Cambridge, Mass., 1932

Harvard Business School, Division of Research, 'Intellectual Innovation at the Harvard Business School. A Strategy', Harvard Business School, Boston, 1991

Heaton, Herbert, *A Scholar in Action – Edwin F. Gay*, Harvard University Press, Cambridge, Mass., 1952

Heilbroner, Robert, *Is Economics Relevant? A Reader in Political Economics*, Goodyear Publishing Company, Pacific Palisades, 1971

Heilbroner, Robert, *The Wordly Philosophers*, 7th edition, Simon & Schuster, New York, 1999

Hely-Hutchinson, John, *The Commercial Restraints of Ireland Considered in a Series of Letters to a Noble Lord*, William Hallhead, Dublin, 1779

Hermann, Benedikt Franz, *Herrn Johann von Horneks Bemerkungen über die österreichische Staatsökonomie. Ganz umgearbeitet und mit Anmerkungen versehen*, Nikolai, Berlin, 1784

Herrnstein, Richard J. and Charles Murray, *The Bell Curve: Intelligence and Class Structure in American Life*, Free Press, New York, 1994

Hirschman, Albert O., *The Passions and the Interests. Political Arguments for Capitalism before Its Triumph*, Princeton University Press, Princeton, 1977

Hobson, John M., *The Eastern Origins of Western Civilisation*, Cambridge University Press, Cambridge, 2004

Hodgson, Geoffrey, *How Economics Forgot History: The Problem of Historical Specificity in Social Science*, Routledge, London, 2001

Hodgson, Geoffrey, *The Evolution of Institutional Economics*, Routledge, London, 2004

Hont, Istvan, *Jealousy of Trade: International Competition and the Nation State in Historical Perspective*, Harvard University Press, Cambridge, Mass., 2005

Hörnigk, Philipp Wilhelm von, *Oesterreich über alles wann es nur will. Das ist: wohlmeinender Fürschlag Wie mittelst einer wolbestellten Lands-Oeconomie, die Kayserl. Erbland in kurzem über alle andere Staat von Europa zu erheben, und mehr als einiger derselben, von denen andern Independent zu machen. Durch einen Liebhaber der Kayserl. Erbland Wolfahrt*, no publisher, [Nuremberg], 1684.

Hume, David, *The History of England from the Invasion of Julius Caesar to the Revolution in 1688*, 6 volumes, A. Millar, London, 1767

Jacobs, Jane, *Cities and the Wealth of Nations*, Random House, New York, 1984

Jenkins, David, *The Textile Industries*, vol. 8 of R. A. Church and E. A. Wrigley (eds), *The Industrial Revolution*, Blackwell, Oxford, 1994

Jones, Richard, *An Essay on the Distribution of Wealth*, John Murray, London, 1831

Justi, Johann Heinrich Gottlob von, *Vergleichungen der Europäischen mit den Asiatischen und andern vermeintlich Barbarischen Regierungen*, Johann Heinrich Rüdigers, Berlin, 1762

Kaldor, Nicholas, 'Alternative Theories of Distribution' in *Review of Economic Studies*, vol. XXIII, no. 2, 1955–6; reprinted in *Essays on Value and Distribution*, Free Press, Glencoe, Ill., 1960

Kaplan, Steven, *Bread, Politics and Political Economy in the Reign of Louis XV*, Martinus Nijhoff, The Hague, 1976

Keynes, John Maynard, *The End of Laissez-faire*, The Hogarth Press, London, 1926

Keynes, John Maynard, *The General Theory of Employment, Interest and Money*, Macmillan, London, 1935

Keynes, John Maynard, 'National Self-Sufficiency' in *The Collected Writings of John Maynard Keynes*, vol. XXI, Macmillan, London, 1972, pp. 233–46

Keynes, John Maynard, 'Herbert Somerton Foxwell' in *The Collected Writings of John Maynard Keynes*, vol. X, Macmillan, London, 1972, pp. 267–96

Keynes, John Neville, *The Scope and Method of Political Economy*, Macmillan, London, 1890

King, Charles, *The British Merchant; or, Commerce Preserv'd*, 3 volumes, John Darby, London, 1721

Koyré, Alexandre, *From the Closed World to the Infinite Universe*, Johns Hopkins University Press, Baltimore, 1957

Kregel, Jan, 'External Financing for Development and International Financial Stability', G-24 Discussion Paper Series, No. 32, UNCTAD, Geneva, October 2004

Kregel, Jan and Leonardo Burlamaqui, 'Banking and Financing of Development: A Schumpeterian and Minskyan Perspective' in Silvana de Paula and Gary Dymski (eds), *Reimagining Growth*, Zed, London, 2005, pp. 141–67

Krugman, Paul, *Rethinking International Trade*, MIT Press, Cambridge, Mass., 1990

Krugman, Paul, *Geography and Trade*, MIT Press, Cambridge, Mass., 1991

Krugman, P. R., *Development, Geography, and Economic Theory*, MIT Press, Cambridge, Mass., 1995

Krugman, Paul, 'Ricardo's Difficult Idea. Why Intellectuals don't Understand Comparative Advantage' in Gary Cook (ed.), *The Economics and Politics of International Trade. Freedom and Trade*, vol. II, Routledge, London, 1998, pp. 22–36

Kuhn, Thomas, *The Structure of Scientific Revolutions*, University of Chicago Press, Chicago, 1962

Laffemas, Barthélemy, *Reiglement* [sic] *general pour dresser les manufactures en ce royaume, et couper le cours des draps de soye, & autres merchandises qui perdent & ruynent l'Estat: qui est le vray moyen de remettre la France en sa splendeur, & de faire gaigner les pauvres…*, Claude de Monstr'oil and Jean Richter, Paris, 1597

Landes, David, *The Wealth and Poverty of Nations*, Norton, New York 1998

Lane, Frederick, *Profits from Power. Readings in Protection-Rent and Violence-Controlling Enterprises*, State University of New York Press, Albany, 1979

Lavinas, Lena and Eduardo Henrique Garcia, *Programas Sociais de Combate à Fome. O legado dos anos de estabilização econômica*, eda UFRJ/IPEA, Coleção Economia e Sociedade, Rio de Janeiro, 2004

Lawson, Tony, *Economics & Reality*, Routledge, London, 1997

List, Friedrich, *Das Nationale System der Politischen Oekonomie*, G. Cotta'scher Verlag, Stuttgart and Tübingen, 1841; English translation, *The National System of Political Economy*, Longman, London, 1885

Lucas, Robert E., 'On the Mechanics of Economic Development' in *Journal of Monetary Economics*, vol. 22, 1988, pp. 3–42

Lundvall, Bengt-Åke (ed.), *National Systems of Innovation: Towards a Theory of Innovation and Interactive Learning*, Pinter, London, 1992

McCloskey, Deirdre [Donald], *The Rhetoric of Economics*, The University of Wisconsin Press, Madison, 1985

McCloskey, Deirdre [Donald], *Knowledge and Persuasion in Economics*, Cambridge University Press, Cambridge, 1994

Machiavelli, Niccolò, *Tutte le opere storiche e letterarie*, Barbèra, Florence, 1929

Malynes, Gerhard, *The Maintenance of Free Trade, According to the three essentiall [sic] Parts...Commodities, Moneys and Exchange of Moneys*, William Sheffard, London, 1622

Malynes, Gerhard, *The Center of the Circle of Commerce, or, A Refutation of a Treatise,...,lately published by E.M.*, Nicholas Bourne, London, 1623

Marshall, Alfred, *Principles of Economics*, Macmillan, London, 1890

Meek, Ronald, *Social Science and the Ignoble Savage*, Cambridge University Press, Cambridge, 1976

Meyen, Johann Jacob, *Wie kommt es, dass die Oekonomie bisher so wenig Vortheile von der Physik und Mathematik gewonnen hat; und wie kann man diese Wissenschaften zum gemeinen Nutzen in die Oekonomie einführen, und von dieser Verbindung auf Grundsätze kommen, die in die Ausübung brauchbar sind?*, A prize winning essay to the Royal Prussian Academy, Berlin, 1770

Mill, John Stuart, *Principles of Political Economy*, Longmans, Green & Company, London, 1848/1909

Mirowski, Philip, *More Heat Than Light: Economics as Social Physics, Physics as Nature's Economics, Historical Perspectives on Modern Economics*, Cambridge University Press, Cambridge, 1989

Mirowski, Philip, *Machine Dreams: Economics becomes a Cyborg Science*, Cambridge University Press, Cambridge, 2001

Misselden, Edward, *Free Trade and the Meanes* [sic] *to Make Trade Flourish*, Simon Waterson, London, 1622

Misselden, Edward, *The Circle of Commerce or the Ballance* [sic] *of Trade*, Nicholas Bourne, London, 1623

Mitchell, Wesley Claire, 'Sombart's Hochkapitalismus' in *The Quarterly Journal of Economics*, vol. 43, no. 2, February 1929, pp. 303–23

Mitchell, Wesley Claire, *Types of Economic Theory, from Mercantilism to Institutionalism*, Kelley, New York, 1967

Monroe, Arthur Eli, *Early Economic Thought, Selection from Economic Literature prior to Adam Smith*, Harvard University Press, Cambridge, Mass., 1930

Montesquieu, Charles-Louis de Secondat, Baron de, *The Spirit of the Laws*, Hafner, New York, 1949

Morgan, Mary S. and Malcolm Rutherford (eds), *From Interwar Pluralism to Postwar Neoclassicism*, Annual Supplement to *History of Political Economy*, vol. 30, Duke University Press, Durham, 1998

Morgenthau, Henry, Jr, *Germany is Our Problem. A Plan for Germany*, Harper, New York, 1945

Murra, John, *La organización económica del estado inca*, Siglo XXI, México, 1978

Murra, John, *El Mundo Andino, población, medio ambiente y economía*, Instituto de Estudios Peruanos, Lima, 2002

Myrdal, Gunnar, *Development and Under-development: A Note on the Mechanisms of National and International Economic Inequality*, National Bank of Egypt, Cairo, 1956

Neill, Charles Patrick, *Daniel Raymond. An Early Chapter in the History of Economic Theory in the United States*, Johns Hopkins Press (Johns Hopkins University Studies in Historical and Political Science), Baltimore, 1897

Nelson, Richard R., 'Economic Development from the Perspective of Evolutionary Economic Theory' in *The Other Canon Foundation and Tallinn University of Technology Working*

Papers in Technology Governance and Economic Dynamics, No. 2, 2006; downloadable at <http://hum.ttu.ee/tg/>

Nelson, Richard R. (ed.), *National Innovation Systems*, Oxford University Press, London, 1993

Nelson, Richard R., and Sidney G. Winter, *An Evolutionary Theory of Economic Change*, Belknap Press of Harvard University Press, Cambridge, Mass., 1982

Nelson, Robert H., *Economics as Religion: From Samuelson to Chicago and Beyond*, Penn State University Press, University Park, 2001

Nietzsche, Friedrich, *Thus spoke Zarathustra*, Penguin Books, London, 1968

Nietzsche, Friedrich, *Werke*, Digitale Bibliothek Band 31, Directmedia (CD-ROM), Berlin, 2000

Nye, John Vincent, 'The Myth of Free-Trade Britain and Fortress France. Tariffs and Trade in the Nineteenth Century' in *Journal of Economic History*, 51, 1, March 1991, pp. 23–46

O'Brien, Patrick, 'Historiographical Traditions and Modern Imperatives for the Restoration of Global History' in *Journal of Global History*, vol. 1, issue 1, 2006, pp. 3–39

Ortiz, Fernando, *Cuban Counterpoint. Tobacco and Sugar*, Alfred A. Knopf, New York, 1947

Ortiz, Luis, 'Memorandum to the King to Prevent Money from Leaving the Kingdom', Madrid, 1558; quoted in Earl J. Hamilton, 'Spanish Mercantilism before 1700' in Edwin Francis Gay, *Facts and Factors in Economic History – Articles by Former Students*, Harvard University Press, Cambridge, Mass., 1932

Paine, Robert (ed.), *The White Arctic. Anthropological Essays on Tutelage and Ethnicity*, Institute of Social and Economic Research, Memorial University of Newfoundland, St Johns, 1977

Perez, Carlota, *Technological Revolutions and Financial Capital. The Dynamics of Bubbles and Golden Ages*, Edward Elgar, Cheltenham, 2002

Perez, Carlota, 'Technological Revolutions, Paradigm Shift and Socio-Institutional Change' in Erik S. Reinert (ed.), *Globalization, Economic Development and Inequality: An Alternative Perspective*, Edward Elgar, Cheltenham, 2004

Perez, Carlota and Luc Soete, 'Catching Up in Technology: Entry Barriers and Windows of Opportunity' in G. Dosi et al. (eds), *Technical Change and Economic Theory*, Pinter, London, 1988, pp. 458–79

Pfeiffer, Johann Friedrich von, *Vermischte Verbesserungsvorschläge und freie Gedanken*, vol. 2, Esslinger, Frankfurt, 1778

Pfeiffer, Johann Friedrich von, *Der Antiphysiokrat, oder umständliche Untersuchung des sogenannten physiokratischen Systems für eine allgemeine Freyheit und einzige Auflage auf den reinen Ertrag der Grundstücke*, Schäfer, Frankfurt am Main, 1780

Pfeiffer, Johann Friedrich von, *Grundsätze der Universal-Cameral-Wissenschaft oder deren vier wichtigsten Säulen, nämlich der Staats-Regierungskunst, der Policey-Wissenschaft, der allgemeinen Staats-Oekonomie, und der Finanz-Wissenschaft*, 2 volumes, Esslingersche Buchhandlung, Frankfurt, 1783

Polanyi, Karl, *The Great Transformation*, Rinehart & Co., New York, 1944

Polanyi, Karl, Conrad Arensberg and Harry Pearson, *Trade and Markets in the Early Empires*, Free Press, New York, 1957

Pommeranz, Kenneth, *The Great Divergence: China, Europe, and the Making of the Modern World Economy*, Princeton University Press, Princeton, 2000

Porter, Michael, *The Competitive Advantage of Nations*, Free Press, New York, 1990

[Putumayo Affair] *Report by His Majesty's Consul at Iquitos on his Tour in the Putumayo district, Presented to both Houses of Parliament by Command of His Majesty*, His Majesty's Stationery Office, London, 1913

Quesnay, François, *Traité des Effets et de l'Usage de la Saignée*, d'Houry, Paris, 1750

Rae, John, *Statement of Some New Principles on the Subject of Political Economy, Exposing the Fallacies of the System of Free Trade, and of Some Other Doctrines Maintained in the 'Wealth of Nations'*, Hilliard, Gray & Co., Boston, 1834

Raymond, Daniel, *Thoughts on Political Economy*, Fielding Lucas, Baltimore, 1820

Reder, Melvin, *Economics. The Culture of a Controversial Science*, University of Chicago Press, Chicago, 1999

Reinert, Erik, *International Trade and the Economic Mechanisms of Underdevelopment*, Ph. D. thesis, Cornell University, 1980

Reinert, Erik, 'Catching-up From Way Behind – A Third World Perspective on First World History' in Jan Fagerberg, Bart Verspagen and Nick von Tunzelmann (eds), *The Dynamics of Technology, Trade, and Growth*, Edward Elgar, Aldershot, 1994, pp. 168–97

Reinert, Erik, 'Competitiveness and Its Predecessors – a 500-Year Cross-National Perspective' in *Structural Change and Economic Dynamics*, vol. 6, 1995, pp. 23–42

Reinert, Erik, 'The Role of Technology in the Creation of Rich and Poor Nations: Underdevelopment in a Schumpeterian System' in Derek H. Aldcroft and Ross Catterall (eds), *Rich Nations – Poor Nations. The Long Run Perspective*, Edward Elgar, Aldershot, 1996, pp. 161–88

Reinert, Erik, 'Diminishing Returns and Economic Sustainability: The Dilemma of Resource-Based Economies Under a Free Trade Regime' in Stein Hansen, Jan Hesselberg and Helge Hveem (eds), *International Trade Regulation, National Development Strategies and the Environment: Towards Sustainable Development?* Centre for Development and the Environment, University of Oslo, Oslo, 1996, pp. 119–50

Reinert, Erik, 'Raw Materials in the History of Economic Policy; or, Why List (the Protectionist) and Cobden (the Free Trader) Both Agreed on Free Trade in Corn' in Gary Cook (ed.), *The Economics and Politics of International Trade. Freedom and Trade*, vol. II, Routledge, London, 1998, pp. 275–300

Reinert, Erik, 'The Role of the State in Economic Growth' in *Journal of Economic Studies*, 26 (4/5), 1999, pp. 268–326. A shorter version can be found in Pier Angelo Toninelli (ed.), *The Rise and Fall of State-Owned Enterprises in the Western World*, Cambridge University Press, Cambridge, 2000, pp. 73–99

Reinert, Erik, 'Karl Bücher and the Geographical Dimensions of Techno-Economic Change' in Jürgen Backhaus (ed.), *Karl Bücher: Theory – History – Anthropology – Non-Market Economies*, pp. 177–222, Metropolis, Marburg, 2000

Reinert, Erik, 'Full Circle: Economics from Scholasticism through Innovation and back into Mathematical Scholasticism' in *Journal of Economic Studies*, vol. 27, no. 4/5, 2000, pp. 364–76

Reinert, Erik, 'Schumpeter in the Context of Two Canons of Economic Thought' in *Industry and Innovation*, vol. 6, no. 1, 2002, pp. 23–39

Reinert, Erik, 'Increasing Poverty in a Globalised World: Marshall Plans and Morgenthau Plans as Mechanisms of Polarisation of World Incomes' in Ha-Joon Chang (ed.), *Rethinking Economic Development*, Anthem, London, 2003, pp. 453–78

Reinert, Erik, 'Globalisation in the Periphery as a Morgenthau Plan: The Underdevelopment of Mongolia in the 1990s' in Erik S. Reinert (ed.), *Globalization, Economic Development and Inequality: An Alternative* Perspective, Edward Elgar, Cheltenham, 2004, pp. 115–56

Reinert, Erik, 'Benchmarking Success: The Dutch Republic (1500–1750) as seen by Contemporary European Economists' in *How Rich Nations got Rich. Essays in the History of Economic Policy*, Working Paper No. 1, SUM – Centre for Development and the Environment, University of Oslo, 2004, pp. 1–24; also at <http://www.sum.uio.no/publications>; and in Oscar Gelderblom (ed.), *The Political Economy of the Dutch Republic*, Ashgate, Aldershot, forthcoming 2007

Reinert, Erik, 'German Economics as Development Economics: From the Thirty Years War to World War II' in Jomo K. S. and Erik S. Reinert (eds),*Origins of Development Economics*, Zed Publications, London and Tulika Books, New Delhi, 2005, pp. 48–68

Reinert, Erik, 'A Brief Introduction to Veit Ludwig von Seckendorff (1626–1692)' in *European Journal of Law and Economics*, 19, 2005, pp. 221–30

Reinert, Erik, 'Development and Social Goals: Balancing Aid and Development to Prevent 'Welfare Colonialism' in United Nations Department of Economic and Social Affairs, DESA Working Paper No. 14, 2006; downloadable at <http://www.un.org/esa/desa/papers/>

Reinert, Erik, 'The Economics of Reindeer Herding: Saami Entrepreneurship between Cyclical Sustainability and the Powers of State and Oligopolies' in *British Food Journal*, vol. 108, no. 7, 2006, pp. 522–40

Reinert, Erik, 'Institutionalism Ancient, Old and New: a Historical Perspective on Institutions and Uneven Development', Research Paper No. 2006/77, United Nations University, WIDER, Helsinki; downloadable at <http://www.wider.unu.edu/publications/ publications.htm>

Reinert, Erik, 'European Integration, Innovations and Uneven Economic Growth: Challenges and Problems of EU 2005' in Román Compañó et al. (eds), *The Future of the Information Society in Europe: Contributions to the debate*, Seville, Spain, European Commission, Directorate General Joint Research Centre. Institute for Prospective Technological Studies (IPTS), pp. 124–52; downloadable as Working Paper No. 5 at <http://hum.ttu.ee/tg/>

Reinert, Erik and Arno Daastøl, 'Exploring the Genesis of Economic Innovations: The Religious Gestalt-Switch and the Duty to Invent as Preconditions for Economic Growth' in *European Journal of Law and Economics*, vol. 4, no. 2/3, 1997, pp. 233–83, and in *Christian Wolff. Gesammelte Werke*, IIIrd series, vol. 45, Georg Olms Verlag, Hildesheim, 1998

Reinert, Erik and Sophus Reinert, 'Mercantilism and Economic Development: Schumpeterian Dynamics, Institution Building and International Benchmarking' in Jomo K. S. and Erik S. Reinert (eds), *Origins of Development Economics*, Zed Books, London and Tulika Books, New Delhi, 2005, pp. 1–23

Reinert, Erik and Hugo Reinert, 'Creative Destruction in Economics: Nietzsche, Sombart, Schumpeter' in Jürgen Backhaus and Wolfgang Drechsler (eds), *Friedrich Nietzsche 1844–2000: Economy and Society*, Springer/Kluwer, Boston, 2006

Reinert Erik and Rainer Kattel, 'The Qualitative Shift in European Integration: Towards Permanent Wage Pressures and a "Latin-Americanization" of Europe?' Working Paper no. 17, Praxis Foundation, Estonia, 2004; also at <http://www.praxis.ee/data/ WP_17_2004.pdf>

Reinert, Sophus, 'The Italian Tradition of Political Economy. Theories and Policies of Development in the Semi-Periphery of the Enlightenment' in Jomo K. S. and Erik S. Reinert (eds),

Origins of Development Economics, Zed Books, London/Tulika Books, New Delhi, 2005, pp. 24–47

Reinert, Sophus, 'Darwin and the Body Politic: Schäffle, Veblen, and the Shift of Biological Metaphor in Economics' in The Other Canon Foundation and Tallinn University of Technology Working Papers in Technology Governance and Economic Dynamics, No. 8, 2006; downloadable at <http://hum.ttu.ee/tg/>

Ricardo, David, *The Principles of Political Economy and Taxation*, John Murray, London, 1817

Robbins, Lionel, *The Theory of Economic Policy in English Classical Economics*, Macmillan, London, 1952

Roca, Santiago, and Luis Simabuco, 'Natural Resources, Industrialization and Fluctuating Standards of Living in Peru, 1950–1997: A Case Study of Activity-Specific Economic Growth' in Erik S. Reinert (ed.), *Globalization, Economic Development and Inequality: An Alternative Perspective*, Edward Elgar, Cheltenham, 2004, pp. 115–56

Roosevelt, Elliot, *As He Saw It*, Duell, Sloan and Pearce, New York, 1946

Roscher, Wilhelm, *Principles of Political Economy*, Callaghan, Chicago, 1878

Ross, Eric, *The Malthus Factor: Poverty, Politics and Population in Capitalist Development*, Palgrave Macmillan, London, 1998

Ruggiero, Renato, 'Whither the Trade System Next' in Jagdish Bhagwati and M. Hirsch (eds), *The Uruguay Round and Beyond – Essays in Honour of Arthur Dunkel*, The University of Michigan Press, Ann Arbor, 1998, pp.123–41

Sachs, Jeffrey, *The End of Poverty: Economic Possibilities for Our Time*, Penguin Press, New York, 2005

Sachs, Jeffrey and Andrew Warner, 'Natural Resource Abundance and Economic Growth' in National Bureau of Economic Research Working Papers, 5398, National Bureau of Economic Research, 1995

Said, Edward, *Orientalism*, Vintage, New York, 1978

Samuelson, Paul, 'International Trade and the Equalisation of Factor Prices' in *Economic Journal*, vol. 58, 1948, pp. 163–84

Samuelson, Paul, 'International Factor-Price Equalisation Once Again' in *Economic Journal*, vol. 59, 1949, pp. 181–97

Samuelson, Paul, *Economics*, 10th edn, McGraw-Hill, New York, 1976

Sanness, John, *Patrioter, intelligens og skandinaver. Norske reaksjoner på skandinavismen før 1848*, Universitetsforlaget, Oslo, 1959

Schmoller, Gustav, *The Mercantile System and its Historical Significance*, Macmillan/Kelley, New York, 1897/1967 (translated from articles in the journal *Schmoller's Jahrbuch*)

Schmoller, Gustav, *Wechselnde Theorien und feststehende Wahrheiten im Gebiete der Staats- und Socialwissenschaftlichen und die heutige deutsche Volkswirtschaftslehre. Rede bei Antritt des Rectorats*, Büxenstein, Berlin, 1897

Schoenhof, Jacob, *The Destructive Influence of the Tariff Upon Manufacture and Commerce and the Figures and Facts Relating Thereto*, Free Trade Club, New York, 1883

Schumpeter, Joseph Alois, *Theory of Economic Development*, Cambridge, Harvard University Press, Cambridge, Mass., 1934; a much-changed English translation of the German original from 1912

Schumpeter, Joseph Alois, *Business Cycles*, 2 volumes, Macmillan, New York, 1939

Schumpeter, Joseph Alois, *History of Economic Analysis*, Oxford University Press, New York, 1954

Schurz, Carl, *Life of Henry Clay*, Houghton Mifflin, Boston, 1887

Senghaas, Dieter, *Von Europa lernen. Entwicklungsgeschichtliche Betrachtungen*, Suhrkamp, Frankfurt, 1982

Serra, Antonio, *Breve trattato delle cause che possono far abbondare l'oro e l'argento dove non sono miniere*, Lazzaro Scorriggio, Naples, 1613

Singer, Hans W., 'The Distribution of Gains between Investing and Borrowing Countries' in *American Economic Review*, 40, 1950, pp. 473–85

Smith, Adam, *The Theory of Moral Sentiments* in *Collected Works*, Cadell and Davies, London, 1759/1812

Smith, Adam, *The Wealth of Nations*, University of Chicago Press, Chicago, 1776/1976

Smith, Erasmus Peshine, *A Manual of Political Economy*, Putnam, New York, 1853

Sombart, Werner, *Krieg und Kapitalismus*, Duncker & Humblot, Munich & Leipzig, 1913

Sombart, Werner, *Luxus und Kapitalismus*, Duncker & Humblot, Munich & Leipzig, 1913

Sombart, Werner, *Der moderne Kapitalismus*, 6 volumes, Duncker & Humblot, Munich & Leipzig, 1928; partial Spanish translation, *El Apogeo del Capitalismo*, 2 volumes, Fondo de Cultura Económica, Mexico, 1946; partial Italian translation, *Il Capitalismo Moderno*, Unione Tipografico-editrice Torinese, Turin, 1967; partial French translation, *L'Apogée du Capitalisme*, 2 volumes, Payot, Paris, 1932

Soros, George, *George Soros on Globalization*, Public Affairs, New York, 2002

Spann, Othmar, *Types of Economic Theory*, Allen & Unwin, London, 1930

Stangeland, Charles Emil, *Pre-Malthusian Doctrines of Population. A Study in the History of Economic Theory*, Kelley, New York, 1904/1966

Steuart, James, *An Inquiry into the Principles of Political Economy: being an Essay on the Science of Domestic Policy in Free Nations. In Which are Particularly Considered Population, Agriculture, Trade, Industry, Money, Coin, Interest, Circulation, Banks, Exchange, Public Credit, and Taxes*, 2 volumes, A. Millar & T. Cadell, London, 1767

Stiglitz, Joseph, *Globalization and Its Discontents*, Norton, New York, 2002

Strindberg, August, *De lycksaliges ö och andra berättelser. Svenska öden och äventyr*, Stockholm, Åhlén & Åkerlund, Stockholm, 1882/1913 (I have found translations into German and Italian.)

Taussig, Frank, *The Tariff History of the United States*, Putnam's, New York, 1897

Tawney, Richard, *Religion and the Rise of Capitalism. A Historical Study*, J. Murray, London, 1926

Thünen, Johann Heinrich von, *Der isolierte Staat in Beziehung auf Landwirtschaft und Nationalökonomie, oder Untersuchungen über den Einfluss, den die Getreidepreise, der Reichtum des Bodens und die Abgaben auf den Ackerbau ausüben*, Penthes, Hamburg, 1826

Tilly, Charles, *Coercion, Capital and European States* AD *990–1992*, Blackwell, Cambridge, 1990

Tocqueville, Alexis de, *Democracy in America*, University of Chicago Press, Chicago, 1835/2000

Tubaro, Paula, 'Un'esperienza peculiare del Settecento italiano: la 'scuola milanese' di economia matematica' in *Studi Settecenteschi*, 20, 2000, pp. 193–223

UNCTAD, United Nations Conference on Trade and Development (2006), *The Least Developed Countries Report 2006. Developing Productive Capacities*, Geneva; <http://www.unctad.org/en/docs/ldc2006_en.pdf>

Uztáriz, Gerónimo de, *The Theory and Practice of Commerce and Maritime Affairs*, Rivington & Croft, London, 1751 (original Spanish 1724)

Veblen, Thorstein, 'Why is Economics not an Evolutionary Science' in *Quarterly Journal of Economics*, XII, July 1898, pp. 373–97

Verein für Sozialpolitik, *Verhandlungen der Eisenacher Versammlung zur Besprechung der Sozialen Frage am 6. und 7. October 1872*, Duncker & Humblot

Vernon, Raymond, 'International Investment and International Trade in the Product Cycle' in *Quarterly Journal of Economics*, May 1966

Verri, Pietro, *Meditazioni sulla economia politica*, Ivone Gravier, Genoa, 1771

Wade, Robert, *Governing the Market: Economic Theory and the Role of Government in East Asian Industrialization*, Princeton University Press, Princeton, 1990

Walde, Otto, *Storhetstidens Litterära Krigsbyten. En Kulturhistorisk-Bibliografisk Studie*, Almquist & Wicksel, Uppsala, 1920

Warsh, David, *Knowledge and the Wealth of Nations. A Story of Economic Discovery*, Norton, New York, 2006

Wells, Louis T. (ed.), *A Product Life Cycle for International Trade?* Harvard Business School, Division of Research, Boston, 1972

Wolf, Martin, 'The Morality of the Market' in *Foreign Policy*, September/October 2003, pp. 47–50

Wolf, Martin, *Why Globalization Works*, Yale University Press, New Haven, 2004

Wolff, Christian, *The Real Happiness of a People under A Philosophical King Demonstrated; Not only from the Nature of Things, but from the undoubted Experience of the Chinese under their first Founder Fohi, and his Illustrious Successors, Hoam Ti, and Xin Num*, Printed for M. Cooper, at the Globe, London, 1750

Yonay, Yuval, *The Struggle over the Soul of Economics*, Princeton University Press, Princeton, 1998

Young, Allyn, 'Increasing Returns and Economic Progress' in *Economic Journal*, vol. 38, no. 152, pp. 527–42

Index

Edison, Thomas 102
Edward III, King of England 17, 209
Egypt 62, 281
Einstein, Albert 44, 149
Eisenhower, Dwight D. 15
El Salvador 116
Elizabeth I, Queen of England 80
Engels, Friedrich 101
England 6, 7, 12, 17, 23, 25, 30, 31, 55, 58, 74–5, 79–81, 133, 135, 136, 167, 251, 255, 266, 302–303
Enlightenment 73, 236, 249
Enron 56
Ernest of Saxe-Gotha, Duke 91
Estonia 115–16, 163
Ethiopia 211, 264
European Common Market 40
European Union 42–3, 57, 61, 62, 251, 266, 267–8, 274, 280, 281
Evans, Peter 221

Finland 130, 146, 191, 244, 273–4, 283, 295
Finnmark 192
Fisher, Irving 213
Fleming, Alexander 148–9
Florence 77–8, 80, 225, 287
Fogel, Robert 46
Ford, Henry 103, 131, 149, 160, 229, 293
Fordism 143–5
Foreign Policy 67–8, 120
Foucault, Michel 200
Foxwell, Herbert S. 239
France 9–10, 55, 81, 90, 119, 246, 251, 267
Franci, Sebastiano 71, 72

Franklin, Benjamin 130, 168
Freeman, Christopher 125, 127, 275, 298
Freud, Sigmund 259
Friedman, Milton 31, 199, 271–2, 273
Fujimori, Alberto 217, 218–19
Fukuyama, Francis 7, 206, 226
Fulbrook, Edward 205

Gadamer, Hans-Georg 44
Galbraith, John Kenneth 18, 56, 134, 151, 179, 272, 273, 291
Galiani, Ferdinando 17, 86, 203, 287
Gasser, Simon Peter 97
Gates, Bill 35, 102, 108, 149, 160, 177, 229
Gay, Edwin 4
Gee, Joshua 165, 166
Genoa 225
Genovesi, Antonio 24, 37, 86
Germany 55, 90–2, 96–7, 127, 152–3, 211, 225, 241, 251, 257, 278, 285
Giddens, Anthony 55
Goethe, Johann Wolfgang von 4
Graham, Frank 38, 110, 301, 309–310
Grant, Ulysses S. 168
Greenland 191
Greenspan, Alan 228
Guatemala 114
Guyana 116

Hahn, Frank 206
Haiti 112, 113, 115, 116–17, 142, 148, 263–4
Hales, John 74

Roosevelt, Franklin D. 168–9, 179, 212
Roscher, Wilhelm 38, 97
Ross, Eric 213
Ruggiero, Renato 67, 245
Russia 118, 163, 180, 236
Rwanda 110, 111, 157–9
Rybczynski Theorem 181

Saami 191–7, 314
Sachs, Jeffrey D. 177, 179, 236
Samuelson, Paul 31, 43, 46, 47, 48, 197, 198, 200, 258
Sanness, John 59, 60
Scandinavia 31
Scandinavian Fallacy 196–7, 240
Schmoller, Gustav 4, 58
Schumpeter, Joseph 8, 12, 16, 21, 37, 39–40, 67, 121, 123, 125, 126, 148, 161, 190, 228, 248, 250, 253, 280, 281, 296
Schweigaard, Anton Martin 168
Scott, Bruce 227
Seckendorff, Veit Ludwig von 90–2, 97, 225
Segovia 85, 284
Serra, Antonio 7, 27, 37, 38, 74, 95, 104, 152, 153, 156, 234, 241, 244, 246, 275, 281, 282, 286
Sigismund, Emperor of the Holy Roman Empire 222
Silicon Valley 57, 213, 214, 276, 284, 302
Singapore 235
Singer, Hans 161, 229, 259, 282, 310
Smith, Adam 11, 12, 16, 21, 24, 25, 30, 37, 38, 40–1, 48–9, 52–3, 57, 64, 79, 97, 106,
121–2, 124, 125, 133, 167, 170, 201, 207, 245–6, 252, 284, 304
Smithies, Arthur 12
Solidarity movement 267
Somalia 199, 224, 287
Sombart, Werner 16, 92, 120–2, 123, 124, 125, 166, 206, 209
Soros, George 208
Soslow, Robert M. 274
South Africa 58, 158
South Korea 118, 142, 244
Soviet Union 15
Spain 57, 80, 84–7, 167, 191, 251, 266, 267, 280, 284, 315
Spann, Othmar 42
Spinoza, Baruch 94
St Louis (Missouri) 137
Stability and Growth Pact (1997) 267–8
Stalin, Joseph 31
Steinbeck, John 152
Stephenson, George 55
Steuart, James 52, 58, 171, 246, 251
Stiglitz, Joseph 215–16
Sträng, Gunnar 254
Strindberg, August 223
Surinam 231
Sweden 59–60, 146, 191, 280, 292
Swift, Jonathan 45, 51
Swissair 164
Switzerland 236

Tacitus 64
Taiwan 6, 142
Tanzania 82, 158, 203
Tartu, University of 116
Tawney, Richard 257
Telesis 97–8

Erik S. Reinert is professor of technology governance and development strategies at Tallinn University of Technology, Estonia, and President of The Other Canon Foundation, Norway. In addition to a PhD in economics from Cornell University, Reinert holds an MBA from Harvard.

PublicAffairs is a publishing house founded in 1997. It is a tribute to the standards, values, and flair of three persons who have served as mentors to countless reporters, writers, editors, and book people of all kinds, including me.

I. F. STONE, proprietor of *I. F. Stone's Weekly*, combined a commitment to the First Amendment with entrepreneurial zeal and reporting skill and became one of the great independent journalists in American history. At the age of eighty, Izzy published *The Trial of Socrates*, which was a national bestseller. He wrote the book after he taught himself ancient Greek.

BENJAMIN C. BRADLEE was for nearly thirty years the charismatic editorial leader of *The Washington Post*. It was Ben who gave the *Post* the range and courage to pursue such historic issues as Watergate. He supported his reporters with a tenacity that made them fearless and it is no accident that so many became authors of influential, best-selling books.

ROBERT L. BERNSTEIN, the chief executive of Random House for more than a quarter century, guided one of the nation's premier publishing houses. Bob was personally responsible for many books of political dissent and argument that challenged tyranny around the globe. He is also the founder and longtime chair of Human Rights Watch, one of the most respected human rights organizations in the world.

· · ·

For fifty years, the banner of Public Affairs Press was carried by its owner Morris B. Schnapper, who published Gandhi, Nasser, Toynbee, Truman, and about 1,500 other authors. In 1983, Schnapper was described by *The Washington Post* as "a redoubtable gadfly." His legacy will endure in the books to come.

Peter Osnos, *Founder*